Red Dust and Broadsides

Red Dust and Broadsides

A Joint Autobiography

Agnes "Sis" Cunningham
and Gordon Friesen

Edited by Ronald D. Cohen
Foreword by Pete Seeger

University of Massachusetts Press   *Amherst*

This book is published with the support and cooperation of the University of Massachusetts Boston.

Printed in the United States of America
LC 98-53049
ISBN 1-55849-209-7 (cloth) : 210-0 (pbk.)

Designed by Dennis Anderson
Set in Trump Mediaeval by Graphic Composition, Inc.
Printed and bound by Book Crafters

Library of Congress Cataloging-in-Publication Data

Cunningham, Sis, 1909–
  Red dust and broadsides : a joint autobiography / Agnes "Sis" Cunningham and Gordon Friesen.
    p.   cm.
  Includes bibliographical references, discography, and index.
  ISBN 1-55849-209-7 (cloth : alk. paper).—ISBN 1-55849-210-0 (pbk. : alk. paper)
  1. Cunningham, Sis, 1909–   . 2. Friesen, Gordon, 1909–1996. 3. Folk singers—United States—Biography. 4. Radicals—United States—Biography. I. Friesen, Gordon, 1909–1996. II. Title.
ML420.C985A3   1999
782.42162'13'00922—dc21
    [B]   98-53049
                                                          CIP
                                                          MN

British Library Cataloguing in Publication data are available.

To Aggie and Jane

Contents

Foreword

Beware starting to read this book late at night.

I couldn't put it down. Two Oklahomans tell a straightforward story so different from what usually gets told. Because they were political radicals, dedicating their lives to trying to find a better social system, they got fired from jobs. They worked as volunteers for numerous campaigns. Then in the latter decades of their lives they became entrepreneurs, free enterprisers of a new kind. They started to publish (using a home mimeograph machine) a small magazine of songs about events of the day. Malvina Reynolds, Bob Dylan, Phil Ochs, and many others first had their songs printed in the little song magazine, called *Broadside*. Later some of the songs were published, promoted, and heard by millions—hundreds of millions, sometimes. But *Broadside* stayed broke.

It's an inspiring story. Two people who started as country folks: a life of cows, chickens, a garden. Old family traditions going back to Germany and Russia, Mennonites on one side, English and Scottish radicals in the other's background. Covered wagons going west. Then during World War II the couple came east, met ballad maker Woody Guthrie and others.

How lucky we are, how lucky future generations are, that these two got their story down on paper. People in other parts of this world need to know that the United States of America, famous for Pentagon Power, famous for Hollywood Hype, famous for wheeler-dealers wallowing in Wall Street wealth, also contains people like Sis Cunningham and Gordon Friesen.

Pete Seeger

Editor's Preface

This joint autobiography has been gestating for well over two decades. In the early 1970s Sis and Gordon, spurred by "Broadsider" Stu Cohen (not related to the editor) and their own desire to set the record straight, began the process by talking into a tape recorder. (These tapes are now stored in the Mennonite Archive at Bethel College, North Newton, Kansas.) After a dozen reels were full of their memories, they hired a friend to make transcriptions, which they next carefully edited for style and content. Following a futile search for a publisher, with some help from Pete Seeger and others, including a temporary literary agent, they sadly admitted defeat. The boxed manuscript gathered dust for about ten years, until their daughter Agnes spruced it up for another go-around with publishers in the mid-1980s—again with dashed hopes and bitter memories.

In the course of researching a study of the folk revival that began in the 1930s and continues to wax and wane up to the present day, I met Sis in 1992 and learned of the Cunningham/Friesen manuscript. I was delighted to have it as a resource and wished to share it. The manuscript seemed to me an essential document that enlarged our understanding of the political, social, and cultural origins of this powerfully expressive movement to meld the authenticity of folk forms with the expansive outreach of popular-culture and mass-media venues. I am pleased and honored to be able to prepare Sis and Gordon's text for publication. Given the advanced age and increasing debility of the authors (Gordon died in 1996), the text we have is necessarily incomplete and fragmentary—especially as it reaches the end of their long and busy lives. This book, nevertheless, presents vivid pictures and moving stories of our country's twentieth-century journey that are available nowhere else. It stands as a monument, albeit unfinished, to an optimistic, oppositional American lifestyle and tradition that may no longer be possible in our cynical age. In the afterword I have tried to fill in the gaps, round out the story, and provide documentation for the historical and social contexts in which Sis and Gordon and their peers lived and worked, sang and struggled. We may never see their like again.

Gary, Indiana

Author's
Acknowledgments

First of all, I would like to say that were it not for the help of our daughters, Aggie and Jane Friesen, this book would never have been produced. Thanks go to Aggie for having spent months going over the manuscript page by page, word by word, and giving it a much needed toning up; to Jane principally for having been our "gofer" during the years of work on the book and seeing us both through our numerous advanced-age illnesses.

Second, many thanks to Ronald Cohen for the years of encouragement he has given us, for lending us his skill as a professionally qualified editor, for acting as our agent in getting the manuscript published, and for writing the beautiful and informative afterword. And thanks to Pete Seeger for taking time from his incredibly busy schedule to do a most complimentary foreword (the thoughts in which I doubt the book really deserves). Also thanks to David Bookbinder for many hours of help in the initial assembling of the manuscript.

I must mention the encouragement we got from members of that group we call "Broadsiders" (the magazine's contributors and volunteers). They were always dropping by or calling on the phone to say "hello" and urge us to "stay in there." Thanks to each and every one of them for their support.

And finally, thanks to Paul Wright of the University of Massachusetts Press for helping our manuscript see the light of day in book form.

I would like to add that in my attempts at song writing I have been most inspired by the following great topical songs written since the '30s: Malvina Reynolds's "I Don't Mind Failing in This World," Les Rice's "Banks of Marble," Len Chandler's "Turn around Miss Liberty," Janice Ian's "Baby I've Been Thinking" (later titled "Society's Child"), Bob Dylan's "Talking John Birch," Vanessa Redgrave's "Hanging on a Tree," Nina Simone's "Mississippi Goddamn,"

Peter La Farge's "Drums," Eric Anderson's "Plains of Nebrasky-O," Buffy Sainte-Marie's "Now That the Buffalo's Gone," Will McLean's "Oseola's Last Words," Pete Seeger's "Bells of Rhymney," Tom Paxton's "Train for Auschwitz," Kristin Lems's "We Will Never Give Up," Mike Millius's "Ballad of Martin Luther King," Woody Guthrie's "So Long It's Been Good to Know Ya," Phil Ochs's "Cops of the World," Carol Hanisch's "Song of the Oppressed," Matt Jones and Elaine Laron's "Hell No I Won't Go!" and Sammy Walker's "Look Away Old Friend," also Julius Lester's "Keep a-Inchin' Along," and his rendition of "Freedom is a Constant Struggle."

Sis Cunningham
New York City
1996

Red Dust and Broadsides

Meeting and Marriage

Interviewer: How did you two first meet?

Sis: Ina Wood called me [in March 1941] and said would we have a spare bed where a couple of my brother Bill's friends could sleep for one night; they'd be coming about midnight. I said sure, the front door would be open, we'd all be gone to bed, but they could just come in and sleep on a duo-bed which I'd have made up for them. We thought they must be from New York, 'cause that's where Bill was at that time. Next morning my father came in from out back and said those two guys were out there lookin' around and they couldn't be from New York—they were too tall and they didn't talk much. I went out, and they just kind of said, "hello" and "thanks for a place to crash," and then they went on their way. I sort of felt the same way my father did. When I saw Gordon I thought, well, yeah, he's not from New York—the way he talked, the "hello" and "thanks"—I knew damned well that he couldn't possibly be a New Yorker. I thought he was pretty tall, too. I had been to New York, but I never did run into anybody there that was quite that tall.

Interviewer (To Gordon): You left early; did you go back to Weatherford?

Gordon: Yes.

Sis: He went right back to Weatherford then, and I thought that was hello/goodbye. It never occurred to me that I'd see him again. But then, two or three weeks later, they had this meeting of the defense committee [Oklahoma Committee to Defend Political Prisoners]. How much later was it? Couldn't have been much later 'cause I remember this was early spring. We were working out-

This unpublished interview was conducted by Stu Cohen of the *Broadside* staff in New York City, in the early 1970s. The transcript is part of the *Broadside* collection.

side, either with the chickens or in the garden. I had started a garden.

Gordon: You were raising okry. Okry and corn.

Sis: I raised more than that, I raised practically everything you could raise in a garden.

Gordon: And chickens.

Sis: I think it was probably a few weeks later that there was a meeting in town of this defense committee and I went to it, and there I met Gordon again; it was announced that he was going to be chairman of the committee.

Interviewer: Who organized that? Bob Wood was in jail at that time.

Gordon: No, he was out of jail at that time—the others also—out on bail but not sentenced.

Sis: Oh yes, they were out. It was Bob Wood who had the idea of the committee, and Gordon was working on a pamphlet, *Oklahoma Witch Hunt.* And so when they had these meetings I went to some of them, and that's how we got to know each other.

Interviewer: Was he good looking?

Sis: Well, sure! Yeah, he was very good looking.

Gordon: Plus, I was a very nonchalant type.

Sis: Yes, he was very shy.

Gordon: I wasn't shy.

Sis: All right, you weren't shy, but I mean you didn't get up and make a long speech about those things.

Gordon: I'd been through more hell than all of those other people.

Sis: Yes, but you were economical, you were certainly economical with words when you got up to make a speech. You didn't just stand up there and talk away for hours like most of them did. So, in that sense, I mean you didn't—you weren't aggressive in that way. But he was aggressive as hell when he sat down to the typewriter and started pounding away on it. He just didn't get up like most people would who were introduced as the chairman of an important committee and aggressively take over. He didn't push himself forward in a crowd or anything like that—he would just get up and in a few words say what he had to say, and sit down. I thought that was great, because I was so sick and tired of long speeches.

Gordon: Which you had been making yourself.

Sis: No! I never did make long speeches. But I guess I was probably a little bit more aggressive than Gordon was. I'd been going to some of the trials, mainly the Ina Wood trials, but not that much.

Gordon: I remember the first time I fell in love with her was in the summer of '41, when—the trials were still going on, but—the Communist Party called a state convention. The members were invited secretly. You know, it wasn't announced. We didn't announce it in the newspapers, and I remember it was in the middle of the summer.

Sis: It must have been June. It wasn't the middle of the summer, because my father died in the middle of the summer, and it was before that.

Interviewer: You were both members of the Communist Party then?

Sis: We sure were.

Gordon: At least we were accepted as members.

Sis: We felt we were, anyway. The "card-carrying Communist" business was—anyway, we didn't go around carrying cards.

Gordon: I'm not sure that I was actually a member.

Sis: Maybe I shouldn't have said that. I thought you were; maybe you weren't. I thought *I* was. I considered myself—in fact, I was sure I was one later on, when they came looking for me all the way up in Watonga after we moved to the acreage near Oklahoma City.

Gordon: Well, that was earlier. That was during the roundup. That was in the fall of '40, after they had made the raid.

Sis: Yes, that was in the fall of '40.

Interviewer: That was when your uncle told them he was going to become a Communist if they didn't stop asking him questions?

Sis: Right. Well, to get back to the state convention, it was in June, near a riverbed.

Gordon: One of the Canadian Rivers, south of Bristol. They had it secret, everything was done in secrecy.

Sis: We had about twenty people there, and the whites were in the minority. Nowadays, you see these articles where it's said that blacks were not drawn to the Communist Party, but two-thirds of these were black.

Gordon: Various people gave reports. I gave a report on the Political Prisoners' Defense Committee; everything was going badly. When the defendants came up for trial they were just automatically given ten years on the hard rock pile at McAlester. Sis gave some report on the women's role, right?

Sis: I don't remember what I reported on there. Something, but it wasn't more than ten minutes. I don't think I ever talked more than ten minutes.

Gordon: Well, anyhow, we sort of went there secretly. We went in separate cars, and it was sort of combined with a picnic. Food was brought, and Sis and I got together there, and she was smoking in those days, and I was smoking, and I didn't have much money, so I had a five-cent package of Target, where you roll your own.

Sis: Me, I had Bugler.

Gordon: No, I had Bugler.

Sis: No, I think you had Bull Durham and I had Bugler. 'Cause I know sometimes you'd have nothing but Bull Durham. That was that dry stuff. It was hard to roll.

Gordon: I guess it was Sis that had Bugler. Anyhow, we shared cigarettes and laid in the grass and listened to the reports.

Sis: Did we do any singing there? Did I take that little old accordion I had along?

Gordon: Yes, we had done some singing.

Sis: I played the accordion and sang "Strange Things Happenin' in This Land."

Gordon: In the middle of it, a couple of farm boys rode up. One was maybe sixteen, the other fourteen, they were doubled up on a horse, and I think they were attracted by the singing. Anyhow, they rode into the midst of the state convention of the Communist Party. So to throw them off the track, so they wouldn't ride back home and say there was something weird going on there, we sang church hymns. Bob told them it was a church meeting, a revival meeting.

Sis: Oh, that's right! We sang—what was it?

Gordon: (Singing) "Shall we gather at the river . . ."

Sis and Gordon: (Both singing) "The beautiful, beautiful riii-verr . . ."

Sis: I can't believe we were singing that!

Gordon: We were on this riverbank.

Sis and Gordon: (Both singing) "Shall we gather at the riii-verr, that flows by the throne of the Lord."

Sis: It goes on and on. You can drag it out.

Gordon: Well, it satisfied these kids, who were used to church revivals and church meetings.

Sis: Was it Sunday? Maybe they thought they were hanging around to watch a baptism or something after they heard those songs.

Gordon: I don't think there was that much water.

Sis: No, that's right.

Gordon: Or I might've baptized you!

Sis: No, there wasn't that much water.

Gordon: Anyhow, Sis and I laid in the grass and shared a package of Bugler and sort of fell, like, in love.

Sis: We sure didn't have a very long courtship. We got married on July the twenty-third. We had met earlier than that, but we didn't really get together till June for any kind of courtship. We were married a month later.

Gordon: We didn't really get together until this state convention of the Communist Party.

Sis: But we'd known each other, off and on, from that first meeting in early March. Hey, you made a leaflet, didn't you, for that big fascist rally?

Gordon: Yeah. It wasn't a fascist rally. That was in September of '41, when Colonel Charles Lindbergh and Senator Burton K. Wheeler were the speakers.

Sis: We were already married then. I got my time sequence mixed up.

Gordon: We got married in El Reno, Oklahoma.

Sis: We started over there with about ten dollars and our car, my folks' car; it was pretty old, and something cracked; we didn't make it.

Gordon: It was about thirty miles. El Reno was the county seat of Canadian County.

Sis: About thirty miles from the edge of Oklahoma City where our acreage was. And what was the crack? Just as we got there, something cracked in the car.

Gordon: The brakes froze or something, I don't know.

Sis: No, something cracked. I don't know what it was. But anyway, it cost us eight dollars to get it fixed, and we only had two dollars left.

Gordon: No, we had more than that.

Sis: What did we have? The license cost two, and we had one dollar left to give the preacher, and when we gave him the dollar and said it was all we had, he looked funny at us, naturally. But then we had to tell him our sad story about how we planned to pay him eight dollars, you know, but . . .

Gordon: We planned to pay him five.

Sis: Well, we told him we'd pay him eight, but we had to spend that on getting the car fixed. We lived just outside of Oklahoma City—about, I would say, about a mile from the edge, right?

Gordon: Yeah. Her folks had ten . . . when they gave up their farm at Watonga, they had bought like a ten acre . . .

Sis: With the equity. They spent the equity.

Gordon: They spent the equity on the ten acres, which had a house on it, on the edge of Oklahoma City. Since then, the city has developed in that direction and beyond, and that ten . . .

Sis: Office buildings, hospitals, stores, garages.

Gordon: The developer paid a hundred thousand dollars for that same ten acres.

Sis: My father died a couple of weeks after we were married. He suddenly got a coronary thrombosis and we took him to the hospital, and he died in a few days.

Gordon: At St. Anthony's in Oklahoma City.

Sis: He just suddenly died. But he'd been deteriorating. After we lost the farm he just never, never was . . . he wasn't the same at all. He even brought a team of horses and a wagon down. He hung onto a team of horses and a wagon when we moved down to that ten acres, and he would say—God, it was just pitiful! You know, he'd say, "Well, maybe I can get some haulin' jobs." That was in 1941. He was seventy-one; he died when he was seventy-one, 'cause he was born the same year Lenin was born, 1870. He brought that wagon and team of horses down there; he just couldn't give it up, that's all, and he kept rationalizing it all, although he knew better. Who's gonna get anybody to haul with a horse and wagon when the truck age had long been in existence? But he took those horses and wagon down there, and he'd say, "Maybe I'll get some haulin' jobs."

Chapter 1

Gordon's Childhood

Dust churned up into the hot summer sky as the Indians in their war paint rode their ponies around and around the small wagon train. Gunshots rattled as the warriors hung on the outer sides of their ponies and fired on the encircled wagons and the besieged whites fired back, some from behind the wheels. The Indians whooped and yelled their war cries, and every so often a brave would tumble into the dust, roll over a few times, and lie still. There were casualties among the whites also; they would stumble out into the open real crazily and fall dead to the ground, occasionally kicking in their death throes. Gun smoke mingled thickly with the dust as the battle reached its climax.

I was only three at the time, and my father lifted me onto his shoulders for a better view. It was, of course, only a sham battle, and all the ammunition being expended were blanks. The year was 1912 and the scene was a dusty old fairground at the southeastern edge of Weatherford, Oklahoma. Weatherford, where I was born on March 3, 1909, is in western Oklahoma in a county named after the loser of the Battle of the Little Bighorn. The Cheyennes taking part in the sham battle were part of the same tribe that had fought the white man for so many years in a valiant struggle to keep their homelands. Weatherford was not far from the site of the Battle of the Little Washita and from where they had started their doomed trek northward, later portrayed in the book and film *Cheyenne Autumn*. At the Little Washita, they had gathered under Chief Black Kettle to sue for peace now that the buffalo were gone. But General George Armstrong Custer, bent on his trail to glory, attacked anyway, his cavalrymen slaughtering women and children. Black Kettle's fighting men, although taken by surprise, resisted furiously and took a heavy toll of Custer's troops before the village was overwhelmed.

Now the brave Cheyennes were broken, humiliated, and reduced to acting as clowns for the amusement of the conquering whites in a Buffalo Bill–type Wild West show on Weatherford's fairgrounds. It was symbolic of the end of the long struggle of the Indians to keep their lands from the encroaching whites; the fighting had become a stage play—a fake representation of what actually had been. It was an admission—an acceptance—on the part of the Indians that the real struggle was over, that they had lost finally and that the white man had won. Naturally this understanding came to me much later, but the exciting sham battle is the first vivid memory from my childhood.

Weatherford, which became a town in 1898 when the Rock Island Railroad tracks reached Custer County, is on what had been the Cheyenne-Arapaho Indian Reservation. My father, Jake, and a number of his relatives had homesteaded quarter sections of land a few years earlier, about four miles southwest of the stage station and post office that became the town. His own parents—in fact, all four of my grandparents—were Mennonites who were part of a migration from Russia to Marion County, Kansas, in 1874. The Friesens were losing their original American farm to the bank when they heard that the Cheyenne-Arapaho Reservation was being opened for white settlement. They sent Jake and his brother-in-law Frank Bergen ahead in a wagon to look over the land to determine if it was good for farming. My grandmother had baked them a bushel basket of zwiebach so they would have food along the way; the trip took them two weeks. They reported back that it was good farmland, so the Friesens made another migration to take up new homesteads. My grandfather Isaac filed on a quarter section; my father, who had just reached twenty-one, took up a homestead adjoining it to the east; close by to the west three of his brothers-in-law, Frank Bergen, J. M. Kroeker, and Dave Bushman, homesteaded their quarter sections. My father's oldest brother, also named Isaac, had become an "ootlander" from the Mennonite sect because he had married an American woman and gone off on his own. Two of my father's sisters remained in Kansas; they had married there. My father's younger brothers, Pete and John, were too young to homestead land, but they had come along anyway. Altogether they made a virtual community: there were all these homesteads practically adjoining each other. Not only relatives, but friends they had known in Kansas: David Harder, Mr. Frank Toews, and others. There was a much larger Mennonite settlement farther south, down around Corn, Oklahoma. The homesteaders there had originally spelled it "Korn," which was a

German word, but during World War I, when patriotism grew to such heights, the postmaster changed it to Corn.

The land the whites settled was what was leftover after the Indians had made their first choices, a quarter section for each headright, and they had chosen almost en masse to settle along the creek and river bottoms, which were more familiar and homelike to them, who were then a stubbornly nonagricultural people. I remember as a child seeing the Indians—after we had moved into town—coming into Weatherford on Saturdays in their buckboards, a couple of men on the seat and the women and children crouched in their blankets in the wagon bed. By this time the men were wearing white men's clothes—pants, shirts, big black hats—but they still had their long black hair braided in the old way, in two braids hanging down in front, down their chests, down to their belts, with red ribbons tied at the ends. They always had some dogs running in the shade underneath the buckboards, their tongues lolling out.

My father had always maintained a close friendship—as close as possible, at least—with the Indians since he had first come to their country. He developed a lifelong friendship with a couple of Cheyenne Indian men who lived north of Weatherford on the South Canadian River bottoms. The men would come to town on Saturdays— Walter Bear Bow and Walter Bear Head. My father would stand on the street corner and talk and laugh with them; I don't know what they talked about, I was just a kid hanging on my father's hand. When he had first plowed up his original quarter section of land, he had planted a cornfield right alongside the road, and he told his Indian friends to spread the word among their fellow tribe members that any time they came by they were welcome to stop and take all the roasting ears they needed, so that the first twelve to fifteen rows of corn right near the road were always picked by harvest time. It was a manifestation of my father's attitude not only toward the Indians but toward his fellow man in general. He was scolded for this in later years, chastised for inviting Indians to help themselves to his corn and accused of considering other people ahead of his own family. This was only one example; he was always ready to do something for other people to whom he was not even related while his own family went neglected and sank into poverty and misery.

There were other manifestations in Weatherford of the disappearing Old West when I was a kid. Old Bill Weatherford, for whom the town was named, still stalked the streets with his Colt .45 on his hip, cowboy hat cocked on the side of his head, long mustache. Weatherford was a bankrupt slaveholder from the Confederacy; I'm not sure which part of the Deep South he came from, but he had owned at least one hundred slaves; sometimes the story grew them to five hundred and even more. After the Civil War he came west, like so many other ruined Confederates, and became a United States marshal, trailing and killing outlaws in what finally became the state of Oklahoma. The territory was a refuge at that time for numerous outlaw gangs; the Daltons, the Doolans, Frank James after Jesse was killed, and many others. I remember one of Bill Weatherford's daughters telling me how he would sometimes stop in at their home to keep overnight an outlaw he had captured somewhere farther west and was taking east to Fort Smith, Arkansas, where the federal court held sway. She said he would never take the handcuffs off these prisoners. When she'd ask him why he didn't at least take the cuffs off so the poor man could eat, Bill would say he was much too dangerous, and he'd chain him to a bed and sit guard over him.

Bill Weatherford established a little general store and post office in the territory. It was a stage station on the line between El Reno and Arapaho, but when the railroad came it bypassed this spot, and the grade was laid down a mile farther south. That's where the town of Weatherford was founded in 1898, right at the time the Rock Island Railroad had reached that point. They say the town was built overnight over a cornfield—shacks, buildings, tents—and when these old buildings were demolished, dried-up cornstalks were found underneath. The Weatherford of that time had the reputation of being the toughest town in the West. Along the main street there were twenty-four saloons with brothels upstairs, one general store, and one bank. The saloons were patronized mainly by boomers following the railroad west to found new towns, the railroad workers themselves, gamblers, politicians, whores, thieves, and criminals keeping one step ahead of the law. When the young scion of the Anheuser-Busch–beer family asked in St. Louis to be taken to the toughest town in the West, they brought him to Weatherford.

Several years after the town was founded, old Bill Weatherford was called upon to lead his last manhunt. A man had murdered his wife and fled afoot west out of town into the canyon, past Banner's Bluff and on toward the Blair place. Old Bill, Winchester in hand and a posse of citizens behind him, persued the killer deep into the canyon. When he spotted his prey, he brought him down with one shot through the head. A buckboard was commandeered to bring the dying man back into town. The buckboard was too short for him, so that his head hung down off the back end, the blood running out of his mouth and nose leaving a trail behind. Half the town, including school children, ran out to meet the posse returning triumphantly with its gruesome trophy.

Of course, the Weatherford I knew during my first six or seven years was not this wild and wooly town; it had changed a lot, become quite a stable community. By this time it had two banks, a weekly newspaper, a couple of grocery stores, some dry goods stores besides its general store, and the saloons had disappeared. There was also a hardware store. One of the incidents my father was bitter about throughout his long life happened when we were still living on the homestead four miles south of town. He had been caught in Weatherford after nightfall—some business had kept him there— and the chimney of his lantern was broken. He happened that night to be completely out of money. He went to the hardware store, run by Sugden and Boyer, and although he had done hundreds of dollars' worth of business there, they refused him credit for a fifteen-cent chimney to put in his lantern so he could guide his way home. That hurt him deeply, and he never forgot it.

My father was a restless man. When I was four and my younger brother, Ollie, was just a babe in arms, he took the family to California and bought a twenty-acre vineyard at Reedley. My grandmother, Mom's mother, went along, as did my half uncle Abe. We stayed there for about a year. The main things I remember from that time were the grapes on the vines and having my right foot injured in a motorcycle accident. Uncle Abe had a motorcycle, and he gave me a ride on the back. My foot got caught in the wheel, which ripped off a couple of patches of skin about the size of a dollar. They're still visible, the scars.

My father took a correspondence course in how to become a real estate agent, so when we came back to Oklahoma he opened a little real estate office a couple of doors off Main Street and went into business. He rented a house on West Main Street. While he was in this business, a real estate company paid the family's train fare to the Rio Grande Valley in Texas to familiarize my father with land for which he might find buyers. Going through Texas, my older brother Eddie, who had a brand-new straw hat, stuck his head out the train window, and the wind blew off the headgear—and of course, the train didn't stop for it. About an hour later he turned to Mom and Dad and told them very seriously in low German, "Well, I guess my hat's in heaven by now." My folks were taken to Brownsville and shown some land around there; the real estate man took them across the Rio Grande to Matamoras, Mexico. What Dad remembered most was a trip to a graveyard—the fact that the Mexican people had to pay rents on the graves by the year. If the families of the dead didn't keep up with the rent, the skeletons were dug up and thrown over a wall into the "bone pile." Dad was stunned to look over the wall and see the mass of mingled and mixed-up skeletons of poor devils whose surviving relatives hadn't been able to pay enough to satisfy the landlord of the cemetery.

On the way back to Oklahoma we were involved in a train wreck. The train we were on jumped the track, scattering cars in all directions. I don't think there were any fatalities. We weren't hurt. But this wreck comes back to mind because my mother was in a whole series of wrecks and accidents paralleling the progress of transportation. As a girl she was in a buggy when its horse bolted. After the train wreck she was in two different car crashes; in one instance she was in a Ford that went off a grade and tumbled down a hundred-foot embankment. Later she was in a Maxwell that crashed head-on with a Metz. As an elderly woman, she was in a bus wreck in Arizona. Fortunately for the other passengers, she never took a plane ride. In none of her mishaps was she seriously injured.

It was in Weatherford that I started to school and went through kindergarten and first grade in a big red-brick building, wooden inside, on Custer Street. The main thing I got out of this education was to get my directions turned backward. I sat in a desk facing south, and the tops of the maps seemed south to me rather than north. That misdirection was permanently implanted in my young, formative brain, and to this day I have to reverse maps to visualize proper directions. (Maybe this same thing happened to Wrong Way Corrigan!) We bought most of our school supplies at Jantzen's Penny Store, where for one cent you could get a red cedar–wood lead pencil, a tiny tablet about three-by-five inches, and, if you wanted to splurge, you could get a little box of Crackerjack for a penny. I was in the second grade before I got a genuine school tablet, which cost a nickel and had a red cover with a big Indian chief's head on it.

In our primer there was a story about a girl who saved some shipwrecked sailors. Her name was Grace. There was an illustration in which she was bravely rowing a boat through a stormy sea on her way to the rescue. I got this mixed up with the religious hymn "Saved By Grace," and for a long time whenever I heard this hymn I thought it was the story of Grace saving these miserable, drowning seamen.

Early in school, in kindergarten, I was introduced to the cruelty of children toward each other. There was a shy, homely little girl named Anna Blumenshine, and we used to dance around her in a circle and chant and jeer, "Anna Blumenshine, Anna Blumenshine, see her bloomers shine." (She probably grew up to become exquisitely beautiful and change her name). I also remember when the toughest boy in town, Burton Brown, somehow got onto the steeply slanted roof of the school building; the men had a hell of a time getting him down. That caused a lot of excitement and turmoil. Burton Brown was bigger and older than the rest of us; he was in the sixth or seventh grade. We used to chant—at a safe distance—"Burton Brown, went to town, with his britches upside down." He was full of tricks he played on the younger boys. More than one involved cow shit. Almost everybody in Weatherford had a cow. In those days you couldn't go to the store and buy milk; you couldn't have milk delivered unless you were of the top-society people and could afford it. Practically every house had a cowshed behind it (ours in play became a pirate ship). It had a little loft to store hay and other feed. Boys were given a dime or so to round up the cows and herd them along the dirt streets to grass at the edge of town. In the evening the boys were required to retrieve the cows and put them in their proper sheds. While meandering along the town streets, the cows would inevitably leave a trail of what we called "cow pies." Burton Brown's bag of tricks included finding a nice fresh cow pie and carefully placing his cap over it. Then he would get some gullible little kid and tell him, "Hey, I got a bird captured under here. I'll raise the edge of the cap and you grab under there with both hands and get the bird." Burton Brown did this once too often; he got hold of a kid whom he did not recognize as a former victim. Instead of grabbing under the cap, this particular kid jumped down hard on it with both feet. Another trick involved telling the boys he had a human skeleton in the loft of his cowshed. He'd invite a kid up to view the imaginary skeleton, some kid who did not know about Burton's secret trapdoor in the middle of the loft. He would say, "Well, walk over there and look in that box, that's where I keep the skeleton." When the kid got on top of the trapdoor, Burton would spring it and drop his victim into the cow shit below.

My brother's and my closest cronies in Weatherford were Louis and Lester Avritt. They were Mexicans; their father was a section foreman for the Rock Island Railroad, and they lived in a house painted Rock Island red on railroad property just south of the tracks. Next to the house was a shed painted the same red in which were kept a handcar and tools. When the tracks in that section needed repair, the Rock Island would send extra workers from El Reno or someplace, and Mr. Avritt would supervise the work. They kept the tracks in shape, examined them for breakage. If a rail was loose they drove in new spikes; if a tie was rotted and looked like it might be a danger, they replaced it. Once a locomotive broke down and was left on a side track at Weatherford. We enjoyed a happy weekend, playing all over it, ringing the bell and pretending to be engineers speeding across the country. Often we'd put our ears to the rails and listen to the singing that messaged the approach of the trains. We stood in the cinders close to the tracks and waved and yelled at the passengers. I understand the Rock Island has closed that line down, and even the depot where we used to sit around the pot-bellied stove and listen to the clicking of the telegraph keys has long since been abandoned.

Once Burton Brown did the lot of us a real dirty trick. Often on weekends the four of us explored and played in a deep canyon behind the Avritt house. Every time we started out Mrs. Avritt warned us, "Look out for gully washers. Come out of the canyon the minute it looks like rain." We built ourselves a camp on a canyon ledge. We had a teepee made of gunnysacks and ate potatoes roasted in our campfire. One morning from the top of the railroad grade we saw our teepee on fire; someone had put a match to it. I forget just how we determined the culprit was Burton Brown, but we were sure of it. Louis and Eddie tried to think of a way to get some sort of revenge. They were afraid to face him, to confront him, so we stayed safely up on the railroad grade. They decided to yell curses down at him but were afraid to curse him in English; he might get after us and beat us up. We looked into the future and visualized him in the canyon, maybe even tying us up and setting *us* on fire. Lester asked Eddie if he knew any German curse words, which Burton Brown wouldn't understand but which we felt would get us our revenge without running the risk of retaliation. All the curse words

Eddie could think of were *du verdamter Dumbkopf*, meaning *you damned idiot*. So we stood up there on the grade shouting this down into the canyon for a long time until we were satisfied. Apparently Burton didn't know any German, for he never did anything about it. I don't know what ever happened to Burton Brown; I would venture the guess that he probably wound up as a worker for President Richard Nixon.

The Avritts were the only Mexicans living in Weatherford, except for a hot-tamale man who pushed his tamale cart around the streets. He had a shack down in the canyon right south of Main Street, and the story went around that somebody one day had discovered hundreds of cat heads behind the shack, implying that the meat in his tamales was cat meat.

Also in that part of the canyon lived an old woman all by herself whom we considered to be a witch. She always dressed in black and came out at night like a bag woman to forage through garbage in back alleys. She never came out in daylight. I never saw her myself, but the whole town believed her to be a witch, and I overheard all the talk about her. I don't know what this belief was based on, for I never heard of any instance where she actually practiced witchcraft. Just the same I was terribly afraid of her. We kids would never go down into that part of the canyon for fear she might grab us and use us in some horrifying rituals. We would stand on the big culvert— it was on West Main Street—where the canyon had its beginning and holler down in the direction of her half-hidden shack, "Hey, you old witch down there!" Then we'd run.

While on the subject of being afraid, it was as a child of two to five years of age that I had instilled into me three more-or-less intense fears, in this sequence: first, of Gypsies; second, of Catholics; and third, of Lutherans. The Gypsies were an immediate threat because they traveled in those days all throughout the country in wagons and carriages. (They started out with horse-drawn vehicles, advanced to Maxwell automobiles, and since have graduated to Cadillacs.) I was terribly scared of Gypsies because I was warned by my parents that they would capture small children and carry them off for the purpose of turning them into Gypsies; I guess in those days it would be called brainwashing. You came to believe that if you got caught by them, they'd make you into a Gypsy child and you'd forget your whole background, lose track of what you had been, and your folks would never hear of you again, never be able to find you. So whenever a strange wagon or carriage came down the dusty road I would run and hide, my little heart pounding.

I had three personal experiences with either real or imaginary Gypsies. The first was on the homestead near Weatherford when I was too small to remember the details, which were filled in later by Mom and Dad. A Gypsy troupe descended on the farmstead utilizing their favorite ploy: claiming an old grandmother was sick and begging for chickens to make soup for her (the Gypsies would gather up free chickens in this way and sell them for cash at the nearest poultry-buying store). When my parents refused, grabbed Eddie and me, and ran into the house, the Gypsies showed their dissatisfaction in various ways. The most spectacular was when one of the Gypsy men climbed onto the windmill, took down his pants, and shit a stream out into the air. The second happened after we had moved to town. I was playing at the edge of the street when a wagon came by with two men in the seat. One of them yelled at me, "We're Gypsies and we're going to kidnap you!" I raced into the house, scared stiff. Actually they were not Gypsies at all, but ordinary farmers. The third instance occurred in western Kansas when I was at home alone; it was a Sunday afternoon, and the rest of the family had gone off visiting. A caravan of Gypsies, this time travelling in cars, stopped on the road, and a Gypsy kid came to the house with the same old story: "My grandmother is sick. Give us a chicken so we can make some soup for her." I was very frightened, but did have the courage to say, "No, I ain't goin' to give you no chickens," dreading the unknown vengeance they might visit on me. But the kid simply ran back to the cars shouting at me back over his shoulder, "You goddamned son-of-a-bitch." The caravan proceeded on its way, presumably hoping for better luck next stop.

My fear of the Catholics was a heritage from the past. Our Protestant sect was founded by a former Catholic priest, Menno Simons, during the Reformation; in revenge of his rebellion the Catholic churchdom martyred innumerable early followers of Simons. This centuries-old fear was renewed during the Spanish-American War, when enormous waves of propaganda were spread in the U.S. charging the Catholics with committing terrible atrocities in Cuba. There were apparently few homes in the country that did not receive leaflets and booklets describing and picturing the horrible atrocities being inflicted on the people of Cuba by the Spanish Catholics. Our booklet had a picture of Cuban children in terribly starved conditions; they were just skin and bones. It resembled photos years later showing the victims of liberated Nazi concentration camps. This anti-Spanish propaganda was spread, of course, to gain the support of the American people for the war against Spain and to justify the acquisition by the U.S. imperialists of the Spanish colonies—Cuba, Puerto Rico, and the Philippines. So that was my second deep fear. If the Gypsies didn't get me, the Catholics would.

Also there existed in me an uneasy concern that I would come to some kind of harm at the hands of German Lutherans. This apprehension has been perpetuated among the Mennonites during the four hundred years since Martin Luther advised the German princes to put the Mennonites to the sword and kill them all. Fear of the Lutherans still existed in our minds; it was taught to us by our parents, who got it from their parents and ancestors going all the way back to 1525 and Menno Simons. But it had grown quite dim by the time we came along; in fact my sister, Esther, married a Lutheran, Walter Reifschneider. Perhaps it was because we had something in common: his ancestors, too, had migrated to Russia, settling along the Volga River. They were known as Volga Germans (it's hard to translate into English, but we in the low German language call them something like "Vulgoah").

Strangely enough I was never afraid of the Indians, although the Indians had been a much more recent threat. In fact, only a short time before I was born there had been the last Indian "scare" in the area. Riders came out from Weatherford to the farmsteads urging all the families to come into town for protection. They warned that Indians by the thousands were assembling on Deer Creek about ten miles east of town and were preparing to go on the warpath to kill all the white settlers. They were described as being in the midst of their war dances. Most if not all of the white homesteaders loaded their families into wagons and buckboards and hurried as fast as they could into town. My parents were among them. It turned out that the whole thing was a hoax perpetrated by these young white jokers, because when scouts were sent out to reconnoiter the supposed war encampment, they reported back they had not seen a single Indian. I suppose I was never afraid of Indians because of my father's friendship with them.

There were very few blacks in and around Weatherford. One was a barber who had his shop in the basement underneath the Emerson Racket Store. He also had public baths in his barber shop. His establishment was patronized mainly by white farmers who generally came in on Saturday night for a haircut, shave, and a bath. The only other black business in town was a dry-cleaning shop. There were two black farmers west of town living on skimpy acreages not big enough to support them and their families, so to eke out a living they engaged in other pursuits. One was a moonshiner. The other was hired by townspeople to clean out their privies. There was as yet no sewage system in Weatherford. The holes under the seats of the outhouses were lined with cement; when they started to get too full he would climb down in there, barefooted and with his pants-legs rolled up, and bail the shit into barrels he had on his buckboard. After he had scooped and shoveled all the accumulations into his barrels, he would haul the contents out to a canyon near his house and dump them. He had a second business going, which was to raise hogs with the slop he gathered in the alleys back of the houses and restaurants. For this he did not get paid; it was sufficient that he got the slop for free. Once, on leaving town with a load of shit, his horse ran away, and in turning a corner the barrels tipped over and the shit sprayed over the front of three or four houses.

The butt of the white jokers along Main Street in Weatherford was a black man they called Rastus. Whenever he appeared walking the street there was invariably a white who would goose him and give out a whistle at the same time (goosing was poking in the ass). This caused Rastus to jump up two or three feet in the air. He carried some kind of skinny little whip, which was really no danger to any-body, but on landing back on his feet he would whirl around and lash out at whoever was tormenting him. He was an elderly white-haired man, but this only seemed to make it all the more fun for the jokesters because he was unable to retaliate in any real sense. All the businessmen along Main Street—the big shots—got a tre-mendous kick out of this cruel torture of a human being. They would stand in the doorways of their establishments and laugh their heads off.

It was during this period in Weatherford that I got my first intro-duction to sex. There was only one Jew, as I remember, in early Weatherford—Mr. Soloway, who owned a dry-goods store called the Dixie. Apparently he assumed that Weatherford had enough ex-Confederates to make a business by this name pay. He sold women's clothes and men's pants, shirts, and coats. His residence was only three doors from us on West Main Street, and he would bring home and pile up in his back yard the boxes in which his goods had arrived from wherever he ordered them. They were wooden boxes piled one on top of the other, and it was in these boxes that I had my first sexual experience, although I didn't realize at the time what was happening; I was so young that the stirrings of sex were just beginning. I was about five. A little neighbor girl and I would go down the alley back of our house, back of her house, back of the Soloway house, and we'd go into the boxes to play house, play like we were husband and wife. We took off all our clothes, but we didn't know the procedure. Sometimes I would lie on top of her, sometimes she would lie on top of me, both of us completely naked, without any idea of what to do next. One thrill we enjoyed was watching each other urinate. I would watch her urinate, then she would watch me, and that caused the very first beginnings of sexual feeling. She was killed in a car crash when she was about thirty years old.

One of the most emotional events I remember from my childhood in Weatherford was the annual Christmas Eve celebration. A big platform was erected in the middle of Main Street topped by a good-sized cedar tree. The canyons around town were full of evergreen cedars from which the people would select Christmas trees; not only could you find them in the canyons but also along the fence rows, where birds, perched on the top strand, would drop the seeds after digesting the outer covering of the purple berries. Virtually every family would gather around the town Christmas tree. There was a Santa Claus on the platform who would hand out little paper boxes full of candy and nuts to the kids. Then the whole assemblage would sing "Silent Night, Holy Night." It was all very stirring to a small kid—even to this day whenever I hear "Silent Night" I get a nostalgic reaction.

Although I have only a dim remembrance of it, a highly touted movie came to Weatherford in 1915. It was a sin for Mennonites to attend a motion picture (a new invention by the devil), but the publicity must have been so forceful it broke down my father's inhibitions, and he sneaked away from mother to see it, taking me and Eddie along. I assume it was "Birth of a Nation," for later on in western Kansas Ollie and I, inspired by scenes from it, carried out cavalry charges, riding stick horses and cutting down the enemy with sabers shaped from laths.

It seemed that some of our relatives were getting into various kinds of trouble, and my father was invariably called upon to straighten things out. Sometimes his solutions were quite valuable and lasting, as in the case of his sister's boy, Jake Kroeker. Whenever his father brought him into town he would go along the gutters and pick up everything he found there and examine it closely, turning it over and over. It might be a piece of tinfoil, a scrap of paper, cigar wrappers, or even half-smoked butts. The townspeople considered this to be strange behavior and suggested to my father that Jake belonged in an institution. But Dad knew it was simply that Jake possessed an unusually inquisitive mind. (At home he had built a working model of a steam engine from sundry odds and ends—he was probably trying to figure out to what use he might put all this junk from the street.) My father got him enrolled in the Southwestern Normal Academy, a division of the school where prospective teachers got training. He rented Jake a room in our house, for which Mr. Kroeker paid a dollar a week. The payment was always in produce, mainly butter and eggs; there was never any cash involved. Cousin Jake went to school long enough to learn accounting; he learned how to balance books and make the sums come out right. Later on he got a job with the Ford Motor Company as a bookkeeper, which lasted his lifetime. And it was my father who rescued him from the difficulties into which he was drifting and set him on the course to a productive life.

The problems my mother's relatives created were more troublesome. Her brother, my uncle Dave Duerksen, had violated all Mennonite principles by joining the United States Army. He served in the Philippines with the American troops who subdued the patriot Aguinaldo. Now he was living in Weatherford with a wife named Mittie. While he was away following the harvest, she carried on with other men. One night there was a fight in her place around two o'clock in the morning, and somebody got stabbed with a butcher knife. The town marshal came to our place to get Dad to resolve the situation; he managed to keep Mittie out of jail, but not to cure her of her unsavory activities.

Then there was a night when we were awakened by another commotion. Mother's half sister, who was just a girl at that time, had allowed her boyfriend to talk her into joining him in stealing one of the first automobiles ever bought in Weatherford. They escaped westward out of town. I don't know whether or not they planned to drive the car to California—the distance was only about fifteen hundred miles. But the alert marshal quickly pursued with a horse and buggy and caught up with them about halfway to Clinton, only twenty miles west of Weatherford. Their stolen car was trapped on high center. (The roads were originally laid out for horse-drawn traffic and became two parallel ruts, and the deeper these ruts got, the higher became the center ridge between them. When cars were introduced the transmissions got caught on the high center; they stalled there. Early motorists learned to carry spades with which to dig their cars loose.) Anyway, the marshal arrested these novice car thieves, handcuffed them, brought them back to town, and clapped them into the town jail, a one-cell concrete blockhouse in the alley back of Thacker's grocery store. Then he came to our house to discuss the situation with Dad. Soon everybody was awake. My mother was yelling and crying, my father was trying to stay calm and work out some way with the marshal to at least get Mom's half sister out of jail. The marshal finally released her in Dad's custody. At the time it wasn't so much a matter of hiring lawyers and battling cases out in the courts. An agreement was reached person-to-person. The marshal would come to our house and ask Dad, "Now look, what can we do here?" and they'd reach some satisfactory mutual conclusion. I don't know what happened to the boyfriend; I think he was told to leave town and never return.

There was a sort of irony in the incident. The first car stolen in Weatherford belonged to Dr. Matt Gordon, who delivered me and for whom I am named. (There were a lot of Gordons around Weatherford whom he had delivered—I can think of Gordon Collins, Gordon Pigg, Gordon Goss, and there were others.) Dr. Gordon and his partner, Dr. J. J. Williams, had homesteaded 160 acres across the road half a mile north of my father's homestead, and my father knew them quite well. They made their calls in those early days by horse and buggy. As soon as Weatherford was founded, they opened an office in town. They were from the South; Dr. Gordon's home town was Florence, Alabama. I imagine my father was quite ashamed that after all the years of their friendship, it was a member of his family who had tried to steal Dr. Gordon's car.

Even without all these family distractions, my father probably would not have been a successful real-estate man. He was too honest and too sensitive. He often said that to achieve success as a real-estate agent, one had to be a crook and a swindler, and he didn't want to be that kind of person. He felt he had been cheated out of a three-hundred-dollar commission by a banker named Galloway. In the early days of the depression, Galloway's bank was one of the multitude that failed. Although it was a national phenomenon of capitalistic collapse, many bankers were held personally responsible by the depositors who lost their life's savings. A number of Weatherford townspeople believed Galloway had stolen their money; among these was Bud Rainey, a son-in-law of old Bill Weatherford, who strapped on his frontier six-gun and began stalking the streets and alleyways proclaiming loudly that he was going to shoot Galloway on sight. His intended victim took Bud's threat very seriously and remained in his house for two or three years behind drawn shades. This situation naturally interfered with the Galloways' social life—they belonged to the very highest strata of Weatherford society. Mrs. Galloway finally got a job at the University of Oklahoma in Norman and spirited her besieged husband out of town in the dark of night. My father maintained that the Galloways had lived those last secluded years in Weatherford on his nine-hundred-dollar life savings, plus the money lost by the other depositors in the failed bank.

Fate eventually intervened in such an absolute way as to change our lives forever. My father and a very close friend of his and our next-door neighbor on West Main Street, Frank Toews, who also homesteaded southwest of Weatherford, had applied for the franchise to operate the Ford agency in Weatherford; they were number one on the list. They were preparing to complete the final negotiations when Mr. Toews became ill with typhoid fever; he got a very high fever and went out of his head. In his last hours, he ran outside and wandered about in his delirium. It took some hours to find him and bring him back, and he died shortly thereafter. Next on the list for the Ford franchise was my father's younger brother Pete, P. E. Friesen, and his partner Jake Bergman. So they got the franchise, and in the succeeding years they became the richest men in Custer Country, selling Ford cars, Fordson tractors, and, later on, Massey-Harris combines. They took a lot of mortgages and foreclosed on these when the farmers couldn't pay, and in that way accumulated a lot of land. If Mr. Toews had not died when he did, this book would not have been written.

My father was ready to move again. His dream of being half-owner of the Ford franchise was shattered. His real-estate agency was becoming more and more distasteful to him. He was weary of the seemingly endless negotiations with the town marshal. When the new widow Toews offered to trade a quarter section she owned in Ford County, Kansas, for my father's homestead, he jumped at the chance. He went to look at the Kansas land, up on the southern edge of Ford near Meade County. It looked good to him, and he made the fateful trade. In the early spring of 1916, my father bought a new Ford car—a Copperhead, so called because of its brass radiator— loaded the whole family into it (at that time there were only the first three children: Eddie, the eldest, myself, and Ollie), and we moved to our new home.

Chapter 2

Sis's Childhood

We plough and sow, we're so very very low that we delve in the dirty clay,
'til we bless the plain with the golden grain and the vale with the fragrant
   hay,
Our place we know—we're so very low, 'tis down at the landlord's feet.
We're not too low the bread to grow but too low the bread to eat.

("The Song of the Lower Classes," words by Ernest Jones, music by Sis
Cunningham, c. 1933)

We were permitted to play with Grandpa Cunningham's Civil
War rifle, but we weren't supposed to take it outside the house.
Sometimes we did though. But only on a sunny day. So long as we
didn't get the rifle wet there'd be no harm done, and we couldn't
have much fun playing with it inside—there was nothing to sight.
And that was what we liked most about it, the dandy sighting gadget
it had. The rifle was big and heavy; it had a long barrel and a thick
stock. We'd place it across a corner of the stoop, then we'd sit on
the lowest step and sight out over the railroad track into the cornfield beyond where we could see amazing targets when we looked
through the little openings in the sight. There was a thing that
snapped up and then another thing you could pull up out of the
thing that snapped up—a dilly for tinkering with. Our Dad had explained that this double sight was so Grandpa could sight an enemy
soldier at close range or way off in the distance—and never miss
when he pulled the trigger. We often wondered how many Johnny
Rebs this rifle had killed. We kids liked to boast of killing quite a
few ourselves.

I was about six the first time we took the Civil War rifle outside.
My brother John, three years older, lugged it out and put it across
the stoop. When it was my turn to sight, I pulled the trigger. He
looked scared and said not to do that—that a shell might be stuck
in there and would get unstuck all of a sudden and shoot somebody.

Or somebody's cow, which was worse. A small metal piece or two—pins or something—were missing in the mechanism, and it had been years since there'd been any ammunition for the old gun. But John was always cautious about everything; he didn't want to take any chances. After all, we weren't even supposed to have it outside. Once when we had it out Dad came in early from the field and caught us. We were so busy sighting that he came right up behind us and picked the rifle up in his big hard hands and carefully slid and clicked the sights into the cradle. He took the gun in the house and stood it up in its corner beside the kitchen cabinet. Later he said in a sharp voice that if we ever was to take the double-loader down he'd use the razor strap on us, damned if he wouldn't. The double-loader was the shotgun. Then he spoke more softly and said, "I'd like ya not to bust that old gun, more than she is already. Play with her on the bed, if you hafta play with her. You know she was your Grandpa's."

He told us about Grandpa, who had died before the turn of the century. Captain William Cunningham of the Eighth Iowa Infantry, Company K, a good soldier for the Union, "damned if he wasn't." He fought in twenty-seven battles, including Shiloh. And he served under the famous Colonel Geddes, a Scotsman like himself, for whom he named one of his three furlough babies. That was our Uncle Ged, one of Dad's half brothers. Grandpa enlisted at the start of the war and served three years, during which time he was wounded twice. Then he re-enlisted for the duration and was wounded again, and they kept him in the army in a special service for a year after the war ended. When he was finally mustered out he was a semi-invalid, and never did get back his full health. And he never got the pension that was due him; he didn't even apply. He said that they knew in Washington what he had done and how bad his wounds were and it was up to them to send him a pension if they were a mind to. If not, to hell with them—and the pension. He figured that he had done as much for the cause of antislavery as his father before him had done, and that was not to be sniffed at.

Great Grandfather Cunningham had come to this country around the late 1830s with a little capital, and he had built a gristmill on the Ohio River at Old Washington near Gallipolis, and it was here that he became operator of a station on the Underground Railway. He built double walls in his mill where escaping slaves could hide out, and my father said no slave was ever caught and returned from his station. (I don't know how long he operated this Underground Railway station, and I don't know how long the mill remained standing, but now there's a main highway built right over the sight.)

Our most famous ancestor was Sir William Wallace of Scotland, who lived and performed his brave deeds in the thirteenth century. My father's given name was William Wallace, and all the way back through the generations there have been Williams and Wallaces— one way of hanging on to what was considered prideworthy in the family, I suppose. Grandpa Cunningham was William, and my two older brothers were William Meredith and John Wallace.

Sir William didn't have a very long lifetime, but he sure made a mark for himself while he lived—he was a kind of military genius for those times. He came from the working class and he was just about worshiped by the common people. In his midtwenties he got the support of a bunch of nobles. They were the ones who wanted to keep Scotland independent, and he won them over because he could lead men in battle better than anyone else. Other leaders might be wishy-washy, but Wallace was never that; he was a constant. He said freedom was a national birthright, and he stuck to it and got the title of Guardian of Scotland, which meant that they put him pretty much in charge of things. Some Scottish historian or other calls him "the noblest and purest of his country's heroes." My father sure felt that way about him, but he didn't put it in those terms, quite. He'd say something like, "If that young feller didn't spear them Englishmen in the belly, he got 'em in the butt and drove 'em t'hell outa there and across the border where they was supposed to be, damned if he didn't." Wallace's men were on foot and they fought with bows and arrows and spears. They'd be greatly outnumbered by English heavy cavalry, King Edward's men. But they'd win. In between these battles Wallace always had plenty of places to hide out, but they finally got him. They ran him down, seized him in the year 1306, and they took him to Westminster Hall and tried him for treason. At the trial he announced that he couldn't possibly be a traitor because he was not and never had been a subject of the king of England. He was hanged that same year; he was about thirty-three. The loyal Scots thought of him as a martyr, and they put up a beautiful monument to him in Stirlingshire. It must still be there, a huge castlelike structure high on a hilltop that overlooks the scene of one of his routs of the British, the Battle of Stirling Bridge.

Grandpa Cunningham was bad-off after the war, but he managed to sire thirteen more children, eleven of them sons. That was quite a lot of fathering, even for those times. Grandma Cunningham had been Alice Smith before she married. She was pregnant or with a child at the breast for over twenty years steady. And she had to bring up two stepsons (the third of Grandpa's war babies died in infancy).

My father was the second of Alice's thirteen, and after him kids just kept coming. The poverty was not just bad, it was about as near to being hopeless as anything I've heard of. I can't begin to describe it the way Dad told it. They scraped an existence from a small farm in Iowa where most of these children were born and two baby boys died. They had to deal with blizzards blowing down across the plains from the north; there was nothing to break the fierce winds that often came at the same time as a snowstorm. But winter or summer, life for my grandparents and their huge family must have been one long scramble just to get what was needed to stay alive.

Dad was named William but they called him Chick. He'd gotten that nickname as a little baby, and it stuck through his life. His brother Ned, two years old when Dad was born, had said just one word, "chicken," when he first looked at Dad, so Chick it was from then on. But the teacher in the school called him William—he got to go through third grade.

When he was nine he was farmed out to better-off neighbors for a dollar a month and keep, the money being paid to his parents and the "keep" being mostly cornmeal mush and a pallet of straw in the attic or barn loft. If he became sick he was packed off home, and there was no dollar that month even if he was only sick a week. In any large family there occurred many bouts with diptheria and pneumonia; these were very critical diseases back then that sometimes lasted a long time. They also had outbreaks of boils, probably because of poor diets, and my father told of a case of bone infection he had that just about killed him. But in spite of all this he grew to six-foot-three in his bare feet and weighed two hundred pounds at age twenty. He used to boast that he had never varied more than five pounds from that weight through his entire adult life (and he weighed the same a year before he died at age seventy-one).

Dad must have done quite well as a hired hand. At thirteen he was considered a full hand with pay upped by fifty cents a month to a dollar and a half. He told of working for a family where the mother had died and there were no daughters, just the old man and some boys. A sickly boy who was not much good at outdoors work did the cooking, and he stirred up some pretty awful messes. At the supper table on my dad's first night at this place a bowl of something that positively stank was put in front of him, and since the others were eating, he put a spoonful in his mouth. He couldn't swallow it—just sat there holding the mess in his mouth. After a while the old man noticed and got red in the face and said, "Spit 'er out if ya don't like 'er. Our boys eats 'er." Dad said he left the table that night and went to his loft. But he learned to eat what was put before him and stayed on there for quite some time. (All the time we were growing up as kids and would show dislike for something at the table, my father would repeat what this old man had said to him.)

Grandpa Cunningham got restless in Iowa. He was always complaining of the cold. His boys were doing all the farm work—he was totally unable to do anything but pull himself up to the table for such meals as they had and carry out his husbandly duties on the straw mattress at night. But as the boys got bigger, the lot of the family was somewhat improved, so they were able to do something about the old man's wish to try to find greener pastures. They got a covered wagon rigged up and a team of fair-to-middling horses and took to the trail headed southwest. They made it to southern Kansas. They lived in a dugout there and it seemed, at least for a time, that it had been a bad move, hard on all of them, but especially the mother and younger children. A little girl, next to the last of the thirteen, died of diptheria in that dugout. Little Hattie, they called her, and she was two years old when she died. My father could hardly hold back his tears when he told how she'd cry for "ba-boodle-ah," which was her word for *milk*. A man who called himself a doctor said not to give milk to a child with diptheria, so they hadn't given Hattie any; Dad figured she'd starved to death. The crying for "ba-boodle-ah" went on pitifully for days, getting weaker and more faint until it sounded like the mewling of a little sick kitten and the tiny body shrunk to nothing. Later on the family learned that milk might have saved Hattie.

The dugout, as they called it, was really only half dug out of the side of a hill; the other half was a one-room sod shanty, a terribly cramped place for such a huge family—and another baby on the way. Seven or eight months of the year the older boys slept outside or in a shed with the pigs or cow. But Kansas was anything but warm in the wintertime, and at night the shanty and dugout floors of pounded dirt were covered with straw mattresses and thrown-down quilts for twelve to fifteen people to sleep on, depending on who was away looking for work.

At age eighteen my father went to the Pacific Northwest and worked for a year as a lumberjack. He said he liked it there and sometimes wished he'd stayed. Going out he "bummed it" because he had no money. But coming back he rode the Union Pacific most of the way and paid his fare—that was some experience for him to boast about when he got home. None of the other boys got quite as adventurous as Chick, anyway not at such a young age. He had the two half brothers and then there was Ned, older than he was. But Ned was just a little retarded—not very bright, they always used to say—and he stayed around home until he was kind of pushed out by circumstance.

My father homesteaded in Oklahoma, making "the run" when the Cherokee Strip was opened for white settlement in 1893. When he talked about this he called it "the race." He made the race on horseback. But there were wagons of all sizes and kinds—there were buggies, two-wheeled shays, even a few of those bicycles with the big wheel in front. Dad told of people on foot, women on horseback, women in big plumed hats bouncing along in the back seats of surries sporting drivers up front.

All these people, horses, and vehicles were lined up for miles and miles at the border of the strip. There were army men stationed at points along the line, and at a certain time they were to shoot their guns signaling for the race to begin. *Bang!* and everybody raced, just tore off across the prairies hell-bent for land. Of course, the horseback riders could go faster; others had their families, their kids, a few chickens, even a pig or two, some household stuff, which slowed them a little. But they went tearing and bumping along in buckboards, covered wagons, spring wagons, ox carts, anything with wheels. Some of the vehicles tipped over; there were some bad spills, some injuries, a few fatalities—this, that, and the other thing. If a wheel worked loose and rolled off, my father said, "kids, dogs, and skillets went spillin' out over the prairie. And if one horse got a broke leg steppin' in a prairie-dog hole, runnin' the way they was, the woman would stay to shoot it while the man jumped on the other horse and rode like the devil back into the race." The people were hungry for land; they went out there and they staked a claim.

The strip opening was the biggest of the land runs they had in Oklahoma. It was called the Cherokee Strip because it had been set aside for the Cherokees. But there really weren't any Cherokee Indians living on it. In the 1880s they had leased the land to cattle ranchers, big cattlemen's associations. There were Cherokee Indians in Oklahoma in the '90s, but they were in the eastern part of the state; the strip was a large area in the northwestern part. The north edge where the people lined up was the Kansas border.

The day of this run was September 16, and it was a mighty day for a lot of people—a greater day than the first opening in 1889, which had been more in the central part of the state. (In her novel *Cimarron*—later made into a movie—Edna Ferber describes the first Oklahoma land run in 1889.) The Cherokee strip opening was *the* race. Of course, there were some crooks, the Sooners. Sooners got in ahead of time and staked themselves a claim illegally, so when those who made the Run legally got there, they would find these guys standing on a claim pretending they just ran a little faster, their horses were a little better, they got there a little quicker. There would be confrontations then. Sometimes a Sooner would win out, and I guess sometimes these honest guys would take their shotguns and blow the damn Sooners' heads off. My father said an honest farmer could tell those sons-a-bitches by their smell. The term *Sooner* stuck, though. Oklahoma is still called the Sooner State, and the football team at the University is called the Oklahoma Sooners. But in those days, the Sooners were crooks—the worst kind. The Boomers were those who had waged the campaign through the '70s and '80s to have Oklahoma lands opened for settlement. Their campaign was the main factor in breaking down the efforts of the Indians to keep their nations going.

The first farm my father claimed—everybody was in a hurry, hurry up, to find something and stake it—his first claim he didn't like. It was bare of trees, and he wanted a little patch of blackjacks so he'd have firewood for at least a while. So he waited until some fellow came by who did like it and was willing to buy it off him. He got twenty-five dollars for it (160 acres) and moved farther south across the Cimarron and paid the twenty-five dollars for a farm he liked better. This one he settled on and lived there for about twelve years; built a shanty and "batched" up to the time he married my mother and brought her there. My mother said Dad's hair was almost completely white when she met him, though it had been dark brown when he was a child. That hair, it was beautiful—a big shock of white hair from the time I first remember him. It never thinned; he had this thick white hair when he died.

Dad's older half brothers and a couple of the others, the ones old enough, homesteaded in Oklahoma the same time Dad did. Other brothers came later until there were a whole mess of Cunninghams right around in the same general locality. It was hard work to clear and break in this land, but the Cunninghams were used to hard work—it was more the tediousness of it, especially during the first years, that almost caused my father to give up and make the long trek back to the state of Washington, back into lumber country. It was harder and more lonely for the unmarried homesteaders, which was what Dad was for seven or eight years. But it was not all bitterness. No life is lived through in utter bleakness; if bleakness it is, then a curtain has been drawn, and behind it people just exist, they do not live.

The Cunningham brothers found a way to lighten their burdens; they formed a baseball team after they were more-or-less settled in Oklahoma. My father was in his late twenties by then and there were enough grown Cunninghams, or nearly grown, to make a team, counting the two half brothers, Ned and Tom. Mostly they challenged neighboring teams just for the hell of it. But two of them, Chet and Chick, became a "professional" pitcher/catcher duo and hired themselves out as a battery wherever they could for three dollars a piece per game, which was a small fortune in those days. Dad used to tell of them getting themselves an engagement across the Cimarron River, and when the day came the river was flooded to the width of over a mile all along where they had to cross over. So they swam the river, played their game, collected their six dollars, and swam back across to where their saddle horses were tied. They got home in time to milk the cows.

Dad would ramble on about those past times: "The country sure was a pretty sight in the early days, damned if it wasn't. Not cluttered up with towns like nowadays. Why, by god, you could ride your horse for miles and miles and there'd be nothin' but open country as far as you could see, just as flat and pretty as anybody'd want; just a cabin here and there and them pretty clumps of blackjacks scattered along. And it'd be in the cool of the evenin' with the sun goin' down across the prairie well—that was about as good a time as could be for anybody that had a feelin' for the land. I don't recollect any better."

He'd tell how he and Chet would be tired after a fast game; it wasn't such easy work. But with the extra money in their pockets, they were lighthearted and at peace with their world. These were the times my father wasn't at all sorry that he had come back to the southwest from the state of Washington and the lumbering. Having a piece of land of his own had turned out to be better than working for wages. "Sure was better . . . back in the early days. Hell, nowadays it's banks and Wall Street grain speculators runnin' the damn country—runnin' and ruinin' it. Times sure ain't like they was by a damn site." Dad finished most of his ramblings on this note.

Some of the aspects of life in "the early days" I gleaned from my mother, who had been a school teacher for seven or eight years before becoming a frontier wife. Teachers of the one-room country schools were required only to graduate from eighth grade and attend six weeks of normal school, which my mother did and began her teaching career at age sixteen. She drove her little horse cart to the school from the home of the farm family she boarded with. Her salary was twenty-five dollars a month, five dollars of which she paid for room and board. She was about five feet tall weighing eighty-five pounds, and she told sometimes of the difficulty of teaching pupils bigger and older than she was, the boys especially. She didn't talk much about her teaching; it must have been very hard. But she remembered the activities connected with the church with considerable fondness. "That was where we girls got to meet fellows—at the church picnics." She smiled and blushed slightly at this. Then she'd explain that she didn't go to dances until after she married Dad because her father didn't approve of dances. But church picnics had the old man's blessing; after all, daughters must find mates somehow. (An amusing little aside to this is that Grandma Boyce leaked out to us what a feller Grandpa had been on the dance floor when he was a young man.)

None of the Cunninghams were religious, but they went to these church gatherings to play baseball firstly, and secondly to look around for a pretty girl to marry. Or maybe it was vice-versa. They needed womenfolk on their homesteads. Chick and Chet had their eyes on Ada and Edna, the little Boyce twins, my mother and aunt. The Boyces were staunch Methodists; the family never missed a Sunday's church service. So the two atheist Cunningham brothers went regularly to church for a time and even learned a few hymns. Chick played fiddle in the church, which was not too easy for him since he played for all the square dances in the vicinity, and this church music was really something else. I think it was during this time that he learned to read notes, to be able to follow the music of the hymns. My mother also played what she called the violin. It wasn't too long before she and Chick were carrying on an intensive courtship.

There were a few changes after Ada married him and they went to live on his claim near Okeene. She discovered what was causing the stomach trouble he'd had since their courtship. She went about making them some coffee and found that his blackened old pot had an inch of dark-greenish crud in the bottom of it; he had never washed the pot in the seven years of his bachelorhood. The first thing Ada did on the day she moved in with Chick—he'd built himself a frame house—was to throw out the coffee pot, and Chick got over his stomach trouble. He also got over going to church; that was no longer necessary.

During their courtship they had discovered something about their past lives that perhaps drew them together more than anything else: that they had been born and spent their childhood days a few miles from each other near Creston, Iowa. But unlike the Cunninghams, who came to Oklahoma via Kansas, the Boyces had made their covered-wagon trek to Missouri, a trip that kept them six weeks on the trail with the half-grown twins and four smaller children. And they took more stuff with them than the Cunninghams—they had more to take—cows, chickens, probably a dog or two, chests of clothes and heirlooms, sacks of seed grain, and the family Bible (which was one item the Cunninghams didn't have, unless Grandmother Alice toted one secretly).

The Boyce family was escaping the cold also. Southwestern Missouri in Ozark country was their stopping place, but they found that the farmland was not what they expected. Grandpa Boyce had known it would be hilly, but he must have had no idea how hilly— and rocky. He couldn't handle the rocks. Some traveler had given him a description of the Ozark country; it was so fine to the eye and so mild-climated—but he had left off mentioning the rocks. So the family made the trek back north, to Nebraska this time and back into the cold. They spent a few winters in blizzards worse than those they'd had in Iowa, then they headed southward again. They settled in Oklahoma this time, on a nice flat quarter section of already-broken land that turned out to be only four miles from Dad's claim.

My mother always felt a kind of wonder in this—being born in the same community and then meeting as grown-ups so many hundreds of miles from the spot. I suppose if you consider the way they traveled in those days and the number of moves made by the two families, you could say it was just a coincidence.

I believe the miracle of my mother's life was that she lived at all. She and her identical twin were born two months premature to their sixteen-year-old mother in January in an Iowa blizzard with no doctor in attendance, only a midwife. The babies were bedded down in shoe boxes lined with cotton and with a bottle of warm water laid in beside each one. An ordinary teacup fitted nicely over their heads—just for measurement purposes, of course. When they were about two weeks old it occurred to somebody to weigh them. The only scale available was one used in measuring produce, so both babies were weighed together in their didies, long dresses, and sacs, and wrapped in receiving blankets. The whole kit and caboodle tipped the scale at six pounds; it was estimated that they had weighed two and a half each at birth. I don't know how they survived, but they both lived to be quite old, Mama well into her eighties, a considerably longer life than my father had.

Her childhood was easier than my father's once they got beyond infancy. Her folks were better off than his. They had more land, better land. They did all their own work same as Dad's family, but they had more to eat, a better house, and better clothing. Grandpa Boyce was not an invalid as Grandpa Cunningham was; restlessness was about the only thing my two grandfathers had in common.

In the Boyce household the womenfolks' skills were varied and adequate; they spun wool for knitting into winter garments, even socks; they bought bolts of cotton cloth and sewed by hand everything the family needed in the way of light garments. The dresses for girls aged twelve and over had no less than seven yards in the skirts, always floor length in those days. They had no sewing machine. We had a foot-operated machine at home while I was growing up, but still my mother hemmed by hand; she said it was softer. I loved to watch her as she hemmed; her needle fairly flew through the cloth. It amazed me; I could never stitch like that. But she had learned to do it as a small child. Imagine doing a mile or so of hand stitching on your year's wardrobe. Each dress required a few hundred feet of it, double seams throughout, lace to whip on, tucking, smocking, and at least two dozen buttonholes. And then each dress had a petticoat of equal yardage to go underneath, Sunday dresses two or three. Not to mention drawers and camisoles. And in addition to their own clothes, the women made the boys' and men's wear, as well as quilts, comforters, featherbeds, pillows, and rag rugs for the cold floors in winter. When did those women can their food, cook, wash, churn butter? They milked cows, too. How did they find time to go to church? Or give birth?

I was the middle child of five—two older brothers and a younger brother and sister. I was born on February 19, 1909, in the same bed I was fathered in. Mama said I was a quiet baby—that none of us bawled very long after we were born—and I think I know why that was: the competition beat us out. The demands of the farm work on our mother's time and energy kept her from picking us up except for suckling. Our parents got up early, went to bed early, and in between they worked without let-up. They had moved in 1907 (the year Oklahoma became a state) to a sandy farm on the banks of the North Canadian River, where I was born two years later. But it was no good on this place. Bill, my oldest brother, developed malaria there. So another move was made, this time to a farm closer to town, and it turned out to be a good move. The land was better, it was good wheat land. But it was then that we really got in the clutches of the mortgage company. There were no improvements on the new farm. Dad borrowed every dollar he could to get a good start. First to be done was to dig a well and set in a pump, the kind that could be attached to a windmill later. Then the building of a barn so the family could be moved to the new place. I was too little to remember, but we lived for a while in a couple of grain bins, the only part of the barn besides the hayloft that had a floor of sorts. Next to be built was a storm cellar. My mother was terrified of wind storms; she had been in a tornado that had blown part of her folks' house away, leaving the rest of it—the floor and one wall—crosswise on the foundation. Nobody had been badly hurt, but even a high straight wind, which we often had on the prairies, threw Mama into a panic; she wanted the best kind of storm cellar that could be built, even if she had to live in the barn the rest of her life. The cellar was of cement with an arched top, all underground except a low brick chimney and the door, which was horizontal but slanted enough so the rain would run off.

All this before the house. However, a house finally was built, my father doing all the carpentry himself, as with the barn. It was a very small house, three tiny rooms with a stoop at the back door and a tiny open porch at the front. A year or so later he put a screened-in porch at the back. It wasn't as roomy as the house I was born in out on the river, but it was much sturdier. It had a solid cement-block foundation; no high wind ever did more than shake it slightly.

But we sure had winds; there was the almost constant singing of the prairie wind in the eaves of the house, varying from a gentle sigh to a wail. We had winds that broke off our trees and sometimes laid the crops flat. But we never had a cyclone make a direct hit on our farm. Several times they came close enough to us so we could see the tail, or the funnel, as folks called it. It came down out of a ridge of dark, greenish clouds that were really moiling around up there, and Dad would use the word *siphon* instead of funnel. "That thing is sucking up everything in the path of it. But if you ain't in the middle, you jist get moved around some." Dad would hold me in his arms and we'd watch from the safety of the cellar door. My mother wouldn't come up to look, but Dad would take us kids up one at a time. I remember being fascinated by all that fierce motion, but some of my mother's terror had rubbed off on me, and I'd start shaking. Dad would take me back down into the cellar. Later we'd hear of crazy things that happened to farms and towns where a cyclone had struck. A house was lifted off the floors leaving supper on the table. A baby was picked up in its bed and tumbled down close by unhurt. A cow was found upside-down in a horse trough kicking her feet in the air, and nothing happened to her but her milk went sour. Of course, animals and people were injured and killed; a town southeast of us was almost wiped off the map.

Dad never seemed to be fearful of this kind of hell breaking loose on the plains—but he *was* fearful of drought and hail. Months of no rain and he would go into a long fit of anger, followed by a spell of despondency. A hailstorm just before wheat harvesting time and there are no words in the language to describe a dirt farmer's torment. But Dad would come out of it, and it was then that he'd read aloud to us, usually it was Robert Burns's poetry or a Dickens novel.

I remember starting school; this was in the town. We had kindergarten before first grade, and kids could start at age five. My teacher's name was Miss Converse; she was a very large and very calm person. I was allowed to stand by her desk while crying, which I did during the first hour of every school day for at least three months. On some days I cried all day and did my ABCs between sobs. Miss

Converse showed no emotion, no irritation, while I stood sobbing between each letter. Afterward she pasted a little red or blue circle in the corner of my school book. If I got through the alphabet without sobbing more than three or four times, I got a gold star in my book.

When a storm came up while school was in progress, I panicked; this went on until I was well into second grade. The teacher of whatever grade I was in—all the teachers were kind—allowed me to put on my hat and coat and stand outside the room door to wait for Dad to come get us in the wagon. Sometimes, if the storm came up during the morning, I stood there for hours. I was too frightened and shaken to take my sandwich from its newspaper wrapping at noontime, so I held the parcel and took it back home when the school day was over. During long cold spells I stayed in town nights with my Aunt Edna and Uncle Jimmy Bloss, who for several years had a little house in Watonga. At these times I always cried myself to sleep; Uncle Jimmy spanked me a number of times for crying.

The school had a large playground in back of it. There was nothing there but bare ground at first, then they put in a bunch of equipment—swings, teeter-totters, and slides. The boards of the teeter-totters (seesaws) were very long so that you went way up in the air when you tottered (or sawed), and you sometimes locked your feet together under the board to feel more secure. Once when I was up—as high as one could go—the school bell rang, signalling the end of recess. The little girl teetering with me jumped off and ran to get in line. Down I went. My ankles got sprained. The pain was unbearable at first and I let out a screech, but I didn't cry; I was adjusted to school by that time. The slide on the boys' side of the playground was very high, eighteen or twenty feet, with the slide part at somewhat less than a forty-five-degree angle to the ladder, making the slide very steep. The girls' slide was lower, with something like a sixty-degree angle, making it considerably less steep. It was slow going, and we envied the boys as they yelled and whooped making their fast descent. Girls were not allowed on the boys' ground during recess and the noon hour. But after school when there was no supervision on the playground we'd go back there and sneak a slide or two, suppressing our whoops so as not to attract attention. I think the great fun of going zipping down the boys' slide was mainly due to its being stolen fun. (Or were we little women's libbers and didn't know it?)

Weary Willie was a little red horse that we sometimes rode bareback to the pasture to get the cows. He wasn't good for much; he was old. There was a time when three of us were going to school in the same building a few blocks from grandpa and grandma's house, and we hitched Weary Willie to a little cart-type buggy we had and the three of us drove to town, unhitched Weary Willie, and left him in grandpa's shed during school hours. After a while Willie got to falling asleep and stumbling while we were driving him. One day on the way to school he fell down, and John, my brother just older than I, struggled getting him back on his feet. We went back home that day and missed school. Dad put Weary Willie out in the pasture where he stumbled around for a few weeks and died. We loved him and gave him a good burial.

The land was good. But to get what was needed to stay alive still meant twelve hours of work a day and sixteen at harvest time. There was so much work to do just to go on existing that my parents could give little time and attention to us individually now that there were five of us. Kids illnesses came and went—had to be accepted as part of living, no big deal. So it happened that what developed into a serious sickness of mine was overlooked for a time. Not that paying attention to it would have done much good, since little or no doctoring was to be had. I had measles followed by scarlet fever. So did the other kids, but they recovered; I had a "back-set." I was bedridden for a year with what was called inflammatory rheumatism, then St. Vitus' dance and a heart malfunction. Later this disease came to be called rheumatic fever, and the aftereffects I had are now generally known as chorea and paroxismal tachycardia. I can remember feeling awfully sick. There was no medicine, not even aspirin in those days, to relieve the constant pain I had in my joints. They'd swell up, get very red and tender to the touch, first the wrists and ankles, then the knees, elbows, etcetera. The fever must have been high; Mama and Dad would appear to be walking on the ceiling sometimes, and the flame of the coal-oil lamp would be close and grow huge, then recede and get small as the point of a pin. But I don't remember any kind of a feeling of depression with the pain— perhaps I was too young to recognize such a feeling even if I had it. I finally managed to get back on my feet and got by with missing only one year of school.

Mama raised chickens. Each year in February she set her 160-egg incubator that she kept in the cellar. She would have nothing but Rhode Island Reds, the chickens that produced the big golden-brown eggs and the chicks with the beautiful tawny coloring. When I became able to help Mama with the housework after my illness, she got her second incubator, and about two thousand baby chicks were hatched each year. That was a lot of chickens, and she worked herself down to skin and bones each spring. The first batch to be hatched had to be brought into the house—it was too cold to put them outside in coops, and we didn't get a brooder house until much later. The corners of our rooms were used; a board would be put across the corner, a little straw thrown in, and a hen "gone to setting" was fooled by having one egg from the incubator hatch out under her, then she'd accept from sixteen to twenty incubator chicks depending on her size. She'd take all she could hover.

It didn't smell too good in our house during this period, with at least eight batches of chickens and mother hens around; we didn't have visitors from town. The Indian women and children came in to sit by the stove as usual while their menfolk were watering their skinny horses at our stock tanks. The road to an Indian settlement went right by our house, and the folks were humped over and shivering in their open wagons, damp blankets flapping around their bodies in the wind. Many of them never talked, just came in to get warm; the chickens in the house certainly didn't bother them. Bill, my oldest brother, spent quite a lot of his time in town, and the chickens didn't bother the rest of us; we thought of the fried chicken we'd have by midspring—at least once a week we'd have it. The chicken raising wasn't for that purpose, though. It was for cash, about the only cash we'd see from one year's end to the next. Wheat money at harvesting time went to pay off interest on the mortgage and any little loans my father had gotten, and to pay off the grocer. Of course we had to buy chicken mash on credit and pay for it later out of chicken money, but we still realized enough cash to get a few "luxuries," like new shoes and stockings once a year, cotton yardage from Montgomery Ward for a few dresses and shirts, which Mama sewed on her treadle Singer. Such coats as we had were nearly always hand-me-downs from better-off cousins; but we didn't have many such cousins, so coats had to last year-in and year-out.

Bill was eight years older than I was. So I didn't get to know him very well until much later. I remember him scaring the hell out of me once, dressing up like a woman and pretending to be one of his high-school teachers who'd come to get me because I'd drawn scribbles all over his report card and one of his notebooks. Bill read

Oliver Twist and *David Copperfield* before he started to school. My mother's teaching experience came in handy; she taught Bill to read with almost no difficulty. When she took him to town school they enrolled him in the first grade, and the teacher remarked that he'd be pretty big in that class. My mother replied that he had other adjustments to make; he'd have to stay in town with his grandmother, and the teacher needn't worry about so small a matter as his bigness. After a couple of days Bill came home to Grandma with a note saying they'd promoted him to the second grade. At the end of the week he came home with a note saying he'd been promoted to third grade. Before Thanksgiving he was in the fourth grade. He was nine then, and smaller than most in his class.

When he was about twelve Bill stopped going to the cellar with the rest of us during storms. This nearly worried Mama to death. She'd cry. She'd say she knew Bill would be killed. I'd be scared too. The wind made a furious rushing sound in the trees, and the claps of thunder came one right after the other. Mama jumped up now and then and wrung her hands. We never could make Bill realize how scared she was. She'd get a terrible pain in her back and have to sit or lie down for a while.

Sometimes when a storm came up in midday, Dad would come in the wagon to pick us kids up from school. Bill usually couldn't be found; we'd have to go home without him. He seemed to hate for any of his school friends to see his father, I suppose because Dad was in his work clothes. He'd be standing up in the wagon in his ragged mackinaw behind a team of work nags. Bill would walk home in the rain and be soaked. He wouldn't ride with us in the surrey either. I thought he was some kind of nut, but he was an intellectual, no doubt about that. And he was a social success; he managed to break down the class barriers in the town as far as his own socializing was concerned. No other farm kid we knew of did that. Later on John was middling. But Bill associated with the top. Dad used to call them the high mucky-mucks of the town, and Bill hobnobbed with high mucky-muck sons and daughters, the offspring of bankers and store owners.

Dad had opinions about each of his kids, and he didn't always keep these opinions to himself. Bill he considered to be a dude. Always he complained that he couldn't get a decent day's work out of Bill, and he grouched and grumbled quite openly about it. Bill was marching to a different drummer. Or sleeping to one. He would go to sleep on the plow, or anywhere, having been up the night before messing around with his high-school bunch.

I guess Bill was really ashamed of the way we lived, ashamed of farm work. However, he got over that as he reached maturity, and in the several books he authored during his life, he always wrote with compassion about the rural poor, deploring the lives they were forced to lead. (I'm referring especially to two of his books, *Pretty Boy*, on the life of Pretty Boy Floyd, and *The Green Corn Rebellion*, which will be dealt with somewhat later on in my story. His first novel, entitled *Townbroke* and never published, was about how as a kid he broke into town society, and takes a crack at his own obsequiousness toward the town's well-to-do.)

Among the things I heard my folks talk about many times was the incident of Bill and the flash-flood scare when he was around ten or eleven. He had ridden the pony to visit Uncle Ned and Aunt Rhody, who lived across the river about six miles away. Flash floods are exactly what they sound like—they happen very suddenly. A cloudburst way upriver that we couldn't possibly know about ahead of time would cause them. There was a general alarm on the party line and Central—that's what the country folks called the operator—gave out the flood warning: *A twelve foot wall of water coming down the North Canadian, creeks running into the river way over their banks, stay away.* I was so small that I remember the details only from hearing my folks tell about it. But I was very sensitive to Mama's frights, and I knew she really had one this time. She listened on the phone and then got a pain in her back so she had to sit down. I think she told John to get Dad from the field or wherever he was; he came right away. Ned didn't have a phone, so they tried to call a family living on Ned's side of the river, but the lines were all down by that time. Dad hitched up the light wagon and drove the three miles to the river, running the horses the whole way. But the water was a raging torrent a mile wide, and what remained of the bridge was way out in the middle of that mile. *He* was scared now. There was no way of knowing if Bill had gotten across the river before it flooded—he was such a dreaming kind of kid he might have walked his pony, in which case he couldn't have made it. Mama told of walking the floor all night; the back pain and collapse were from the first shock of hearing about the flood. Dad stayed up all night too. They didn't find out until the middle of the next day that Bill had made it and spent the night safely with Uncle Ned and Aunt Rhody. The river went back to its banks about as quickly as it had got out of them, and the phone lines were put back. All in all, I think Bill must have been more of a headache to the folks than he was a help. But I could tell they knew he had brains by the way they didn't come down on him too harshly.

John, the second boy, wasn't much of a farm worker either. I remember him as the sensitive one—he cried openly when any animal on the farm got hurt: a horse cut up in a barbed-wire fence, our little dog getting a leg cut off in the mowing machine. He cried to hear about a little boy we didn't even know being burned to death when a farmhouse caught fire. We were at a fair once and all having one of the few good times our family ever had when all of a sudden John began crying and wanting to go home. My folks thought he was sick—he'd had a bottle of strawberry soda pop—so we got in the wagon and went home. He jumped out of the wagon before we got to the driveway and ran pell-mell to the house. We found out it was his rabbit; he'd forgotten to put it in its chicken-wire cage and thought the cat would surely get it. He found it safe, and he turned it loose way out in the field (where a cat or dog probably did get it; it was a young cottontail crippled in one of its hind legs).

The worst time for John was when Prince, a dandy two-year-old workhorse Dad was just starting to use in the fields, had an accident and had to be shot. Prince—one of a team, Prince and Pilot—was cavorting in the corral, throwing his front legs up in the air, when he came down and impaled himself on a fence post. John watched in horrified silence—and so did I—as Dad put his back and broad shoulders between Prince's front legs and slowly lifted him off that post. The colt's guts came out, and he fell over on his side pitifully struggling. Dad ran to the house for the gun. John didn't stay around for the shooting. For a week we saw his tear-streaked face only briefly each day when he came into the house for a bite to eat; he stayed out in the blackjacks.

We had another young workhorse Dad called Hypockets because of his high rear end, and he was a kicker. One day Dad came in from the field in the middle of the morning, unharnessed the horses, and started up the slope toward the house painfully dragging one leg. John was suddenly there—he appeared from nowhere. He started walking along beside Dad crying and grabbing him by the hand to try and help him; he was pint-sized then and couldn't really help. I went to the cellar to get Mama, who was down there putting away cans of fruit or something. Dad had a great, ugly, livid swelling on his leg just below the hip where he said Hy had kicked him that morning; he'd gone on to the field and stayed with the mowing as long as he could. This injury didn't lay him up, it just slowed him down; it festered, and bone splinters would come out. I remember Mama wouldn't dress the injury when John was in the house—it started him crying. (It's no wonder John died of a heart attack in middle age—he was too easily hurt.)

I remember John finding some money once—quite a lot of money—when he was about half grown. There were three-hundred-some dollars in an envelope he found by the tracks while he was on his way home from town. He didn't come home but took the envelope straight to the sheriff; it turned out to be the payroll the section boss had lost. They gave John some small pittance, like three dollars—which I suppose seemed like a lot to John—then they patted him on the shoulder and said "good boy" (I'm sure they did that). Dad and Mama listened to John's story; they were very quiet, just looked at each other. Somehow this story got out, and Dad said when any of the townspeople or neighbors said something about it to him they spoke well of John, but then they would sort of snicker and act like they thought Dad had sired a fool. I remember wondering afterward what Mama and Dad really thought about John being in such a hurry to get to the sheriff. Three hundred dollars was sure a lot of money. Neither one of them ever said a word, though, about what they thought, just what other folks thought.

Jim, three years younger than I, was the one I felt closest to. Madge, six years younger, was the baby, and all of us were supposed to look after her. I could get Jim to play farm with me. I would take a stick and mark out the fields on the ground and draw a yard and a house and barn, sheds and chicken houses, and even find some pretty weeds to be the trees. Little sticks would be the horses and cows. And we'd make people out of twisted pieces of paper, a mama, a daddy, and kids. We would play farm for as long as we could, usually until Madge got tired of nobody paying attention to her and tore up our farm by running back and forth through it.

Jim was always getting hurt when he was little. He got hurt more than all the rest of us put together. A big old setting hen chased him once, and he fell down so hard he broke his arm. It had to be set, and when we thought it was all well, he fell off a haystack and broke it again in the same place. Two or three times he bit his tongue so bad that his lower teeth came through and he'd have blood all over him before we could get him to the house. One of these times was when he fell eight feet through the hay throw in the barn and struck his chin on the manger on the way down. He was always falling off of something and gashing himself. He had the whitest hair I ever saw when he was a little guy, and a gash on the head always looked worse than it was, the blood showed so on that white hair. But the damnedest thing was his poking grains of wheat into his ears. He'd sit in the granary and he'd get this intent look on his face and poke away. The folks had to take him to town a couple of times to see the doc about his ears—they'd get to hurting—and the doc would give him ether and take out swollen grains with inch-long sprouts curled around them. After this would happen Mama would say to me, "Watch him in the wheat bin—watch him!" She knew by that time there was no keeping us out of the wheat bin—it was a great place to play, to run from one wall to the other sinking our bare feet in above our ankles with each step and falling down and getting half buried in wheat. And chew a handful of it into gum. The bin would be about three-fourths full of the seed grain for the fall planting, so it was just a few months of the year that we got to play in it.

In spite of his trouble with accidents, Jim was good about the chores from the time he was little. Whatever he was given to do he tried to do his best; it was as though he realized his shortcomings and made up his mind to overcome them. He soon got to be Dad's best helper around the farm. And he began to want to learn everything about the machinery. We had some kind of old car from the time Jim was seven or eight, and he wanted to know what made it run. Later on Dad got an engine to run the pump when the wind was down, and Jim soon got to be an expert at fixing it when anything went wrong; and he was doing all the mechanical jobs around the place by the time he was twelve. It was then that he stopped having all those accidents. He loved cars. By the time he was ten he would shut his eyes and listen when a car went by and he could tell you the make and the year—he never missed. By sixteen he was in the "car business." He'd drag home abandoned autos hooked on behind our Chevy. He'd prowl junkyards for parts. Then he'd carefully disassemble the wrecks and organize the parts in piles. He'd do this—make these piles—all over a large space between our house and the car shed. He had so many piles that they spread right over the path from the house to the privy. Then he'd warn us all that on penalty of death we weren't to stumble over any of this stuff or disarrange any of it in any way. He'd spend all the time he could squeeze from farm work and school to work with his car parts. Out of all this indescribable junk he'd assemble a heap that would purr beautifully, and he'd sell it for twenty to thirty-five dollars, depending on whether it was a Ford/Chevy or a Buick/Dodge. Clear profit—it hadn't cost him a thing but fifty cents or so for some grease, the kind Dad greased his plow wheels with. Plus gas and oil, of course.

Later Jim got a craze to be a musician. He listened to Bing Crosby on the radio and learned dozens of pop songs and played pop music on clarinet, saxophone, four-string banjo, and guitar. Of all the kids in our family, Jim could do the most things and do them well. He kept branching out in many directions like a young piss-elm tree. There was even a time when he was around twelve that he collected and read pulp western story magazines and filled his Big Chief school tablets with his own penciled stories of cowboys and outlaws. I used to read them—they weren't at all bad. That period lasted about a year.

My sister Madge, the youngest of the family, took after our grandma Boyce in looks—a very pretty girl and popular with the boys, even in grade school. She seemed to be the most easy-going of all the kids—didn't care "whether school kept or not" (an old saying meaning to be carefree). Once when she was about three we were playing in the barnyard and it was freezing weather; the stock tanks were frozen over. John put a board, a two-by-six, from rim to rim of one of the tanks to form a bridge, and we took turns "walking the plank." The three of us were having a lot of fun, as fun went in those days on a farm, and Madge wanted to do it, too. We let her. She fell off the board first thing and cracked the ice, going under completely. John fished her out and she was breathless for a minute, then she began to giggle. We hurried her to the house and caught hell from Mama. Madge was none the worse off—seemed to have enjoyed the whole thing, including the hell we got, or more likely the attention she got. Anyway, later on we discovered her tugging at a board trying to get the end of it up to the rim of the tank. She wanted to do it again.

There was an old swimming hole known as Marshall Lake out near the river; it had no connection with the river but was fed by a deep underground spring and was said to be bottomless (the West was strewn with "bottomless" water holes). They put up a fifteen-foot diving board for the older kids, and Madge climbed up there and jumped off feet first. She was four that summer; she couldn't even swim yet. But Dad or John would be down below to swim her to the edge of the water where she lost no time in climbing right up for another big splash. I remember feeling foolish—"chicken," they'd say now—and I went through agony to learn to dive off that board before the summer was over. I was ten.

So it went. There were other times when Madge made me feel chicken. When she was a teenager she managed to get the little things a girl wants—some nice underwear, stockings, face powder—a feat I had not been able to accomplish when I was her age. How did she do it with no money to spend? One day I found out. We were in town and I had just complained about not having a decent hand-bag. I didn't have any handbag with me. "It's too shabby," I said. She pulled me into a store that specialized in women's stuff, and there we were in front of a rack of leather bags. "Nice," she said. "Hold my purse." I started to ask what she was going to do, but she gave me a look and I took her purse to get it out of my ribs. With a quick flip she slipped the strap of one of the twelve-dollar bags over her shoulder and in almost the same motion poked the price tag inside with her finger. She took my arm, and we were out of the store and down the street; then she took her purse from me and switched the new one to my shoulder. "What do you mean your pocketbook is shabby?" she said.

Madge nearly died of Bright's disease when she was eighteen. The aftermath of the disease was a long one—she was in and out of hospitals. But soon she went about her business, got married at twenty-two, and was widowed at twenty-three by a tragic accident. She went through a period of grief and lost about thirty pounds. But she bounced back and married again a year later. She had a kidney weakness her disease had left her with, and she had to have her two daughters by caesarian section. In her late thirties she had a radical mastectomy. Later she had some strange kind of disease—very rare and very painful—that causes a deterioration of the tissue between the skin and muscle over the entire body. There was no known cure. When Madge was three she wasn't afraid of anything—she remained the same all her life. Her time of birth may have been to her advantage; she was born at a time when our parents were settled, as settled as it was possible for them to be. Or Madge may have gotten her fearlessness from Dad, who had only one fear of a personal physical nature, fear of the tachycardia an early disease had left him with.

John and I were born at a bad time for Mama—not that any time was especially good—but let's say a *worse* time. She went through the last months of her second pregnancy while on the move. Dad didn't think he was doing his best at farming on his claim near Okeene; he wanted a change. He sold out and bought the farm on the Canadian River nine miles from Watonga. Anxious to get going, he pulled up stakes before the folks on the new farm had vacated the house, and John was born in Watonga at Grandma Boyce's house, where Mama had been temporarily dumped. So they took John as a teeny baby to the new place. Then when Mama had her third pregnancy they found they couldn't stay on the riverbank—the land was too sandy for wheat, the river was eating into the east side of the farm, and Bill had malaria from too many mosquitoes. But at least Dad stayed this time until after I was born. I believe all this had an upsetting effect on both John and me. A mama bird with her nest threatened is a mighty nervous mama bird. And a mama cat without a place under the porch has got to find a place quick or her kittens don't do very well.

I was born at a bad time, and the year of sickness took a chunk out of my childhood. But I wasn't beyond looking around for satisfactions. In spite of all the chores I had to do, I wanted to raise flowers in the yard, and some vegetables besides potatoes, potatoes, potatoes. We had to help in the potato patch, planting and debugging. I planted lots of seeds, but my flower beds and my garden failed. If the chickens didn't scratch and peck off the young sprouts, the wild rabbits got them. A couple of springs of this failure and I gave up. But there was something else I could do, and I felt good about it. When I was six Dad taught me to play chords in several keys on the piano. We'd visit Grandma and Grandpa Boyce on Sunday afternoons, and Dad would bring along his fiddle and show me the chords. I caught on very quickly. Later I learned to fit these chords to any tune I wanted to play on the piano. In winter, when my chores were somewhat lighter, I'd stop off at Grandma's and play her piano a while before going on home from school. After I was well we started to go to square dances during the times when the work wasn't so heavy on the farm. The whole family would get in the wagon and go to a neighbor's house, and my father would play fiddle. If they had a pump organ I played chords for him. Once in a while there'd be a banjo player, but mostly not. We even had a few square dances at our house, but our front room was too narrow—it cramped the dancers. And none of the farmers' haymow floors were any good for a barn dance—not our kind of farmer anyway. Sometimes we'd go as far as ten miles to a square dance—kids wrapped up in old quilts slept on straw in the wagon bed on the way home. Mama sat and dozed and even Dad claimed to doze most of the way home, his way of boasting a little about his horses. The horses would get us home from anywhere, no matter how far it was.

It's hard to describe those square dances. They were not what most folks nowadays think—and not as pictured in the movies. They weren't rollicking affairs where folks joked and laughed—they were serious. The farmers and their wives were perpetually tired, their faces pinched with hunger and their brows puckered with worry. It was as though in a kind of desperation, these folks were seeking a release, which, try as they might, they could not find. They danced hard, but they didn't smile. Their stony faces resembled the faces of Indians engaged in a spirit dance. And my father often fiddled as though he were battling demons. I guess that was about it—the demons being drought, hail, grasshoppers, and, worst of all, the grain speculators of Wall Street.

From age eight I did most of the housework from early spring on into the fall. Mama was outside most of the day in her faded, ragged old dress splotched with chicken dirt, or she was in the cellar tending incubators. While school was on, the housework was saved for me to do when I got home. It kept. But I didn't keep too good—at least I didn't thrive. The responsibility was too great. I wasn't recovered sufficiently to take it in my stride as a stronger child would have. I got over Saint Vitus' and became afflicted with "workitus." (To this day I can't take a vacation, can't get away from work, not even for a short time—not even when weariness has progressed into that state that is best described as raw pain. Changing type of work or mode of work is the only thing that helps, and that is not always something you can do overnight.)

The chore I hated most was cleaning the cream separator. It was better when we used to put the milk into gallon crocks and let the cream rise, then skim it off with a dipper or large spoon. But Dad got this machine, and most of the year I had the nasty cleaning job to do every day. The mechanism had a lot of pieces to it that had to be taken apart and washed, spouts that had to be cleaned out by poking a rag through them. The machine operated on the centrifugal principle, and there were forty-eight light metal discs about three and one-half inches wide; they were cone-shaped, and to clean them you slipped them off their turning spool onto a giant twelve-inch safety pin with a handle, and you swished them in cold water (all the parts had to be rinsed first in cold water), then you piled everything into the heavy metal bowl (after you had removed it from the top of the separator), and you poured boiling water carefully over all those pieces. There were so many parts they filled the big five-gallon bowl. It really wouldn't have been so bad except that when we got jammed up on school mornings and the separator was left for me to do after school, the discs would all be stuck together and they'd have to be pulled apart on the pin and washed separately with cold and then hot soapy water before scalding. It was messy and took a long time.

The separator was operated by turning a crank. It turned hard, so Dad or one of the boys usually did that part. I didn't mind at all turning the crank after I got strong enough; I thought it might develop my spindly arms. But I never could see that it helped.

There was butter to churn and mold for selling in town. We had a churn with cranks at the top for two-hand operation, and the dash went round and round instead of up and down as on the old-style barrel churn. The tank of the churn was square and hard to clean. Our butter mold was shaped so a newfangled sharp-cornered rectangle of butter came from it weighing exactly one pound. I liked our old mold better; it made pretty rounds of butter with a bunch-of-grapes design on top. We sold our butter for fifteen to twenty cents a pound.

Washdays were dreary. We had a galvanized metal washtub about two and one-half feet across, a washboard, and a big oval-shaped vessel called a boiler that you put on top of the cookstove. Those old cookstoves had four lids that you picked up with a lifter if you wanted an open flame. The boiler fit over two holes on the cookstove. We rubbed clothes on the washboard with a bar of soap—there was no powdered soap in those days. We chipped bar soap into the boiler and added a couple of tablespoons of lye. After the tub washing, clothes were put into the boiler and allowed to boil for about twenty minutes, with a stirring now and then. Then they were taken out and rinsed in cold bluing water. Sometimes we'd have to have two or three tubs of wash water before we could get all of our washing done. In the beginning Mama had only one tub. She'd have to dump the wash water out and then rinse the clothes in the same tub, pouring clean cold water in. It was easier when she got another tub. The new tub was about three feet wide, and more comfortable for taking baths than the old one.

I did most of the house cleaning, such as was done, but Mama would take the last suds on washday and scrub the kitchen and milk room with a broom, swishing the thick, brown, sudsy water out over the stoop and down the steps, and then rinsing clean with what was in the rinse tub. She would do this, tired as she was, every last washday. Water had to be entirely used up—it was hard to carry by the bucketful thirty-five yards uphill from the well. Mama had to do that a lot of the time herself. I did it too, as did Jim and John.

Carrying that water made us satisfied with one bath a week, fewer in winter. Three or four kids bathed in the water heated in a kettle on the cookstove. After the kids, Mama got into the same water, and sometimes Dad. But a lot of times Dad just sponged himself off with a soapy rag squeezed out in the washpan we used for hands and face. He was too big and uncomfortable in the washtub. Of course, Bill took his baths at a different time, we never knew when or where, but we knew he took them because he always looked and smelled clean. He did everything a little different from the rest of us. Grandma Boyce told Mama he took baths at her house sometimes (she had a town tub—a regular bathtub), but not when Grandpa was home, as he was stingy with water. When we littler kids used their water closet we had to line up so only one flush was needed for the lot of us. Town water had to be paid for. Each of us was given one sheet of toilet paper and weren't to pull any off the roll ourselves. I hated that. In the privy at home we had Montgomery Ward catalog pages, and how good it would have been to use more of that nice soft toilet paper! Dad used to say he would never use that damned water closet, and I don't think he ever did. After we got our own piano he never went to the Boyce's house in town; the piano was the only reason he had ever gone there.

Money matters worried me. Dad would get in a pitiable state when he had to go to the bank for a loan. His suit of clothes was at least fifteen years old, so he gave up on it and wore overalls and the lighter of his two work jackets. His ancient mackinaw, shredded at the cuffs and bottom and double-patched at the elbows and down the front, simply couldn't be worn into the bank. Sometimes he'd be able to get a loan and sometimes not—that's the way it was with the dirt farmers, and they'd get bitter and read their *Appeal to Reason* and talk Socialism, the Eugene V. Debs variety. But I was too young for politics; the misery just went deeper inside me.

However, there was one way—albeit a negative one—that I sublimated my misery over the pitifulness of my parents, and that was to consider the plight of the Indians who came by our place and stopped in so often during the winter. These were the remnants of the Cheyennes and Arapahos who were forced south more than a half century earlier from the game-rich plains of Nebraska, eastern Colorado, and Kansas, and especially the Smoky Hill country, where buffalo were in abundance until the mid-1870s. The descendants of these Indians never took to farming. Then the territory was opened for white settlers, and for the Indians what was called "head-rights"—each head of family was to get a quarter section of his choice to "repay" him for giving up his homelands. But the Indian was a ward of the white man's government and subject to the directives of easily corrupted Indian agents. If a white man wanted a piece of land belonging to an Indian, it was easy for him to bribe the Indian agent for approval of a purchase; the final swindle was complete. The law was that an Indian could choose his 160 acres; what he ended up with, after all the chicanery of the white man, was the worst of all possible land along rivers and creeks, too sandy for anything but weeds, sand cherries, and cottonwood trees. But these Indians did do some planting on their worst of land. Corn, for instance.

Beat-down as they were, the Indians made an effort to maintain family relationships. In the rickety wagons that turned in at our place there would often be a mother, father, children, and once in a while a grandmother or grandfather. An old hound dog with its ribs sticking out so far you could play a tune on them would be trotting along between the wobbly wheels. Dad greeted these neighbors in a word or two of their own language and asked the women—or women and children—to come in by the fire and get warm. They knew English. Though we'd known some of these families for years, they'd never get down out of their wagons without some urging. They'd come in and sit by the stove, their coarse blankets adding a fresh outdoor damp to the wood-smoky air of our cramped room. They looked hungry, and for sure they were. We wouldn't be eating too well ourselves during the winter months, but there'd be a piece of bread and butter or some cracklings for the children. The women would accept nothing, but they let their children have what we handed them.

Only once in a very long while would one of the menfolk come into our house. They'd be down by the water tanks with their horses, getting some indication from Dad as to when he might be butchering. There was a period in my early childhood when this rule was not strictly followed, during my year-long illness with rheumatic fever. The Indian chiefs (I assumed at age seven that all Indian males were chiefs) stood by my bedside and called upon their gods to make me well and healthy again. But I, in my sharp perception, concluded from the half-amused expression on their faces that they had about as much faith in their gods as my atheist father had in a white god. I later learned that one of these Cheyennes was a legitimate chief by the name of Chief White Fool.

At butchering time the families came by and got everything we didn't use; they had their way of preparing these leftovers to eat. And their emaciated dogs got something, though we always had a couple of dogs of our own to wolf down the entrails. A lot of farmers used the brains, but my folks didn't. We used the pig's head for headcheese, everything except the ears and snout. But the pig brains and the whole head of the calf we gave to our special family, the Man-on-the-Clouds. Or to old Chief White Fool, who, incidentally, had a fascination for our party-line telephone, which was hooked up while I was sick. I was so young then that I took the condition of the Indians for granted and thought we were doing them a kindness by giving them our waste. I don't know how my folks felt about this at the time; I believe they thought they were doing what they could to help. It was only much later that I developed contradictory emotions about throwing a hunk of waste to the men and women everything had belonged to in the first place.

John Big Nose was in my class for a few years in the town school. And because he was bigger than the other kids he sat way at the back. That's what I thought then; it was because he was bigger, or perhaps because he didn't raise his hand to answer questions like the other kids. He sure could draw better maps than we could—he could draw better *anything*. All the kids could see that. I can remember wondering why there were Indian children in school through the sixth grade, but none after that. But I didn't have the nerve to bring the question to the attention of my teachers. The only answer I got was from Dad, and that wasn't very satisfactory. He simply said most white folks "don't like Indians and don't want them mixin' with their kids in school or anywhere."

The Indians suffered; their deprivations were worse than ours. But ours were enough to blot out any thought of theirs most of the time. When Mama lost hundreds of her just-feathered-out chickens in a prairie downpour, she would be in a pitiable state. Chickens had no sense; they'd run into the weeds and drown. Mama brought in tubs full of them and put them by the stove in an attempt to revive them. You realized then how skinny they were. A few would come around. Mama and I would hold the poults up by the legs and try to shake water out of them. If they gasped and gurgled up some water, then most likely they'd be up in a few minutes running around the floor defecating. Most were stone dead, but Mama didn't want to give up. If she revived one, her weary face lit up, and she had a little victory gesture of clasping her hands in front of her chest before picking up the next one to work on. I wanted so to be able to help Mama at times like these. And to help both Mama and Dad when the grain crop failed or was destroyed.

One year all the wheat burned up in a threshing-machine fire; I think it was the first year Dad used a header instead of a binder, and the wheat was all in two long stacks with the thresher in between. A spark from the machine ignited one stack, and it all went up in flame and smoke. What could kids do? I thought at such times that I didn't deserve to live—I could do nothing. One little girlfriend in whom I confided told me to pray: "Go to Sunday school, Agnes, and pray." But there was a rock wall between me and trying to find peace of mind by praying—I was an atheist. My Dad was an atheist, his father before him had been one, and I was one too. I didn't know clearly at the time what an atheist was. But I knew we never prayed. We didn't go to church, we didn't say grace, we didn't believe in a heaven in the sky or hellfire below. We cussed if we felt like it. The frontiersmen, my forebears on Dad's side at least, were not the "Bible totin'" kind. (They did tote guns; Granpa's Civil War rifle had been kept in working order until no more ammunition could be obtained for it.)

So it was that religion didn't help me—I had none. But I needed something to hang on to, and since I set so much store by hard work I got the idea that by working still harder and taking on more responsibility, the condition of the family would be smoothed over somehow. So I worked harder, did huge washings, chopped cotton, picked it, shucked corn, did more chicken work, more milk work, patched and sewed. But we still had disasters. On top of the big disasters—hail, fire, drought, threats of foreclosures—we had lesser ones: blights, boll weevils, grasshoppers, dirt storms, influenza, bugs in the potato patch, drowned chickens, farm animals dying from barbed wire and bloat.

Some things happened to me personally, things that caused me secret humiliation. I was around eight or nine and there were these friends of John's, Arn and Bub Brucker. Bub was John's age and Arn was two years older, about fourteen. They came on Sunday afternoons to our place—their folks were religious and never worked or made their boys work on the Sabbath. The three boys played lasso in the barnyard. They got Dad's lasso rope and drew straws to see which one got to stand on the low roof at the end of our hog pen and try to lasso one of the others who were supposed to stay inside a circle marked on the ground. (They weren't good enough with the rope to lasso a kid running.) The one that escaped being lassoed got to take over the rope and try the same on the others. They kept some kind of score by marking with a nail on the side of the barn.

One day I was up in the haymow watching; they knew I was there. Arn looked up once and thumbed his nose, and I went back from the door to climb the pile of hay and listen to the pigeons cooing up in the peak of the barn roof. Of a sudden Arn's head came up through the hay throw and he heaved himself onto the floor and scrambled up the hay where I was.

"Show me where you pee through," he said.

I pointed to the back haymow door. If I leaned back when I squatted I could pee out the door onto the manure pile down below.

"Naww," Arn said. "I wanna see on *you* where you pee through." I didn't like what he said; I got up but he grabbed me, pushed me to my back, and pulled my bloomers down. I hollered but nobody heard me; John and Bub were laughing and making noise way out in the corral where they were trying to lasso Midget, our saddle pony. Jim was in the house with a broken arm or something. Arn got my pants down. He looked at me and said: "You got the skinniest laigs I ever seen. You look like a skinned rabbit; you ain't got no hair there at all." He laughed and let go of me. I made it off of there in one jump and swung down the hay throw, yanking up my bloomers as I cleared the manger. I flew up the hill to the house and got down under the first covers I could find. Mama was in the cellar and didn't see me in all this pell-mell, and I never said anything to her or anybody about the terrible embarrassment of that day.

I had a little friend around this time who lived a mile or so farther out from town, and we used to visit each other. She'd turn our girl talk to the subject of sex. She said she was going to "do it" with a boy the first chance she got.

"Do it?" I said.

"Yeah, you know. What I been watchin' my mother and father doin' at night."

"You been watchin'?" I said with a certain amount of incredulity.

"Yeah. Watchin' and listenin'."

I didn't say anything. But I hoped she'd tell me more. Finally she said, "You mean you ain't never watched?"

"No," I said, kind of ashamedly, "just cows and things."

"But it ain't like that," she said. "Cows don't do it to bulls, but my mother does it to my father. I seen her. I could do it to a boy; I know how. It's stupid if you don't know. I bet you don't. *You'd* have to get boys to show you, and they'd know you was stupid."

I thought about being stupid. I didn't like being stupid; it humiliated me.

When I was ten I fell in love. It wasn't like the way a little girl gets a passing fancy for a little boy; I was deeply, overwhelmingly in love. I stayed in love with Jack as long as he lived, and for some time afterward. A little girl's newly found love is a source of strength to her; but it is also a source of pain, especially if the object of her love is nearly twice her age. Jack was Bill's age, and it was unthinkable to let anyone know how I felt about him. I had to keep it inside myself and, however sweet, it was a load to carry.

For several years Jack had been coming out to the farm—he was a town boy—to shock wheat with Bill at harvest time. My job was to bring sandwiches and cold drinks to the boys wherever they were in the field at midafternoon. I had always thought of Jack as another big brother; he tweaked my chin and made jokes, laughing with his black eyes and making faces at me. I was Bill's little sister. But one magic summer day as I was carrying out my chore, our hands touched for a second as I handed Jack his dipper of lemonade. He took the dipper and drank; I went into shock. Nothing like this had ever happened to me before, though I'd had dreams of sweet love with boys my own age ever since I could remember. The thing that took hold of me in the wheat field that day was no dream.

Jack studied the piano, had been given lessons since he was a little boy, and it was told around that his mother virtually chained him to the piano for hours each day. He played classical music for his mother, jazz for everybody else. During school term he played at the weekly high-school assemblies, and the younger grades got to go sometimes. I wasn't doing so well with my school work; I was hanging on to a golden thread that held my days together. When That Day would come and I'd be watching Jack as he played, I hated myself for being a little kid. If I could only grow up—*fast*, within the next few minutes—before Jack got up off the piano bench and, with his black eyes shining, went to sit beside a smiling girl his own age.

Bill and Jack went off to the university. The nine months stretched out long until the next June when Jack came again to work in the harvest and heaven came back to earth, a kid's heaven with some hell mixed in because I couldn't show any of this strong feeling I had.

There was a smallpox scare in our area of the country. We all went and got vaccinated, every big and little kid of us, and Mama and Dad too, since there were known cases of the disease close around and there had been a few deaths. Jack was sent home sick from the university infirmary and a week later he was dead of smallpox. His mother hadn't wanted him vaccinated, so Bill thought, and had talked him out of it. This death was one of the more sobering tragedies of our community, and other folks talked about it too. They speculated about Jack Leish not having been vaccinated. Some gossips said that his mother hadn't wanted it because she was afraid of the sore getting so bad on his arm that he'd have to stop practicing the piano. Vaccination in those days was not done by means of shots but by scratching a patch of skin until it was bloody and then putting the vaccine on. Huge infected places sometimes resulted, which made the arm swell up. We never believed what the busybodies said about Jack's mother. When he died she became a recluse; she shut herself in the house with the shades pulled down, and her old man, one of the town's two practicing lawyers, had to bring her food. She lived on that way for a number of years. As for myself and my grief, it was at least two years before I finally threw away a little picture of Jack I had stolen from Bill's collection of snapshots.

"Win the War with Wheat." That was the slogan raised all over the wheat belt shortly after our country's entry into World War I. The government was in collusion with the big wheat farmers to grow more wheat, so millions of acres which should have been left in pasturelands were put into wheat. This was the case all through wheat country, from Texas to the Canadian border. The land was already overfarmed even before we got into the war. We had dirt storms coming all the way from the Dakotas as far back as I can remember, but they were spaced. It was the frightful abuse of the plains land during and following the war—and for profits, what else?—that laid the basis for the dust-bowl disaster of the following decade. No act of God that!

The price of wheat climbed to $2.60 a bushel. My father was not among those who had pasture to add to his wheat acreage. But it was this high wheat price that caused him to nearly kill himself farming another 160 acres on the shares. He was trying to make up for all the bad years we'd had. Bill was financed in college. Fifty dollars a month! That was what our parents laid out for Bill's university education, *our* parents who had never seen spare cash before. Now they had it to spend for what the dirt farmer usually considered the "unnecessaries." A short time before this we'd traded chickens or eggs for subscriptions to papers and magazines, the *Appeal to Reason, The Farmer/Stockman, Capper's Weekly, The Pathfinder*— this was our cultural expenditure. A few fryers, a couple of fat hens, three dozen eggs. But now, great day, we had some cash!

Chapter 3

Gordon in Kansas

The first few nights after we arrived in western Kansas we stayed with the Reverend Wilhelm Schlichting, the spiritual leader of the Mennonite settlement in that particular area. It had rained the night before we first drove over for what was to be, for us kids and mama, our original glimpse of our new home (the quarter section was about twenty-two miles southwest of Dodge City, a mile from the Meade County line, and close to Crooked Creek). Most of the land was now one big green field of wheat—winter wheat that had renewed its growth very early in the spring and at this stage was three or four inches high. The field was all full of jackrabbits, scores of them, crouched down and grazing on the wheat with only their brown backs showing.

As soon as our Ford stopped, we were out of the car, exploring every part of the farm. We raced through the wheat, putting the rabbits to rout, climbing old wheat stacks, stacks of straw that had been there a number of years, the straw turned virtually white, the stacks full of holes dug by burrowing animals (not jackrabbits, which live out in the open).

We explored the place where the original homesteader had settled in the northwest corner of the quarter section. There was a hole in the ground where his dugout had been, now filled with dried Russian thistles. The trees he had planted in his yard were still there: two cottonwoods now fully grown, a row of four mulberry trees, and about twenty black walnut trees planted along the fence row. The walnut crop was generally good; numerous Saturdays Ollie and I sat under the trees cracking the walnuts between brick halves and picking out the meat with the pointed ends of safety pins.

We gradually widened our explorations. It did not seem strange to us at the time that our land was virtually surrounded by farms the original homesteaders had abandoned, leaving only traces that they had once settled and lived there. These vestiges consisted uniformly of the inevitable holes where their dugouts had been, the trees they had hopefully planted, shards of broken crockery and bent, rusting nails where their front yards had been. A half mile to the west of us there was the remnant of a dugout, a row of box elder trees, and another row of mulberries. To the northwest the remains of a sod house, the roof gone and the walls crumbled down to the level of the windows. To the southeast a shack, only one small room and the clapboards unpainted and decaying, unoccupied for many years, had been built beside the now weed-filled hole of the dugout. To the northeast there was a place showing no sign of human habitation, but a small grove of box elder trees regularly spaced proved that man had been there. A half mile to the east the original settler had left only one apricot tree, now old and gnarled; it bore fruit only once during the seven years we lived in western Kansas—one lonely misshapen apricot. This homesteader had plowed up forty acres of buffalo sod before giving up. The field was taken over by bunch grass, waist-high, tough and unmanageable. No plow could tear up the deeply embedded roots; no livestock would eat the grass. It was an abomination. But the field was interspersed with Spanish daggers (soapweed), and it became a place of ephemeral beauty on midsummer nights when the moon would turn the torpedo-shaped blooms into gleaming silver. It was only much later that we began to wonder why all these settlers, who must have come there soon after the Civil War (the Homestead Act was adopted in 1862), had deserted their homesteads.

As I said, there were no buildings on our farm. My mother's brother Dave, who had learned the rudiments of carpentry, soon arrived by train and, with my father's help, built the structures necessary for a farm. First they built a barn, quite small, with room for four animals and the Ford. We lived in the barn while the house was being constructed. Then came a small combined chicken house and granary with a pigpen in the back. And finally an outhouse—a two-holer, a small circular hole for the kids and a larger one for the adults. The whole works was laid down on buffalo grass on a twenty-acre piece of pastureland in the southwest corner of the quarter section.

Uncle Dave, who had so upset his relatives by becoming a soldier and whose irresponsible wife had caused us so much trouble back in Weatherford, was now a changed man. He had seen the light, had been reborn. In fact, he had become extremely religious; in truth you might say he was now overly religious—a Holy Roller. When he was up on the ridgepole of the house he would pray continuously and loudly. Sometimes he would throw his head back and speak directly to God. Occasionally he would break into a long discourse, speaking in the unknown tongue. Sometimes in the middle of the night he would remember something he had forgotten to tell God during the day, so he would climb back on the roof, even if it was after midnight, to shout up into the sky. Once, when the house was barely finished, a fierce thunderstorm came along after midnight. Uncle Dave climbed upon the ridgepole to intercede with God to spare his creation. There he was on top of the house, legs spread apart, arms outflung, head thrown back, rain pouring down his face as he shouted his prayers. Every few seconds his form would be outlined by a bolt of lightning, and his prayers were drowned out by rolling peals of thunder. Eventually the storm subsided, and Uncle Dave came down convinced that he had finally reached God's ear and gotten a favorable response.

I was deeply ashamed of my uncle's unrestrained religious antics. In fact, this feeling of shame had originated back in Weatherford. Dave had become a Holy Roller shortly before we left, and his group held a series of meetings in an old dilapidated wooden church south of the tracks. It was the blacks' church, apparently the only one made available to them. They put on such a spectacle that the more dignified townspeople would gather around the church at night while the Holy Rollers were doing their thing inside and look in through the windows and laugh and guffaw and holler at the scenes being presented. The Holy Rollers were rolling, of course, and jumping for joy over the pews and over each other; they were screeching in the unknown tongues; they were collapsing in trances in the isles, thrashing and jerking around; the whole congregation would join in screaming and praying simultaneously. Great cries of "Glory Hallelujah!" shook the building.

My folks went to observe several of the meetings, but we, too, stayed outside. So here I was, a six-year-old kid, extremely impressionable, outside mingling with all these respectable townspeople, hearing them jeer and laugh, and all the while aware of the fact that one of those participating in this comical production inside the church was my own Uncle Dave.

Despite the interruptions caused by our carpenter's continuing religious requirements—sometimes he stopped his hammering and nailing and sawing for an hour and more to deliver a speech in the unknown tongue—our little house on the prairie was finally finished. It wasn't much of a house; the dimensions could not have been more than fifteen by twenty feet. On the ground floor were three rooms: a bedroom, a living room, and a kitchen just large enough to cook and eat in. There was a little narrow staircase leading up to the second floor, which had two little rooms so tiny that the slope of the roof was half of the ceiling. In other words, the walls went up about four feet and then sloped up to the ceiling. There was a little attic where a lot of junk accumulated over the years, absolutely valueless—trash, yellowed newspapers, a gunnysack full of worn-out shoes, unfitting clothes sent us by charitable relatives.

After the house was finished, Uncle Dave left for California, where he remained for the rest of his life. He sent us letters once or twice a year, but his handwriting was so pitiful nobody could decipher them. Eddie visited him once in San Francisco in the '30s and found him living in a rooming-house cubbyhole along with his box of tools and a million religious tracts.

Dad bought for the farm four young mules. But it was immediately obvious that we boys on whom Dad was going to depend for an awful lot of the farm work were too young to handle these mules; they were too wild, too dangerous. He sold them and bought four older, safer mules—a couple of buskins, Julia and Jenny, a white mule named Caesar, and Fanny, a black mule with one eye gouged out. Jenny, the youngest of the buskins, died right away of colic. But we had Julia all those seven years we lived in western Kansas. Caesar died in the interim of the "blind staggers." He staggered around in a circle for a while and then keeled over and lay on his side with his top feet going like he was running for about another hour. Then he died. The passing of these farm animals was our first close experience with that phenomenon known as Death. By this time we were getting terribly poor, so all my father was able to buy was an old worn-out horse, Bob, and a young filly we simply called the Young Mare. She proved to be the fastest horse for miles around.

Our first crop in Kansas was a good one, and our lives were quite happy. With Ollie clinging to my waist I explored the countryside on Julia. She couldn't run very fast and she had the wheezes, but she proved very gentle and considerate; whenever we fell off she would stop in her tracks so as not to step on us and wait patiently for us to get back aboard. We went fishing on Cripple Creek. The creek bed was dry for miles except when it rained hard, but there were a couple of deep holes where the water was trapped year-round. The fish we caught were of the lowest order, mud cats and carp, but to catch one of these was as exciting for us boys as it must have been for Hemingway to pull in a big one off Cuba. We put out a trap line and made the rounds on Julia.

Eddie, being the oldest, was assigned to farm work, but I was given over to mother to help in the house. I washed dishes and scrubbed floors, and on Saturdays I'd dust the sewing machine and operate the hand washer, a very primitive type one step above a washboard.

Ollie was too young for school that first year, but Eddie and I started up in the nearest rural school, Wilburn. There had originally been a town nearby called Wilburn; it appears on the earliest maps of Kansas and was a stop on the stage line between Dodge and Meade. Now it was the headquarters of the Van Riper ranch; Van Riper raised white faces, Herefords. The schoolhouse, built on his land, was a one-room affair with a big pot-bellied stove in one corner; there was a bell tower on top, and on the front of the school-house was a cloakroom we called the doghouse. In back was a coal shed and the outdoor toilets, one for the boys and one for the girls. Each had a little stockade around it so you couldn't see the kids entering the toilet itself. We used this stockade for various extraneous purposes. During recess or the lunch hour we'd assemble inside it, work up hard-ons and determine who had the longest pecker, using a two-by-four for a measure.

Once we all made ourselves corncob pipes. We took pencil stubs and pushed the lead out and used these for pipestems. Finally the big day came: we went into the stockade, stuffed our pipes with dried alfalfa, and lit up. The teacher couldn't help but observe the cloud of smoke; at first she must have thought the shithouse was burning down. When we filed into the schoolhouse smelling like smoked hams, she quickly caught on. She made us take the pipes out of our pockets and throw them into the stove. From then on, whenever we wanted to smoke, we didn't do it en masse (we made cigarettes out of dried alfalfa wrapped in thin paper from a "Monkey Ward" or "Rears Sawbuck" catalog).

Our predecessors had left various graffiti. The big boys would squat over the hole on their heels. Sometimes they missed the hole and somebody had printed a slogan on the wall to this effect: "If you

make a deposit here, please do not leave any change on the counter."
Then there was this little poem:

> Two little girls dressed in white,
> Started to heaven on the tail of a kite.
> The kite tail broke and down they fell,
> Instead of going to heaven they went to hell.
> (Signed) Shakespeare

Another was quite obscene. It was a parody of the song "Casey
Jones":

> Casey Jones at half-past four
> Fucked his wife at the station door.
> He mounted to the cabin with his pecker in his hand
> And pissed out the window on a bald-headed man.

Our farm was located on the western edge of the Mennonite settlement. We were the only Mennonite kids in Wilburn, a joint Ford
and Meade County school district; the school just to the east of us,
Lakeside, had a student body made up principally of Mennonite
children.

Pacifism is the Mennonites' main tenet. Thousands were martyred, boiled in oil, crucified upside down, tied together in bunches,
and driven out on thin ice. Often before being executed they were
dragged from town to town in cages and exhibited like wild beasts.
They did manage, however, to invent and build the dike system.
This drew the attention of a Polish baron who invited them to come
and drain his swamps. My ancestors were among those who accepted this invitation. They lived in the region near Elbing and Dan-
zig for about a century. Napoleon is supposed to have complained
that although he had exempted them from military duty, fifteen
thousand Mennonites were in Blucher's army when it fell upon his
flank in the late afternoon and insured his defeat at Waterloo. I'm
sure this is an exaggeration, but undoubtedly many Prussians escaping from Catholicism adhered to the nearest Protestant organization, the Mennonites, without giving up deep in their hearts their
arrogance and militaristic instincts.

Late in the eighteenth century, Russia was looking for settlers to
develop land in the Crimea seized in war from the Turks. After long
and hard bargaining, the Mennonites achieved a one-hundred-year
pact distinctly advantageous to them. They were exempted from

military duty and crown taxes; they were to keep their own language and their own school system. Once the pact was safely signed by both parties, the Mennonites went by wagon train to settle along the Molotchna River.

Early in 1870 the Czar informed the Mennonites that the pact, which had about ten years yet to run, would not be renewed. It so happened that at the same time the Santa Fe Railroad was sending agents to Europe to seek immigrants to farm the land along the tracks it was laying in Kansas. Many Mennonites saw the chance to migrate to America as a direct gift from God. All four of my grandparents were in the group that migrated from the Molotchna to Marion County, Kansas, in 1874 (they crossed the Atlantic in steerage on the ship *City of Brooklyn*).

They established near Hillsboro a village they called Gnadenau, meaning "Valley of Grace." My father was the second child born there that fall. They brought with them a variety of wheat known as Turkey Red. I can remember my older aunts describing how their father sent them into the granary to pick out one by one the fattest and best grains to take as seed to America. It was a hard winter wheat that flourished widely when the Mennonites introduced it into this country—Kansas became known as the breadbasket of the world. It was by this circuitous route—Holland, Prussia, Russia, central Kansas, Oklahoma—that the Jacob Friesen family reached Ford County.

Each succeeding year after the first in western Kansas brought increasing poverty; hard times seemed to come down on us with greater and greater force. One year our crop was wiped out by hail. Everything was ripening; we had a big field of wheat and smaller fields of barley and oats. The corn was half grown. A big hail storm came during the night and smashed everything flat to the ground. Another time a dust storm came and blew away the topsoil just as the wheat had barely sprouted; you could look along the drilled rows and see the grains lying exposed, each with a sprout sticking out like a little tail. A grasshopper plague wiped us out another year when the crop was almost ready to harvest. The grasshoppers came out of the northwest by the millions. All day long they filled the entire sky, almost blotting out the sun. You could stand in the shade at the side of the house and look up and see the diminished sun glistening on their wings. It was like a snowstorm, except that snow is silent, while hoppers make an endless whirring sound. Millions would detach themselves from the massive flight and land in the fields. These grasshoppers would cut the wheat halfway up the stems so that the heads would fall to the ground, where the grains could be eaten more leisurely. The main flight lasted only about a day, but the stragglers kept on coming in waves. The county gave out green arsenic to the farmers with instructions to mix it with wet bran and spread it along the fence rows surrounding the wheat fields. My father, Eddie, and I mixed bushels and bushels of this poison and spread it and spread it. It did absolutely no good; the grasshoppers were simply too numerous. Those that landed along the fence rows were just lighting there at random, and they would eat the bran and die, but in the meantime the vast majority would fly over the fences and straight into the wheat fields and start eating away. By the time the plague ended, the wheat fields looked as though they had been harvested by a header.

We had devastating dust storms long before that region became part of the famous dust bowl of the '30s (in fact, the Mennonites remembered a fierce dust storm that darkened the sky when Kansas was mainly a prairie). This dust must have come principally from the stretches of sand hills that cut through the buffalo grass in many areas. In our time the dust was still fine and powdery, although by then most of the land had been plowed. An added evil was the Russian thistle—it seemed that the Mennonites had brought the seeds of this pernicious weed mingled in with their hard winter wheat— which spread all over the West. They grew high as a man's waist when ripe and were three or four feet in diameter. Green at first, they turned black in the late fall; their main stem, sometimes an inch thick, would let go, and they would tumble miles in the wind, scattering their seeds by the millions.

As they were blown along they would catch in the three-stranded barbed-wire fences. In turn, the dust would settle against and on them. Many a morning we would wake up to find our fence rows like long sand dunes with only the tops of the fenceposts showing. You could walk right over the buried fences. One fall we suffered a real catastrophe from a combination of unusually strong wind and thousands of Russian thistles being blown across our farm. Two brothers named Hamer had homesteaded a quarter section a half mile to the northwest of us (the crumbling walls of their sod house and a windmill still remained on it). They had moved two miles to the west and farmed this original homestead only sporadically. This particular year they had not farmed it at all, and the result was about a hundred acres of full-grown Russian thistles. One night a windstorm sprang up from that direction. It lasted for two days, growing in intensity and bringing all those thistles with it. The force exerted by this combination was incredible, unbelievable. Our fences were completely destroyed. The thistles jerked out the staples on the leewardside of the posts, stripped off the barbed wire and rolled it along, twisting the three wires into a single strand. If the staples were on the windward side, the thistles simply snapped off the fence posts and added them to the jumble. In some instances the barbed wire was so twisted together that knots appeared, as when rubber bands are rolled until they form knots. It took us days to repair the damage. We tried untwisting some of the wire, but most of it was beyond salvage. There was nothing to be done but throw it away. The snapped-off fence posts, now a foot shorter than before, were replanted. My father located some secondhand barbed wire, rusted but still usable. Another indication of how powerful this onslaught had been was the fact that the wind bounced the Russian thistles so high they ripped the telephone lines from their twenty-foot poles; we were without telephone service for more than a week. The repair work was made all the more difficult because some of the telephone poles were broken off at the middle and had rolled out into the dirt roads.

All the while our family kept getting poorer and poorer. Although our clothes were reduced to rags and our lunches to dried biscuit sandwiches of lard sprinkled with sugar to make them more palatable, we did have some happy times in school. It was exciting to play such games as Andy Over, Run Sheep Run, and, when it snowed, Fox and Geese (in this game you trampled a big circle with four spokes in the snow, and whoever was "it" had to chase and tag the others and corral them in an area in the center of the circle). Though there wasn't too much room in the school yard or many places to hide, we also played Black Man, Charades, Blind Man's Bluff, and Hide and Seek. We had a small basketball court but no ball. But it was the unhappiness I remember most. We boys would eat our lunches in the coal house. Hidden away in there the older kids would get us younger ones to fight for their amusement. Almost every day they would goad me into hitting a boy named Orville Dillard. He was about my own size—we were fifth graders—but too mild in nature to strike back. But the older boys pushed us violently together, and I kept bloodying his nose. The whole idea was disgusting to me—it was revolting—apparently this was a sport handed down from previous generations. It all came to an end one evening when we were walking home the long way past Way's grove. Mr. Dillard intercepted us by stepping out from behind a tree into the middle of the road. He had in his hand a piece of barbed wire, actually a double strand twisted together, about three feet long. He kept slapping it against his leg as he faced me, and I knew instantly what he had in mind. My heart started pounding in fear. But he didn't hit me as I expected him to; I knew he had every right to. Instead, he only warned me: "You leave my boy alone, you hear me? You understand? If you hit my boy once more, I'm goin' to beat the shit out of you with what I'm carrying in my hand here." I never hit Orville again no matter how much the older boys goaded me and sneered at me for being a coward. In fact, Orville and I became friends after that.

When the United States got into the middle of World War I, the government laid down a heavy hand of propaganda to inflame patriotism. Wilburn School was not excluded. Every schoolhouse was ordered to put up a flagpole and fly Old Glory high. Such a pole was implanted in our schoolyard, and the children were assigned to raise the flag in the morning and lower it in the evening, carefully fold it, and deposit it on the teacher's desk. We had to learn and sing such songs as "Over There," "She's a Grand Old Flag Though She's Torn to a Rag," and "Never Bite the Hand That's Feeding You."

Ollie and I (Eddie had graduated and gone his way) became more outsiders than ever. We were considered Germans although our ancestors had originated in brave little Holland. I got into real trouble. I was quarreling with Roy Hamer, who was my age and in my class, one lunch hour, and he suddenly called me "You goddamn Dutchman!" In my confusion, all I could think of in response was "You goddamn American!" He informed the teacher, Miss Calvert, of what I had said, and she kept me in after school. "You are a traitor to the United States," she said. "You can be sent to prison for life. By law that is what should be done to you. But I am going to be good to you and only expel you. Don't you ever come back to this school again." So there I was, an eight-year-old kid who actually knew nothing of the war being fought in faraway Europe, or what it was all about, branded a traitor, lucky to escape a lifetime behind cold prison bars. I was too disturbed to tell my father what had happened, but when I refused to go to school the next day he wormed the whole miserable story out of me. He went around to see the school-board members and the matter was straightened out; I was allowed back into school.

During my last year in Wilburn Rural School our poverty was complete. Naturally we always went barefoot during the summer months, but my father was able to obtain for us some kind of footwear when school started, even if only a pair of tennis shoes. That summer the crop had failed again, and he had absolutely no money. I begged him and begged him to somehow get me some shoes as the opening of the school year drew closer and closer. But I was still barefoot when school started. I was deeply ashamed to be the only kid in school without shoes, and already in the eighth grade at that. I could not play with the other kids all over the schoolyard and was restricted to hanging around in a small area in front of the schoolhouse. Each summer the yard was overgrown with sunflowers; a few days before school began one or another local farmer came with a mowing machine and cut down the sunflower crop, leaving stubs too sharp to be navigated with bare feet.

September went, then October; chilly November arrived and I still had no shoes. The teacher, Miss Rexroad, began to prepare the pupils for Literary Night, an event designed to show off the accomplishments of the children to their parents. The kids recited memorized poems, sang little songs, put on skits. The main feature of this particular night was an enactment of Longfellow's "The Courtship of Miles Standish." I competed with another boy for the main role and won the audition. Though I put extreme pressure on my Dad, on the night of the event I was still shoeless Gordon Friesen. I couldn't bring myself to appear in front of all those people barefoot, so I stayed home. Literary Night was held on Friday. By Monday word had spread throughout the community that night was a fiasco and a failure because the lead actor in the main show had failed to appear. I had planned to use for an alibi that I was sick. But Dad, sharing my shame and unwilling to confess that he was too poor to buy his son a pair of shoes, had made matters worse by telling those who confronted him that: "Aw, he just didn't want to go."

I was attacked from all sides. Adults gossiped about it on the general telephone line. One of the school kids even tried to beat me up; I succeeded in warding off his blows. But I steadfastly refused to divulge the real reason for my seemingly erratic behavior—competing for the role, winning it, going through rehearsals, and then blowing everything by absenting myself at the showdown. Miss Rexroad, trying to recoup her loss of prestige as an instructor of the young, rescheduled the performance for two weeks later. I was plunged back into my agony. Fortunately our brother Eddie, who had been away working, reappeared at home a few days before the deadline. He agreed to let me borrow his shoes for that one night. They were much too big for me, and on top of that they were the long, latest style of men's footwear known as "needle-nosed." When I put them on I looked like the letter "L."

My integrity restored, I made sure to be one of the first to arrive at the rescheduled event, disappointing those who had predicted Friesen again would be a no-show. Fortune continued to smile on me. As Captain Standish, I was to sit behind a desk and receive and send out messages. The Indians brought their war-threatening bundles of arrows and flung them on the desk. I did not even get up to instruct John Alden to carry his marriage proposal to Priscilla. So I was able to keep my needle-nosed shoes hidden under the desk throughout the play. During the intermission I managed to keep them out of sight under the edge of the curtain. I remained there immobile while the other kids mingled with their happy parents; one girl even came up to me and asked: "Why do you keep standing there?" I only smiled enigmatically. When the curtain rose for the second act I was once more safely behind the desk. It is proper to say here that when "The Courtship of Miles Standish" reached its conclusion we received a standing ovation.

Incidentally, I finally got my shoes when the snow began to fall and my father managed to squeeze his last ounce of credit out of the Fowler General Store.

The hard blows of fate gradually taught us that it was impossible for a family to make a living on a quarter section of land on the western Kansas plains. To the west of us were several farmers who had taken advantage of the stipulation in the Homestead Act that permitted the homesteader to double his holdings by planting a grove of trees on an adjacent 160 acres of prairie. This was aimed at getting some trees onto the region of America believed in the early 1800's to be the Great American Desert. These groves, as I recall, were some twenty acres in size. The surviving trees were mainly

cottonwoods and mulberries. There were few cottonwoods Ollie and
I did not climb in Way's grove and the Hamer and Hatfield groves;
we picked many a pail of mulberries.

Families like the Ways were well established and could survive a
drought or two, but Ollie and I, riding all over the countryside, also
pried into the lives of poor devils hanging on to existence by a feeble
string. Frequently, some shadow of illegality was involved. Two
miles southwest of us in a two-room shack lived the Francis family.
It was said of Mr. Francis that as winter approached he would break
into a store and allow himself to be arrested so that he could get
through the cold months inside a warm jail. His wife and children
were left to survive as best they could; one of their boys, Johnny, was
in my class in Wilburn.

When the Francis's moved away to Dodge City, the shack was
taken over by a Mr. Willup, seemingly a bachelor. One summer he
started digging a well. He got some neighbors to help him. They
were puzzled. "What in the hell is he digging a well for? He's got a
windmill." He quit at thirty feet down, never bothering to reach water. The mystery was solved shortly thereafter when his shack burnt
to the ground. Ollie and I prowled through the ashes. There was a
rumor that he had burglarized a hardware store in Ashland and stolen some guns and a bushel basket full of lead pencils; we had
laughed with the rest of the community over the idea of the now
vanished Mr. Willup stealing all those pencils—he couldn't even
write. We found a half dozen shotguns and rifles, the wooden stocks
burned away and the barrels bent into hairpin shapes by the heat,
and a knee-high mound of pencil leads, the wood covering destroyed
by the fire. What was more, we discovered the reason for the well.
There was a ladder going down about six or seven feet. Here Mr.
Willup had dug a horizontal tunnel that led under the shack. At the
end of the tunnel he had fashioned a space big enough to contain a
twenty-gallon crock of mash and a still. Mr. Willup was a bootleg-
ger! The shack apparently went up in flames the first time he fired
up the still, for only one batch of kaffir corn mash had been removed
from the crock. We wondered aloud why Mr. Willup had toiled the
whole summer digging a well when the still ended up under his
floorboards anyway; he could have saved himself all that work simply by digging a space under the floor.

A similar disaster happened that same fall to the Kissingers, who
lived close by the Willup farm. Ollie and I had a scary run-in with

the Kissinger bunch. There were four or five men in their gang—tough, black-bearded, like an outlaw band in western movies. It was a Saturday afternoon and we had come upon one of their mules, which had strayed. This was at the abandoned Record place, where there was a long barn with a granary room at one end. We drove the mule into the barn and all the way back into the granary shed, closing the door behind it. A few minutes later we spotted the Kissingers riding up, hunting their lost mule. Scared stiff and feeling guilty as hell, we quickly hid in the farm's one-room shack. There was an old table left behind by whomever had once lived there, and by climbing on top of it we managed to scramble through a trapdoor into the attic. Through the cracks in the rotting clapboards we watched the Kissingers below us searching for their stray. They looked in the barn, but their mule was not in sight; they milled around on their horses in the yard asking each other what could have become of him.

Suddenly the mule began to bray, and one of the Kissingers yelled out: "I'll be a son-of-a-bitch!" They knew the mule couldn't have gotten in there on his own and then closed the door behind himself. And they suspected that those responsible were still around somewhere. Their suspicion wasn't lessened even after riding up to the shack and peering in through the windows (the panes long since had been shattered). They kept riding around the shack yelling: "We know you're in there somewhere, you little bastards! You little devils are gonna get it, don't think you won't! We're gonna skin you alive." One Kissinger was carrying a shotgun, which he waved in our general direction. We scrambled around trying to find something with which to defend ourselves, but all that was in the attic was a scattering of dried corncobs. If they had dismounted and come into the attic, they would have found a six- and a ten-year-old pissing in their pants, convinced that death was at hand. But they finally rode away, driving the mule ahead of them. We took care to stay away from that area for a long time.

Early in the fall on a hot afternoon, with a strong south wind blowing, the Kissinger place caught fire. My father took the back seat out of the Ford, stuffed in a barrel of water, and raced to the scene. I was along attempting to hold the barrel upright. Neighbors gathered from all around to lend a hand, but it was soon obvious that the Kissinger house, two rooms and slightly better than a shack, was doomed. I remember Mrs. Way running around yelling: "I smell rubber burning." She had bought four new tires for her Ford roadster, and someone had stolen them a few nights before. The implication, of course, was that the Kissingers had committed the theft.

Some men dashed into the blazing structure to rescue what they could. They didn't come out with any tires, but they did push out a sewing machine and a feather bed. In their confusion, or for lack of plain common sense, they left these salvaged items on the north side of the house within easy reach of the fire. The sewing machine burnt up and the ticking was scorched off the featherbed. The brisk wind blew the feathers northward for half a mile, leaving a white swath resembling a snowfall. The feathers stayed there for months, but the Kissingers disappeared immediately, perhaps joining their friend Mr. Willup on some distant frontier away from the law.

Ollie and I combed through the ashes and found a few pennies. We discovered that the Kissingers had done what Mr. Willup should have; they simply dug under the floor and placed a still therein. But obviously there was a similar flaw in both their operations. The Kissinger house, too, went up in flames the first time they lit up the still. We also located the spot where the Kissingers were fermenting their mash. Here they showed a mark comparable to genius. They had buried a barrel in the ground right up next to the pig pen. The theory was that the stench of the hogs would overpower the alcoholic smell of the mash should any snooper come around. When we kids removed the covering from the barrel—a piece of old canvas held down by boards—we saw two little snakes wiggling around on top of the mash, obviously getting high.

As a person grows older, memories of his youth flood his mind, crowding on the heels of each other. The mirages I saw as a boy in western Kansas keep reappearing in my dreams in many variations. They were awesome sights. We'd generally see them to the north or east just as daylight was coming. Whole towns appeared in the sky shortly before sunup. They hung there five degrees or so above the horizon. The most prominent structures were the grain elevators towering above the other buildings. The towns themselves were too far away to be seen—I don't remember ever seeing movement of any kind. There was always a space between them and the ground, a gray foggy emptiness. As the sky grew brighter, they slowly vanished, beginning from below; the last vestiges to fade were the tops of the grain elevators. We could never determine the exact towns these mirages reflected; the real towns must have been at least a couple of hundred miles distant somewhere out there on the plain. The impression of these mirages on me was so intense that I am sure it is the origin of dreams I now have more and more frequently. I see whole cities, mountains, elaborate steel frameworks suspended silent and motionless, often directly overhead.

Another manifestation of nature that filled me with awe was a cloudburst at close quarters. A dark mass of cloud some two miles away would suddenly release its accumulated water. It was as though millions of gallons of rain were dumped abruptly from some huge receptacle. The rain came down like the dropping of a vast irregular blue curtain, and it fell with what seemed deliberate slowness. When it reached the dry earth it stirred up great clouds of dust that rolled ahead of the now driving rain. Sometimes this could be witnessed without a single drop falling where you stood. Occasionally only one farmer's land was involved, and the old joke went around that he had prayed harder than his neighbors.

After a general cloudburst, all the gullies and draws were filled with raging water. Eddie and Ollie and I plunged in wearing our overalls, enjoying the time of our lives. Crooked Creek, mostly dry in its upper reaches where we lived, became a roaring river. Such sudden influxes of water were not without their tragedies. A young man we knew up near Fowler started home from town with his wife and two kids in a buggy after a cloudburst had passed. A draw that had been dry when he crossed it earlier was now a torrent. But he had chores to do. Leaving his little family behind he tried to cross the stream. The force of the water overturned his buggy, and he jumped onto the back of one of his horses. The horse went down, and the man scrambled onto another one. It sank and drowned, too. His body was found next day caught in a barbed-wire fence stretched across the draw, now dry and harmless. (Thirty years later, back again in Oklahoma, seven of my relatives were drowned in a similar cloudburst.)

All over this part of Kansas were hollow places in the prairie, quite large in area, which, during rare and unusually heavy rainfalls, turned into lakes; they had no outflow, not even into Crooked Creek. This happened only once in the seven years we lived there. The homesteaders didn't plow up these hollows, for they never knew when they might become sudden lakes drowning out whatever crops were growing there; as a result they were left to the buffalo grass and used for pasture. In the one flood we experienced, the biggest lake was about two miles east of our place on the farm of a man named Kroeker (no relation to our Kroeker). They named a rural schoolhouse Lakeside after its location near this particular hollow. Our father took us to see the new lake the next morning; to us it seemed like an ocean, this body of water transported overnight to the plains. Ducks soon appeared, followed by hunters with shotguns from the surrounding towns. Ollie and I gathered up the spent shells, hundreds of them, of every color in the rainbow. No rains came to replenish the evaporating water; the edges of the lake receded day by day, and by springtime it was again a dry hollow. We never got our hands on a duck, not even a wounded one. But we went everywhere, except perhaps in the summer months when we were working in the fields after Eddie went away. On the heels of a windstorm, we were out looking for arrowheads and other relics of the Old West. With the topsoil blown away, we found them and sites where the Indians had made them; these we could recognize by the chips of flint scattered around. We found huge slugs from the buffalo skinners' guns, bullets from Sharps .45 to .70 caliber rifles. The only physical evidence we located of the millions of buffalos that once roamed the prairies was a lone buffalo horn. That is, unless you count the buffalo wallows left in the unplowed pastureland. Here the buffalo had come for generations to roll and coat their hides with mud, deepening the holes with each visit. The circular "wallers," when the buffalo no longer came, were some thirty feet across and about three feet deep. We crouched in them and fought the Indians one more time, firing our wooden guns at imaginary circling, howling Cheyennes. In school, in our history book of Kansas, we learned all about the battle of the Arikaree and how the Cheyenne charge on Beecher's Island was broken and thrown into confusion when a sharpshooting trooper picked off their leader, Chief Roman Nose. We knelt in the protection of the wallers shooting over the rim, singling him out. We shot many Roman Noses square between the eyes, and then we rushed out to slaughter his fleeing followers with our stick sabers.

Other reminders of the vanished West were the wagon ruts in the buffalo grass the homesteaders had not turned over, all headed northeast toward Dodge City. They were made either by chuckwagons of cattle drives from Texas, following the same route of preceding ones, or by stagecoach lines. We, too, drove many cattle herds to the railhead at Dodge, riding our lath horses and wearing our pistols that fired rubber bands cut from old inner tubes.

We learned much of our western lore out of two books awarded as premiums to people who subscribed to certain periodicals; salesmen traveled through the countryside trading subscriptions for chickens—you did not give them actual cash. One of these books was a biography of Buffalo Bill given out by Senator Capper's *Weekly*; we adopted Mr. Cody as our hero and fought our own, invariably victorious, hand-to-hand duel with Yellow Knife. The other was *Dodge City, the Cowboy Capital,* awarded with a year's subscription to the *Dodge City Daily Globe.* From it we became familiar with the lives and exploits of Wild Bill Hickok, Wyatt Earp, Bat Masterson, and the like. There were pictures of immense stacks of buffalo hides ready to be shipped east, and a little further on, photos of equally enormous piles of buffalo bones for which a market had developed. The bone hunters had picked the prairies clean. That was why we, with all our scouring, had been able to find only that single buffalo horn.

A neighbor, Epp, who had a son, Peter, my age, took me along to the celebration of the fiftieth anniversary of Dodge City in 1922. It was a great adventure. Merchants displayed the six-guns of the frontier marshals in their store windows. We went up to take a look at Boot Hill (I understand it is now a lucrative tourist attraction). For lunch we bought and ate a mushmellon in the sand under the Arkansas River bridge. There was the usual parade. It featured in the lead float the only survivor of the early days, an aged black man, Ben Hodges by name, who had allegedly been a horse thief. Some cowboys had caught him out on the prairie. They had wanted to hang him, but there was no tree around. They solved their problem by taking a knife and cutting the main tendons back of his heels; in other words, they hamstrung him. This put an end to his career by making it impossible for him ever to mount a horse again. He was unable to lift his feet and spent the rest of his life shuffling along the streets of Dodge, outliving all the big names. Once a lowly horse thief, on this day Ben was an honored celebrity. Rotarians and Kiwanians followed his float in the parade. Some were dressed as cowboys in chaps and ten-gallon hats, riding their prancing horses and shooting blanks into the air; there were also women and girls in cowgirl garb, twirling ropes. Other contingents included businessmen costumed as Indians, feathered headdresses and all.

The only real Indian we met while living in western Kansas was a young hired hand known as "Indian Joe," who worked for various farmers. We were very mad at him because one summer he rode across our patch of watermelons and "plugged" almost every melon (to plug means to cut a triangular piece out of a melon to see if it is ripe; if green, and even if the plug is replaced, the watermelon will rot). Although ours were big and promising, unfortunately they were all still green. Indian Joe was responsible for the Wilburn School obtaining a Victrola and some records to go with it. The school gave box suppers for the purpose of raising money. The women prepared the box suppers, and on a certain night they were put up for auction in the schoolhouse. The man who bid the highest got to eat the supper in the company of the woman who had put it together. Indian Joe came to one of these box suppers, and he and another man apparently recognized the box prepared by one of the prettiest women in our neighborhood, Grace Waters. They started bidding against each other. While the ordinary box brought fifty cents or seventy-five cents at the most, Indian Joe won Grace's box with a final bid of fifty dollars—obviously, he had saved up a considerable sum by working in the harvest and eating other peoples' watermelons. I don't know how much Grace enjoyed eating her fried chicken and mulberry pie with an Indian, but she was a daring young gal, the first female in the whole neighborhood to appear in public in bloomers. Indian Joe's contribution paid the major cost of a Victrola. One of the records that came with it had a deep voice singing a song with a line in it that drove us boys into hysterics. We were convinced the man was singing: "Your big black balls and pecker." The teacher could never understand why we would start giggling and then, unable to restrain ourselves, break into loud laughter. It was just too much for us. Years afterward I ran across a poem by Rudyard Kipling that appears to be what the singer was braying. The actual line goes: "You big black bounding beggar." The whole poem is about some "Fuzzy Wuzzies," black troops fighting for the British imperialists.

In our isolation, Ollie and I invented a whole imaginary town and peopled it with characters just as imaginary. We called the town Loopton and outlined it by scratching marks in the yard with sticks. There were stores, of course, but the main action generally took place around the bank and jail. The bank was continually being robbed, and we captured and jailed the robbers. Our citizens each had individual characteristics to fit their names. There was Strong Weed, the leader, and his less forceful but still straightforward brother Stout Weed (we never heard of a real-life Weed until Patty

Hearst's lover made the papers). Wire Flit was also a handy man when the going got tough. Spike Kidney was a humorous guy, a jokester. Flinger Eye was evil and mysterious; we suspected he was a spy either for the Germans or Mexicans, and perhaps for both. The man was perpetually being put in jail; he invariably broke out, and it took us hours to hunt him down in the cornfields. Poop was the town clown. We chose the roles we wanted to play, but the unchosen ones were just as active as we were. Frequently, invading armies tried to overrun Loopton, and we had to muster all our forces to repel them. The enemies were Mexicans or Germans. World War I was going on, and a few years earlier American forces had gone into Mexico to try to capture Pancho Villa. To us the Mexicans were Canadian thistles, a plant with a bristly bulb on top; the Germans were sunflowers. With our trusty lath swords we rushed among them and chopped off their heads. We didn't have any female characters living in our town, but there was one instance with budding sexual overtones. An army of Amazons ten feet tall with enormous breasts swarmed into Loopton. We put up a fierce defense and managed to kill them all.

On cold days when we had to stay inside we put out a little newspaper called the *Loopton News.* We never had any paper, so we'd use the blank sides of sales announcements which might come in the mail. With stubs of pencils we drew little comic strips on the edges of newspapers where the print ended—by this time we were getting the *Dodge City Globe* free in exchange for a half column of neighborhood news Eddie sent in twice a month. Our strips dealt mainly with war, with American troops defeating Mexicans and Germans. The characters were stick men, but you could tell them apart by their headgear. The Americans wore peaked campaign hats, the Mexicans sombreros, and the Germans spiked helmets. Ollie "published" a famous photograph Strong Weed had made in a battle. An enemy had shot a bullet straight into his lens at the instant he snapped the picture. The developed photo showed a jagged hole in the center where the bullet had entered.

I had an intense, all-pervading, painful desire to read; if they had been available I would have read thousands of books beginning at the age of about eight. But we had only the two books about the West and three others we had brought from Oklahoma—*The Last of the Mohicans* by James Fenimore Cooper, Jack London's *South Sea Tales*, and *The Count of Monte Cristo* by Alexandre Dumas. I read these over and over again. Eddie had subscriptions to *Boy's Life* and *American Boy*. But he always remained aloof from us, and I could read them only when I sneaked into his little room while he was away in the fields. He seemed absolutely determined that I should not read. One summer he borrowed three Tarzan books from Jimmy Francis. He tried every which way to keep them away from me. First, he hid them under his mattress, then at the bottom of a gunnysack full of old shoes in the attic, and eventually under a stack of hay in the barn. But I found them every time. And before he returned them I had devoured *Tarzan, The Return of Tarzan,* and *The Beasts of Tarzan*. Once I got hold of a dime and sent in for a six-month subscription to *Tip Top*, a small four-page magazine. Eddie intercepted most of these at the mailbox and tore them to pieces.

Another manifestation of my urge to read was when our father took me and Ollie to Fowler, which happened once or twice a year. He would give us each a nickel to spend. Ollie usually got a box of Crackerjack; I invariably exchanged my nickel for a copy of the Sunday *St. Louis Post-Dispatch* or the *St. Louis Globe-Democrat*. Incidentally, we had to hide all our English-language literature whenever other Mennonites visited us. The sect had a great dread that its members would drop away from their religion once they learned English. I remember my Aunt Lena, one of my father's older sisters, telling me a pathetic story about "Yosh," as they called Dad. When he was around eighteen he found a copy of the *Kansas City Star* alongside the road, brought it home, and hid it in the barn hayloft. He would sneak up there to read it, and the family caught him in the act. "We knew then he was lost," my Aunt said, tears streaming down her face.

To get ahold of a little cash we set out a trap line each winter as soon as the furs got prime. Dad bought us a dozen rusty, secondhand traps from a man running a store in Fowler, a Mr. Frazer. He had hundreds of such traps hanging from the ceiling in his basement, traps he had bought from departing homesteaders. Ours were Victor No. 1's. First we set these out in rabbit runs until we caught a jackrabbit for bait. An older neighbor boy, Jupe Blanchette, showed us how to kill them. You took the rabbit by the hind legs and swung the back of its neck real hard against a fence post. This would break its neck. We'd nail a piece of the rabbit to a fence post or a tree and set a trap under it. Mainly we trapped for skunks. In the frosty morning, before going to school, we galloped around the trap line bareback on Julia, she wheezing at every jump. It was a disgusting matter to kill a skunk we had found in a trap. Just as we had no money for a saddle, we had no money for a gun; besides, we were pacifistic Mennonites and were not allowed to touch a gun. So we had to club the unfortunate captive to death. More than once there was only a gnawed-off foot in the trap. We gave little thought to the pain the desperate animal must have suffered while chewing off its own foot to escape, only regretted the loss of the dollar and a quarter the pelt would have brought. Almost invariably the skunks pissed on us as we clubbed them; more stink was added while we skinned them after school. The result was that we, our home, and the school-house stank throughout the season. One winter we trapped enough skunks so that by Christmastime we received a check from the Funston Fur Company in St. Louis for six dollars and some cents. Our heads were full of exciting ideas of what we were going to do with this money. First of all we planned to resubscribe to *American Boy.* We also hoped to buy some new clothes to replace our rags. But when Dad took the check along to Dodge City to cash it, he spent all the money for groceries. He bought two forty-eight-pound sacks of flour, lard and baking powder to make biscuits, sugar, and a gallon bucket of syrup. Anyhow, all the money went for food. It was a terrible disappointment to us boys, after all our work and high hopes. However, it turned out to be enough food to see us through until spring, considering the small rations we were on.

Once we caught a little baby civet cat; it was so small that when the jaws of the trap sprung together they killed it. We didn't think it worth skinning—it was so tiny—and threw it out on the road. But Dad retrieved it, skinned it, and sent the skin to a fur company in St. Louis. It was so small he mailed it in an ordinary envelope with a two-cent stamp. They sent him back a check for one cent! After all his efforts he lost a penny.

We raised a pig each summer and butchered it in the fall. I could never endure the killing. It squealed loudly as my father threw it on its side and stuck a sharpened knife into its jugular. Then he let it back up, and it would walk quietly around the pen bleeding to death. Finally it fell over, gave a few kicks, and expired. My parents, being of peasant stock, had learned to utilize every part of the pig; even the tail was saved for bean soup. All of it was gone by the first of the year.

All the meat we had during the spring and summer was young

jackrabbit (the full-grown rabbits were too tough and presumed to be diseased). On the corn sled I drove, with Ollie trotting along behind, we carried a monkey wrench hooked behind the seat. We kept our eyes open for baby jacks; whenever we spotted one we stopped and chased it down, throwing the wrench at it as it dodged up and down the corn rows. The minute we hit one we grabbed it and twisted off its head so it would bleed thoroughly. I remember one little head that came off bringing with it the lungs and heart; I can still see that tiny, wildly beating heart. By lunchtime we had half a dozen. Ollie and I would quickly strip off their skins and gut them. My mother would cut them into pieces, soak them in salt water for about fifteen minutes, and then fry them (like you fry chicken). At suppertime the process was repeated. Our record catch for one day was seventeen.

The worst thing about poverty is being cold. Hunger you can stand, hunger you can put up with. But cold is something that simply becomes unendurable. Our beds were ticking-stuffed with wheat straw. For covers we had rags, homemade quilts patched and re-patched, with only shreds left of the cotton inner lining. On some of those bitterly cold winter nights in western Kansas, you couldn't even fall asleep. First your legs would get cold, your thighs, then your feet and hands, and finally the entire body. We tried to stay by the stove downstairs as long as we possibly could. In the first years we had coal to burn. Then it became cow chips, which we got from across the road. It seemed that the cattle on the Van Riper ranch had bunched in this particular corner for years. Each evening Ollie and I took a wash tub, the bottom of which had practically rusted away, and filled it with cow chips as high as we could. The trouble was that they burned so quickly, consisting as they did of dried digested grass. One of the last winters we were there—and this was a real tragedy—we burned corn, bushels of it, to keep warm. We had had a fairly good crop, but the price was so low it was cheaper to burn shelled corn than to buy coal. In fact, my father got only enough money for a whole wagonload to buy my little sister a pair of shoes. That winter we kept from freezing first by burning up all the cobs and then by burning the corn itself. This had a lasting effect on me. I could not help but wonder about a system that made it necessary for us to burn up the very food we should be eating.

I think I first started becoming an atheist as a kid in western Kansas. There were several obvious reasons for this. The main one was that as our poverty grew worse and our suffering and misery increased relentlessly, my mother, who remained deeply religious till the day she died, persisted without result in appealing to God and Jesus for our economic salvation. She saw to it that we attended the Reverend Doctor Schlichting's Mennonite church every Sunday. She personally went out of the house every evening after dark and prayed to God and Jesus to save us from our misery. We could hear her out there behind the barn. She would be crying out and weeping as she pled for sweet Jesus to do something to save her and her family, praying also to God to give a helping hand. What to me was the most disgusting part of this agony of hers was that during the winter months she went into the outdoor privy for a little warmth in which to carry on her praying, kneeling on the floor and placing her clasped hands on the seat. I was both revolted and frightened by this behavior. It did not take me long to realize she was never getting any response; as we sank into worse and worse poverty, she prayed louder and wept louder, and all the while it grew more obvious that all this was futility. Sweet Jesus wasn't going to help us, God wasn't going to help us.

It gradually began to occur to me that perhaps there was no Jesus and no God. Maybe it was just a delusion on her part. Nor was this only a personal problem with her; the whole fake was shared by her tortured coreligionists. Reverend Schlichting in his sermons put special stress on the part of the Christian religion that made the most of a loving Jesus and a loving God and assured us They were actively involved in alleviating the suffering of mankind. He preached over and over, "God is love, Jesus is love, They want us to be brothers, They want us to practice brotherhood to the fullest extent, Jesus will personally look after the poor, Jesus will look after the children of the poor"—in other words, the most positive elements of Christian brotherhood (some of this philosophy, misguided as it may be, still remains with me). At the time I quickly noticed that very little, in fact none, of this precious brotherhood was being practiced. Here we were getting hungrier, freezing at night, and no one seemed to give a damn. It was just complete hypocrisy on the part of our fellow human beings. Jesus may be concerned about a falling sparrow, but he sure as hell never gave a damn about us. I was ashamed of my mother; I was particularly ashamed of her stupidity. Here she was, spending hours hollering up into the sky, calling on something that wasn't there at all.

Then at night, after my mother was through with her praying and everybody had gone to bed, she would scold and berate my father, holding him responsible for the trouble our family was in. Their bedroom was right below the tiny one Ollie and I occupied, and I could hear her down there until two or three o'clock in the morning scolding poor Dad. Whenever he answered her, which was infrequent, he was so meek and mumbling I never did get the drift of how he was responding, but I could hear Mom quite distinctly. "Why didn't you keep the homestead in Oklahoma? You had a good piece of land there. Why did you make that trade? Why didn't you keep us in California? Why didn't you keep your real-estate agency in Weatherford? Why are you always helping out other people? Why can't you think of some way to help us and the children?" This went on night after night. I resented her bitter tongue-lashing, but I also pondered the mistakes Dad had made. I frankly developed contempt for both my parents—almost hatred.

I began to doubt my father's judgment. After all, he came out and looked the area over before he made the trade; he was in the real-estate business; he must have known something about the value of land and how and why the previous owners lost it. The remains of abandoned homesteads were all around us; even our own quarter section showed that the original homesteader had left it. Why hadn't my father noted all this? I started wondering what had happened to all these first settlers. Why hadn't they been able to stick it out? What had occurred? It had been virgin prairie when they first came. There were still a few families of the original homesteaders still there. Why didn't he ask them some questions? Right north of us were the Reardons; they had managed to hang on; they still had their sod house, which they now used for storage. They had built a regular house alongside it. Dad could have asked old man Reardon, who might have been able to tell him, although he stuttered, so you could hardly understand him. Dad might have asked him what happened to so-and-so over there, what happened to so-and-so, what happened to the family that homesteaded our own place. I couldn't help but feel that my father had made a very serious mistake in trading his farm near Weatherford for this piece of Ford County land. He should have looked more closely into the deal before he made it. All this was building up in my mind.

One thing my mother held against my father was definitely true: he was always assisting other families and neglecting his own. During the great flu epidemic of 1918 he was away from home taking care of at least a half-dozen stricken neighbors. He cooked soup and fed the bedridden; he did their chores—milking the cows, tending the livestock, even gathering the eggs. He saw to it that the sick were kept warm. He had this incurable streak of humanity in him. There was another influenza epidemic in the community in the late winter of 1920. My father, who was a good Republican—the loyalty of many farmers to this party evolved from the fact that the Homestead Act was adopted during a Republican administration—was appointed the census taker for Wilburn and Concord townships. (Concord adjoined us to the north.) While taking the census he stopped in on an isolated family in Concord. Repeated knocking on the door brought no response. Dad knew somebody had to be at home because there were seven members in this family, so he started to open the door. There was some obstruction in the way, but he managed to push it back far enough to get a look inside. He saw that the obstruction was a dead body on the floor with the head pushed up against the door. He squeezed his way in and found four of the family dead and the other three sick in bed unable to get up. He made some soup and hand-fed the still-living. The four bodies he carried behind the corral and covered with earth—in shallow temporary graves so that regular funerals could be held later. Strangely enough, none of us ever got the flu despite my father's contact with so many who had it.

Death was all around us. There were two cemeteries close by, one at the Mennonite Church and another on top of a hill a mile south of us, where the early settlers had buried their dead. In the center of the latter was the grave of a Union soldier with a little wooden picket fence around it; on patriotic holidays someone would stick a little American flag on top of it, but his own relatives had long since left the scene. A clue to what happened to the original homesteaders might be that most of the graves in both cemeteries were small; they were the graves of children. They had probably died of unattended frontier diseases—I would guess most often diphtheria, smallpox, tetanus, or pneumonia—for which there were no cures, even had a doctor been available. While we lived there the question of a doctor rarely came up. I was taken to a doctor in Minneola only once during these seven years (I got poison ivy on Crooked Creek so bad that both my eyes were swollen shut). In later years when I thought about the vanished homesteaders, these little graves seemed part of the answer. It was simply too far from civilization to try and raise children. They died off like flies, and their parents buried them and departed.

The newer graves in the Mennonite cemetery were mainly those of Reverend Schlichting's boys. There seemed to be a genetic disease in his family, limited to male children. At least half of his male offspring were afflicted with it. It was a degenerative illness, destroying their muscles. The first symptoms came early when they were about two, three, or four years old. First their legs began to wither; he would bring them to church with him on Sunday carrying them in his arms. When they got to be about ten or twelve years of age, they died. I remember one night when he got on the party telephone line and called up his brother Henry Schlichting, who lived about two miles south of us, to tell him that his son, also named Henry (Heinrich), was dying. Of course, when there was a ring on the rural line everyone rushed to the telephone to listen in. Consequently, the whole community was listening when Reverend Schlichting asked his brother to hear Heinrich's death throes. The father held the receiver down close to his son's mouth and everybody could hear Heinrich's wails of pain, his agony, his whimpering and crying— "Mother help me, father help me"—growing weaker and weaker all the time. I guess Dr. Schlichting did have enough experience to tell when a human being was dying, because he held the receiver down there until the very end. There were a few faint moans and convulsive gasps, and the Reverend Dr. Schlichting announced: "Well, he's gone now. He's in Heaven now. We'll have the funeral on Sunday." It was a hard, cruel world.

My mother had a large metal trunk that she had shipped from Weatherford when we moved. It was full of odds and ends—clothes, papers, letters. I hung around fascinated whenever she'd rummage through it, and one day I noticed a little packet of about six pieces of cedarwood tied together with string. The pieces were about four or five inches long, a quarter of an inch thick or so. They all had the indentations of teeth bites. I asked my mother what these sticks were. And she told me this story to explain them:

It happened in western Oklahoma the year I was born. Uncle John was my father's youngest brother, the youngest member of that Friesen generation, and at the time was living on the old Grandfather Friesen homestead. My father's house was a mile to the east. Uncle John was already married and had two small children, babies. He had borrowed a horse from my father, and one morning he brought it back. He had a piece of flannel wrapped around his throat. My father asked him about it and Uncle John replied: "Oh, I picked up a sore throat somewhere. It's just a cold. I'll be all right," and he went back home. But it turned out to be a first symptom of tetanus—we called it lockjaw. It was harvest time and he'd taken off his shoes and socks as he worked barefoot in the granary shoveling wheat. While working he stepped on a shingle nail, which punctured his heel. A few days after he returned the horse, his family sent word to my father that Uncle John was worse. Dad rode over and found Uncle John in bed. Someone had gotten the old Dr. Schlichting—he was the father of Wilhelm Schlichting of western Kansas (many of the Schlichtings practiced primitive homemade medicine; it seemed to run in the family). Dr. Schlichting had "treated" Uncle John by applying a piece of salt pork to the puncture hole in his heel. This, of course, was a useless gesture, and Uncle John became sicker and sicker. During the next three or four days— here is how mother described it—Uncle John died slowly in the most horrible, painful, torturous way; spasms would increasingly overtake him, and he'd arch up so that only the back of his head and his feet touched the bed. These spasms were accompanied by a locking of his jaws. To keep him from biting off his tongue, my father whittled these little cedar sticks and held them between Uncle John's teeth.

My father insisted all the while that Dr. J. J. Williams be called, but the rest of the family members opposed it. Afterward my father talked to Dr. Williams who said: "Why didn't you call me in at the beginning? We might have been able to save him." When Uncle John was dead, my father took his clothes out to wash them and hang them on the line. From one of the socks he shook out the piece of salt pork. The little sticks of cedarwood with their teeth marks were divided up by family members as momentos of Uncle John's death. (Years later a neighbor woman told me how she, as a little girl, had cared for Uncle John's children, John Jr. and Bertha, in the shade of a cottonwood tree while their father was inside the house dying.)

My mother's father, Cornelius Duerksen, married in Russia and had several children. He brought his family to Gnadenau in the Mennonite migration to Kansas. When his first wife died he married again, to Maria Toewes, by whom he had six children, five boys and a daughter who became my mother. When he died, when my mother was seven, his widow, my grandmother married Jacob Hildebrand. They had two children. My mother remained bitter all her life at the way the local Mennonite hierarchy treated newly made orphans. They were divided up as servants among the various Mennonite families—all except the youngest, George, who was just a baby learning to walk. He was left with his mother, who'd had absolutely nothing to say about the disposition of her six children. My mother, Maria, was awarded to the family of the Reverend J. W. Weibe, a leading figure who with a partner had founded a new Mennonite branch, the Krimmer Mennonites. His innovation revolved mainly around the process of baptisms—he dunked his members backwards into the water instead of face-down. Or was it vice versa? Maria became the slave of the Weibe household. She had to do the cleaning and washing, and no matter how cold it was she was sent out morning and evening to milk the six or seven cows. Her clothes were hand-me-downs from the Weibe girls, who then taunted and laughed at her for looking so funny in the too-large dresses. Her life with the Weibes was three years of torture, which she never forgot or forgave. Her mother meanwhile was put to work in the fields. She took little George with her and tied him to a tree or a bush while she worked.

The Mennonites must rank among the world's worst hypocrites. They make a big deal about their extreme pacifism and refusal to fight, but history shows them quick to jump in and exploit for their own enrichment the spoils won in other men's wars. In Russia they took advantage of the land taken from the Turks by the Czar's soldiers. In Kansas they gobbled up prairie still red with the blood of slaughtered Indians. If they really believed in their principles they would give the land and the profits they've made from it back to the Indians.

My older aunts, offspring of my grandfather Cornelius Duerksen's first wife, used to tell me about conditions they remembered from Russia. Cornelius was both a school teacher and a farmer; the youngest aunt explained how she would hide in the closet and listen in on the classes her father thought she was too young to attend. For harvest time the Mennonites would hire wandering Russian serfs. At mealtime they would set a large bowl of clabber milk out in the middle of the yard and the Russian workers would gather in a circle around the bowl and eat the contents with wooden spoons. This particular aunt told me how offensive this mistreatment was to her, how sorry she felt for the Russians who after many hours of hard work in the wheatfield were slopped like hogs. So one day when her parents were away she decided to cook the workers a decent meal of meat and cabbage, and pies to go with it. It must have taken the serfs some time to get over their surprise and astonishment before they devoured this unexpected meal she had set before them in the shade of a tree. When her parents learned what she had done, they scolded her severely and warned her never to do such a thing again.

My step-grandfather, Jacob Hildebrand, also told us terrible stories about his time in Russia. A small, grotesque-looking man with a huge nose and large flapping ears, he was considered to be somewhat addled. He attributed this to the fact that kerosene had been poured on his head to kill lice when he was a boy, and somehow the kerosene had penetrated into his brain, causing damage to his thinking processes. Sometimes he would develop the illusion that he was back in Russia. He cautioned Ollie and me during these episodes always to carry a bullwhip when we walked along the road. "If you meet a Russian or a Turk," he advised us, "give it to 'em with the whip." He also gave us advice on what to do should we meet up with a camel (this was western Oklahoma)—"Stay away from them as far as possible, or else they will blow snot all over you." To him the Russians and Turks were despicable and treacherous, and unrehabitable thieves as well. Russian beggars, he said, would kill rabbits and wrap the hides around their legs, the fur inside and the bloody part of the skin showing. They would then exhibit their legs, which appeared diseased, to gain the sympathy of those they were begging from.

To foil Russian thievery, the Mennonites kept vicious dogs. During daylight the dogs were chained to the house, at night unleashed to attack intruders in potato patches, smokehouses, and other places that needed guarding. Ironically, Grandpa Hildebrand's own mother was inadvertently killed by such dogs. She was the village gossip, and hurried from house to house to spread some juicy scandal. On one occasion she came into some unusually scandalous gossip. In her excitement to spread the story, she hurried too closely to a pair of chained dogs, which leaped upon her and tore her to pieces. In western Kansas a Mennonite neighbor, a Mr. Kroeker (his wife was Wilhelm Schlichting's paramour), also told me a story about these dogs back in Russia. There was a disturbance in his family's potato patch one night. The dogs were unchained and sent on their mission. "We knew they got some of those rascally Russians," he said, "because the next morning we found blood on the plants."

I remember the first car wreck in our area, which was announced over the rural telephone lines. Some young man living north of us in Concord township was racing his car along the road leading to Dodge when the car went out of control, jumped the ditch, and crashed up against a telephone pole. It came to a stop with one of the rear wheels spinning free in the ditch. The young man was thrown under this wheel. My dad piled us boys into the Ford and raced to the scene. By the time we got there, the victim had been rushed away, and somebody had shut off the motor of his car. There was a big crowd standing around surveying the scene. The wheel had spun against the man's head for some time, and there was a big pool of blood in the ditch, and the wheel was covered with bits of brain matter.

My mother gave us a lecture based on this incident—a warning that death could strike at any instant. She was always predicting or prophesying that if you committed any kind of sin, never mind how small or insignificant your misbehavior might be, God would strike you down. She would continually tell us exemplary tales. I recall one in particular that she told over and over. A boy had disobeyed his parents, then proceeded to climb up on top of a windmill tower in the middle of a storm. God hit him with a lightning bolt and knocked him to the ground dead as a doorknob. There was another favorite of hers: a disobedient boy fell under a disc that cut his body into little bitty pieces. I think she overreached herself, because it dawned on me quite early that the punishments God was handing down were far out of proportion to the sins that were being committed. After any indiscretion on my part she would predict, *Gutt vaught de shtroufe*, which was low German for "God will punish you." Another thing she brought me up with was a fear of my heart stopping suddenly. She told me instances where God had stopped peoples' hearts, causing them to die *"pletzlish,"* instantly. She had me worried about my heart all the time. If you ran too fast your heart would stop. If you got too thirsty and drank cold water in gulps your heart would stop. If you drank too much vinegar your heart would stop. She also kept predicting, "God will make you go hungry some day." This last prediction had little effect on me; we were already going hungry.

As the years went by I grew to despise both my parents; my mother for her desperate stupidity, my father for his weakness and helplessness, his inability to take any steps to halt and reverse the misery remorselessly enveloping us. It wasn't until long afterward that I began to realize we were all victims of the same anarchistic system; they were just as much victims of it as we the children, and there was no reason to hold against them personally the suffering we and they mutually endured. It took a long time, but I forgave them.

My mother never learned about the more serious pranks I participated in. One spring the place where Ollie and I were almost cornered by the Kissinger gang was planted in corn. A drought came that summer, and the corn never grew taller than a man's waist; it never reached the stage of putting on ears. The man who owned the farm—he lived in Dodge City—decided to put a herd of horses in the shriveled cornfield and thus regain at least a part of his investment. He hired a man named Shorty—we never learned his last name—to live in the shack and wrangle the herd. He had a two-horse buggy and would take us along on drives around the countryside. It so happened that a series of revival meetings was in progress at the Concord church; we attended nightly in Shorty's buggy, but we never went inside. Instead, we carried out all sorts of devilment. We stretched a wire between the outhouses. Then we would hiss and spit through the window screen at someone inside the church. He would finally become so infuriated that he would jump up and rush out after us. We would lead the chase to the wire and duck under it—it was about neck high. He, unaware of the wire, would run at full speed directly into it. The wire would catch him under the chin and send him crashing upon his back. We ran on laughing in glee and listening to the wire hum like a guitar string. A lot of folks came to these meetings in buggies. The front wheels were smaller than the rear ones. We would exchange a front wheel for one on the back on opposite sides of the buggy, so that when they drove home the buggy would rock like a ship. One churchgoer who had a car kept a jug of whisky at his feet by the gear shift. He drove with one hand and used the other to hoist the jug for a nip every so often. To sweeten his drink we pissed into his jug while he was in the church drinking up more religion.

Another of our devious practices was sabotaging the private telephone line Reverend Schlichting had rigged up between his house and that of his mistress. While he was engaged in preaching at night services, we boys would cut out a length of this line, say ten or twenty feet, and hide it somewhere in a field. The English-speaking neighbors said if they had a preacher like that they would rotten-egg him. But with the Mennonite community it was like the old joke about the man who when told he was being victimized in a dice game responded, "Yes, I know, but it's the only game in town." Reverend Schlichting was all we had. He was afflicted with troubles of his own. His barn burned down, destroying his prize stud horse. He took on as a hired man a deserter from the Bulgarian army. Nobody ever learned his real name; he was simply called Tom Bulgar. He impregnated the oldest Schlichting girl, Lizzy. "I was always afraid something like this was going to happen," her mother said, "and I tried to keep an eye on them. But he did it while I was away getting water." (The well was a quarter mile from the house.)

Lizzy's father married them, and they rented the old Ratzlaff place. After bearing four children, Lizzy died in childbirth that was too complicated for the Reverend Dr. Schlichting and his assistant, Mrs. Kroeker. Mr. Kroeker had anticipated something like this, for he told around that Lizzy, a few days before her death, had described to him a dream in which she had gone to Heaven. The last we heard about Tom Bulgar was that the authorities had taken away his oldest daughter, twelve years of age, because he had gotten her pregnant. And his boys were developing the Schlichting muscular dystrophy disease.

The reverend's oldest son, George, was drafted into the army early in World War II. He was glad to go since it won him release from the reformatory at Hutchinson where he had been incarcerated for holding up a filling station at Lakin and where there were too many bedbugs to please him. He was trained as a tank driver and was one of the first Americans captured by the Germans—at the Battle of Kasserine Pass in North Africa. He was a prisoner of war throughout the remainder of the conflict. He later died in Reedley, California.

The decline of our family in western Kansas could be traced by the deterioration of our Ford touring car. The folding top went first, then the windshield; Dad replaced the bottom glass with pieces of cardboard to serve as a windbreak. The brass radiator sprang leaks, which were diminished by crumbling dried horse turds and dropping them inside. The light system disintegrated, and we traveled the country dirt roads at night with a lantern hung up front on the radiator. It was hard to start the Ford in wintertime. We got the engine running in two ways. We jacked up one of the rear wheels and put the car in gear—this made the cranking easier. Then we had a rag fastened to one end of a piece of wire. Dipping the rag in kerosene, we lit it and used the flame to warm up the carburetor. Once when we stalled on our way to town, Dad warmed up the carburetor by pissing on it. When the coils gave out, one of us boys would crouch on the floorboards and flick them with our fingers. The inner tubes, patched and repatched, finally were discarded, and Dad drove the Ford with only the casings stripped over the rims of the wheels. Occasionally one of the tires would come off the rim and roll on ahead of the car; we had to catch up with it and force it back on. I recall once when Dad took Ollie and me along to Fowler with the car in this condition and left us sitting in the front seat while he went about some business. A man came along, stopped and walked all the way around the car, finally saying, "Well, I'll be goddamned. This is the first car I ever saw with all four tires flat." We were terribly embarrassed.

The year I graduated from the eighth grade, I worked all summer for a young farmer named Don Stone. I was up at dawn feeding and harnessing the horses, and I plowed, listered, and cultivated until sundown. I was to get a dollar a week. All day long my head was full of big dreams about what I was going to do with the money. I planned to get myself some clothes and scour the homes in Fowler for a possible job where I could do chores in exchange for room and board. This was so I could go to high school; I was desperate to continue my education. I never worked so hard in my whole life; sometimes on hot afternoons Mrs. Stone would not even bring me a drink of fresh water. I got so thirsty my mouth filled with cotton, and I drank from the green slime accumulated in the stock tank on the old abandoned Hamer place across the fence. At the end of the summer my father told me he had taken a bull calf in exchange for my wages. Naturally, after all those dreams, I was terribly crushed. I laid awake nights planning to run away from home: I would walk to Fowler in the night and hop a freight train. I never did get up enough courage to carry out this plan. I went back to the Wilburn School and hung around there for a month or so before the teacher told me I no longer belonged there and to stay home.

In the spring of 1923 my father's brother Pete came from Weatherford and took us out of our miserable existence. The farm and the livestock were turned over to the bankers. Uncle Pete bought new tires and tubes and had the Ford fixed so it would run again. He took my mother, Ollie, and my three litter sisters in his car, while Dad and I followed behind in our rehabilitated Ford, the rear end packed with what personal belongings we had, and in this fashion we returned to western Oklahoma.

Chapter 4

Sis: Youth and Politics

There are strange things happening in this land,
There are strange things happening in this land.
Oh the landhog boasts and brags while the tenant goes in rags,
There are strange things happening in this land.

("There Are Strange Things Happening," words by Sis and Chick Cunningham, 1937, ©1976, based on the original song by John Handcox)

Getting through high school was painful, the first year sharply so. I was a mess emotionally, always getting crushes on boys who never reciprocated. The only thing that got me through was that I could play pop music on the piano; that was my touchstone to belonging. If we hadn't bought the piano the year before I entered high school—wheat was still bringing a good price then—I would have figured a way to drop out, even though I had always been a good pupil. My main trouble was my physical setup. I was tall and weighed ninety-five pounds. And that's thin. I had no figure; I was a stick. I wanted desperately to have dates like my girlfriends, but what boy would be attracted to a stick? I was sick because I couldn't get dates. But I did get invited to parties because I could play good dance music, and there were pianos in a lot of the town kids' houses. In this way I managed to face up to my first real encounter with self-doubt at age thirteen.

We were in poverty again; wheat prices were down. I had no decent clothes except what I could make with Mama's help. No store-bought clothes, no beauty parlor "marcels." But in spite of my sensitivity about this—and all my other sensitivities—I muggled on in the place I was able to establish for myself and never got completely isolated. I suffered from envy of the other girls' burgeoning female attributes: swelling bosoms, rounding thighs, hips bursting out all over the place—delectables for the high school boys to "acci-

93

dentally" bump against turning corners of corridors and going up stairways. I *saw* this. It never happened to me.

Two girls I had gone through grade school with still showed me occasional friendship, and I clung to them for a time. But then Mabel came into town school from way out in the wheat lands, and she became my main friend after a transition during which my two older chums, myself, and my new friend formed a kind of foursome. When it came time for the end-of-term freshman picnic at Roman Nose Canyon, the four of us were getting ready to climb onto the truck hired to haul the class when three high school boys drove up in a touring car with the top down. They stopped and looked over the four of us. "I choose Gladys," said the prettiest boy; "I choose Bonnie," said the grinningest; "I choose Mabel," said the tallest. The first chosen girl giggled; the second chosen put her hands to her face to smother her giggle; chubby Mabel blushed morning-glory pink. Then all three climbed into the car with the boys and took off in a cloud of powdery town dust. I was left standing there. I wanted to go home. Get lost. Be swallowed up by time and the elements. To hell with the others, but how could Mabel? I started to walk toward the edge of town when another country girl, Elmo, who had observed the little scene, ran up beside me and took my arm. "Roman Nose Canyon, Agnes," she said, then she led me back to the truck. And I went to the picnic after all. Elmo and I were pals that day; it was a good day, and I forgot about Mabel and her tall boy.

Roman Nose Canyon had always been to me a cherished place—its notched rim, the sudden sheer drop down to its floor, where an ancient Indian trail wound alongside a clear stream trickling between round stones. Its walls of red earth were striped with gypsum, red cedar, and chinaberry—all this held recollections of stories I heard in childhood. The great warrior chief Roman Nose of the Southern Cheyennes had made the area around this canyon his stopping place when for many years during the past century he had taken his braves south from the Smoky Hill country in central Kansas for winter hunting in the Red River Valley. The favorite camping spot of Roman Nose had been by a big spring the Indians called Everlasting Waters, where a clear, cold stream gushes from the side of a knoll at the awesome rate of six hundred gallons a minute. Henry Roman Nose, also a chieftain and said to have been a son or close descendant of the great chief, was with Black Kettle in the Battle of the Little Washita in western Oklahoma, and when the territory was opened for settlement, Henry chose as his allotment 160 acres encompassing the old Cheyenne camping site.

Henry Roman Nose died when I was a little kid, but his son John, probably the grandson of the great chief, was around for quite some time, and my Dad often pointed him out to us standing arms-folded on the sidewalk on Saturday when the Indians came to town. I do not know, nor have I been able to learn, just when this land where the Roman Nose family lived was "purchased" by a white man to become a part of his several thousand acres of holdings. But around the mid-'30s the land became the property of the state, the white owner collecting all the revenue from the "resale," and was then within the boundaries of a state park built by Roosevelt's Civilian Conservation Corps, the CCC boys. At the entrance to this park stands a great grotesque sculpture of an Indian head about fifteen feet high—a huge cigar-store Indian without a body.

The original chief Roman Nose never surrendered; he was killed in 1868 in the famous Battle of the Arikaree—one of the encounters often portrayed in western movies of the Indian-fighting variety, but depicted in a way sympathetic to the white man. Roman Nose, together with several bands of Sioux and Arapaho, had villages in the buffalo-rich Smoky River valley of central Kansas, not being inclined to move below the Arkansas River as Black Kettle and other chiefs had done at the white man's request, accompanied by promises of food and blankets. General Handcock and fourteen hundred Bluecoats then burned the villages of Roman Nose and his allies, destroying all their lodges, tepees, their buffalo robes and stores of food, the women and children barely escaping death. In retaliation, the braves took action to stop all travel by wagon train, stage, and rail through the land that had been and was still considered by the Southern Cheyennes their rightful home and hunting ground. Handcock was recalled by Sherman, and a six-man commission was set up to move the Cheyennes "peaceably" from along the Smoky Hill to a reservation well below the Arkansas, which would include the Arapahos, the Kiowas, Comanches, and prairie Apaches. Roman Nose and his followers had no intention of signing any treaty that would displace them—they would fight, though the warrior chief knew he'd be killed. Colonel Forsyth's scouts were in the vicinity, but knowing the Indians were aware of their presence, they had retreated from their campsite with a war party in pursuit. In his feathered bonnet and war paint, and riding full speed at the head of his braves, Roman Nose charged the center island of the dry Arikaree where the soldier scouts had taken cover. Thirty braves in the front ranks were killed along with the great chief, but the remaining Indians pinned the whites down for eight days, and until reinforcements arrived, they ate the carrion of their dead horses.

Now the great heart of the Cheyennes was stilled, and they were driven with the Arapahos to a reservation in the red-dust country of Oklahoma, where they were gradually decimated by starvation. The mass slaughter of Indians in the earlier notorious Sand Creek Massacre was repeated in the Battle of the Little Washita, the soldiers led by Custer, in which Black Kettle met his death. This battle was in the fall of 1868. About a year later a party of several hundred Cheyennes escaped northward in an attempt to reach the homeland of the Northern Cheyennes. But Sheridan's soldiers were in pursuit, and only a small, tattered, starved band of stragglers were able to conceal their tracks in the snow and reach their destination in the Powder River country.

There we sat on the rim of the canyon that spring day, Elmo and I, and breathed the air around chief Roman Nose; it was fresh, bracing, and I felt a surge of the nearest thing to happiness I'd known in a long time. My father was said to resemble a picture somebody had seen of Roman Nose. I looked like my father, who claimed to be one-eighth Blackfoot. (I never did get the straight of that. But I've seen a picture of Roman Nose, and Dad did bear a striking resemblance to him.) Clambering down the walls of the canyon, stepping into niches kicked out by the feet of many picnickers, and clinging to bits of brush, I was proud of my Indian blood and my Indian looks.

I did better after the first years in high school. I actually overcame my sensitiveness to a degree and began to consider athletics as a way of building myself up physically. We had a girl's basketball team. But wouldn't you know it, basketball practice was after school, and I had to get right home; work waited for me each day. Once I stayed, and while the girls were getting into their practice duds I went out there on the court of the great wooden cavern of a gym and threw a few baskets. *Whoa!* I got a spell of tachycardia and thought it would never go away, which scared me. Usually it went away in a few minutes; this time it was closer to a half hour.

Well, I learned basketball was not for me. Now I'd be reconciled to giving it up and go in for mental development. I joined the debate team and started a school newspaper called the *Shotgun*. Dad suggested that name, and our staff of five kids was called—what do you think—the Ramrod. Light stuff was in a column called "Birdshot," and heavy editorializing was in "Buckshot." My cousin Jack, in his mid-twenties, was editor of one of the town weeklies, and he printed the paper for us. It was quite a well-structured little sheet, and I entered the state competition for high-school editors, sponsored by the university, where awards were given. I think I won tenth honorable mention, which was thought to be pretty great for a farm-kid editor from a little bitty town school. Numerous larger schools entered and got nothing.

Piano playing was still my best talent, though. But to stay up at night and play and then do my work the next day was not enabling me to gain weight. When the school instituted a program of health examinations, I came out low kid on the totem pole with a "Card of Red—Trouble Ahead." I was said to be twenty-five pounds underweight. My friends got a "Card of White—All Right" or at worst a "Card of Blue—Will Do." Well, I nearly dropped out of school for the second time. I was scared half to death by the threat on my health card, and I thought sure I wasn't long for this world. The confidence I had carefully built up was shattered, and I was a trembling wreck. I begged my kindest teacher, the one who advised kids, to tell me what to do. There was no medical follow-up, just this terrifying warning: TROUBLE AHEAD. This teacher taught literature and had introduced me to many wonderful books. But when I asked for her advice about my health, she had none to give. She committed suicide the next summer by drowning herself—so the story was— in the deep muddy lake made by damming up the stream from the Spring of Everlasting Waters. They said it was because of her bad health.

I had nobody's advice but my own, and I began to try to slow down. I had enough trouble behind me; I didn't want to plow straight into more of it. So I stopped going out anywhere at night, but I couldn't stop helping with the housework and chores. My poor little Mama got pyorrhea and was suffering. I could see she was in constant pain; she got thin as I was, went on like that for a time, and then had all her teeth pulled out, making only two trips to town to see the dentist. She didn't have any decayed teeth, just sick gums that nothing could cure but that a good diet could have prevented. I've often tried to imagine how it was to have all her teeth pulled with no Novocain. A breath or two of laughing gas, but Mama said they sure were stingy with that. Knowing her, she never uttered a sound while sitting in that chair. But she slowed down noticeably in spite of making a great effort to go on as usual.

The "porch" got to smelling so bad I couldn't think of having Elmo or Mabel come for a stay-all-night. The porch was our milk room, where we had a cream separator and, in all but the coldest weather, earthenware crocks and gallon jars of milk in various stages of souring for cheese and butter making. The porch was called that because it originally had been a porch, screened in first and then boarded over as the family grew and the milk operation was crowded out of the kitchen to make room for a cot bed. As for the little old kitchen, it was still crowded, since that's where we both cooked and ate, and now a kid slept there.

An outsider used to some comforts and at least a semblance of order would have found nothing to admire about our tiny house, except its basic sturdiness. The main house (excluding the porch) stood strong under its four-sided roof and above its cement-block foundation. But inside nothing was ever really in order. There was clutter, a messy look about the place; there was the smell of clothes and bedding too long in need of washing. And in the cold months the sour-milk smell and soft-coal smoke from the little heating stove mingled with the acridity of lard being rendered on the wood-burning cookstove. In times of drought there was a layer of light brown dust on everything in the house (the soil in our immediate vicinity was not red; we got red dust when the storms blew up from the northwest).

One lucky thing, I suppose, was that we had no carpets to clean. I wanted carpets, pretty rugs; I wanted curtains, bright chintz or bro-caded ones like the town girls had in their houses. But the best I could do was to try to hang up some ripped-open feed sacks. It was hard to make them look good; you could seldom get two feed sacks to match. We got some cretonne once at seven cents a yard, but it faded to look like flour sacks the first time it was washed. Once in a while we put varnish on the pine floors, but with all the feet and the small space, no varnish could last more than a few months. I once ordered some linoleum for the kitchen, a remnant from Sears Roebuck, and when it came it didn't cover more than half the floor, small as the room was. We put the linoleum down, but very soon the edges got all cracked, not reaching the walls, so we pulled it up and burnt it in the back yard, making a lot of smoke and stink.

Mama said it was too bad we hadn't gotten the kitchen floor covered while the wheat was bringing a good price. During this period of my life I must admit that I was ashamed, in a way, of how we lived. I tried very hard to improve the situation in the house, telling myself it was because of Mama. But mainly it was because I wanted to have my girlfriends visit. No matter how much effort I put out, the mess just wouldn't be straightened nor the smell gotten rid of. We didn't have bedrooms for sleeping and other rooms for other things as my friends had in their houses—somebody slept in all three rooms, even after the "little room" was added.

The little room was a lean-to addition Dad put onto the back of the house at the time when he figured I was too big to be sleeping in the same room with older brothers, or with him and Mama. It was never finished. The walls were one thickness of board; it had no foundation but was propped up on piles of cement blocks at each outer corner, so it was cold as the barn in winter and, since the ceiling was the roof, hot as hell in summer. The inside was never painted, and the boards turned dark with the russet knots and the brown lines of the wood grain making distinguishable patterns on the walls and ceiling—human faces, the waves of the ocean, a galloping horse. And where the rain had leaked in, making streaks, you could see a high log stockade, or the bars of a jailhouse. There were two beds in the little room and a very old bureau with a crazily blotched mirror that made you look chinless or with one eye or the top of your head missing. There was a thing called a "safe" (lord knows why) which was just a cabinet with shelves and doors that once had glass in them, broken out long before I could remember. And boxes—god, the boxes. Whenever we were short of kindling and Dad wanted to bust up a cardboard box to start a fire, Mama wouldn't let him. Everything Mama wanted to save she would put into boxes and put them in the little room. When she was ailing and Madge and Jim played inside on rainy or cold days, some of the boxes got broken open and the stuff spilled out so that there was not a bare space on the floor except when Dad kicked a path to his bed from the door, which opened not off the house but off the back stoop.

The stuff that Mama saved and filled the little room with was mostly rags: boxes of old stockings and socks gone to threads; musty ancient quilts to be mended someday; worn-out shoes mostly without mates; hers and Dad's wedding clothes; *Saturday Evening Posts* torn and with covers missing (Grandma Boyce subscribed and brought us bundles—she was addicted to the kind of fiction they printed; we looked at the pictures); some smooth boards for shelves that never got put up; a legless hobby horse that had been Bill's, then John's, then mine; two great hand-carved wood picture frames, intact (would be worth a fortune now as antiques); a rolled-up bed pad stained with mildew and baby piss; a large metal doll's head waiting for a rag body; a small stuffed doll's body with the china head jaggedly broken. Nails driven into the two-by-fours spaced along the walls held a dozen or more threadbare coats and frayed sweaters, hanging there so long that the collars were uniformly the color of dust. The drawers of the lopsided bureau held not the clothes anybody wore, but more of Mama's stuff she was saving. Dad kept his clothes on top of the safe in a Van Camp's pork and beans box (we bought this goodie by the case at harvest time, on credit till the wheat was sold). And the Civil War rifle had a new resting place in a corner of the little room.

The ancient double bed where Dad and Mama slept was one of those contraptions with thin, much-chipped enameled curlicue iron bedsteads that had once been an even white, and which sagged in the middle from too few slats and worn springs—something from a Walker Evans photograph, except Evans hadn't taken his pictures yet. And I believe the little room would have stymied any lesser photographer, just as it would have presented a word problem for any lesser writer than a James Agee. The other bed was a metal couch with let-down sides that were never let down, so it was always jammed tightly between Mama and Dad's bed and the wall. Their bed had a mattress of sorts—much-patched—while the couch had a thin pad; kids usually slept on it, including myself, when we had relatives overnight or the time Grandpa Boyce lay sick with pneumonia in the other bedroom and died there. Or when I was sick and the little room was too cold Mama had me sleep there close to her (both my parents had to concern themselves with the fact that I might have a recurrence of rheumatic fever). When I had a fever from any small illness such as a simple cold, I was made to stay in bed during the day; it was times such as this that I reveled in adventures conjured up by the shapes on the walls and ceiling.

Mice skittered around in the little room, had babies there, and left their little traces in amongst the rags, on boxes and tops of things, the droppings and the dust almost never brushed off and swept out. Lots of little spiders spun webs, ants got in, little trails of them, and straightaway made paths to the kitchen via the porch, since the west wall of the porch was the east wall of the little room and there were cracks at floor level. I never could figure out why the ants didn't go straight through the porch from outside—perhaps it was a special magic the little room had, which was beyond the sphere of mere human sensitivity. Grass snakes crawled in, mud daubers daubed out nests in upper dark corners, and since there were no screens on the two narrow windows, birds flew in and fluttered frantically about, having a harder time finding a way out than a way in, Madge and sometimes Jim (and sometimes me) jumping about the beds trying to catch one. Hordes of flies buzzed continually in the summer and specked up the walls, chickens came in pecking up crumbs left by the kids eating handfuls of uncooked oatmeal. Ladybugs, inchworms and even centipedes found easy access to the little room. Bedbugs we didn't have; there was coal oil to take care of that.

Mama was weak for a long time after her tooth trouble; I was worn down taking care of necessaries. So the little room was allowed to go its own way, to develop an air of its own, a personality, an odor, an insouciant inimitable individuality to be everlastingly stamped upon the memory of those burdened by the necessity—or pleasured by the privilege—of crossing its threshold.

At about this time, on long winter evenings by the light of a coal-oil lamp, I began to read in earnest. My brother Bill had left quite a few books around from his college days. Fielding's *Tom Jones* was the first I pulled off the shelf; that got me started. Soon I was into Balzac, Goethe, Tolstoy, James, Austen, Hardy, and the Brontës. Then Zola. Then *The Rubáiyát*. Among Bill's books was a set of the complete works of Shakespeare, and I read over again the Dickens novels Dad had read aloud to us as children. *Tale of Two Cities* had been too much for me before; now it became my favorite of the Dickens books. There were not many books by American writers, but I remember Dreiser's *Sister Carrie* and Sinclair's *The Jungle*; there were a few others. The reading at night did me a world of good. I got less nervous; I got outside myself to some degree, which I believe to be good for any adolescent, though so many of them did not (and do not) have the store of good literature at hand that I was fortunate to have. If these books had not been there, right on the shelves in our house, I'm sure I would not have discovered them until much later.

The process of getting outside myself coincided with a growing interest in our early ancestry, intensified perhaps by the reading of historical novels. I wanted to begin with a set of great-grandparents and move backward. My mother seemed to know very little about her predecessors other than that her father was French (the name had been De Boyce, or De Bois) and her mother was Dutch. But my father knew something of his, and I prodded more information out of him by bringing up ancestor William Wallace, whom he loved to talk about. He would complain that Sir William's genius and out-standing achievements were sloughed over in our American history books. He maintained that after Wallace's execution, Scots patriots, invoking his memory, rallied and saved Scotland from the bloodiest of takeovers by the English. Religious differences were peripheral. Dad was an atheist, and he was not hoodwinked by the history lessons we kids had in school; he had his own interpretation of the centuries of strife in western Europe, especially in the British Isles and, more especially, in Scotland. Behind it all was greed for land and wealth. Deliberately obscured but always present behind all religious turmoil was the struggle for economic domination on the part of kings, overlords, and leaders, who succeeded in brainwashing great masses of people to do their bloodletting for them. Religious fervor was whipped up to put men behind spear, bow, musket, and cannon. (What I learned from Dad in my teens I never forgot.)

When he had finished with Sir William—for the time being—he "reckoned as how," since I was of the female gender, I'd like to hear about Molly Haney. (Funny thing about Dad: he read in perfect English, but when he talked he favored colloquialisms and slang; he cussed like hell when he was angry, but that didn't happen often.) He said to put about five *greats* in front of grandmother and that would be Molly Haney's relationship to me. I've come to believe since then that more *greats* are needed.

Molly Haney was poor, and she lived and worked in a lower-class district of Edinburgh. When she went to church—which was often—she wore much-mended clothes and sat on a stool behind the pew holder. On the morning she heard the preacher, also named Haney, begin his sermon in English, she jumped up and threw her stool at him, shouting in Gaelic, "Don't go speaking that foreign language in here, y' bastard!" She was joined by other crones, and they shouted the preacher down. Each had her very real reason for such an act of protest, and ancestor Haney had hers, which was that

Preacher Haney was worse than a bastard, he was a renegade. For it was the Haneys who were related to the Wallaces going all the way back to Sir William.

Molly Haney was caught up in a whirlpool of religious strife that coincided with the economic squeeze on Scotland by England, the likes of which had never been known before. The squeeze was even joined by certain big landed interests among the Scots themselves. Working-class women were beginning to lead mass demonstrations in the streets of Edinburgh and Glasgow. Molly Haney was battling the devilish encroachments on the ways of life of the poor, their difficult but tried-and-true means of providing oat cakes and salt mutton for the family table. The English were trying to force hated foreign ways of doing things down the throats of a simple people who wanted only to go on living as they had for centuries. This was the basic element of discontent, not anything of a strictly religious nature, or even of anything having to do with language, since Gaelic had almost gone out of public usage in the Scottish Lowlands three hundred years earlier. Molly Haney's parish may have been the only one in Lothian in which the ancient tongue was still spoken. I like to picture my rebellious ancestor not as the old woman my father talked about, but as she was in her twenties, roaming the Scottish moorlands: Summer ebbs into autumn, and the intense purple of the heather on the rolling hills repeats itself in the clear, still waters of the loch. There is a light dappling of cloud shadows on the hills. And yonder, like a fresh picnic cloth tossed carelessly down, a tiny patch of bog cotton gleams white in the sunlight. Feeling her beloved land—surely the most beautiful land under heaven—threatened by a frightening outside force, she is deeply disturbed.

But I am shaken back to reality; my dream in technicolor fades. Molly Haney's bairns were many, and she worked as a charwoman. It was little time she had for heather gazing and reflecting on what form her rebellion should take; she simply knew, intuitively perhaps, that her condition could only be worsened by the changes she saw taking place. The use of English in her little church, where only Gaelic had been spoken for centuries, was but a symptom of further intrusion from the south, where her people already had all of that evil they could take. It was in the veins of her husband that Wallace blood flowed, but she was one with her children, and this blood certainly flowed in theirs. She had to resist the ravages of change in whatever way she could for their sakes. That a Haney cousin, however distant, could be guilty of passivity in the face of a threat to all that was good and acceptable in life was perhaps to her the last straw. So she threw her stool at him.

The Cunninghams were from the general area of Scotland known as Bobby Burns country, though the Burnses were border highlander, the Cunninghams border lowlander. Burns was the only Scottish literary figure my father ever talked about. He used to read Bobby's poems to us, and he liked to preface his reading with the story of Burns being called before a subversive-activities examining board for being in sympathy with the American revolutionists. To be harassed in such a way was troublesome to Burns only because of the threat to his livelihood; he couldn't earn a living writing poetry, so he held a government job, some small post that gave him an income, however meager. But impoverished and little-known as he was during the thirty-seven years of his life, Robert Burns was to become a national hero, loved for his unique contribution to his country's culture, honored for his political astuteness and daring—too bad Burns is so often skipped in our classrooms.

Cunningham—or Cunninghame—means "home of the rabbits," and there was a county in Scotland by that name. When this county was abolished (I do not know the circumstances) most of the Cunninghams followed the MacDonalds into Ireland to become a part of the settlement known as the Scotch-Irish—the same MacDonalds, incidentally, whose grandmother or great-aunt Flora saved bonnie Prince Charles from certain execution by the British by disguising him as her maidservant. This was after the prince's ill-fated confrontation with King George's troops on Scotland's Culloden Moor in 1746, an attempt to win the throne he considered rightfully his. The highlander MacDonalds' exit had been some time before that of my ancestors', but they settled in the same place in Ireland. Great-grandfather Cunningham brought his wife and son, William, to America shortly thereafter, where he was to build his Underground Railroad station on the Ohio River.

Nothing I'd learned in school was of a nature to make me proud of ancestors such as Sir William Wallace and Molly Haney and my great-grandfather. There was the possibility that Dad was wrong and Wallace *was* a traitor. And that Molly Haney was some kind of low-caliber misfit, nothing else. My great grandfather must have been doing something wrong—he came to this country with at least some money and ended up a poor man with no property to pass on to his children; also, unless we were to disregard our school books, he performed a disservice by helping slaves to escape. I remember being deeply disturbed by a passage in our American history text-book that said that a great percentage of slaves were contented with their lot, as they were well taken care of by their masters, fed well, and given medical care and good roofs over their heads, and that they were generally made unhappy by emancipation. But I did not have the courage to insist that this particular passage be debated in the classroom, and so there were a lot of times in school when I just turned my mind into a blank—which resulted in my getting most of my education at home.

I had begun to wonder why we were poor. We *were* poor, there was no doubt about it; the price of wheat was hitting some kind of bottom. I was trying hard to figure out reasons by myself; I didn't like to talk about this directly to my folks; they were clamming up more and more all the time, and I didn't like stirring up hornets' nests. But I got up the nerve to ask Dad once if there were any really well-off people among our immediate ancestry. He said my grand-mother, his mother, whose name was Alice Jane Smith, was sup-posed to have inherited some considerable property in Gallipolis. Her mother, Jane Shepard, had this property. But Alice's two sisters married some rich dudes who got lawyers' services and beat Alice out of her share. He named the families the sisters married into, but names don't matter now. One owned a steamboat line to New Or-leans, the other was made up of politicians and prominent newspa-per people. The Smiths, one of whom was Alice's father, also owned a newspaper in Gallipolis. There was a story Dad heard his mother tell that he thought she must have gotten from being around news-paper people so much, from listening to what they talked about but seldom printed.

It seems that during the French Revolution a huge section of the nobility—some 150,000—fled France to save their necks from the guillotine. A lot of them had stowed away a good deal of money in foreign banks (just as the rich do now), and there was a group of these dudes in London who got together and bought the southeast corner of Ohio from some slickers in order to escape the ugly de-mocracy that had taken over and was choking them (surely this wouldn't happen in America). The ships bringing the Frenchmen and -women landed at Alexandria near Washington, D.C., this being the nearest port to the land they had bought. But how near? They had no idea of the distance, and they began walking in the general direction, taking with them their fine clothes and their cases of wine, true noblemen that they were. They took no tools. Five hundred started out, two hundred made it. Not a one could have survived the first winter if the earlier settlers had not done most everything for them: built their huts, nursed the sick, hunted game for them, and showed them how to do simple farming. But once settled in Gallia County (French County) they decided to adopt American customs, and they held a meeting and elected a president; then someone made a motion that they have a dance every Saturday night, which motion was duly passed without opposition. My father's comment on this was that if his propertied grandparent descended from these dudes, he was glad of his Indian blood to balance things out. And when I'd question him about that, he'd say the facts were blurred since having Indian blood had been considered so shameful that the family consistently had tried to hide it. It was hush-hush.

In my last year of high school I was nominated by my class as candidate for the "Best All-Around Girl" contest. Nothing could have surprised me more, and of course I was flattered and highly pleased. I did not care at all when the medal finally went to a junior who was a star of the basketball team; the fact that my own class appreciated me for what I was pushed my self-confidence up no end, and I began to plan seriously on going off to college the following fall. I even tried to decide what my major would be. It might be journalism, it might be English lit. Then again it might be music; I had become a singer in the eleventh and twelfth grades, participating in district contests as soloist for my school. I was all agog making my decisions. I graduated high school in the spring of 1926.

But where was money for college to come from with the price of wheat still going down? My brother Bill, now a teacher and beginning to write for pulp magazines, was going to put me through at least one year at the university; he had been promising for some time to do this, and I had counted on it almost up to graduation time. Then he got married, and that was the end of that. Somebody suggested raising turkeys; they'd bring a good price in the fall. So Mama and I lost no time in getting turkey eggs from neighbors and hatching them out in one of our incubators—fifty of them. They grew like mad and started to feather out, a healthy, squawky lot. But we lost them all in a prairie downpour. Young turkey poults are crazier even than chickens. They hold their heads up, open their mouths, and let the water drown them, resisting all efforts to drive them into coops. So the university was out of the question, out of bounds, beyond reach; I was never to take my first class there.

But I went to college, anyhow, at the Oklahoma State College for Women; I got a job as a waitress in a cheat joint that worked poor college girls to death for a pitiful twenty-four cents an hour, which I was just stupid enough to think was good pay. What's more, if you ate a hamburger they took from your wages what it cost other customers. The result of this was we starved ourselves. I was high on college and didn't realize what I was doing until—wham!—I collapsed: a hyperthyroid condition brought on by overwork and malnutrition, the worst thing that could have happened to a young person with my medical background. The school medico telegraphed my parents, and they came the eighty miles to get me in their old Dodge touring car. It was midwinter. I spent a couple of months at home walking the fields until early spring. I didn't read, I didn't play the piano, I didn't go to town or leave the farm except to follow the back roads that led to patches of timber out toward the river. I watched the wheatfields turn a deep intense green while the scrub oaks were still bare-branched. Early varieties of weeds sprung up by the side of the road, and bunch grass put up tiny shoots in among the dry clumps of the year before. My mother took off two incubators of baby chicks and put them in the house. In the yard the several southern maple and white ash trees, and the one catalpa tree, formed buds—the trees that had been planted by Dad and Mom when I was a little kid. Again I took a walk toward the timber to catch the blackjacks in bud, and on out to the river to examine the cottonwoods. I didn't garden—I just watched Dad sprinkle in a few radish and leaf-lettuce seeds, the things that could be planted very early in the spring.

John was at the university; I believe Jim was in his first year of high school, and Madge was in about the seventh grade. But I was wrapped up in my problems and didn't notice them much as they came and went; I was just barely aware of their existence. Then all at once I sprang to life. Was it spring busting out all around? I don't know. But suddenly I was throwing a few duds into a suitcase with my favorite books and bugging Jim to drive me into town so I could catch a ride to Weatherford with our cousin. I could enroll in Southwestern's (Weatherford Teachers' College, later Southwestern Okla-

homa State University) 1927 spring term, as teachers' colleges did
not go by the semester system as my other college had. The cousin
attending Southwestern knew of a family needing a college girl to
do housework for room and board. So I got situated immediately.
There was a lot to do in that household, but it was far better than
the cheat joint at the girls' school. And I got into some extracurricu-
lar music activities right away—the chorus, the girls' trio, and the
mixed quartet—riding a kind of a crest again.

I went straight through spring term, by which time I was dis-
gusted with work in a private home: cooking family meals, being a
petty chambermaid, delivering and fetching kids, running my legs
off on errands. So I got a job hashing in a teachers' boarding house
for the summer. I went home for the two holiday weeks in late August and early September, exhausted to the point of near illness.
I think my folks felt I was in for another collapse, so they made
arrangements for Mama to go with me to college in the fall, since I
would not stay home. John had quit the university and favored going
to a teachers' college, so we got a tiny place in Weatherford, furnished it with a few beds from home, and Mama, John, Madge, and
I set up house there, leaving Jim and Dad home to hold down the
farm as best they could. I wouldn't have to work—I got a student
loan of $250. Things went uneventfully for six months, then Mama
got to worrying too much about things at home. The arrangement
would never have worked out for that long if Jim hadn't been most
unusual for a boy—he did housework with never a complaint, took
care of Dad, went to school, and did his share of the farm work. The
only thing neglected temporarily was his used-car business.

Early in the spring we gave up the house and Mama went home.
Madge stayed with me in a cheap housekeeping room till her school
term ended, and John and I went to our classes. I had a summer term
to go yet before I qualified for my Life Certificate, good for a teaching job anywhere in the state. Before term's end I landed a job, or,
more accurately, it landed me. In summer, high-school superinten-
dents from outlying areas came to the college to hire teachers; that's
how I got hired for my very first teaching job.

Term's end at Southwestern meant the end of a nine-week term.
The college operated by the quarter system because of the economic
setup of the area. Here we had a perfect example of economic deter-
minism. Though Weatherford was not in the Cotton Belt proper, the
teachers going to their jobs fanned out over the southwestern por-

tion of the state to the Texas border, most definitely cotton country, in which the rural schools, except a few new consolidated junior/senior high schools, were closed in the fall for cotton picking. Kids from the age of seven on picked cotton. A teacher could enroll in the fall at Southwestern and complete a term of credits before his school opened.

My teaching job in 1928 just happened to be in one of these consolidateds, an innovation in Oklahoma and found only where the farmland was most productive. The new brick one-story building was smack-dab on the flat treeless plain, nothing to be seen under a mile away but cotton fields. The town where the teachers roomed, Alden, had a population of nine prior to our arrival: a storekeeper/postmaster and his wife, a preacher and wife, an unmarried preacher, the school superintendent, his wife and two kids. Town buildings consisted of two churches, a general store/post office, and four residences, in one of which we had our rooms. We three teachers increased the town's population by 25 percent, if you visualize things by statistics.

My salary was nine hundred dollars a year, a veritable fortune; I could send my folks forty or fifty dollars a month and still have loads of spending cash—which went unspent, saved for college the next summer. But that's about all I got out of my work—money. Teaching was not what I had expected, not what I wanted. What did I want? I wanted to quit after a week and go back to school. And I didn't care if it meant working for room and board. However, being most keenly aware of how my folks needed that green stuff, I stayed. And I sent them money every month—twenty-five dollars, saving more for my next year at college than I had originally planned, now that I knew I didn't want to go on teaching. My folks would make out; Mom and Dad were leather-tough. The money I sent was mainly so that Jim and Madge would stay in school and not feel that they had to go out and get jobs away from home. Things would surely get better on the farm. (As a matter of fact, things were to get worse. The Great Depression hadn't really set in; it wasn't yet 1929.) Naturally, I would do everything in my power to help the folks stay on the farm. I had a feeling, a foreboding, that if they lost their land they would die—not figuratively, but actually. (I was not too far off; a decade later, when they did lose it, my father lived less than a year afterward.)

I was twenty when I finished my first year of teaching. I faced a hard decision; the school board begged me to come back. But I yielded to my own feelings and quit. I went back to school for the summer and enrolled again in the fall, applying for and receiving a fellowship in the music department, which paid me just enough to take care of room and board. I hashed at meal time for clothing and expense money; I had blown my savings during the summer. It was really wonderful to be doing just what I wanted to do. I had a pleasant roommate; we had a housekeeping room and could cook our own meals if we wanted to.

I was all settled in when my folks called me on the telephone. The landlady where we roomed said, "It's your mother, Agnes." God! Had Jim killed himself in one off his wrecks of cars, had Madge run away, or had that damned old kicking horse, Hypockets, finished off poor Dad? Flashes of bloody disasters! To get a long-distance phone call in those days could mean nothing else but some kind of bad trouble. But Mama didn't sound desperate, just quite concerned, as she first said for me not to be scared and then told me the music teacher in Watonga had just quit her job that day, finding that she was pregnant, and would I come home tomorrow to be her replacement. If I'd get home quick, the job would be open.

I said nothing. Of course I was relieved that no member of the family had met disaster. On the other hand, my insides started churning around something awful because *I* was facing a disaster; it was *me* that I was concerned about now. What worse thing could possibly happen to me than to have to make the decision whether to stay or go? I tried desperately to stall.

"Oh, Mama, I'm glad nothing bad happened. But Mama . . . please, Mama, I don't want to teach now. I'm all started in the fall term here and I can't possibly drop out. . . . I mean, I don't see how I can. I know it's hard for you and Dad to understand. . . . I know that. But I got this job in the music department. . . . It took some wangling. The best break I ever had and I . . ."

"But you can always go back to Southwestern later, and this job here, why it's exactly what you've always wanted; and we want you home so bad. You used to say you wanted . . ."

"But, Mama, I *don't* want it *now!* I want to finish something I started here. I want . . ."

"Dad and Jim will drive to Weatherford in the car and get you tomorrow morning and you'll be all set for Monday—to start here, I mean."

"But Mama . . . I . . . I . . ." I couldn't think what to say.

"Madge liked Mrs. Jenkins, but she said you'd make a better music teacher—she said that. Here, Dad wants to talk to you. Hold on a minute. Here's Dad."

"Sis? That you? Hello?

"Hi, Dad."

"Now we'd sure like it for ya to come on home. We sure . . . Are ya there? Hello, Hello?"

"I'm here, Dad."

"Guess my hearin' ain't holdin' up too good. We'll come over there, me and Jim, drive you right on home so you don't have to . . . have to . . ."

"Well, Dad, you see, I thought I'd try and . . . I mean I'd made up my mind just this once to . . . Oh well, I guess I ought to come. I guess I could come. But there's my credits. I'll lose my credits that I've already started to work on. I'll . . ."

"We can be over there by ten o'clock. Git an early start and we could git there nine o'clock."

"That's all right, Dad. Ten will be fine. I'll be ready. Bye."

I hung up and cried most of the night. My deep conflict at the time was sex, though it wasn't clear to me then, backward as I was in these matters. I had developed what they called in those days a deep crush on a piano-playing college boy, Marcus, who, incidentally, hadn't given me more than a couple of glances, if any at all. I was also studying piano, and under the same teacher, making it easier to speak to Marcus occasionally, stammer a few words, and glow a little in his presence. I had entertained the idea that I had a chance, that chance now gone forever. When I laid down I dozed and had nightmares of Dad getting himself primed to go to the bank and try for a loan: his big, taut frame, his funk of hopelessness and helplessness as he dug through his box of pitiful clothes, then his going off in the cold without anything on; but it would be me standing naked in the bank, and crying. Then it would be Mama crying, holding a drowned, half-grown chicken up by the feet and shaking it so that its darkening bulb of a head snapped back and forth on its long scrawny neck, it wiggling from her grasp and running around the room still dead, its eyes closed, its skinny body turned a livid blue. I saw the wheat stacks go up in leaping flames that formed into a great leering, heaving face in the sky and laughed down at us. Then there were hailstones as huge as goose eggs knocking off wheat heads and leaving little bloody stumps over acres of fields, through which Mama was walking toward me in her torn sack dress and long apron all caked with brown chicken crud, stockings gone to threads around her ankles, her eyes half hidden by dirty strings of graying hair. Taking my hand, she led me away from Marcus, and her smile was a bloody slit from having her teeth all knocked out by the hailstones.

Then I came awake, packed my suitcase, and sat waiting for Dad and Jim to rattle up in the old Chevy hardtop.

I first went to Commonwealth College in the summer of 1931. My brother Bill and his wife, Clarice, who were teachers there, were returning after a leave of absence. I had just finished my nine-month teaching term in Watonga. The two of them, their cat, and I got into their Ford runabout and took off from Oklahoma City, happy to be heading east and out of the dry winds and the dust.

The experience of Commonwealth that summer blew my mind; that was a godawful beautiful place, and I cannot find words to relate what this experience did to me emotionally. It was like a shock, the delicious shock of cold water after heat; you have to think of what I had just come out of to understand why. I was exhausted physically and blanked-out emotionally from three years of cramming public-school music into the heads of kids from kindergarten through high school, and following the cut-and-dried curricula handed down to all teachers from the deadwood state board of education, even though I did break out of it some to write my own little musical plays for the kids.

Well, so much for that. I spent the summer at Commonwealth in a kind of euphoria. The manner of living here was rough and frontiersy, not unlike what I was used to on the farm; so I was able to fit in without a ripple in that respect. The happy difference was that I suddenly felt plunked down in the midst of friends. And I realized this was the ingredient that had been missing during my teaching years—friendship. I had been without close friends except for the members of my family.

There were other differences, like the natural surroundings: I immediately loved the pungent woods smell and the sound of the creek waters tumbling over stones. And to have a great library a few yards from your doorstep! The library was unbelievable; books I had only dreamed of—they were here. I felt I had been brought to this place on a magic carpet.

In the summer there was only a fragment of a student body. Throughout the mornings little knots of students sat around their teacher or discussion leader under the shade of ancient oaks. The edge of the high bluff overlooking Mill Creek and a six-mile-wide valley was a favorite place for such little gatherings. Evening sings were held almost regularly on this bluff. In the afternoons students and teachers alike were divided into work crews: garden, office, cannery, kitchen, etcetera. No one had to stick with the same crew for long if he didn't want to; it was pretty much up to the individual what he or she worked at. If you wanted to cook, you damn sure got a chance to, but you had to work under the supervision of a kitchen manager. When we all sat around preparing vegetables or fruits for the cannery, we mulled over some theoretical question or other, and teachers and students got into such arguments that it would have been impossible to tell which was which unless you knew. It was one such session that first introduced me to Karl Marx's theory of dialectical materialism, and I was so fascinated that I decided right then and there to spend as much time as possible at Commonwealth, at least for the next few years.

At the end of the summer—that enchanting summer just had to come to an end—I faced up and returned to my teaching job. But I resolved that I would save more money—not turn it all over to my family that they might remain on their mortgage-ridden farm, much as my sympathies were with them. They would make it without so much of my help. Or they wouldn't make it. A small acreage might be better for them, anyway. So I did save quite a bit of my salary with the idea of having enough money to pay my tuition at Commonwealth for two years at least. As I recall it was around forty dollars a quarter, there being four terms a year. That was quite a lot of money, but not too much that I couldn't save it up if I was careful.

My public-school job was more of a grind than ever, day after day of sameness so sharply in contrast to the remembered summer at Commonwealth. That deeply gratifying life among friends—it was going on every moment at the college, and every moment I was missing out. This kind of longing is like an affliction; it eats the flesh. I quickly lost the few pounds I had gained. I was young, yet old. I felt drained, wrung-out, work-worn and weary, years of grind behind me. When the term that seemed to stretch into a decade finally ended, I hugged and kissed good-bye the last of my pupils— I was on my way. I sold my Ford to Jim for half its worth, the deal being that he drive me to the college. When I arrived on the campus—for the second time—my friends wanted to put me straight to bed and feed me up; I must have looked a sight to these vigorous folks of the happy, satisfying life. But they didn't put me to bed; I went first to the old swimming hole in the creek and then visited everyone who had been there the summer before, talking them half to death. I didn't need food—I needed these people, this change of atmosphere. I immediately felt great.

At suppertime we sang "The Internationale." Somebody remembered how much I loved the song; it had been eons, so it seemed, since I'd sung it or heard it sung. Now I would see that it was sung every day. "The International Soviet shall be the human race." Beautiful! The family of man; the concept of the human race being international. It didn't occur to me then that we were missing black faces in our family of man, in our human race. I don't know if it occurred to anyone else there at the time; the question wasn't discussed.

This summer promised an even greater degree of euphoria than the one before. I felt a security in having enough money for several tuitions, with some to spare for Bugler rolling tobacco and a once-in-a-while bottle of moonshine—though the latter was the least of one's needs; you could get high just being there.

I asked Ray, the industrial manager, to put me in the garden for the four hours of work each afternoon. He advised me against it, thought I was a bit touched to want to try it in view of my fragile physical condition. I insisted I wasn't as fragile as I looked and I was used to the heat (it was 100 to 112 degrees in the shade when the sun shone; I wouldn't care to guess what it was in the sun). It got hot, all right, but we took a break after two hours for a little swim, and I thrived. I started to gain weight; I put on twenty pounds during that summer. But along about mid-August I was taken out of the garden and put into the office—not *forced* to change jobs, but talked into it since I was a good typist and they needed me to type letters for the coming fall fund drive. No mimeographed form letters ever went out in the donation-getting, they had to be originally typed. There were also letters to prospective students, and quite a bit of general office work. I loved every bit of this work, and I was always hungry when mealtime came. Back on my job in Oklahoma I had forced myself to eat. Being around what to me were kindred spirits made all the difference.

In the evening there was always a get-together of some kind.

Sometimes a few of us would go off into the woods, light up a little campfire to keep away the bugs, and just sit and talk. On moonlit nights the woods scene sent me into a dream world—such exquisite patterns the shafts of light made on rock and undergrowth. At other times I sat in a daze of wonderment, listening to the young people talk—what a wide variety of subjects they discussed. Most of them were way ahead of me in worldly wisdom, or so it seemed. I felt embarrassed at what I considered to be my lack of sophistication and decided to set myself up a strict regimen of reading and study; I was not going to sound stupid when I opened my mouth, so for quite a while I kept my mouth shut—except when it came to singing. We sang a lot at these campfire sessions, some old folk songs but mainly the great songs of the labor movement, which I had heard for the first time only the summer before: "Brother, Can You Spare a Dime," "Hold the Fort," "Solidarity Forever," and the more humorous songs of the Wobblies, "Hallelujah, I'm a Bum," "Pie in the Sky," "Casey Jones, the Union Scab," and countless others.

The nights were cool, and I slept soundly on my lumpy little mattress in the dorm room, lulled by the symphony of small night creatures, beautiful to my ears. On the stark plains of home we hadn't much of this—just crickets. But here, plunked down in the middle of the lushly wooded Ouachita range of the Ozarks, there were crickets, yes, but there were also cicadas, katydids, tree frogs—all kinds of little things making night music, rubbing wings or hind legs together or inflating and deflating vocal balloons at the throat. Not too far away there'd be the call of the Chuck-will's-widow and the many nocturnal birds of the deep woods.

Commonwealth was located about halfway between the town of Mena and the Oklahoma border. Across the wide valley north-by-northeast was Rich Mountain, the highest ridge between the Rockies and the Alleghenies. Most of the college buildings, one-story frame structures, were on the bluff directly above Mill Creek; a few farm buildings were in the near valley just on the other side of the creek. The main hiking trail for the students was across that valley and up Rich Mountain, which provided the elegant ruins of the once-famous Wilhelmena Hotel.

It was around midsummer that Bill and Clarice; Lucien, the college's young director; Ray, the industrial manager; his wife Chucky, the office manager; and I; plus another student or two rolled up some old blankets; packed chicory coffee, salt pork, cheese, and bread; and took off across Mill Creek valley through cleared fields and into lush woods in the fullness of summer glory—my first trip on this well-trodden trail. It was almost dark when we got to a favorite camping spot about a quarter of a mile from where Rich Mountain's incline begins. We pitched camp, ate supper, and rolled up in our blankets to sleep, with the idea that some of us would go on up the next morning, but at daybreak everyone except me thought of something urgent that needed doing back on campus. Besides, they'd all been to the top before.

We broke camp, and they headed in one direction and I in another—I and my little Brownie box camera. There was no cheese and bread left, but they had assured me that I'd find an abundance of blackberries about halfway up, and they weren't fooling. I even found some before I got to the incline. Besides blackberries, I found a woodthrush's nest with bits of blue eggshell, saw a screech owl with his funny close-together ear tufts and his bright yellow eyes looking out at me from the entrance of his hole in a hollow sycamore, watched the back end of a skunk disappear into the blackberry bushes, and almost stepped on a garter snake, the longest one I'd ever seen—at least four feet; and I wouldn't care to numerate the squirrels, rabbits, chipmunks, red-headed woodpeckers, cedar waxwings, and hummingbirds that scurried away or took wing at my approach. On the Oklahoma plains, except for rabbits, there was nothing like this, ever! Here the wildflowers, the different kinds of trees and butterflies, the fragrances that seemed to me from another world, were almost beyond belief. I wished that I had a person along to share *ohs* and *ahs* with. The dogwood was so beautiful even when not in bloom, its spaced, yellow-green leaves playing counterpoint to the dark, fernlike foliage of the black locust. And yonder was a silver maple upstaging a stand of young pines.

The top of the mountain seemed to get farther and farther away, but I made it at last, and the old caretaker gave me a drink of cold sweet water and agreed to snap the camera so I could have a shot of me standing atop a stone parapet of the old hotel ruins. I had to show them back at the campus that I had actually been to the top. The sun was bright and hot, a quarter of the way up in the east over the distant hazy ridges of the Ozarks. I went to the rim of the mountain, the side I had just climbed, and, finding a shady spot, I sat down with my back to the old hotel and looked off in the direction of the Commonwealth College campus.

I took a few slightly mashed blackberries from my shirt pocket—
that stain wouldn't come out at the college laundry—and as I slowly
ate them I fell to thinking. I was physically tired, and my exaltation
over the beauty of the place slowly gave way to contemplation as I
weighed my feelings for this and that person at the college. I decided
that I liked just about everybody.

Suddenly it occurred to me that perhaps most of the Commoners
were Jewish. Yes, of course, they were Jewish. In the community
where I'd been raised—also in the places where I had taught—there
had been no Jews, or hardly a one. I had heard people make slurring
remarks about Yids and Kikes and so on, but how this attitude in
small Oklahoma communities had originated I did not know. I began to puzzle, sitting alone on that ridge above the world, why had
I not thought of this before? Or wondered who was Jewish and who
wasn't? Counting the summer before, I had spent about four months
at the place. Among the older folks at the school, those near thirty,
there were Levy, Freeman, Stein, Englestein; the middle people—I
never thought of their last names—Mark, Charlotte (Chucky), Her-
shel (Hesh), Leah; and the kids, Mimi, Sam, Shoshana (Shonnie),
Moe, and so on. Well, who was Jewish and who wasn't? They were
working people. And the youngsters were working-class kids who'd
grow into working people. So that little thought problem evaporated
in thin air.

I took off my old tennis shoes; my feet were scalding. Toes cooled,
I could think better, and with my big toe I dislodged a small stone
and sent it bumping down the steep incline. A harvest mouse skittered into a grass tuft, and a small yellow-breasted bird with long
tail feathers shot up from a low branch, where it had been trilling
away in a manner to burst its throat.

I had read the aims of the school in old *Fortnightlies*, the college
publication, and listened to discussions when administration members got together in the evenings. The idea was to build "an institution which will serve as a model for others of like character the
world over, and in which ambitious youths without money may
avail themselves of the benefits of higher education and thereby prepare themselves for service directed toward the enlightenment of
the masses and the reconstruction of society to the end that parasit-
ism be eliminated and equality of opportunity be established; and
with this hope uppermost in our minds we face the future with confidence." There was not one full-blooded Indian and not one black

person at the school. I'd already met folks of several nationalities there—some of whom had come to this country fairly recently. Something was not quite right about the situation. I had to think the problem out.

I did think on it as I went down the mountain and across the valley back to campus. But there was ambivalence in my thinking. No doubt about it, Commonwealth was wonderfully stimulating; a person could grow and develop rapidly there—and what's more, be happy doing it, be alive, be part of something big pushing out into the future. On the other hand, the institution just was not what it claimed to be; it had lofty ideals it didn't quite adhere to, and this caused in me ripples of uncertainty. I delved further into back copies of *Fortnightlies*. The philosophy of workers' education is based upon a sense of social responsibility and refusal to accept the status quo. This is the substance of what I read, and it made sense. Yet Commonwealth had been in existence nine years as a labor college, an institution set up to further workers' educations, and all this time only white folks could come to it. Was my thinking too simplistic? Frankly, I didn't know at the time. I was twenty-three years old, had worked hard since I was eight years old, and had four years of wage-earning behind me. I certainly ought to be able to think clearly on the matter. And yet . . .

The fall term was getting ready to open, and I for one hurried to pay my forty dollars. I wonder if very many folks who have heard a great deal about Commonwealth College know how small it was. Forty-five or fifty students was about the average for the fall, winter, and spring terms. The fall of '32 had over eighty enrolled, and more were on their way from all over the country. I was wishing that I had studied harder the last term—I was scared of meeting all those brilliant young people. If the ones I'd already met were a sample—young men and women from New York, Chicago, Detroit, Milwaukee—what would it be like to have a big bunch of them around? I really did get apprehensive. But when the first of the new students arrived, my apprehensions disappeared in a breathless happy wonderment. Nothing like this ever!

Nothing like this ever: not for me, not for Commonwealth. Classes got rolling. The "commons," our combination dining room/ meeting hall/theater (there was a low platform for a stage at one end) was overflowing at mealtime and usually at night for some kind of get-together, orientation session, or whatnot during the first sizzling week.

Hank was from New York. Or some very big city in the East. He was about twenty-five and had more information in his head than most folks store away in a lifetime. I don't know why he singled me out to talk to shortly after he got there, except that I was from such a different background and this fact interested him. Or maybe he enjoyed the way I hung on his every word. I'd talked to quite a few northern urban folks the two summers I'd been there, but Hank had a way of putting new meanings into things. As he talked he reached right into whatever he was talking about, pulled out the substance— the core—and spread it out for you. He was a thinker, but he never tried to go over your head. Hank had light hair, but his skin was the kind that took on a heavy tan, which he acquired within a couple of weeks, since he asked right away to be assigned to outdoor work—late gathering of crops: squash, turnips, cabbages, and the last of the tomatoes. He worked for a few days on the wood crew and got blisters and had to go back to the fields. That sun still came down fairly warm, and the guys would rub olive oil on their backs and legs and work with just a pair of very short shorts on. So Hank was nut-brown all over, except for the shallow stripe covered by the shorts.

Our letter campaign was over, and there was not too much to do in the office. And I thought the glorious, golden, spicy fall days would be the best time of all to be outdoors. (Or was it Hank's figure out there bending over the rows that tempted me from the office window?) Anyhow, I asked to work in the garden again. The girls who worked outside usually wore shorts and halter tops. But me, I wore a sleeved shirt and overalls, since no amount of sun could make me immune to sunburn.

I was out in the very early fall in the pole beans, and Hank was working in the next row. He straightened up and mopped his brow with a red handkerchief.

"Did you ever read anything about a black man named Du Bois?"

"No," I said. "Black people I know are named Washington or Jones or Harrison—names like that."

"Well, I want to tell you what this man Du Bois said, and I think he's got the situation sized up about right."

"There was Mr. Porter who leased a farm just west of us—farm belonged to the bank. He and my father used to talk across the fence, and Mr. Porter came and had supper with us once in a while." I was remembering our black neighbor in Oklahoma, and Hank's remark had only half-registered, so I quickly said, "What about this man Du Bois? I'm sorry, I was remembering."

"William E. B. Du Bois said that the future of this country would be decided by what happens to the blacks—it pivots on the race question." Hank stooped over to gather a fallen pole-bean vine and place it back on its support. "You see that, don't you? Looking backward in the history of this country, black labor was the basis of the economy, and without it the white power apparatus would have been up shit creek without a paddle; and looking forward the white working class and poor haven't got a chance as long as the blacks are held down and kept out of unions and so on—and out of schools like this."

"My father used to follow Debs a lot in his thinking," I said. "And Debs tried to get black workers accepted into the Railway Union way back before the turn of the century. I guess Debs believed like your Mr. Du Bois." I didn't say anything about my forebodings on Rich Mountain that summer day a couple of months back. I still wasn't ready to condemn the school and didn't know if I ever could. It had been and still was my Shangri-La.

"Do you know the whole story of how Commonwealth started?" Hank asked me. "Why in hell did they start it in a place where blacks can't even stay overnight?"

"I don't know a whole lot," I replied. "But I know Kate O'Hare was a follower of Debs, and she was one of the original trustees. You've got me curious, too." A bit of a pretense, since I had been more than curious—I'd poked around a bit. I told Hank some of what I knew: when the O'Hares, Kate and her husband, along with William Zeuch, the former director, first established the college, it wasn't in Arkansas; it was in Louisiana. Something went wrong there—I didn't know exactly what—and then *this* place was located. They had bought this land with a grant from the Garland Fund, one of Roger Baldwin's enterprises. Baldwin was a militant socialist and president of the ACLU, which Hank knew. I told him that Commonwealth had been given quite a sizeable sum, and the staff lived in tents for a while until they could knock a building together, but that I did not know what the criteria were when they chose this site—perhaps the main one was the beauty of the natural surroundings. "They sure picked a place dreams are made of," I said. "The land isn't too good, except for what's been cleared down on the valley floor; my father had better land on his quarter section in Oklahoma. But this place, god it's beautiful. It gets me—and it gets you too, Hank; I can see that. Hey, have you been over to the spring yet? It's a jump and a stone's throw from here—that's why I always like to work in this field. Let's get a drink."

I took off running toward the edge of the field and to the spring, hidden deep in a woodsy hollow pungent with the smell of pine and thick with dark-green, briary underbrush with a few giant old oaks providing solid shade to the spot. My long overalls and long-sleeved shirt served me well as a shield from the spiny thorns that stuck out every which way from the bushes along the path. So I got there, had my drink of cold, clear water from the dipper left hanging there, and wondered how Hank was making it in his short shorts and no shirt. I started back toward the edge of the woods and there he was sitting down nursing a long, bloody scratch across his bare chest.

"Look out!" I shouted, pointing behind him. He turned his head and stood up very quickly, for there was a huge black snake beginning to take off into the bushes. "Harmless," I said.

"I *know* that. You didn't give me time to look at it, f'chrissake. *You* startled me—not the snake. I know that thing's harmless."

"But *that* isn't," I said, pointing to the spot where Hank had been sitting.

"What isn't?"

"That's poison ivy. Where were you when they had the orientation session on poison ivy and coal-oil lamps?"

"What's a coal-oil lamp, f'chrissake?"

"That's what you light with a match in your room at night. Otherwise known as a kerosene lamp. But in Arkansas and Oklahoma it's coal-oil."

Then I told Hank Bill's story of Lolly, a one-time Commonwealth student from the big city who, after attending the orientation session on coal-oil lamps, went to her dorm, lit a lamp, and threw it out the window. She went to the supply room for another lamp, lit it, and threw it out the window. After the third lamp Lolly gave up and went for advice. The instructions had been that if a lamp sputtered and popped, sending up a smoky, erratic flame, something was wrong; the wick might be twisted and the flame could possibly crawl down to the oil in the lamp's bowl and cause a fire. Since the wooden dorms were made of tinder, one was to quickly blow the lamp out in such a case. Lolly had understood *blow* as *throw*. I told Hank that I didn't think he would ever take so small a thing as a coal-oil lamp that seriously, no matter how it sputtered, since he hadn't even bothered to find out what it was he'd been lighting every night.

And yet it wasn't only big things that Hank took seriously. He had adopted a campus kitten nobody wanted—a scrawny, mangy-looking little thing—and had given it an imposing name: some martyr of the labor movement, Sacco, I think it was. I've never seen anyone so fond of a pet. I believe the kitten stood for something—perhaps it personified the underdog. It would not have survived without special consideration, and Hank knew that. He always brought it to meals, where it sat beside him on the bench and ate bits of food from his fingers. He came to the kitchen early in the morning and begged a half cup of milk from the breakfast crew, which he warmed before taking it back to his dorm room to give to his kitten. The kitten thrived.

There was considerable harvesting and canning to be done in the month of September. Of course, the cannery was busy from late-spring-berry season right through to October, putting up the produce in gallon tin cans. Corn was canned in early August when still green, while the ears for animal consumption were left in the fields to ripen and get hard in the sun. The sweet-potato and peanut harvests were in the fall—there were still lots of tomatoes ripening in the garden acres close to the campus. For any of these operations—canning or harvesting a certain fruit or vegetable while at its peak—special enlarged crews were organized. For the young people from the cities, as most of the students were, there was novelty and a certain excitement in this harvesting and preserving of food. Few had ever participated in anything like it. But by mid-October it was finished, or nearly so, and the restiveness began.

It rained a lot, and the dorms were damp and chilly in spite of wood fires in tiny heating stoves. Students stayed around the huge fireplace in the commons long after supper, and they talked and complained about how the place was run. There was a nucleus of about ten or twelve who seemed to know more than the administration about organizational techniques; I believe they must have been politicized before they graduated from elementary school. Several were Communists, some had trade-union experience, some had helped in the organization of the great hunger march of the year before. A couple of the young men told of witnessing President Hoover's troops led by Douglas MacArthur attack the Bonus Marchers the previous summer, shooting into the crowd and killing some, mercilessly driving women and children from the encampment with tear gas and bullets. Such students were seriously in search of basic knowledge of world affairs.

William Z. Foster was the Communist Party's candidate for president in 1932—his third time to run. Norman Thomas was the Socialists' candidate. With election time almost upon us, what was more appropriate than for the students to organize a straw vote? In the process of working for his candidate—Foster—Hank got up a wall newspaper called the *Red Menace*. The Socialists had one, and the journalism class had one. I remember I was a "Jimmy Higgins" for all these projects, typing and pasting up, and especially drawing caricatures of various campus personalities. My sketches were on all the wall newspapers, including one called *The Dodo*, put out by a very young group of campus humorists, the "Disorganized Order of the Disorganized Orders."

As I recall, William Z. Foster won the straw vote for president, though I'm not sure; I do remember for sure that Hank talked me into voting for Foster, whose running mate was a black man, James W. Ford. It didn't take too much doing to swing my vote. I was beginning to spend later and later hours in the library studying *Das Kapital* and reading a biography of Marx, and by the time the straw vote took place, I had mastered the theory of surplus value, and dialectical materialism was beginning to come within my grasp. As a matter of fact, we were witnessing a practical example of dialectics at work right on our campus—quantitative changes taking place with each student meeting, with the qualitative leap not too far ahead.

Class attendance slipped—the students were having too many meetings lasting into the wee hours. Who needed classes on revolutionary theory—a revolution was about to be experienced! The students bustled about during the day, criticizing and making suggestions for how this and that must be changed—this teacher was completely worthless and that one had better shape up or else. Within the nucleus of ten of the most dissatisfied, there were two who were real leaders, Hank Forblade and Jack Cope. By the time Lucien Koch, the college's twenty-four-year-old director, got back from a fund-raising tour in early November, the place was in the process of being systematically taken over by the students. The administration, instead of calmly assessing the situation, started to grow quills like a porcupine. Looking back, I believe you could describe the mental state of some of its members as verging on panic. I say *some*, certainly not all. Anyway, the situation worsened by the hour. I managed to attend most of the student meetings, sticking it out until midnight at least. A big discussion point was the admission to Commonwealth of black students and the acquiring of at least one black teacher (I can't say *hire*, because nobody at the college was paid a salary; staff and maintenance people were allowed a small cigarette-and-shoe-leather stipend).

Nonmilitant students, also in attendance at meetings, argued that this was entirely too much to expect, and that it was dangerous to even think about. To something like that Hank would counter with: "Its a hell of a lot more dangerous, in the long run, *not* to think about it. And *not* to do something about it. What's the idea of danger?"

"That goes without saying," the answer would be. "Getting the blacks killed and getting the college burnt to the ground."

"This college is most likely going to get burned to the ground anyway, and as for blacks getting killed, nobody says we have to get them here next week. We want much more representation on the administration staff, then we would be able to thrash the question out and propose that the school be moved to a location where blacks could be accepted. Our proposal as we've written it up is for the immediate *consideration* of admitting black students, not immediate admission—as Dave and Lucien keep throwing at us when we try to get a chance to talk things out."

"I still think we're moving too fast," the student who had started a Socialist Party group on campus said. "Let's just draw up a proposal for some more student representatives and drop the subject of black students for the time being. Every association member [who jointly owned the college land and equipment] I've talked to has made it pretty clear that the black issue is simply nonnegotiable, period."

"What is this property supposed to be worth?" Hank asked. "Anybody here know?"

I spoke up. "About thirty or thirty-five thousand dollars, I think."

"How many people are in on the ownership?"

"I'm not sure—about ten, I think."

"Well, that eliminates *that*, then."

"Eliminates what?" I asked.

"Property considerations. Divide thirty thousand dollars by ten and what have you got? Only three thousand dollars. Nobody—not any of *those* people anyway—are going to compromise principles for any three-thousand-dollars' worth of property. Now if it was a matter of three-*hundred*-thousand-dollars' worth of property to be divided . . ."

"Wait—wait a minute," I said. "Do you mean to say you thought that . . ." I hesitated, and everybody looked at me. "Oh, nothing. Skip it." I did not want to get into this any further here. But I intended to take it up with Hank in private. After all, my own brother and sister-in-law were members of the association.

"I don't know what you people are getting at," said the socialist student. "But this school has been here for nine years. They have a fund-raising apparatus set up that works and that very possibly might get thrown out of kilter if the school were to move, say north somewhere."

"Now," said Hank, "we're getting into something. *We* can attend a school like this—learn labor history, study the political and economic background of the mess this country's in, and so on and so on, for chrissake—only because a fund-raising apparatus has been set up over a period of years. Money is being sucked up from all kinds of sources, but black students can't take advantage of it. All right then, this school that professes to make workers' education available to all, no matter how poor and whether they do or don't adhere to any creed or 'ism'—this school is saying in effect, 'Come one, come all—if your skin is white.'"

There was silence for a full minute while this soaked in.

"But we're learning here how to go out there and work for equality," said the socialist student. "We've got to have a certain amount of peace and quiet to study in. Blacks should set themselves up a school like this up north."

"With a gift from the Garland Fund?" said Jack. The Communists and various militants smiled and gave each other knowing looks.

"I've got it," continued Jack. "They'll do it with what they save up picking cotton. The average cotton picker can get sixty cents a day in midseason when the pickin's good. His wife and kids work for nothing."

"All right, let's get serious." Hank took over again. "Just what are we supposed to be doing here—what has the school been doing for nine years? Educating young people for participation in the bringing about of a new social order; that's what all of you heard at the orientation sessions. A school is going to educate people for a new social order—white people only? For chrissake, that's something like feeding hay to a cavalry horse when right under its belly is a mortar shell ready to explode. Where's the hay goin' to go, for chrissake?" Hank had colorful analogies, you could say that much about him.

"I'm asking for a vote on our proposal, a show of hands. Everybody in favor." Hands were counted; "All those opposed." Hands were counted. Those in favor won. A few of us abstained. Intellectually I was convinced Hank and his group were correct. Emotionally, I was still wavering. The school must be given time to move to a suitable location. It would take a lot of doing. Were the militants going to bring things to a head before anything constructive could be done? I had to have a private talk with Hank.

The meeting adjourned with the singing of the "Internationale," and students divided into groups and went off to dorm rooms to hold bull sessions till the wee hours. I believe most of them were still vague about just what specific proposals were going to be made to the association. Negotiations for the admission of blacks could be effectively carried out only if there was more student representation on the administrative body. I believe that was clear. Majority dissatisfaction with at least two teachers—there was no doubt about that.

The association was also holding meetings almost nightly, and as Bill Cunningham's sister, I was welcome to attend them. At the first one I went to after the trouble set in for real, I got the feeling that Bill was the calmest person there, even though his wife was soon going to have a baby and he had every reason to be nervous. He may have had more of a feeling of security than the others; he could always go back to his job of teaching regular high school in Oklahoma. Besides, he and Clarice had a small but steady income writing for the pulp magazines, so a threatened disruption of the school would not mean that they would face a depression-crazy world with nothing in the hand. I sat in at the association meeting and kept my mouth shut. But I listened:

"Jack and Henry cannot possibly have as many followers as they profess to have." ... "Oh, I believe they do have." ... "But they're such kids; they show their lack of maturity every time they open their mouths." . . . "On the contrary, I think Henry has a hell of a lot of experience behind him. And charisma, which the students go for." . . . "But his smart-alecky attitude. When he talks to me I want to slap his face!" . . . "Never mind his smart-aleckyness, I think he's dangerous. Have you noticed how he uses the other students? That poor Myer, for instance, who used to run Henry's errands for him and follow him around like a puppy, or like that kitten of Henry's." (Myer was a plump, awkward fellow who liked to boast having been a charter member of the Young Communist League, which couldn't have been true since he was only twenty.) "Never mind Myer; Jack is the one Henry respects, and he'll go along with Henry absolutely on the black question." . . . "None of those disrupters have the slightest notion of what it's taken to set up a labor college like this and keep it going." . . . "But you can't just classify the whole student body as disrupters." . . . "If it comes down to it, and if things don't quiet down, they've got to be expelled." . . . "Who?" . . . "Those two. I don't have any intention of allowing them to stay around here. There's too much at stake." . . . "But they haven't really done anything yet—let's not jump to conclusions." . . . "I've come to a conclusion. Why, the college has ceased to function as a school! I had three in my class this morning." . . . "I bet it was the Socialists. Or the neutrals. They seem to be trying to make up for the troublemakers' disruptiveness." . . . "Well, I don't think it's factional, or ideological in the usual sense. I think it's personalities. Personalities, I tell you! Maladjusted personalities who'll never fit in anywhere!" . . . "I agree, they've got to go." . . . "Please don't do anything hasty. I suggest we give it another few days at least." And the meeting ended on that note.

I went to these meetings honestly trying to get the point of view of both sides. But one morning the *Red Menace* wall newspaper had a story about a certain student who was becoming notorious on campus as an informer—no names were named, but obviously the article referred to me, as I was the only student also attending association meetings. I yanked the story down, ran to the young men's dorm, and almost knocked Hank's door off the hinges. I found him hunched down on his knees, pouring his little half cup of warm milk into the kitten's saucer.

"I know you couldn't have done this, but did you say something to inspire it?" I thrust the piece of paper at him. He stood up, took the paper, and slowly read it. "Where was this?" he asked. Using my most sarcastic tone, I replied, "Printed in the *Red Menace*, where else?" Hank burst out laughing.

Here was this deeply serious guy, amused at something I thought was serious. I had scared the kitten, so Hank reached down and pushed its tiny nose into the milk. "Well?" I said.

"No, I didn't do it. And I didn't say anything like that. But I think I know where it came from. It wasn't up there last night. And I don't think very many saw it. So forget it." I demanded to know who did it. Hank picked up the kitten, stroking it between the ears with his thumb. "I said forget it. It was done for kicks, f'chrissake. To get you riled up—and that's just what happened. Obviously, Sis, you know, don't you, that I don't take that *Red Menace* project seriously as a movement activity—it's for relief, like taking a piss, for instance. We started it to see what kind of reaction we could stir up, I suppose, but mainly it's a takeoff on the *Campus Bluff* [the wall newspaper of the journalism class]. The really serious business of this school will be decided, but not by means of wall newspapers. Come on, let's see if there's any oatmeal left in the commons." I was getting educated.

Myer, the kid who'd been Hank's yes-man, showed up at supper that day with a black eye. I knew Hank was getting sick of Myer's stale puns and his referring to himself as the original "XYZ heller" (ex-YCLer). Once, maybe, but twenty times? So Myer was no longer being asked to do bits of research when Hank was busy writing articles to send off to various left-wing magazines and newspapers. Myer was obviously jealous of Hank's friendliness toward me and had begun to make a pest of himself. When he showed up with that shiner, I knew he'd been the one responsible for the informer story. I suppose down through the years every "utopia" has had its Myer.

The situation grew more complex by the hour. When the kitchen manager was no longer allowed to enter the kitchen and no association member could make a phone call from the campus, that was serious. The gist of the matter was that a phone call was made or word was gotten somehow to the sheriff in Mena that help was needed to remove some troublemakers from the Commonwealth College campus. When the sheriff and his deputies showed up in their Black Maria, there was no feeling of relief on anyone's part—it was an ugly day. Hank and Jack, the two who had actually been expelled but were still there, immediately agreed to leave peaceably.

They seemed not quite to believe what was happening. They did leave, taking two-thirds of the student body with them.

I was not quite what anybody would call a class-conscious activist when the student strike at Commonwealth and the departure of so many of the group shook the school to its very foundations. I thought Hank Forblade was a great guy in spite of the lack of patience he showed toward the end. I realized that I would likely never see him again when he gave me the faintest trace of a smile as he raised his hand in a gesture of good-bye. Basically he was correct, I was convinced of it. But emotionally I was a southwesterner and needed time to sort things out. The college administration had made a very grave mistake in calling in the law, of that I was certain. Principles had been compromised for expediency—it had been the easiest way out of a difficult situation.

Everyone who stayed—teachers, maintenance people, and students—shared this bad feeling. Anything but calling the cops! Lawmen were tools of the bosses; there was no way of getting around the fact that a hasty decision had not only nullified the ideas and loyalties the college had been attempting to impart to its students, but also compromised some of its most basic ideals. Early in the term, at one of the orientation sessions, there was a detailed description of the school's trip of the previous spring into the coal fields of Harlan County, Kentucky. Lucien, another teacher, and three students had driven into the area with "Food for starving miners and the Bill of Rights for sheriffs," as the streamers on their car read. Lawmen asked them to turn back, and when they refused they were dragged into the woods and severely beaten. The lesson of the orientation session was clear: not only by word but by example, Commonwealth teaches confrontation with lawmen if necessary to protect workers' interests in any situation.

Now the college had called in the law, showing a greater degree of impatience than the "immature" student strikers had shown. Henry Forblade had a point in his favor. Theoretical training was very important, but to provide it took money. And the money for this school was coming from wealthy white intellectuals. Where could blacks obtain funds to set up schools for themselves? If they couldn't get theoretical training, what kind of justice was that? You had to go out there and do some confronting for them, or with them, or something. You couldn't just let that kind of inequality go unchallenged.

To Henry's way of thinking, he was challenging a kind of inequality he couldn't go along with. Old John Brown—you came around to thinking about old John Brown.

All night I lay awake, seeing over and over again Hank's trace of a smile—mirthless, almost a grin. He hadn't gone triumphant. He wasn't proud of the fact that the majority had joined him. He was surprised and perhaps a little perplexed. His face held a question— what was the answer? This was not the answer, not clearly anyway. I don't think anyone slept that night. It was a weary, haggard, depleted little group that straggled to the commons next morning for breakfast. It was true, I was never to see Hank again. He enlisted in World War II, attained a petty-officership and died at Anzio in the advance of the beachhead there. He was commended for bravery in setting an example to the troops in his command and was awarded a Congressional Medal of Honor posthumously.

It was several months later, and well into spring, when I fully realized why my brother Bill had been so calm during the big upheaval at Commonwealth. He had a book in gestation—a book that had virtually nothing to do with the immediate surroundings—neither as to place nor time—so he was basically in a position to be objective. Commonwealth was a good place for a fellow like Bill to concentrate on his writing, since few stringent demands were made on his time; he could sit at his typewriter more or less when he felt like it and work with few interruptions. And, unlike many a young writer, he knew there was always a table to put his feet under when he was hungry. Besides his and Clarice's many short stories accepted by the pulps, he had finished his autobiographical novel, *Townbroke,* and sent the manuscript off to various publishers, only to have it returned accompanied by formal rejection slips.

The new book growing in his head was a different kind of novel, and I became aware of it one glorious day when I went with him to visit an old hill farmer, Clyde Washington, in his mountainside cabin a few miles from the campus. The dogwood was in full bloom, wood violets peeked out from the wild tangle of fern fronds carpeting the shady floor of the woods, and when he came out onto a cleared bench of grassland, the meadowlarks almost drowned out whatever conversation we tried to carry on. And so we came to Clyde Washington's cabin set on an incline with wild grape vines all below and above it.

I knew Clyde as a talented and forceful square-dance caller who came to the commons on a once-in-a-while Saturday night to put us through the intricate figures of the Arkansas dances—much more complicated than the kind I'd cut my teeth on in western Oklahoma, but performed in the same stern ritualistic manner as the plains folks performed theirs. Often I watched Clyde's stony face as he barked and yodelled his dosidoes and allemande-lefts. And that was how I knew him. Bill got to know him in a different way—he interviewed Clyde to get material for his new book on the Green Corn Rebellion, since Clyde had been one of those who, in a spirit of patriotism and in all innocence no doubt, had hunted down farmers suspected of taking part in the "Oklahoma insurrection" of 1917 and turned them over to the sheriff for arrest.

The Green Corn Rebellion was essentially an antidraft action and not really a rebellion from the viewpoint of an outsider. Inwardly, those farmers were rebelling like hell—not only against going to war but against their insufferable economic condition. Many were followers of Eugene V. Debs's Socialism. They read the *Appeal to Reason*, and because of having voted Socialist in an election or two, they were grossly discriminated against. They'd been denied farm loans; many had been subjected to foreclosures and forced to become tenant farmers at a time when small independent farming was supposed to be on the up-and-up. (The up-and-up business was and still is a myth—there never was such a thing, not so far in the twentieth century, anyway.) So the dirt farmers in Arkansas, Oklahoma, and parts of Texas had organized themselves into various groups, most notable of which was the Working Class Union led by H. H. (Rube) Munson, a former Wobbly. This organization grew to a membership of around fifty thousand by the time of this country's entry into World War I. Munson had been at Commonwealth (that was before I came there), and Bill knew him. He had served five years of a ten-year sentence at Leavenworth as a result of his activities in connection with the Green Corn Rebellion, an action long developing but triggered by President Wilson's draft call in June 1917. A group of tenant farmers southeast of Oklahoma City met in a schoolhouse, raised a red flag, and drew up a Declaration of War on the United States.

For some time it had been preached to the Oklahoma tenant farmers by unscrupulous—or perhaps merely careless—local socialist leaders that the capitalist system under which they'd suffered such grave abuses was in the process of being overthrown all around the country, and a farmers' and workers' republic was in the process of being set up; thus were the assurances passed down by means of speech-making and leafleteering from headquarters in Oklahoma City. The farmers were certainly ready for a farmer/worker republic, but they were far from being ready to engage in the necessary struggle to achieve it, since they had no arms except .22-calibre rifles, possibly one shotgun for every six men, and not more than a day's supply of ammunition at any given time. Nobody had any money, nor was any raised for them. They were presented with an elaborate plan for a march on Washington, the immediate aim of which was to stop the draft and secondarily to stop a capitalist war. The U.S. government would topple without its war, and the farmer/worker republic would take shape. The farmers had understood that the march was starting from rallying points all over the U.S.; they even had pieces of paper on which were written the names of a dozen localities in Oklahoma from which contingents were on the way and a promise of forthcoming directives as to the next move, central meeting point, travel routes to Washington, and the like.

About one hundred men from the area around Sasakwa occupied a high spot of ground called Spear's Bluff, hoisted a red flag, and waited there for two days and nights for further orders—which never came. In the group were a number of blacks, a few Indians, and only one person with any military experience, a black man who'd served in the U.S. army and fought in the Spanish-American War. He was made military leader. He took command reluctantly, as he felt no group of whites would submit to being disciplined by a black. And discipline, he said, was the basis of any military action.

He didn't have much time to find out if he was right about whites not taking orders from blacks. At Spear's Bluff, as it turned out, there occurred the only actual confrontation between the rebels and the law, and this confrontation became known as the Battle of Spear's Bluff, even though the defenders fired not a single shot. When approached by a bunch of men who'd been quickly deputized for the occasion, the farmers retreated and scattered into the fields with sheriffs' and deputies' guns blazing away at them. Those who lived close by sneaked home, to be dragged out, beaten, and arrested later. Others hid out in the tall corn, living on *tomfuller*, which was the Indian word for corn cut from the cob and boiled over an open fire.

The distraught farmers were abandoned by those trusted ones who had drawn up the plan for the rebellion, and now they were at the mercy of bands of vigilantes who tracked them with trail hounds and ruthlessly persecuted them. Less than a hundred had occupied Spear's Bluff, one bridge over the Canadian River had been set afire, and a sheriff was killed by a bullet in the back accidentally fired from the gun of a deputy. But over one thousand poor, bedraggled dirt farmers were rounded up and put in a stockade at McAlester. Some were held a while and let go; others were tried, convicted of treason, and served terms of from one to ten years in federal prison. Many were beaten and gunned down, others hounded off their rented land or forced to give up what nebulous claim they still had to farms they owned. Families were shattered; wives and children starved. The number victimized in one way or another rose to countless thousands before the whole thing cooled down. As one deputy said years later, "I didn't want to fight in any damn rich man's war either, but I kept it to myself back then."

So Bill wrote his book. And I believe I can say in all sincerity that if, during the year or so following the student strike, Commonwealth served no purpose but to provide Bill Cunningham a good place in which to write, its continued existence was worthwhile. Bill felt that he was getting on the right track in beginning to produce historical novels. He often repeated a quote from Aristotle: "The artistic representation of history is a more scientific and serious pursuit than the exact writing of history. For the art of letters goes to the heart of things, whereas the factual report merely collates details." Everybody left at the school attended Bill's class in creative writing, including the teachers, and at least half the folks there were working on novels. Many of Bill's lectures dealt with the works of the great nineteenth-century historical novelists to illustrate the premise that a writer could best advance an understanding of history by dealing pictorially with people's reactions to events, and conversely by showing the way those reactions shape events to come.

That Bill was not a latter-day Emile Zola and that he did not produce an American *Germinal* was the fault of the times and not due to lack of talent or effort. *The Green Corn Rebellion* was printed by Vanguard in 1935—it's now long out of print. But some day this work will be taken out of mothballs and reprinted for its historical value, if for no other reason.

Henry Forblade had been prophetically right in at least one thing he said: that the school would most likely be burned down whether or not it admitted blacks. Commonwealth College weathered several near closings in the late 1930s. It was put to the torch in the late fall of 1940.

Mr. and Mrs. William Wallace Cunningham, their five children, and Grandmother Boyce, in front of family residence, near Watonga, Oklahoma, summer 1916. Sis Cunningham *far left*. (Cunningham/Friesen Family Collection)

William Wallace Cunningham, Sis's father, near Watonga, Oklahoma, 1938. (Photograph by Eli Jaffe, Cunningham/Friesen Family Collection)

Birthplace of Sis Cunningham, 1909, near
Watonga, Oklahoma. (Photograph taken c. 1959,
Cunningham/Friesen Family Collection)

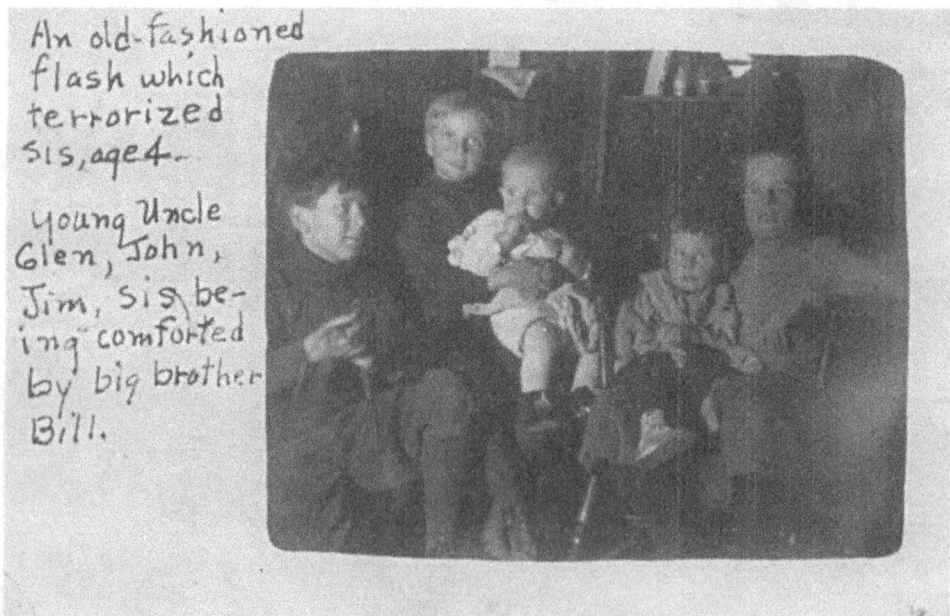

An old-fashioned
flash which
terrorized
Sis, age 4.

young Uncle
Glen, John,
Jim, Sis be-
ing comforted
by big brother
Bill.

Sis Cunningham, age four, *fourth from left*, with,
left to right, Uncle Glen Boyce and brothers John, Jim,
and Bill, March 15, 1913. (Cunningham/Friesen
Family Collection)

Weatherford, Oklahoma, high school football team, 1927. Gordon Friesen *far left, tip row.* (Cunningham/Friesen Family Collection)

Marie and Jacob Friesen, Gordon's mother and father, near Weatherford, Oklahoma, mid-1940s. (Cunningham/Friesen Family Collection)

Sis Cunningham, first teaching job, southwest Oklahoma, c. 1928. (Cunningham/Friesen Family Collection)

The Commonwealth College faculty, late 1932. Sis Cunningham, *far right*. Her brother Bill Cunningham, *third from left, back row*. (Cunningham/Friesen Family Collection)

The Commonwealth College faculty and student body, c. 1932–33. Sis Cunningham, *fifth from left, second row.* Bill Cunningham, *sixth from left, first row.* (Cunningham/Friesen Family Collection)

Faculty of Southern Summer School for Women Workers, Ashville, North Carolina, 1937. Sis Cunningham, *third from left, front row.* (Cunningham/Friesen Family Collection)

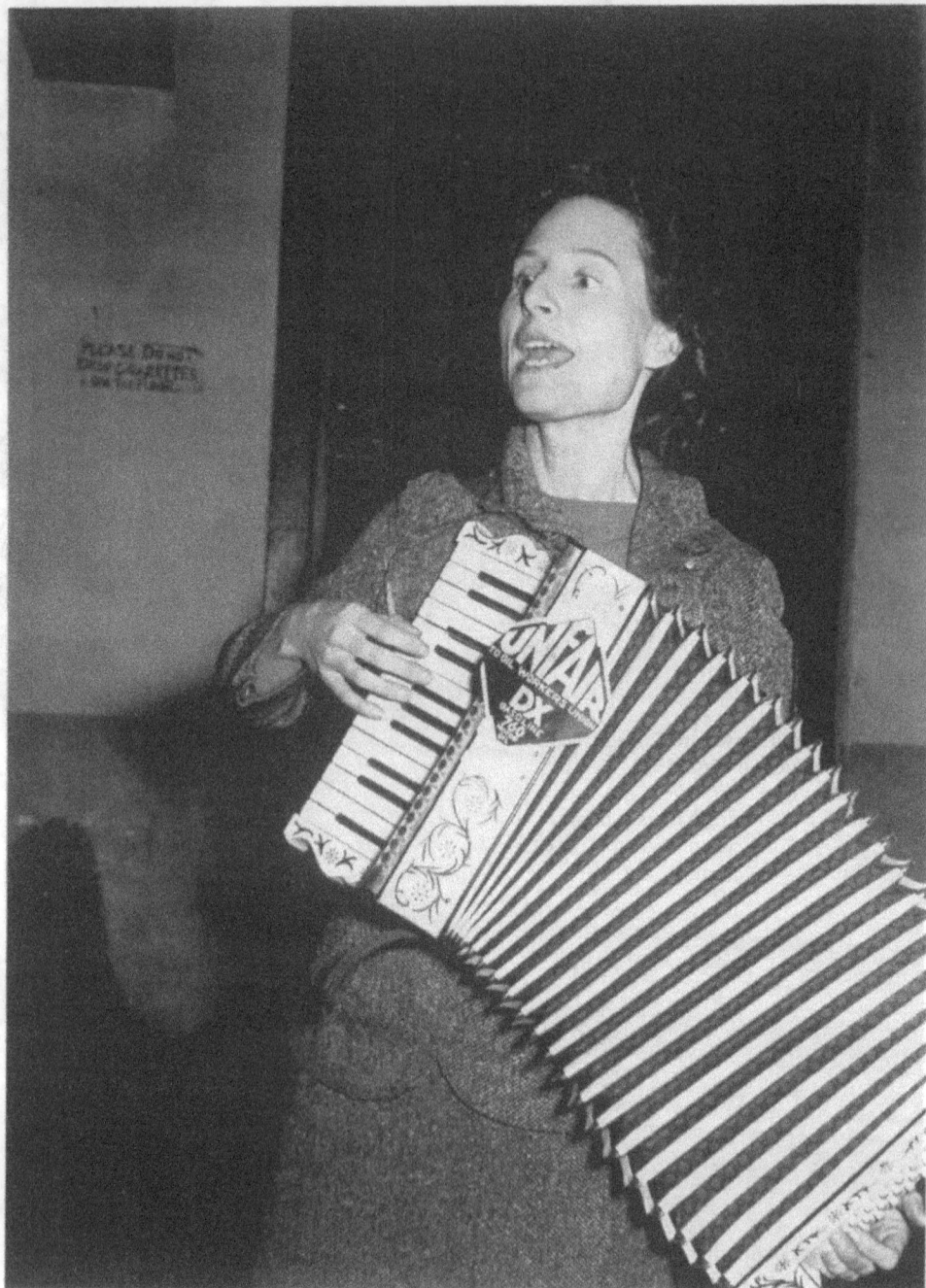

Sis Cunningham, Bristow, Oklahoma, 1940.
(See photograph of 1985 poster at end of gallery.)
(Photograph by Russell Lee, Farm Security
Administration, from the Library of Congress.
Reproduced with permission.)

The Almanac Singers,
1942. *Left to right:*
Woody Guthrie, Millard
Lampell, Bess Hawes,
Pete Seeger, Arthur Stern,
and Sis Cunningham.
(*Broadside* Collection)

Gordon Friesen,
New York City, 1942.
(Publicity photograph
by Helen Themill, for
art exhibition,
Cunningham/Friesen
Family Collection)

Gordon Friesen and
daughter Aggie, West 106th
Street, New York City,
1949. (Cunningham/Friesen
Family Collection)

Jane Friesen and
friend Victor, site of
Frederick Douglass
Housing Project
construction,
New York City, late 1950s.
(Cunningham/Friesen
Family Collection)

Village Gate *Broadside* benefit
concert, New York City, 1963. *Left
to right:* [unidentified], Pete Seeger,
Pat Sky, and Peter La Farge.
(*Broadside* Collection)

Detail of exhibit shown at union Solidarity Day rallies,
Oklahoma, 1985, with picture of Sis Cunningham from the 1940s.
(Photograph by Jim Cunningham, Cunningham/Friesen Family
Collection)

Chapter 5

Gordon in the 1930s

I kept up my love of reading—all the books in the state correspondence library. I was given by the druggist copies of unsold magazines whose covers had been returned to the distributor. Thousands of magazines—Mencken's *American Mercury* (I was greatly influenced by its iconoclasm), *Harper's*, *Atlantic Monthly*, the old *Golden Book*, a progressive but short-lived *Plain Talk* (the original, not the later thing by same name). I read every pulp imaginable, plus books from the state library: H. G. Wells, Arnold Bennett, Willa Cather, Edith Wharton, Theodore Dreiser, Thomas Hardy, Tolstoy, Anatole France, Dostoevski, Turgenev. Later, I got books brought back by my cousin from trips to Oklahoma City. I was greatly influenced by Sinclair Lewis (*Main Street, Babbitt, Elmer Gantry, Arrowsmith*). Hemingway seemed superficial, Faulkner rambling on and on about a South that no longer existed, if it ever did. And, of course, later on, *Grapes of Wrath*, the only important piece Steinbeck ever did (the first talking movie I saw was *Grapes*). Mencken and *Elmer Gantry* finished off whatever religious sentiments were still left from my Mennonite childhood. I became quite cynical, but did not start to think about social problems until the Great Depression worsened.

I had done some beginning writing in high school; I wrote mainly sports for the high-school newspaper, the *Weatherford Broadcaster*, and I also did a lot of ghostwriting for students at Southwestern State College. Central State in Edmund had correspondence courses where students could earn extra credits; one correspondence course was worth two credits, and these could be added to the credits students were earning by actually going to school at Southwestern. Quite a few students were doing this to hurry up their education. I took a whole batch of these correspondence courses for students I knew; in fact, that was about the only formal college education that I ever got in my life. I took correspondence courses in everything imaginable. Central State would send out questionnaires and mimeographed lists of questions, suggestions for what textbooks to study, what additional reading to do.

I took courses in American literature, English literature, civil law—I learned all about torts and maritime law—took courses in economics. I can still remember how the law of diminishing returns goes. I took English history; I learned all the names of the British kings and queens, from the Normans and even earlier. I used to know them all by heart. There were others, too. I got paid fifteen dollars per course, and I guaranteed passing grades so that my "clients" could get the credits. I did pretty well; a lot of them got *A*'s and *A*-minuses. I did that for several winters, several school seasons. This was in the early '30s, when the depression was really deepening, plus we had the added phenomena of the dust storms and the droughts. Corn fields dried up, cotton developed nothing but "bollies," little wrinkled bolls that don't really open; it was too damn dry. Anyhow, money in our family was extremely scarce; for a while I was the only source of cash. The money I earned all went for food—sacks of flour, cans of lard, buckets of syrup. It was like western Kansas all over again.

Then I began writing news stories from Weatherford and the surrounding territory there, first for the *Clinton Daily News*. Clinton was the largest town in Custer County. At that time it had a population of six to eight thousand, three or four times as large as Weatherford, and there was a man there, Buff Burtis, publishing a daily paper; a very small paper, but it came out daily. It was four sheets, sometimes six, and for the next several years I wrote reams of stories for that paper, mainly about things going on up at Southwestern. I covered the sports up there at the college. Southwestern at that time had a wrestling team that became nationally known, one of the top wrestling teams in the country. I think one year they were second only to the Oklahoma Aggies—from Oklahoma A&M College at Stillwater, which also turned out many top-flight wrestlers. I not only wrote about wrestling, but also about all the other sports— football, basketball, track. They even had a golf team, of which my brother Ollie was a member. I wrote about news from the town, elections, the streets being paved, a new water well being dug, accidents—two cars crashed head-on in the middle of Main Street, people got hurt in town and out on the farms, people were killed by lightning, maimed or killed by runaway horses.

Another big news item was the paving of Highway 66; they were making it ready—making a trail, as it were—for the Okies to get to California on. Up until that time it was a dirt road, terribly muddy during the rains. Dozens of cars would get stuck—in fact, there were farmers around there who made money using their teams to drag cars out of the mud. I wrote about hailstorms, everything I could think of. Historical background stories. I wrote a lot on the founding of Weatherford, the settling of Custer County, how it got its name. General Custer is supposed to have crossed the South Canadian River at a point that also bears his name—Custer City—and lost two artillery pieces in the quicksand. This story was considered to have at least enough historical value to name a town and a county after him. I don't think he was connected with Custer County in any other way. Of course, there was the Battle of the Little Washita in which he massacred the Cheyennes, who were looking for a peace parley—that happened on the Washita River, two or three counties west of Custer. The early-day outlaws who had roamed through there, the first settlement—I wrote reams of stories of that nature. The pay was very small; I got so much an inch. I was what is known as a stringer. I expanded the operation gradually by writing the same kind of material, and getting more or less the same kind of pay, for the *Daily Oklahoman and Times* in Oklahoma City; I sold some stories, mainly about animals, to the *Denver Post.* I remember once writing a story that ran a whole column down the page, for which I got a check for one dollar. I wrote for the *Kansas City Star*, the Tulsa papers.

My major source of income started when I began writing for the Associated Press and United Press bureaus in Oklahoma City. First I would cover the spot news: storms, wheat was in a bad shape or it was doing good—it was going to make twenty-four bushels to the acre, it only made eighteen the year before—the economy was improving. Of course, in between the dust storms there was one good crop year out of three. And a lot of stuff about the dust storms, the dust bowl, refugees leaving—that was somewhat later on. Then I began to branch out into feature stories. They had a lot of newspapers to fill up all over the country, and they would send a file of these stories to their member papers; the more circulation they got, the better I got paid. My brother Ollie helped me a lot during this whole period; he was like my legman. I had to keep some money coming; there wasn't actually enough spot news happening. I used to think up angles on these feature stories and occasionally embellish them a little bit as time went on.

One of the stories I wrote during that time was about a guy who became known as "the flying farmer." He'd built his own airplane out behind the barn. It was one of those one-seated biplanes, of the old category, with double wings. He'd constructed his own struts, built his own cockpit, almost everything from the ground up—or from the air down, whichever way he put it together. It was quite small, maybe fifteen to sixteen feet long. Anyway, he made the framework of the wings and covered them with this cloth, whatever kind of cloth they use or did use on those little biplanes, and painted it with a coat of shellac; I assume it was shellac, or maybe varnish. He built it in the corral out in the back of the barn and set it in the sun to dry. A couple hours later, when he went to check it to see how the drying process was going, he found one of his cows licking the shellac off, and that infuriated him. In a burst of rage he grabbed a nearby rock and hit the cow in the head, hit it so hard he killed it. So in order for this not to be a total loss, he quickly butchered the cow, cut it up into pieces of meat, piled the meat into the back end of his car, and raced around the neighborhood selling it to other farmers for so much a pound. In the process, he almost broke even. The cow had cost him $32, and the meat he sold brought in $31.75, so he was out only a quarter.

Then he went ahead and dragged the plane out of the corral so the other cows couldn't get to it. I called it a one-seater, but he did have room in there for his dog, pressed up close beside him. He had a collie dog that he called Lassie. This was before TV was invented, but maybe he got the name out of one of those Terhune books. Anyway, the big afternoon came when he was going to make his first test flight. He took off OK, but his motor was so small that the engine didn't have enough power to gain any kind of respectable, satisfactory altitude; he only got up about thirty feet, fifty feet at the most, and he couldn't get it up any higher, hard as he might try, so he flew along at this altitude for twelve or fifteen miles till he ran out of gas and landed in some pasture. He landed safely, but he had to call up his wife on the phone and tell her to bring the car and trailer to carry the plane back home again. It seemed like he was never able to solve this problem. He got a little higher-test gas, but even that didn't help. But he kept flying around, just barely clearing the telephone lines, and complaints came in that it was dangerous because he was flying so low. Some farmers claimed—farmers out in the fields—that he came so low that the air suction pulled their straw hats off their heads, and they lost them somewhere in the weeds. And one farmer said the plane had flown so low over his chicken house that it frightened the setting hens so that they left the eggs and refused to go back, so he lost that whole crop of chicks.

Then he got into trouble with the state highway department. They reached the decision that his plane was a menace, a danger; it might fall onto the highway and kill motorists. So they passed a regulation forbidding him to fly over any state highway. Now he had planned originally—and that's where he got the term "the flying farmer"—to use the plane to take his eggs and cream and other produce into town to sell them. But it so happened that the state highway—Highway 66—ran between his farm and both Weatherford and Clinton, so at this point he got really mad at me. My byline had been on the stories that had described his progress, so he rushed over to my place, gave me a terrible bawling-out, and threatened to sue me for ten thousand dollars. I don't know how he developed that figure and besides, it was purely academic—I didn't have ten cents. It bothered me some; I thought maybe I'd gone too far. I had held him up to ridicule, an offense on which he might be able to bring suit.

Shortly after that he got a telegram from a CBS radio show in New York City called *We the People.* They had a weekly network show a half an hour long, as I remember, in which they asked people who had done unusual things to tell their stories. So *We the People* invited him to New York to go on their show, and they would pay the expenses for transportation back and forth and his stay in New York—they were going to get him a hotel room for three days, and they would show him some of the sights. He jumped at the offer; he went to New York and had a great time there.

He was especially pleased by one incident. When he went up on top of the Empire State Building, he was wearing a black leather jacket such as aviators in the old movies liked to dress up in while they were in flight. I don't think he had one of those tight-fitting helmets, one of the Lindbergh-type helmets, but anyhow, just a couple of months before there had been the case of the cat they called Wrong Way Corrigan, a young aviator who had flown a small plane (I don't think it was as small as the one the flying farmer had) across the Atlantic from the United States to Ireland, as I remember;

I don't think he got to London. He had done this without clearance, and the government got on his back for having made an illegal journey, so he had replied that he got mixed up, he was mistaken, he thought he was flying west (he took off from Long Island or somewhere) across the United States, when actually he had been going east across the Atlantic. He never did explain how it was that he couldn't tell the difference between land and water (maybe the cloud cover was so thick he couldn't see what was below him), but anyhow, the thing was like a joke, and he got this title, Wrong Way Corrigan. So when my farmer friend was visiting New York, a lot of tourists up on top of the Empire State Building mistook him for Wrong Way Corrigan, and the flying farmer got to share in some of that glory. They crowded around him, and if they asked for his autograph, I don't know what he put on there. But he was proud of that.

Then came the night the show *We the People* went on the air. The show's writers prepared the script for him, and the contract he signed limited him to the reading of this script. The payoff was that they had prepared the script from clippings they had gathered of my stories. So there he was, telling a whole nationwide audience all the things I had written about him, so his law suit went out the window; how could he sue me if he himself was there personally attesting to what I had written, stating everything as facts? Anyhow, he never visited me any more. I never got any more threats. He did come back to Weatherford, and I understand that later, in World War II, he had a good-paying job in an airplane factory in Wichita, and that's the last I heard of him.

Most of the stories I wrote did have a basis somewhat in fact, and some did some good. I once wrote a story about the Weatherford fire department. They had only one fire truck, which they had had for thirty-odd years. The motor was shot, they could hardly get it underway, and whenever there was a fire like up towards the top of the hill past the high school, they would phone ahead and ask the principal to turn out all the boys so that when the truck got up there they could help—get behind it and push it to wherever the fire might be. The fire chief was a guy named Ralph May. The whole thing was a volunteer operation. I don't know whether May got any money or not, but the volunteer firemen didn't; they had to do it for the good of the city. He complained about it. One of the things he complained about the most was that the fire truck traveled so slowly—I don't know how much horsepower it had, maybe a half or a quarter of one horsepower—anyway, it moved so slowly that boys on bicycles would pass the fire truck racing to the fire. This offended him, so I wrote a story about it. It was distributed very widely, and he got four or five hundred letters and telegrams from sympathetic people all over the United States. To me, the most interesting telegram he got was from some small town in California; the guy wired our chief that they had had the same trouble, so the city fathers had solved the problem by passing an ordinance making it illegal for boys on bicycles to pass a fire truck on the way to a fire.

Another story I did that also had a factual basis, although not as clear-cut as the fire-department one, was about a farmer on a rural route near Weatherford who was celebrating his twenty-fifth wedding anniversary. He and his wife had gotten married as a result of a strange mix-up of letters. Twenty-five years earlier, when he was still single, he had composed two letters, one ordering a shotgun from Montgomery Ward in Chicago, the other a proposal of marriage to his girlfriend who lived not far away. He got the letters in the wrong envelopes, and so some clerk, order-filler, or whatever she was at Monkey Ward's, got the proposal. I never heard what happened to the woman who got the letter ordering the shotgun. But anyway, this young woman at Montgomery Ward answered him back and accepted the proposal of marriage. I was not too sure whether all this had really transpired; I'd seen similar stories (a lot of my stuff was based on stories that were quite common in the American press). So, not being sure, I wrote the story with the fellow's name spelled backwards. The man to whom this supposedly happened lived near Weatherford. He, too, got a lot of response, just as the fire chief had, but there was no address for him other than town and state. The letters piled up in the Weatherford post office. Again, there were four or five hundred of them, including one from Robert Ripley, who wanted to put this item into his "Believe It Or Not." Here the letters were, piling up, and the Weatherford postmaster, Jerry Crabtree, didn't know what to do with them. There was no such man listed in Weatherford or on any rural route branching out of Weatherford. Crabtree grabbed Ollie one day on the street and asked him what the hell was he going to do with all this mail. Where was this guy? How could the mail be delivered? So Ollie told him the man lived a considerable distance south of town, and it might be that he was on another rural route, one that did not originate in Weatherford. Ollie conjectured that it might be a route coming out of Eakley, and suggested that Crabtree package up all this mail and send it to the postmaster at Eakley, which Crabtree did. And again, that's the last we ever heard of that particular story.

I had the honor of bringing to Weatherford, along about the middle '30s, the first national convention that the town has ever had. This was the convention of an organization that I, as founder, gave the title of the Amalgamated Brotherhood of Chemical, Mechanical, Physical, Spiritual Gold Restorers of America, Inc. Its main, announced, single purpose of existence was this: considering the fact that America was in the depths of a depression and the economy was in such a desperate position, we should seek out and dig up the millions, even billions, of dollars in gold buried all over this country and restore it into circulation so that the depression could be overcome and the economy once more put upon a stable base.

The existence of this gold was a long-established legend of America. There are Gold's Little Acres everywhere, and there was a book written some years ago tracing all the locations throughout the West where gold was believed to be buried. Again, there had been literally hundreds of these stories; there were hundreds of maps circulating at that time, and they all had a more-or-less common description. Each legend followed almost step for step the legend of all the other gold burials or hidings. The basic story goes that a wagon train was returning east from the California gold rush and other gold locations, loaded down with gold that had been mined and was being brought back to the eastern states. There are whole books about this; all through Texas, New Mexico, Oklahoma, Colorado, wherever, there are points these wagon trains managed to reach before they were wiped out. In almost every instance, the wagon train was surrounded by Indians; the Indians attacked, overpowering the members of the wagon train, killing them off one by one. Finally there were just a few left, and they took the gold, buried it, and built a campfire over it so that the ashes would cover up the fact that the earth had been disturbed. Often there was a survivor, and he was badly wounded. His body was stuck full of arrows like a porcupine full of quills, so the Indians overlooked him; he was the only one they failed to finish off, and in his dying condition he managed to crawl, in some cases several hundred miles—astonishing as that may seem considering the shape he was in—to some point in civilization, an army fort or a settlement. Just before he died he told the story, and generally drew out a map in the sand showing where the wagon train was when it was attacked, and gave pointers as to how it could be located. If he was so close to death that he could no longer draw the map, in his dying breath he whispered the directions to somebody standing by, who then became possessor of the coveted knowledge and quickly drew up his own map.

Of course, there are other, similar legends. Some individual had some gold, and before he died he buried it out back of the barn, or down under some mulberry tree or along a hedgerow. There was an extensive search going on during the middle of the depression for gold, which was understandable: there were so many people who had nothing—who had no jobs, had lost their farms, had become drifters, and were in a psychological mood to consider seriously that there might be some truth to these gold burials or caches. Around Weatherford and other southwestern towns, farmers were surprised mornings to find huge holes dug on their farms during the night—six feet deep, freshly dug—and they'd wonder who in the hell did that and what was the reason for it. It was nighttime seekers looking for hidden gold. They usually had old ragged maps to go on that some con man had sold them.

I put out a newspaper story calling for a convention, the purpose of which was to help America recover from the depression. I wrote that the chamber of commerce was going to give a luncheon to the delegates, and that certain preparations were being made to assist in finding the exact location where a particular wagon train had buried its hoard, which I estimated to total at least five-million-dollars' worth of gold. In the depression days, when jobless men were desperate, there were opportunists who took advantage of them by selling them gold-finding contraptions. There was an outfit in Arkansas that advertised widely in order to sell these devices, such as the Spanish dip needle. This particular device had a flexible handle three feet long and a torpedo-shaped object at the point of it that contained certain chemicals. It was like a water witch. You walked along holding this thing out in front of you, and supposedly whenever you passed over gold, the point would dip, regardless of what you were doing: holding your hands perfectly still, adding nothing to the operation it was performing. The scientific theory behind the instrument was that all metals give off a minute quantity of gas as they decay, and this gas is emitted from the surface. The gold sniffer was a boxlike contraption full of chemicals that would react to the gas given off by gold. They were sorted out in such a way as to respond to gaseous gold, or goldish gas. The little box had batteries in it, and whenever the thing sniffed gold it would set up an electric current, which was transmitted to the batteries and set bells ringing like on the old-style telephones. What else did they have? They had a gold buzzer. I don't know exactly how it worked, but with this thing you had earphones, and whenever you passed over gold it would buzz in your ears; the buzz got louder the more directly over the gold you were. If you were walking and the buzzing diminished, you knew you were "getting colder," as we said in kid games, so you came back; in this way you could pick the exact spot.

The physical gold restorers in my organization were just to dig at random wherever they felt like digging, not depending on any of these several contrivances—forget science, just go on digging and digging until finally, like in those Western movies, they'd find the nuggets, the glory hole, or a vein. It so happened that we didn't have any successful members in the organization; in fact, I can't remember one. But very common and generally always occupied—there was a big demand for them—were the spiritual gold finders. They were the ones who were like mediums—knew how to contact the spirits who might be drifting around, circling around a certain area, and would try to get in direct contact with these spirits, who were apt to know where the gold was.

In fact, there was a famous—we considered him famous—medium in Oklahoma, who was in great demand. I don't know what his full name was; he was known as Woody. This was long before we heard of Woody Guthrie; Oklahoma was full of Woodies then. Anyhow, Woody was about forty or fifty, a very thin man—thin face, a beaky nose—and even in the hottest weather he wore a scraggly, matted fur coat that came clear down to his ankles,and he would never take it off. I think it had been worn by a spirit or something, or it was a symbol to spirits to trust him and give him their precious information. And he wore an old dirty hat perched on top of his head. He came from somewhere around Ponca City, and he had all his front teeth knocked out. He told us that some bank robbers had captured him and abducted him to Texas to try to find some loot that had been stolen by a rival outlaw gang, who had buried it somewhere. They forced Woody, practically at gunpoint, to try to find out where it was buried, to contact his spirit or the spirits who might be in that area. But he hadn't been able to locate a dime, so one of the bank robbers had knocked his front teeth out with the barrel of his gun and kicked him out, told him to get lost. But that hadn't hurt his reputation. After all, they were looking mainly for paper money; they weren't looking for gold. And Woody's specialty was gold.

I remember we took him out with some local gold addicts to the Washita River near Clinton and watched him in operation. He would go into a sort of trance, and he would cry out, "Ohhh, beloved spirits, Ohhhh, spirits who are such friends of mine. Where is the gold? Show me, show me, show me the gold." He'd prance around a while in a kind of circle, and then he'd suddenly take off running as fast as he could go, his derby hat flying off his head and his fur coat flapping behind him. He'd head in a direct line where the spirits supposedly had shown him the gold. And you had to run with him, because he was so overcome by the power of the spirits, their force was so strong, that they sent him headlong in a straight direction to where the gold was, and if anything got in the way—like a tree— he'd run smack-dab into it. So we had to run along with him, and if it looked like he was going to run into a tree, we'd sort of jerk him around it.

He located what he claimed was a very big gold deposit in the Washita River bottoms, and these dudes from Weatherford had brought their shovels and spades along. They dug there a long time and finally unearthed some old tin cans, and there was some speculation that maybe the stupid spirits had mistaken tin for gold.

Anyhow, Woody was going to come to our national convention in Weatherford. He'd been glommed onto by a rich widow in Ponca City. Her husband had been an oil millionaire, and she brought him in a chauffeur-driven Cadillac, the chauffeur in his uniform proudly up front, she and Woody in the back seat. They came to the convention. The publicity release announcing the convention had tied into it a number of variations on these legends: the wagon train loaded with gold that the Indians had overpowered I placed at the foot of a butte south of town called Ghost Mound. It originally got the name Ghost Mound because some lover's rejected girlfriend had jumped off of it and committed suicide, and her ghost was still supposed to be wandering around there. But I changed the ghost into one of the people who had been killed in the wagon-train disaster. The delegates were to be given an opportunity to contact this particular ghost, who would be in a position to show them where the gold was buried because he'd been there when it was buried.

Then we also had another Woody. This Woody was a skeleton—with the feet missing—supposedly one of Custer's troopers. Ollie and our cousin Menno Dirksen found the skeleton in the Washita River bottoms in a sand bank. The water had washed the feet away, but the remainder of the skeleton was there; we knew it was a soldier because with the skeleton were some old army buttons and a canteen, one of those old-time army canteens, round and flat. And I think there was a belt buckle. Anyhow, we finally decided it was one of General George Custer's troopers who had been killed in the battle of the Little Washita, where Custer had attacked Black Kettle and his Cheyennes. Black Kettle and the Cheyennes had set up a teepee camp there; they were on their way north to try to make peace, and Custer, to get some glory, attacked them. He was able to overrun the women and children and kill them, but he also lost twenty or thirty soldiers when the braves got their weapons and started fighting back. This battle had taken place about twenty miles upstream from where we found this skeleton. Cousin Menno took the skeleton home in a paper carton; the bones came apart. He took it home and stuck it under his bed, although his father, my mother's brother Jake, was a minister, and he was very uneasy about having that skeleton. He thought he should be given a Christian burial somewhere. I don't know if he ever was.

Anyhow, the delegates to this gold restorers' convention were also to be given the opportunity to talk with this skeleton. I can't remember what information it was that he would be able to transmit to them, maybe where there might be some gold up the Washita River. I appointed Menno president of the Amalgamated Brotherhood. This story was widely reprinted and put on the radio all over, and he began to get great quantities of mail from people announcing that they were coming and were glad to hear that this convention was going to be held. In the story he had been described as a mechanic, which was his occupation. He was about twenty years old. Anyhow, so much mail came that the postman came to be able to recognize it. For instance, one letter came addressed in a scrawled penciled hand just saying "A Mechanic, Weatherford, Okla," and the postman knew exactly who it should be delivered to.

Now my old friendly enemy, Jimmy Craddock, editor of the local paper, the *Weatherford News*, was unaware of all this; the only paper he read was his own. So when the day of the convention dawned, Menno, who had received boxes and boxes full of mail from a lot of desperate people all over—some came from as far away as Ohio, many from Arkansas, Texas, Colorado, and Kansas—Menno got cold feet and left town, vanished. So the president of the organization was missing the morning the delegates began to arrive. They assembled in the streets, and they had all this stuff with them—the Spanish dip needles and the gold buzzers, spades and shovels and gunnysacks to take the gold home in. So they were more or less left milling around in the streets, and Craddock couldn't figure out what the hell was happening. Where were all these guys coming from? The whole town was full of them. They were leaderless. They found their way up to Menno's house, his folks' house on the west edge of Weatherford. His mother was also taken by surprise. Who were all these people on the porch, pounding on the door? She showed good sense; she wouldn't let any of them in. Some of them threatened to break the door down so they could talk to the skeleton, Woody.

But then our good friend and loyal citizen, Charley Kendall, took over. He was attracted to this business of discovering gold, had gone into it, studied it. He took over, and he led them, a long caravan— some came in trucks, old jalopies, and of course the widow in the Cadillac—he led this whole caravan to Ghost Mound. It was in July; the temperature was 106 degrees, hotter than hell. They went to work up there. Ghost Mound was a fairly big butte. They went all over it with their sniffers and Spanish dip needles, and around about two o'clock they were getting hungry for the lunch the chamber of commerce was supposedly going to prepare for them. Of course, there was no lunch.

As I remember, a big quarrel broke out over who was to get the services of Woody, the medium. They accused the rich woman from Ponca City of trying to keep him all to herself. They pointed out that here she was in a Cadillac, they knew she was rich, she didn't need the gold. Why didn't she release Woody from his contract to her and let Woody help them? Here they were hungry and in a rage, broken shoes—they really needed the gold. But she wouldn't give him up. Of course, there were other mediums, none of high-echelon quality like Woody; but there were other mediums in this gathering, they just couldn't find anything of consequence. Then a sharp quarrel broke out that almost led to violence. The faction whose faith was in the sniffers had located the gold at one spot, but Woody denounced them as fools, claiming that he had located it at another place. So the argument raged as to who was right, where they should dig; as it turned out, nobody was very anxious to dig anyway. Ghost Mound was really a hard rock pile, and the temperature was 106, the sun was blazing down—this was two or three o'clock in the afternoon. They were hungrier by the minute. So at this point, somebody located a wild plum thicket, and a shout went up concerning this discovery, so the factions forgot their differences, all raced over there, and filled themselves up on wild plums, which had to take the place of this celebrated, nonexistent chamber-of-commerce banquet.

Meantime, all kinds of rumors were spreading around Weatherford, headed south in the direction of Ghost Mound. It so happened that an airplane flew over town, a casual plane just passing through, but the rumors spread widely that it was a government plane, that a great quantity of gold had been discovered and the United States government stepped in to confiscate it. It was illegal to have gold when they needed it badly in Washington. Anyhow, a lot of townspeople began rushing out there in cars with arguments going back and forth among the students and professors up at Southwestern, some believing the rumors, others scoffing at them. One of the biggest scoffers was a professor who all day had been sneering at the idea; it was a whole lot of stupidity, some phoney crap. But then when the rumor came that gold had actually been found, he was seen getting his car out of the garage; he put a shovel in the back, raced down to the filling station, and had the attendant fill it up, telling him, "They found gold, I'm gonna get my share of it, by god. I'm gonna get my share." He said, "I can't live on the wages they pay up at Southwestern."

Then the day grew into evening, and the whole thing petered out. People started going back where they came from. I still think Weatherford—Mr. Craddock and the chamber of commerce and the Kiwanis and the Rotary—didn't act properly and responsibly. They didn't acknowledge, appreciate, or handle in a dignified manner the only national convention that was ever held in Weatherford, Oklahoma; they didn't respect or honor these delegates who had come from so many parts of the United States to take part in this first—and as far as I know last—convention ever held by the Amalgamated Brotherhood of Chemical, Mechanical, Physical, Spiritual Gold Restorers of America, Inc. If they had really put their shoulders to the wheel and done something to further this movement, it might at least have helped to slow the depression, which continued to grow; and to shore up the economy, which continued to collapse.

If I remember the date, it was 1940, although it may have been a year or so earlier. Southwestern State Teachers' College went up in flames. There was quite a bit of mystery around it. The building burned was the administration building, what they called the Ad building; four stories, each with extremely high ceilings—twice as high as usual, making it a very tall building in our one-to-two-story town. It was the first building that had been built on the campus, dating from about 1905, when the state institution was first set up as a teachers' college; in those days it was called Southwestern Normal. It was built on a high hill just at the north edge of Weatherford; the hill sloped all the way down through town to the railroad tracks, which were on the south edge of town. The interior was all wood— the floors, stairways, panelled walls—the wood had been hauled in from elsewhere. There wasn't that kind of timber around Weatherford. The Ad building could be seen from miles around because of its location at the top of the hill. In fact, there was a rural school district about seven or eight miles southeast of town that called itself Normal View because they could see the Normal from there.

Throughout the years the building had been swept—the floors, the stairs going clear to the top—had been cleaned with a cleaning substance like wood shavings soaked in oil; the building was permeated with this substance, so it was a real fire trap. I remember in the '20s before a college gymnasium was built, they played basketball on the top floor. It was like an attic up there, but with room for a court and baskets and wooden bleachers, and before each game there was a formal warning that in case of fire, people should go under the northern bleachers to the door to the fire escape, which ran down the back of the building. So, the whole building was a tinderbox. The files and records were stored in the basement, where they had some kind of brick vault; I don't know if it stood up under the fire.

It was graduation day, and that evening they had had the graduation exercises. Weatherford at that time had a population of twenty-five hundred people—a permanent population—and the student body was one thousand or close to it, so there were about two hundred young people in the graduating class. The ceremonies were held in the science building, which was more or less a modern structure with an auditorium in it. Afterward the caps and gowns were stored in a closet in the Ad building, up on the third floor. I guess it was about two o'clock in the morning when the fire broke out. There had been some political struggles between various factions of the students—a radical faction demanding a new president, the other faction supporting the incumbent—and some politicians had been drawn into the controversy. The governor of Oklahoma, as I recall, was Leon "Red" Phillips, who had been at a function of some sort at Elk City, which was about thirty miles west of Weatherford, also on Highway 66. Just as he and his entourage passed Weatherford on their return to the state capital, Oklahoma City, the fire broke out. They could see the building was going up, and Phillips is supposed to have said, "I knew politics was hot in Weatherford, but I didn't know it was this hot!" He had a suspicion of arson.

The building went very quickly and made a tremendous blazing scene that could be observed for miles. The first theory was that some student had stuck a lit cigarette in his gown after the graduation ceremony and it had smoldered there and set fire to the other graduation clothing. The Weatherford fire department was absolutely helpless. They had one fire truck, which they drove up there, but the water pressure was so weak that it barely came out of the nozzle of the one fire hose; it was like one of those old comedies before the talkies came in, where a comedian turns the fire hose on the fire and a little dribble of water comes out, or he fires a bullet at somebody and the bullet just drops out of the end of the barrel onto the ground. So there was absolutely nothing they could do. The student body assembled on campus, or at least a goodly portion of it did, including, I imagine, most of the graduates, and as the thing went down in smoke and flame (mainly flame, there wasn't too much smoke, it burnt too fast), they sang the Alma Mater hymn, "Hail to Thee, Good Old Southwestern," and there were tears in their eyes; it was described as a heartbreaking scene, with the governor of the state himself in attendance.

Ollie and I had gone to bed—we lived in our folks' farmhouse two and one-half miles southwest of town—when the Associated Press woke us up by calling to ask us to cover the story; they said, "How come we have to call from Oklahoma City ninety miles away to tell you that your own college is burning up?" That was an indication of the kind of news hounds—really on the ball—we were. Ollie answered the phone and said, "Really?" They said, "Well, look out the window!" So we looked out the window and there was—oh God!—

this tremendous fire. So he got in his little Model-T Ford, and he drove in and filed a lot of stuff on the incident. I think we finally got a check for fifteen dollars for the night's work. And later on there was an investigation, and the county attorney on the case happened to be my old friend Milton Keene, who'd got himself elected. He told Ollie, "I think you and Gordon burnt that place down your-selves so you'd have a story to sell the Associated Press." He said it facetiously, and that's all it deserved. Keene's investigation led no-where, but because of the mystery that surrounded the fire, Ollie and I carried out our own investigation. We reached the conclusion that it definitely was arson; here's the picture as our observation and investigation built it up:

The fire didn't just start in the closet that held the graduation caps and gowns, it was started there deliberately. Someone had gone in there and set the fire and then run back down the stairs to the first floor. One fact that caused suspicion—in other people, too; it was brought to Keene's attention—was that the main-entrance doors on the first floor, which were always locked at night, were swinging open. This was noticed before the fire had been observed. These main doors were reached by an outdoor set of steps, the steps going up over the two smaller doors to the basement. (It was a semi-basement, being two-thirds above the ground.) The main-entrance doors were flapping open, so we decided that whoever set the fire came running down from the third floor, opened these doors, and was going to run down the steps to get away. But just as he was about to do so, a car came up the hill with its lights shining on these doors. He didn't want to run out into the glare of those headlights, so he ran down the inside stairs leading to the basement, up a few steps and out the smaller doors into the little area right under the steps of the main entrance. Then he ran around the back of the building where he couldn't be seen, and ran northward. (The building faced south.)

We knew this was what happened because there was a plowed field right north of the Ad building, and across this plowed field we discovered the tracks where a man had been running. It had been fairly freshly plowed, the tracks were quite deep. We were real detec-tives—we weren't like Sherlock Holmes because we didn't have all that deduction going on, but we could see what was in front of our eyes. The man had been running, because the tracks were some dis-tance apart—at least five feet. And halfway through the plowed field

we found an empty pint-whisky flask. The cork was gone, but when
we smelled it, we could smell gasoline. In other words—this was all
supposition—he had emptied this flask of gasoline onto the caps
and gowns and put a match to it and then made his escape. We could
track him all the way; he ran straight north all through this plowed
field, but then we came to grass, like a pasture, and we couldn't tell
which way he turned from there, whether he turned east or west, so
we lost the trail at that point. But we've always been convinced that
it was a case of arson and that the perpetrator, whoever he was, had
some very real, deep-down reason for burning down the old Southwestern Normal.

So much for the great detectives who, in our minds, at least, not
even having available the great powers of deduction of Sherlock
Holmes or the investigative resources at the command of our county
attorney, resolved what must have been one of the first times a college was put to the torch prior to the student turbulence of the '60s.
I can't remember offhand any other cases we solved. "Hail to thee,
our Alma Mater, May our hearts be true to the old white and blue."

When I went to Oklahoma City in the spring of 1941 to become
chairman of the Oklahoma Committee to Defend Political Prisoners, defending four Communists, I was paid fifteen dollars a week,
which was to cover all expenses—food and lodging and so forth—
and I rented a room in the Travelers' Hotel. It wasn't really the lowest kind of hotel—it was somewhere in the middle. Office expenses
for the committee were paid separately. In the Travelers' Hotel I had
a small room for three dollars a week; that was long before inflation
closed in upon us all. Many nights we had interminable strategy
meetings; I would arrive back at the hotel at two o'clock in the
morning. There was a night porter, a black man named George. At
that time black men—and also black women—had no last names.
George was around middle age. He had to sit back in the lobby in
one of those stiff wire chairs like you used to see in barber shops.
The chair was placed back by the water cooler, and George was told
to stay there while he wasn't cleaning spittoons or sweeping up.

I would straggle in at 2 A.M. and flop down and talk to George; I
got to know him pretty well. In his youth he'd been a worker on the
railroads in the South—he came from the South. I had developed an
interest in folk music, and I would encourage him to talk about
songs and to sing some of them. He sang in a fairly average, cracked
voice, mainly the railroad work songs. He had the folk philosophy

of the railroad workers, which is that you can't build a railroad unless you sing to it. You couldn't line a rail properly unless you sang, twelve men on one rail, in rhythm, "Line 'em—line 'em." It was a kind of chant they did and it was the only way they could put rails together straight.

Many nights we just sat there and talked, and I got him to tell me other things about his life. He had been in World War I, a member of a black battalion or regiment or whatever they were called, and they weren't allowed to go to the front; they were held back in reserve to do menial clean-up, such as clearing the bodies off of the battlefield after the battle had ended. They were not allowed to have rifles because a black man was not supposed to shoot a white man, even when the white man was, as in this instance, the enemy. After the war ended in November of 1918, he and his contingent had been kept over there for another six months to go into the Argonne forest and find the bodies of the dead, the American dead who were still rotting under the leaves there. He told me how they would go out in trucks, he and five or six other blacks, and find the bodies. First they'd pile them up. By this time they were pretty well rotted, not much more than skeletons, and he explained to me the scientific technique of picking up a skeleton. He said back of the knee there's a big muscle connected to the thigh and the middle of the calf. They'd stick a pickaxe under this muscle, and that way they could lift up the whole skeleton. That muscle was the last to go.

George worked all morning each day in the Argonne forest collecting the skeletons of soldiers, the white American soldiers who had been given a privilege that he had been denied—the privilege to go out there and get themselves killed by the Germans. They would pile up a mass of these skeletons—twenty, thirty, forty—then they would wait for the truck to come and pick them up. And while they were waiting they'd eat their lunch; they would sit beside the rotting skeletons eating their sandwiches, laughing among themselves because those skeletons were all white men.

After I had known George a couple of weeks, he told me about this: when people were coming in and out of the hotel lobby, he'd have to sit on that stiff-backed metal chair back by the water cooler, stay in his place, as it were. But after the lobby got empty and there were a dozen easy chairs scattered around, he said he would go and sit for a few seconds in each chair, so that the next day he could laugh at the white people who came along later and sat in these same chairs. He laughed at what their reaction would have been had they known they were sitting in the same chair that a "nigger" had sat in.

There was an Indian living at the Travelers' Hotel, and he and I became close friends. He was a wheeler-dealer trying to make a little money here and a little money there; in fact, he seemed to be doing pretty good—he said he had a son in the Oklahoma Military Academy, which I believe was located in Claremore. He was a kind of double agent; he operated as a spy at the state capital for both the Democrats and the Republicans. He found out the secrets of the Democrats and put his information in a drop the Republicans had for such purposes. Then he'd sit in on a confidential meeting of Republicans and drop whatever he found out into the Democrats' box. He got paid by both. But there wasn't enough bread coming in on that bit, so he had another racket certifying people as osteopathic doctors. His certificates were handsome-looking things, all in green ink and italics and with a fancy border. My friend used to come up to the office of the political prisoners' committee and bring me some material, which I would cut onto a stencil and run off on our mimeograph—a leaflet that he would then send out by mail to everybody whose addresses could be gotten. I didn't charge him anything for running these off; I thought the whole thing was damned funny, and I used to laugh my head off. Besides blanks for filling in name, address, and age, he had a few medical questions, such as what the person's pulse rate was. I don't think he asked for blood pressure, but anyone could take his own pulse if he had a watch or a clock with a second hand. Anyway, these questionnaires were to be returned with five dollars, and the person was sent his certificate, or medical license, showing that he was now a doctor; the word *osteopathic* was stuck in somewhere in small letters.

But this wasn't the end. The real money was not in these five-dollar fees. Now that he had made you into a certified doctor, he would follow that up with an offer for a diagnosing machine, for which he charged something around $350. I don't know how much profit he made on each of these sales, but it was considerable. The machine consisted of a chair with phoney electrodes or something that were strapped to the patients' arms. The thing had a huge face with a dial on it, and when switched on, the dial would turn until the needle got to the proper diagnosis—diabetes, heart trouble, prostate disability, declining sexual powers; I think it had about fifty different diseases. If a woman was put in there, the dial might indicate a fallen womb. I don't recall whether it diagnosed pregnancy. It had every imaginable disease on there. It was said to mainly stop at kidney trouble—everybody in Oklahoma was drinking 3.2 percent beer or home brew, and many of them actually had kidney trouble, so perhaps the machine was rigged to stop there; I don't know. I do know Oklahoma was full of these so-called doctors, and you couldn't really call them quacks because many of them seriously believed in this whole operation.

So the Indian was just a case of a man trying to get along in the modern world. I don't think he was any worse than the brokers who are now operating the Wall Street stock exchange; they're probably carrying on just as much of a racket as the Indian was—and on a bigger scale. I've forgotten his name. On his leaflets he called himself Chief something-or-other. And there was a folk belief that Indian chiefs had certain powers. The medicine shows going through the country selling snake oil on Saturday nights in the small towns spieled that the snake oil was produced by Indian chiefs.

Oklahoma at that time was also full of "Jesuses." Every Saturday night in the little towns, Jesuses would appear. They had beards (this was long before the hippies) and long white robes, and they stood barefoot on the street corners holding up the crosses on which they had been crucified—and collecting money. It must have been very bewildering for the primitive believers in religion to see so many Jesuses everywhere. But it was just another of the rackets, the con games—phoney certificates, carnival concessions, snake oil, Jesuses—all part of the same thing.

Chapter 6

Sis in the 1930s

Back in cottonland, livin' in a tent
Car broke down, and money spent
Preacher says pray for your lives
Union man says "Organize"
Well the very first meetin' we did call
Them bullets came through the church house wall
Planters don't 'llow no Union here
Machine gun's speakin' it mighty clear.

("Sundown," words and music by Sis Cunningham, 1937, ©1975)

It was in the late '20s or early '30s and the scene was somewhere in cotton country. At settling time, a black sharecropper took six bales of cotton to the plantation manager who, after doing some figuring in his black notebook—or pretending to do so—told the cropper that the cotton brought in exactly balanced what was owed for "furnish," interest, and so on, plus the half that went to the owner of the land. Great day, thought the cropper. It had never happened before: he would come out a little ahead this year. When he reported happily to the manager that he had still another bale of cotton to bring in, he got this reply: "Well, damn you, why didn't you tell me in the first place! Now I'll have to do this figurin' all over again so's to git it to come out even."

I first heard that story told by a black sharecropper on the floor of the Southern Tenant Farmers' Union convention in 1937. I was a delegate at this convention, which was held in Muskogee, Oklahoma, in midwinter. It was a four-day affair, and those sessions were held in a hall with cracks in the walls you could throw a boot through. The weather was freezing, and I remember wearing boots and pants, though women didn't usually dress like that in public back then. Those in attendance agreed this was the biggest convention they'd had, in spite of weather drawbacks and late arrivals. And for certain they'd never had one as big afterward.

My feelings on the second day, after the rank-and-file delegates had arrived exhausted and half-frozen, was that these folks were in desperate need and deadly serious, or they wouldn't have nearly killed themselves getting to this meeting. Their faces were twisted into attitudes of suffering and revolt; their bodies were set in positions of strain. The leaders were in good shape—warmly clothed, comfortably housed in Muskogee's Huber Hotel. And they looked like they'd had enough to eat. As I sat there in that cavern of a hall and looked around, I wondered if ever a meeting like this could be held in which everyone present was on an equal footing as far as their personal well-being was concerned. Not yet, not yet.

Those who came were black, white, Mexican American, Indian, and mixtures. There were preachers and atheists, Communists and Socialists, and folks who said they were just plain Democrats or just plain people. They represented a total membership of around thirty-five thousand—small considering the land area covered by the Cotton Belt at that time, but sizable when you observed the almost insufferable conditions under which these folks lived and worked, and understood how hard and even dangerous it was for them to communicate with each other in their localities; sizable when you considered the fact that they maintained their activity in spite of substantial odds against them. Uppermost in their minds were basic problems of getting back on the land they'd been driven off of, how to feed their kids and get a roof over their heads and a floor under their feet. And certainly not least, how to dodge bullets from the machine guns of night riders hired by the big planters.

Survival was the immediate issue the rank and file had come to talk about. Ownership of land—to own and clear "forty acres and a mule"—that was somewhere off in the future, pushed aside for the time being by necessity. As a means of survival, the cooperative farm was a favorite dream of many, and we listened to a report on one such project called the Delta Cooperative founded by Sherwood Eddy in northern Mississippi. It was small, only two thousand acres, with twenty-nine families living and working there. But the important thing was that these families were black and white, and they had managed to raise a bountiful crop of cotton and enough fruits and vegetables to last them the year. I have forgotten some of the reports I heard at this convention, but this one I remember.

Each session opened with singing, usually led by A. B. Brookins or John Handcox or a choir from a local church. We sang one or several of the most loved songs: "Before I'll Be a Slave, I'll Be Buried In My Grave," "Hungry, Hungry Are We," "Roll the Union On," "Strange Things Happening in This Land," and, of course, "We Shall Not Be Moved" (though a lot of the folks already had been moved). After prayer and singing we had an opening address by a union leader or a visiting dignitary. One such dignitary was Walter White of the NAACP, who I was to meet on other occasions. We also had STFU bigwigs Howard Kester, J. R. Butler, Harry Leland ("H. L.") Mitchell, and Odis Sweeden. But this was the only time I was to meet Gardner Jackson and the two black leaders—Owen Whitfield, Missouri organizer, and E. B. McKinney, vice-president of the STFU.

Gardner Jackson was the man most of the other leaders took advice from—he was chief fund-raiser. He had been in Chester David's Agricultural Adjustment Administration in the very early Roosevelt years, but Davis had gotten him fired in February 1935 for carrying his liberalism too far. (Henry Wallace, head of the Agricultural Department, had been proposing the same reforms that Jackson had, so Wallace was put in the embarrassing spot of announcing the firing.) Whitfield was a minister of the gospel, a spell-binding speaker and crack organizer. He was his own man and didn't feel he needed advice from anyone, not even Jackson. The white preacher, Claude Williams, I knew quite well from the time I attended Commonwealth; he had been active in Arkansas for a number of years. The previous summer Williams and Willie Sue Blagden—a bouncy, talkative young Socialist whom I had also met at Commonwealth—had been stopped on their way to a meeting by a group of planters and hired thugs, dragged into the bushes, and beaten. The incident had triggered nationwide publicity for the STFU and provided a perfect opening for all sorts of racketeering outfits to jump in and raise money for the poor sharecropper. (The sharecropper, of course, never saw the first dime.)

The justice department under Homer Cummings was at the same time supposed to be conducting an investigation into the practice of peonage in the South. The supposed investigation had gotten no press coverage, while the Williams-Blagden beating had gotten plenty—especially Willie Sue's involvement—and had even drawn a message of indignation from President Roosevelt. Blacks were beaten routinely throughout the South; even if a black was beaten to death the news got around only by word of mouth. But welts on the behind of a white woman—this was a story. Newspapers big and little carried detailed accounts. It got into a nationally popular magazine, *The Literary Digest*. Some papers even went so far as to run a photo of Willie Sue's bruises, while the regular press gave no publicity at all to the case of Eliza Nolden, a black woman who was beaten to death by the same thugs who had delivered the blows to Willie Sue.

A lot of the things we heard at Muskogee had not been written up anywhere except in the STFU paper, *Sharecroppers' Voice*. We listened to firsthand accounts, not only of beatings, terrorization, and jailings, but of families, including old folks and babies, being evicted in freezing weather without so much as a tent to crawl under. Folks were there who had witnessed brutal murders; some told of their organizers and active people among their friends having disappeared without a trace. We wept at the story of Frank Weems as it was told and retold there under a big banner stretching high along one side of the hall: WHAT MEAN YOU THAT YOU CRUSH MY PEOPLE AND GRIND THE FACES OF THE POOR. Those who had traveled farthest to get to this meeting were the ones straight from the area where the planters' terrorizing practices were worst. Except for a few, the names of the victims have been forgotten, seldom spoken or written down. But if they had been able to make their assessment of the situation felt, if they could have prevailed over the so-called leaders, we'd probably have a different story to tell today. Owen Whitfield, a black man and very much in the background at the time of Muskogee, was to emerge later. The top three—Mitchell, Kester, and Butler—were white men. Telegrams of congratulations were received from William Green, Henry Wallace, Hugo Black (then senator from Alabama), Rexford Tugwell, John L. Lewis, Norman Thomas, and Senator Robert Wagner of New York, among others.

It was not specified in the rules and regulations of the STFU that a small farmer doing his own work could not be a member; neither was such membership encouraged. The leadership was mainly against it. I was for it, and I had a few rank-and-filers on my side. After all, the dirt farmer was a dirt farmer, and it made little difference whether he had to deal with some shitheel of a landlord living in the area or an absentee outfit such as a bank, a mortgage or insurance company, or any gang of land-speculating crooks, the biggest of which had headquarters on Wall Street. We seemed to have made our point; no rules were made denying membership to the farmer who worked his quarter section of land.

I was living with my parents at this time; they were still holding out on their quarter section. When I got back from the convention I sang for my father John Handcox's "Strange Things." He listened and as I finished the song he started in:

> There are strange things happenin' in this land
> There are strange things happenin' in this land
> Too much cotton in our sacks, so we have none on our backs
> There are strange things happenin' in this land.

Other punch lines were: "Oh the farmer cannot eat cause he's raised too much wheat," "Lots of groceries on the shelves but we have none for ourselves," and "Oh the rich man boasts and brags while the poor man goes in rags." We both threw in verses, each beginning and ending with "strange things happening," until we had about twelve new verses in all.

Also, while getting a little rest from the rigors of that cold four days in Muskogee, I began writing a ballad based on the story of one of the women rank-and-filers who had impressed me immensely. It was a story of the more specific strange things that were happening in cotton country. This song, entitled "Sundown," took me a long time to write; I kept going back to it and working on it between busy times. One verse of it goes:

> Hurry, hurry through the long long days
> And a fightin' the gnats from out-a my face
> The boss he says, when the crop's all in
> He don't owe us nothin' but we owes him
> When we pays him off at forty percent
> Our share a the cotton done came and went
> We's livin' in slavery, but thinkin' free
> Goin' to find us a better place to be.

The song tells a more-or-less typical story of a family trying to find a better place to be, getting into a similar or worse situations, and finally returning to the old location and putting up a fight. Our songs usually ended on a note of optimism. In the face of personal disaster, weak union leadership, and a government that didn't bother to assess the real depths of rural impoverishment and work out meaningful remedies, where else could we give vent to natural human optimism than in our songs? We tried to get as much as we could into our songs, but we couldn't get everything in—statistics, for example, a few cold facts and figures needed to round out the picture.

There was a new situation in the time of the Great Depression, especially through the southern and southwestern states, that greatly accentuated the horror of the countryside. This was that for the first time since emancipation land tenancy was on the decrease. And this decrease did not coincide with an increase in the number of farmers owning land; on the contrary, each year saw fewer owners and larger holdings, a trend that had begun to develop a number of decades before. The special tragedy of the '30s was the general downgrading of tenants and sharecroppers to the status of day laborers, despite governmental claims that the New Deal was alleviating agrarian distress.

Going back to the period immediately following the Civil War and moving up to the onset of the depression in the late '20s, land tenancy in the Cotton Belt had steadily grown to a point where 1.75 million families were involved; considering the fact that families tended to be large, that was a lot of people. Of this total number of families, about 40 percent were black. But when the general classification "land tenancy" is broken down into its three categories— cash renters, share tenants, and sharecroppers—the last category, worst-off in terms of poverty and oppression, was close to 80 percent black.

Cash renters were comparatively few in number; they paid the land owner a set sum in money or crop for the use of the land, and their yearly cash income varied from around $100 to $250 except in years of crop failure. Share tenants, the largest of the three groups, owned their own work animals, farm implements, and the like and turned over to the landowner one-third, sometimes one-fourth, of the crop. They usually broke even or, in a good year, cleared up to $150. Sharecroppers, comprising a third of the total, owned nothing but their labor power and turned over half of the crop; they almost always came out in the hole.

Cotton tenancy on any level meant a life of endless toil and humiliating defeat. But in the case of the sharecropper, he sold his muscle power and that of his family to the owner in exchange for the barest subsistence, a fraction above starvation level. He was better-off than the peon, or convict slave, in only one way, though to him an important one: he could keep his family working right along beside him in the cotton fields, if his wife stayed alive and could raise his kids up past the age of six.

Any improvements a sharecropping family made—fixing the roof, putting up a woodshed, mending fence—were all to the good of the boss; the tenant was never recompensed. If evicted a few days after he made the improvements—and this happened often—he was just out his effort and whatever money he'd spent. Also, and this was saddest of all, no produce could be raised for the use of the tenant family, just for the big house's table, and only if assigned to do so. Same with chickens, turkeys, hogs, and the like. Cotton was grown right up to within a few feet of the sharecropper's shack and outbuildings, if there were any.

The sharecropper was spoken of as being absolutely dependent on the landlord; in many cases even the year's food (called "furnish" and consisting of fatback and cornmeal) was supplied to his family, and the cost of this, plus exorbitant interest, was deducted from his half of the crop at season's end. Seldom, however, was the landlord's dependency on the cropper family spoken of as such. In reality it was from this labor that he extracted the greatest percentage of profit, other than peon labor, which was widely used on many plantations.

The migration of blacks to northern cities began in earnest as early as 1915, so by 1930 the number of white sharecropper families had increased and many whites had become tenant farmers, as figures previously given indicate. They were for the most part the small-owner farmers who lost out to the banks. Very few black families had managed to become owners even of a small patch of land. With no land to lose, they lost their status as sharecroppers.

The Cotton Belt—King Cotton's domain—extended through ten states, from the seacoast of Georgia and the Carolinas on west to cover a considerable part of Texas and Oklahoma, with the Missouri boot heel and a small area of delta land above it thrown in. More land in this vast area was devoted to cotton than to all other crops put together. And the cotton produced added a billion dollars a year to the world's economy—no small contribution. But the price paid in human degradation and broken lives has never been adequately assessed. And if there are no words with which to document this, then how to describe the period in which cotton tenancy collapsed, bringing an even darker pall of misery and hopelessness held over to this very day in our rotting cities teeming with refugees from the land? Not to mention the thousands of rootless migrant families—our country's harvest of shame. All over the country, the small family farm was becoming a thing of the past, devoured piecemeal by an insatiable, rapidly growing agribusiness.

If a positive move had been made back then in the '30s toward land ownership for all dirt farmers, either cooperative or individual or a mixture of both, millions would have stayed on the land and farmed as their folks had before them. They'd have stayed on the cotton farms of the South and wheat farms of the Great Plains, the rich corn and sugar-beet land of the Midwest, and would not have followed the millions already displaced into urban centers. In the '20s there were 6 million such farmers, a big portion of whom would have returned in the '30s if New Deal promises had been fulfilled and they'd been given a chance at land ownership, even on a minimal scale. The farm cooperative movement, which various New Deal agencies were created to promote, never even got a good start. The Resettlement Administration was the most notable of the agencies, but it misfired because government could not go up against the profit makers. In too many instances, government was the profit maker—senators and congressmen with their hands in the pie, and too many of the agency bigwigs themselves mixed up in the corruption.

Very early in New Deal days, Secretary of Agriculture Henry Wallace said, "It seems to me that it will be virtually impossible for America to develop a rural civilization which affords security, opportunity, and a fully abundant life for our rural people unless she acts to convert tenants of this sort [share tenants and croppers] into *owner farmers.*" But the opposite happened. Instead of Wallace's proposed conversion of tenants and croppers to owners, the '30s saw millions of mortgaged small farmers losing their ownership status, some becoming tenants but more leaving the land altogether.

Roosevelt left much of the decision making on matters of economic recovery to Harry Hopkins, Louie Howe, and others who formed a group known as the brain trust. The Department of Agriculture under Wallace set up a program in 1933 called the Agricultural Adjustment Administration, which went into effect in the Cotton Belt as a "plow-under" arrangement, since that year the cotton was already sprouting in the fields before a plan could be cooked up to satisfy the boys in Washington. The next year it was acreage reduction before a seed hit the ground. And so on thereafter. Growers had gotten thirty-five cents a pound for cotton in 1919; in 1932 they got five cents. Three years of cotton surplus had piled up. So it took some doing in the agricultural department to draw up a plan for 1933 that could head off a major disaster. The plan involved cotton contracts, which were agreements whereby planters would plow up one fourth of their crop and get paid parity, in this case the average amount of profit they'd gotten during the five years between 1909 and 1914, which had been designated the base period. The planters were then to share this parity money with their tenants and croppers. The whole idea was known as the economics of scarcity—less production would cause prices to go up.

It so happened that these cotton contracts were routinely violated. How else could it happen when the agents of enforcement, the AAA county committees, were themselves planters? The law made them the judges. Tenants and croppers judged no longer needed due to acreage reduction were simply evicted. Evictions should have totaled roughly one-fourth, since one-fourth of the land was left idle, but in fact the evictions amounted to more than that—much more. After all, a former cropper now living in a tent or a cowshed nearby could be hired as a day laborer any time he was needed. And there was yet another factor contributing to the downgrading of hundreds of thousands of families: the increasing use of machinery. A machine is cheaper than many bent backs and pairs of hands. There was a diabolic catch-22 here for tenants and sharecroppers: not only were they denied their share of parity money, but they had to stand helplessly by and see the landowner use these shares to buy additional new machinery with which to replace their labor. A landowner, simultaneously, had the double advantage of dispensing with his tenant and, with the aid of his new machinery, raise just as much or more cotton on three quarters of his land as he could before on all of it.

The Southern Tenant Farmers Union was organized first near the little town of Tyronza, Arkansas, in July of 1934. That was in Poinsett County in eastern Arkansas, some distance from my stomping ground. I got involved in Oklahoma about two years later, when the main tasks were to try to stop a wave of evictions and to help fight for the tenants' share of the subsidies for those on the verge of giving up and hitting Highway 66 for California—as Oklahoma's dirt farmers (mostly white) were beginning to do in great numbers.

In the period of its onset, the STFU carried out at least one notable unified action—a successful pickers' strike in the Mississippi delta area that upped the pay rate from around forty cents to seventy-five cents per hundred pounds. This was in 1935. The spring of '36 saw the bosses ready with a reign of terror, and when a choppers' strike was called to establish the rate of a dollar and a half for a ten-hour day, the aim was not achieved, but they did raise it to one dollar in most localities, a gain made at the cost of many lives and thousands of evictions—in the Arkansas region especially.

As a pressure group in Washington, STFU representatives seemed on the surface to be getting somewhere; they succeeded in holding some hearings. But in reality their activities led nowhere—the situation worsened. Their lobby focused on the Resettlement Administration to arrange long-term loans to tenants and croppers so they could buy a piece of the land they were working. The Bankhead-Jones home-ownership bill, then in committee, was quietly being emasculated, and when finally passed, the tenant farmer's situation had "progressed" one step forward and two steps backward. There would be loans, but he simply could not qualify for one; time had elapsed, in which the landowner had kicked him off the land and just maybe hired him back as a seasonal worker. He no longer even had a house—he and his family lived in a tent or abandoned chicken coop.

There were farm loans—yes, indeed. They were going to owners, and with these loans they bought up foreclosed family farms to add to their ever-growing domains. So the Resettlement Administration could better have been called the Unsettlement Administration. The country hadn't got rid of Hoover yet. And Roosevelt was coming up for re-election. Them that's got are the ones that get—that's the way it still had to be. The wording in the farm law as passed was in effect that loans would go to those who had demonstrated their ability to manage. Translation: the more land a man owned, the more he had demonstrated his ability to manage, so to *him* would go the loan.

The big boys in Washington were sending agents and researchers out into the field to scout around on big expense accounts. These agents made "acceptable" reports, which were passed around in

mimeographed form and released to the press. There was one notable exception, a woman, Mary Connor Myers, who patiently collected hundreds of affidavits of sharecroppers cheated of their part
of the parity money. She put these in her report, which might as
well have been filed in the nearest wastebasket—none of the material was ever released to the press. "Why, something like that could
upset the entire AAA program!" were the hollers that went up, and
further inquiries were stonewalled. The boys sat at their desks and
read good reports and formulated their ideas and read more reports
while the cries of the suffering grew weaker and weaker.

What happened was Washington began to rationalize. One AAA
bigshot made a report in which he said, to paraphrase, "we can take
pride in the fact that we've helped the farmer; the tenants and sharecroppers are only 'a little worse off.'" Statistics show that in the
early '30s tenants and croppers comprised three-fourths of those
who did the work of raising and harvesting the cotton. So, going
by this, one-quarter were helped, three-fourths were worse off!
This was what they took pride in. Words are wonderful things for
twisting.

FDR meant well in trying to do something to help the poor
farmer, but his failure was in not knowing the real situation himself;
he left too much to the brain trust. Actually, the AAA program as it
worked out was not his program at all. Everything in the original
program that might have helped was scrapped, and all procedures in
Washington were under careful scrutiny of landowner representatives. There's a familiar ring to that, even for those who weren't
around or cannot remember the '30s. It was feared that southern
Democrats would look elsewhere politically and the entire New
Deal would meet an early death. Eleanor Roosevelt was much less
cautious, and railed away openly at AAA bigwigs who talked one
way and acted another, but her efforts came to naught, and her opinions went the way of Mary Connor Myers's reports.

It was "Strange Things Happening In This Land" that became the
theme of our organizing drive in my home community. Here we all
worked together: the dirt farmer, tenants with no land to farm, the
elderly and the unemployed. We were battling for WPA (Works Progress Administration) jobs for everybody; even the farmer with a little
land needed to supplement what scanty income he could scratch
out after the big owners took their lion's share. A lot of old Socialists
joined up with the Veterans of Industry of America, and so we all

joined. This organization was misnamed—the "America" part—as I don't think it ever spread beyond the Oklahoma boundaries. The VIA was primarily for the aged and unemployed, and its leader, Ira Finley, was a blatant ignoramus. He was a kind of scaled-down Huey P. Long. But we rank-and-filers had a feeling that if we got big enough we could roll it over the demagogues, and so we built a huge chapter of the VIA and had everybody in there together—STFU folks, Farmers' Union folks, all ages and colors—meeting in the county courthouse once a week and packing the place with lots of music and singing between the speeches. Even the vestibule outside the courtroom was filled with people standing, listening, eagerly waiting to get a look inside. The kids worked on skits, and at the VIA convention that year our delegation provided the music, led the singing, and performed dramatic sketches on the tragedy of workers without jobs, farmers without land, old folks without pensions or anything to live on. In a positive vein we did skits urging people to go after WPA jobs.

I never received pay for any of this activity; it was something I felt had to be done. At the time I was making a kind of living playing the piano in a dance band made up of my brother Jim, my sister, myself, and a guitar-playing friend. My father joined us if there was to be square dancing; he was still the best of fiddlers, though his hands were beginning to get stiff from too much heavy work. He helped us to build our great wash-tub bass, which was our show-man's piece, and we all had a crack at plunking it. As for our music, we were flexible and often alternated old-time with modern country and tin-pan alley tunes.

My health was better than it had been for some time, and I found the extra energy to head up a relief committee of union and VIA members to get emergency help for the worst-off families. If we got nowhere with the local relief authorities, we'd go around to grocery stores for canned goods and to bakeries for stale bread, which we distributed ourselves. Needless to say, it was a makeshift kind of relief, and if I had it to do over, I believe I would take down my father's shotgun and go big-game hunting. Getting donations of food and clothing is one of the lower and less-dignified ways of surviv-ing—and I don't recommend it unless it is most clearly a means to an end, as if a great social change is just around the corner and you don't want to get so hungry and so cold that you miss it.

Sometimes I'm quite sure that the singing we did in those days was a part of our survival mechanism at work: the seemingly endless chanting of "We Shall Not Be Moved" when we knew damn well that if we didn't have to move today, it would be next week, or next month, or certainly by the end of the year. The answer to the question Why do hungry people sing? may lie in the premise that emptiness of the stomach, though fatal if endured up to a point, is not the most acute hunger suffered by human beings. That other hunger, the one reaching out for human togetherness, is satisfied when folks meet in a common cause. And they sing.

In the summer of 1937 I took a break from my attempts at organizing and worked as music director at the Southern Summer School for Women Workers near Asheville, North Carolina. Here in the foothills of the Great Smoky Mountains, beautiful in the way of the Ozarks, I was able to get a respite—not in any sense a period of calm, but at least a change. I met for the first time women from the textile mills. Most of them were physically exhausted from long hours at the loom, but mentally alert and eager to grab on to every moment of instruction in labor history and class-struggle theory the school could offer them. There were also union women from the hotbed of sharecropper struggles in Missouri and Arkansas, just as at Muskogee. But here I would get to be with them over a longer period of time. The floods of the St. Francis and other delta rivers had been worse that year than for decades, and Myrtle Lawrence, in her late forties but looking nearer seventy with her weather-worn, grief-lined face, sang for us the now well-known and oft-printed "Song of the Evicted Tenant" made up by her eleven-year-old niece, Icy Jewell.

Myrtle dipped snuff, and when we had evening sings on the wide porch of the long dining/rec hall, she would tilt her chair forward and spit way out over the railing before she'd start to sing. Her eyes were usually drawn almost shut, but at times like this she opened them, and you could see their deep blue color as she forgot herself in the spirit of song. She knew all the songs we sang at Muskogee and more. The Wobbly songs "Pie In the Sky" and "Casey Jones the Union Scab" were new to her, and she loved them. In the mimeographed songbook made up for the students to take home with them, I put my Dad's version of "Strange Things Happening," and that may very possibly be the way it got started on its long trek.

The school was the site of a regionwide labor conference to close off the seven-week term. Howard Kester was there, and he didn't seem to want to recognize me when he saw me, though we'd been on the resolutions committee together at Muskogee. I think both he and Mitchell felt that any new face at a convention of the STFU— and I had been a new face at Muskogee—was suspect if it looked like there was a brain behind the face. They seemed to have had me pegged as a red, though I certainly hadn't gone along with the "divide by tenure" policy of the Communists. (I've heard it said since that both of them "saw red" at any hint of criticism or disagreement from any source.)

There were no black students at this school, and again I came to the conclusion that important changes in our socio-economic setup were way off in the future if the people who called themselves progressive leaders and educators could not face the problem of racial segregation squarely, but kept skirting around it.

On the way back from the school a bunch of us detoured by way of Washington, D.C., and spent a day picketing with unemployed hunger marchers and visiting their muddy tent city, where they had been encamped for several days. I ran into some former Commonwealth students and they were singing "The March of the Hungry Men," to which I had written a tune while at the college. The car was headed toward New York, and I went along for the ride, staying in the city for a couple of months before going back to Oklahoma.

It was during this short visit that I became fully aware of the widespread ramifications of the Spanish Civil War, which was raging at the time. An old friend from Commonwealth days, head of the Federated Press in New York, gave me a chance to attend a showing of Joris Ivens's movie "Spanish Earth" and do a review of it for the news service. The experience jolted me into a clearer understanding of what was going on in Spain, that the fighting was the result of a fascist coup overthrowing a democratic government elected by the people, and the people had risen up in resistance. I hadn't really been clear before as to what was happening there. That was it for New York City; I was on my way home, where I hoped I could put what I'd learned to some use.

Steinbeck told the story in *Grapes of Wrath*, Carey McWilliams told it in *Ill Fares the Land*, but best of all, shortest, and most memorably, Woody Guthrie told it in many of his songs. The poor farm families of Oklahoma were going, going. Translated in terms of human misery, the statistics of this period are beyond the scope of imagination. Actually no one has yet written it the way it was. The people who survived tell of blank spells lasting over a period of time in which they don't recall what happened. Their minds couldn't quite deal with it. One set of statistics that sticks in my mind has to do with the deaths of babies. They were born and they died—18 percent among white migrants, over 30 percent among blacks. And it's commonly known how government figures underestimate things like this, give only a part of the picture. For example, this is infant mortality, babies of a year and under. It was a very rare exception to know a family that hadn't lost children well above the infant stage. Conversely, you ran across children who had lost both parents—teenagers struggling to take care of younger brothers and sisters were not uncommon sights in the shack towns.

The split in the STFU began to surface shortly after the union's annual executive board meeting in the fall of 1937. The battleground was set then for the factional turmoil that was to rage for nearly two years and finally to reduce the STFU to a few scraps of paper. The board members voted to join up with a newly formed CIO union under the leadership of Don Henderson—the United Cannery, Agricultural, Packing, and Allied Workers of America (UCAPAWA). Mitchell and Kester were wary, but they went along because they saw the merger as an expedient way to get tied in with the CIO. They were getting little or no help from the AFL—William Green sent telegrams to their conventions, that's about all. And they got turned down by John L. Lewis when they were feeling around for a direct CIO tie-in.

Within six months Mitchell was figuring ways to back out of the deal with UCAPAWA without causing STFU to disintegrate. Kester gradually pulled out of union work altogether to devote himself to pepping up religion so the young people of the South wouldn't all leave the church. Williams had no intention of pulling away from UCAPAWA; W. L. Blackstone, a white union official who had earlier been appointed to Roosevelt's special committee on tenancy, sided with Williams, and so did McKinney, vice-president; while Sweeden, a half-Cherokee Indian and top organizer in Oklahoma, managed to keep a good deal of the autonomy he'd always had. At the next board meeting, in September of 1938, Butler, Mitchell, and their followers on the executive board expelled Claude Williams for allegedly trying to capture STFU for the Communist Party; they expelled Blackstone for going along with Williams, and McKinney for "Garveyism."

Williams was then director of Commonwealth College, where "Communism was propounded openly." Everybody knew Don Henderson was a card-carrying Communist. This was too much communism, especially for Norman Thomas–brand socialists, and the gist of the story is that the split had happened. The STFU took back McKinney as a rank-and-file member, but though Claude Williams put up a strong fight, he was out, and so was Blackstone. Owen Whitfield, the most down-to-earth organizer the union had ever had, was working closely with Henderson and had very little to do with the Memphis office, despite still receiving one hundred dollars a month from STFU and replacing McKinney as vice-president—on record at least. Sweeden suddenly up and left Oklahoma, turning his locals over to other UCAP organizers, one of whom, Otis Nation, I was to meet later.

I was merely keeping an eye on these later developments, not participating in them. For some months I had been holding down a WPA job while trying to be active in the Workers' Alliance in Oklahoma City. I wanted very much to be able to stand up to the rigors of full-time organizing so that I could ask for pay, something more than the $7.50 a week I got for a while from the Workers' Alliance in Tulsa. I hated to have to find some other means of earning my bread. But I had to face it, I was not strong enough to do this kind of work. Still and all, looking back, the ninety-five pounds of me stood up to quite a lot of wear and tear.

My job was in the education and arts division of the WPA. It was part-time, after school on week days and six hours on Saturdays—music, arts, and crafts supervision of elementary pupils. The school to which I was assigned was in a working-class community complete with its own stores, post office, churches, etcetera—a suburb of sorts some distance southeast of Oklahoma City. To get there I rode the bus through the black ghetto that was along the eastern edge of the city.

On my first day I boarded a bus downtown, checking with the driver if it was the right one to get me to Locust Grove or whatever the name of the place was. He said as near as any bus would. It was about 2 P.M., and the bus was full of black people, some of them coming back from the farmer's co-op market on the west side, where they could get food cheaper than anywhere else; others of the riders were part-time cleaning women and laundresses on their way home

from a morning's work. On such busses there was a front seat facing
to the side where an occasional white rode, but if no white boarded,
a black was allowed to occupy the seat.

When I got on, an aged black woman was sitting in the white seat,
clutching a lapful of heavy-looking bundles. She started struggling
to get up, and I said, "No, please stay. You have the packages—I
have none." The white bus driver turned and glared at me, muttering
something about losing his job and that I'd better sit there in that
seat. But the old woman, pretending not to hear him and certainly
not giving a damn one way or the other about his job, smiled me a
thank you and remained sitting. As we rattled on east through the
black section of town, the bus gradually emptied, and I sat down in
a vacated seat back a ways. When the woman with the bundles got
off, the driver looked back at me and said, "Please, lady, don't you
know what you're doin' ain't allowed?" I replied that I would be getting off soon and he could rest assured I wasn't going to report him
to his supervisor or any of the authorities, that he needn't worry. I
thought for a minute that he was going to just sit there and not drive
on till I'd moved. But the bus lurched forward and he kept glancing
out from side to side as though afraid of being caught violating the
law. As a matter of fact, I guess it was me violating the law. Oklahoma, as you may know, got itself admitted to the Union in the year
1907 as a Jim Crow state.

Shortly I was the only passenger left—or so I thought. When I got
off at the last stop, I found myself in bewildering surroundings. I'd
been given instructions that to get to my school from the bus stop I
had to follow a footpath south through an abandoned oil field. But I
could see no path—just some old derricks with crosspieces missing,
rusty rigs, stagnant pools of oily water, mud everywhere, weeds and
brush. I just stood there while the decrepit bus made a half-circle
turn. I started to wave for it to stop. Niggerlover that I was in the
eyes of the driver, I thought he'd deliberately dropped me off in the
wrong place. But I hesitated too long—the bus rattled on in a west-
erly direction back toward the city. I considered the situation for a
few minutes and decided that I couldn't be too far off course. As I
started walking into the oil field, I heard a small voice behind me
say, "That's the wrong way, miss, the path is over that-a-way; it's the
only path they is that gits you anywhere." I turned and I guess I
stared. A black boy of about twelve stood there digging his bare toes
into the sandy shoulder of the road; I hadn't seen him get off the

bus. He must have seen my surprise. "I rides that bus all the way from the market and I seed what you done." He was offering something in the way of an explanation of his presence. "I thought I c'd mebbe hep you."

I mumbled some kind of thanks; I couldn't stop staring at this little fellow—I guess it was in disbelief. I pinched myself hard on the wrist and said it looked like I could use some help all right, as I could see no path. The boy came a few steps closer and pointed through some brush, saying I'd find a path there; then he gave me careful direction as to which fork to take to miss the muddiest places, and when I got to the other side of the "dirt pile," as he called it, there'd be a bois d'arc (bodark) hedge. I'd see the school down a hill, and the houses where white folks lived. "But do you live near here?" I asked.

"No'm, I lives back 'bout a mile and a half—I lives in Oklahoma City."

And I said, rather foolishly, "And you rode past your stop to come out here?"

"Yes'm. I heard you ast the bus man the place and I knowed you'd git lost. We plays yonder on the rigs when we ain't doin' cleanup at the market, and I knows this place. We plays as far as the dirt pile."

I thanked him again and told him I'd be okay now. Then I offered him a dime of the thirty cents I had, a nickel for the bus fare back and a nickel for a bottle of pop or something. He refused the money. "I didn't do no work, miss, and we always walks home from the dirt pile." Now I felt not only foolish but just a little cheap. What this boy had done was in the spirit of returning a favor; money didn't figure in such an exchange, not even to one so young.

I followed the path about ten yards and then looked back. I saw him standing there, a man in a little boy's body. I waved; he waved back and then disappeared. Though I kept looking for him on the bus right up to the time my job ended a few months later, I never saw him again.

It's a touchy undertaking to try to convey to others my emotional reaction to this experience. I was really indebted to this boy—and I hadn't even asked him his name. If he hadn't been there, I most likely would have waited an hour and caught the next bus back, in which case I would have asked to be transferred to a different job. As it was, the job turned out to be quite satisfactory, much more so than clerical jobs I'd had. I truly believe that this boy somehow changed the course of my life, and for the better. What I had done on the bus was nothing, and the incident would have been immediately and completely forgotten if what followed had not happened. But it *did* happen. And in the wake of the experience I must forever try to see through the eyes of a black child growing up in an overtly Jim Crow world.

Around this time I became a member of the National Association for the Advancement of Colored People. Our city had a thriving NAACP chapter, and I believe it was in 1938 that I went along with a small group of folks to meet two of the younger Scottsboro Boys at the train. They were to be guest speakers at a defense rally for those of the nine still in jail. Roscoe Dunjee got the welcoming committee together. Dunjee was a black journalist who had gained considerable notice as editor of the *Black Dispatch*, the most widely circulated newspaper for blacks in the Southwest—perhaps in the entire South, though I can't say for sure as to that. He was a brilliant man and a militant fighter who later became a strong supporter of the Committee to Defend Political Prisoners in Oklahoma during the witch-hunt period. His managing editor, a young black woman also militantly active, and Bob Wood, Communist Party state secretary, were the other welcomers besides myself. Wood was a white man, so the four of us made for the best possible balance racially—that was Dunjee's way, and if in the late '30s anyone was to make Jim Crow knuckle under in a completely segregated locale, he was the one to do it. I believe the two young men we were to meet at the train were Willie Roberson and Roy Wright, but I could be mistaken—one of them may have been Olen Montgomery. Four of the nine were out free, and the rally was to raise funds for the defense of the five still in jail.

The way those trains were set up—the Jim Crow trains—was in such a way that the black folks would get most of the coal dust, cinders, and smoke; the Jim Crow car was just back of the baggage car, then came the cars for whites. We got to the station. The train pulled in and stopped in such a way that a railing across the narrow platform divided the area of the Jim Crow car from the area of the two white cars. There was a little gate in the railing. As we approached the gate, a white guard came over and said, "Don't take that white lady through that gate; just go yourselves. The white lady shouldn't go through that gate." "You goin' to stop her?" Wood asked. He was a very dark-complexioned guy, his curly black hair clipped close; besides he had a heavy tan from being outside so much organizing farmers. I suppose the guard thought him to be light-skinned black. "Hurry up, go through, but don't take the lady." I was "the lady"; the managing editor of the *Black Dispatch* would have been referred to as "girl." We could see another guard keeping the white folks with their suitcases from alighting and motioning a group of white welcomers back toward the station door. Dunjee fingered the catch on the gate and swung it open. I felt heavy with the weight of eyeballs upon me. "Lady, don't go through!" barked the guard. Dunjee, one of the coolest characters you'd ever hope to meet, replied for me, "Well, if this lady wants to go through this gate, I guess she'll go; you can't very well keep her from it. You can't interfere with her civil rights; she has an absolute right to go through here if she's a mind to." His presenting the matter as a civil-rights thing—a white woman's civil rights being violated—seemed to baffle the guard. He became flustered; didn't say anything else, just stood there. We opened the gate and went through, and we were all right there to meet the two Scottsboro Boys as they stepped down.

The arrival of the young men had not been announced; the NAACP was taking precautions against trouble at the railroad station. Without secrecy as to who the guest speakers were to be and just when they would arrive, there might also have been a "welcoming" party of Ku Klux Klaners at the train. As it was, the only incident was the comparatively quiet one of a guard trying to keep me from going through a gate. Of course, it was a most interesting and memorable experience for me.

We went on and had the rally a few days later after the boys were settled in a hotel in the black section of the city. Nobody knew that the Scottsboro Boys were there until they were secure inside the black community, then Dunjee publicized in his paper that the rally would take place and who would be there. A lot of people came; the large hall was packed. There was no incident of violence, and I believe that was due to Dunjee's careful supervision of the entire affair. Walter White, national head of the NAACP, came to give the main address, and each of the young men made a short speech; funds were raised for the defense of Heywood Patterson, Charlie Weems, Andy Wright (older brother of Roy Wright), Ozie Powell, Eugene Williams, and Clarence Norris. (The story of this case is documented in Heywood Patterson's book *Scottsboro Boy.* Patterson escaped from Kilby prison in the late '40s and, though quite ill when he got out and shortly to die, he was able to write his book in which he describes the hellish tortures he endured for some seventeen years in southern jails and on prison farms. Norris's experience was much the same. The culmination of his story appeared in many newspapers in November 1976; after a fight of many years' duration, he won a full pardon from the state of Alabama.)

My personal experiences with Jim Crow in Oklahoma call to mind something that happened in the state about twelve years later, when I no longer lived there. The town of Norman, fifteen miles south of Oklahoma City and home of the state university, was a lilly-white town. Black domestic workers, porters, scrubwomen, and the like, rode the Interurban from Oklahoma City in the morning and back in the evening, not being allowed to spend the night within the city limits of Norman. In June of 1950 the first black student, being assured the help of the NAACP, battled his way to admission to the University of Oklahoma. The case was known as *McLaurin v Oklahoma State Regents for Higher Education*. McLaurin's "victory" was qualified by the stipulation that he sit in the classroom separated from the white students by an opaque screen and visible only to the instructor, and that he be assigned a separate chair and table in the library and in the cafeteria. This case demonstrates the "progress" made in our state against segregated education by 1950.

The last three years of the '30s were crazy with issues, all screaming for attention. In our state we had Jim Crow. You couldn't ignore the blight that kills when you knew it was killing not only black people but you as well. As an active member of the Workers' Alliance, you couldn't sidestep the uphill struggle of your group to see that everybody had work, or were on relief if they couldn't work. There was the plague of the rural areas, farm families thrown out on the road to starve to death, and the agricultural union split all to hell. Above all—right then—there was Spain. Money was needed, lots of it, to keep up the campaign to end our government's idiot neutrality policy and insure our aid to a people being slaughtered by Franco, Hitler, and Mussolini fascists. If democratic Spain lost her war, a chunk of our world would die—that made it our war.

There was only the thinnest of lines between these issues and problems; for the most part they overlapped. I wanted to be right in there helping to find recruits to go over to Spain and fight for the Loyalist cause. I was still working with children in a WPA program and mistakenly thought I could combine my bread-and-butter job with my political activity. I was training a group of kids in folk dancing when I got my idea of killing two birds with one stone. I sent notes home for parents to sign, giving permission for their kids to perform at a Spanish fiesta. I explained that the affair was to raise money to aid the courageous people of Spain. The fiesta was held in the garden of a well-to-do supporter of our cause, and a large group of people came. The kids were a hit; they were happy.

Result: I got fired from my job. Not because of the political motivation of the affair, but because "two Negroes" had been present. I told the supervisor who called me on the carpet that there had been actually *three* Negroes there, one being the hostess's maid who helped serve the food. The supervisor said, "Well, naturally I had no complaints about *that*."

I was tired, very tired. Luckily I got invited by friends to visit them in Arizona, and I lost no time taking them up on it. I reasoned that I could work for the cause no matter where I was. And I could also keep up with news of the sharecropper struggles. A continuing bleak world climate was causing all progressive-minded folks to take stock. It looked bad for democratic Spain—and earlier I had talked a friend into joining the Eugene V. Debs Brigade, a small group that later merged with the Abraham Lincoln Brigade. Then Munich happened, and I found myself becoming increasingly active in the League Against War and Fascism in Tucson while sponging off my friends so I would not have to take a job. Our group worked day and night planning and putting on rallies. Then suddenly we realized it was too late to press further for a U.S. lifting of the arms embargo to Loyalist Spain; her final denouement came in February of 1939, when the French sold out the Loyalists and drove evacuees back across the Pyrenees by the thousands after seizing their arms, which they turned over to Franco's forces. Several personal friends and acquaintances of mine were volunteers in Spain—all but one came back. In a manner of speaking, all of us, even if we never left the United States, had to come back from Spain.

I now began to look around for work. I really needed a job, but I found nothing available but domestic work, so I hung on with my friends as long as possible. The Arizona surroundings bowled me over. I had an overwhelming desire to get right out there and walk barefoot in the moonlight through the mesquite-dotted desert and bury my feet in the pale yellow sand—similar to what we used to do in the bin of threshed wheat back home. I wanted to lie back and peer up at the stars through the spiked arms of a giant Saguaro and inhale the airborn sage deep down where it can be tasted. We had to go out a ways to see the buttes, which were at their best by the light of evening or very early morning. But right from our back yard I could look off through the prancing heat-devils of midday at those low, sometimes choppy, sometimes rolling blue mountains, which at day's end turn orange-gold and all shades of red, deepening to purple, then to indigo, and finally to livid black under the light of the stars.

In the month of June I got a job on a dude ranch for boys. School was out and the over-privileged kids had gone home or to Europe. But there were the stable hands, a small construction crew putting up a building, a cook, cook's helper, a waitress, a chambermaid, and a few guests housed in individual cabins. I was partly in charge of two seven-year-old girls, one the child of the husband-and-wife team who owned the ranch/school, the other her guest—both spoiled brats. These children had a nurse/governess, but she was a professional and given to hauteur—slept late and didn't do a lick of work. The boss at the time was the wife, the man having gone east to round up rich kids for fall. M'lady, the girls, and the governess occupied a stone house with nine tremendous rooms. My day was like this, every day:

6 A.M.—Out of bed. Hurry to house and adjust outside awnings: down on east side, up on west. Run, don't walk, to dining pavilion, help set up for breakfast. Take fifteen minutes to grab a bite.

7:17—Get children up, dressed, and to breakfast. Back to house, clean their room. Hand-wash two sets of kids' playclothes plus two ruffly dresses, hang to dry in sun, dresses starched just right.

9:00—Mop stone floors in all nine rooms with cold water—buckets of it (the floors aren't dirty, it's for cooling). Clean M'lady's room.

10:15—Put M'lady's coffee to perc, time it ten minutes. Arrange coffee tray, sugar, and creamer; cup handle, spoon at proper angles.

10:30—Serve coffee to M'lady, sometimes joined by governess, in the den. Tray to be removed 10:45, meanwhile check on children and report to M'lady as tray is removed. Wash and put away coffee things.

11:00—To garden to pull or pick a few vegetables, take them to cook to prepare for children's lunch. (A meager garden, nothing in it for grown-ups.)

11:15—Adjust awnings all around house at half mast—twenty windows.

11:45—Take girls to dining room for lunch. Eat own lunch—twenty minutes. Help in kitchen while the workmen eat; set up trays to be taken to M'lady, governess, and guests.

1 P.M.—Oversee quiet hour for children, read or tell stories. Bed them down for naps, stay with them until they fall asleep, get a word or two from M'lady if late to your next chore, "Take it out of your siesta time."

1:30 (subject to some variation)—Take in and sprinkle down the clothes you washed that morning.

2:00 (subject to some variation)—Siesta time; go to your bunkhouse and drop onto cot in a state of semicoma.

2:45—Girls up, dressed in fresh clothes, and out to play. Awnings adjusted again: down on south and west sides, up three-quarters on east and north sides.

3:30—M'lady's tea, similar procedure as morning coffee.

4:00—Iron kids' clothes, playsuits, and especially dresses without a crease.

4:45—Get children in, instruct them to undress for bath while you examine bathroom for scorpions and remove same. Bathe and dress children for dinner, put them quietly (?) at play in their room. Clean bathroom, scour tub, basin, and toilet bowl. Governess will take children to their dinner. (As far as I could see, that's all she did, except put tape on their cuts and scrapes. Not being a professional, I wouldn't be trusted with that.)

6:00—Eat your own dinner—help allowed thirty minutes *if* they can get to next chore on time, which for you is exactly at

6:30—Get children into pj's, after which, thank god, M'lady takes them over while you hurry back to dining room for cleanup.

7:30—Final adjustment of awnings, all the way up all around; water the children's vegetable garden. Through about 8:15. You wanted so to watch the buttes change from vermillion to purple. But everything looks purplish by this time, so you drop onto your cot and into oblivion.

When I had earned enough money to do me for a few weeks, I took off for Tucson. On the trip I felt like I was coming out of a deep fever, or returning from some netherworld. I had to get back to what was for me the more real world, and I managed to do that only to plunge right into another kind of subreal circumstance—but more believable within the span of my experience.

I returned to Oklahoma City in the late summer of '39 and, resuming my membership in the Worker's Alliance, I began going to the community camp to conduct meetings. Called Elk Grove by the city dads (God knows why), it was the worst of the Hoovervilles I'd seen. It was situated on the banks of the river that ran along the southwest edge of the city and was estimated to have had three thousand people living—or existing—in it, but I can't vouch for that—I never counted them. Even the word *existing* isn't right, because one begins to think of how many folks, especially kids, found these foul camps a place not to exist in but to exit from. Death came calling every day, and there'd be a funeral, usually a double or triple one, in a hovel called the church house. Rent was extracted for the ground the folks built their hovels on, and there was only one water tap for the whole camp.

These were the dispossessed who had not had the wherewithall to take off for California; a small percent were returnees. What could anyone do to help? Most of these folks were too weak from starvation to work in the WPA; relief was two dollars per person per month; you could help them battle for that. Or you could find some five-gallon tin containers to flatten for patching roofs. Some were living in sections of sewer pipes; the depression had interfered with the laying of these pipes, so many were available for living purposes. Single men had plywood boxes, the kind that coffins come in. I met a man and his wife who had a home in a piano crate. More cheerful than a coffin crate? Hard to tell.

It was the discovery of families coming back from the Okie trek and finding no help, no understanding of their plight and nothing but hovels to call home that caused me to scribble down in a notebook (misplaced for a time) the verses to "How Can You Keep On Movin' Unless You Migrate Too," a song about the Okies who got as far as the border of California only to be told by border guards, "No more migration into this state. Turn around and keep moving." (This song has been commercially recorded twice that I know of without name of author. My name was lost, the song was not.)

As the year 1940 approached, more than ever within my experience up to then folks were evaluating, probing, and re-evaluating the signs of the times. Hitler's armies had taken Prague in the early spring of 1939, and in the fall invaded Poland. The USSR, which in 1937 and 1938 sent planes, armaments, and men to the aid of democratic Spain in an attempt to counterbalance Hitler's and Mussolini's aid to Franco, was at the same time trying to form a pact with Britain and France. Efforts in this direction had failed, and still failed after the defeat of the Loyalists. And so in late August of 1939, the Soviet government signed a nonaggression pact with Germany in a desperate effort to give its underdeveloped military time to gain strength. When this happened screams went up in this country from the very same elements who had prevented our government from aiding the Spanish Loyalist cause—that fitted. But what didn't fit were the screams going up also from some liberal and left-wing groups. We girded ourselves, knowing the worst was yet to come. But we took time out to read Steinbeck's *Grapes of Wrath* and to go see the movie when it was released in February of 1940. This was a subject close to home.

My new WPA job was in the cultural division as the others had been. This time we had the privilege of organizing our own classes in a location of our own choosing, and I chose to teach music to children of packinghouse workers. Other than teaching the children a few of the good-old Wobbly songs, I did not mix job and political activity this time. But I had to be involved in the movement, good party member that I was, so shortly after my classes were set up in the union hall of the packinghouse workers, a bunch of us enthusiasts got together to form a peoples' theater. We were among those who could not work openly as Communists because of our various jobs; there were about ten of us. We met a couple of times to talk, and then we got busy.

We tried out in Oklahoma City with skits for the Letter Carriers' Union, to which one of our group belonged; they were just getting organized, but they already had their own song, "When Our Union Gets So Strong There'll Be High Elation." I played it for them on the accordion, and we raised the roof with it. I can still feel their elation singing that line. But the main thing we wanted to do was to work up a repertoire suitable for tenant-farmer and sharecropper audiences and go out into the countryside where we felt the main need was. The project as we conceived it was quite like the peoples' theater I had participated in at Commonwealth, and though the makeup of this group was quite different, the spirit and dedication was the same. In our tryouts before city audiences, we knew we could work well together, and to overcome a feeling of temporariness we set about choosing a name. It didn't take us long; we talked it over one evening, recalling that Oklahoma was dubbed in some history books the "little red island of the West" (a lot of the soil was red, and the area had been bypassed by very early settlers because it was Indian territory, hence the term *island*). And there was the dust. We became the Red Dust Players.

We were going to follow the red-dusty roads and search out any remnants of tenant farm organization left in Oklahoma in the early fall of '39. The total membership in our state was estimated to have been only around thirty-five hundred souls, at most four thousand. Sweeden had left Oklahoma so suddenly that there was as yet no way of assessing the true situation. We did know that the most active of the union folks, those who had built locals of the Southern Tenant Farmers' Union, had long since been driven off the land. But we would find new leaders. Now, under the jurisdiction of the newer and more vigorous UCAPAWA, the union could be revived. Soon we had skits and songs ready—enough for a show—and Doria, our director, had us booked solidly every Saturday for months ahead, mostly in the cotton country south of Oklahoma City—southeast, southwest, and almost to the Texas border—and some midweek gigs to boot. Red Dust Players performances were free; not only were they free, but we took along as much supper as we could in boxes and baskets. While we usually ate along the road somewhere, we'd always have sandwiches and graham crackers left over, so that at least the kids could share in our comparative affluence. We knew people were hungry.

Doria, in her early twenties, was a housewife, and we had another housewife, Virginia, mother of two small children. We had one dirt farmer, Jelly, who lived with his wife, Mildred, and his parents on their truck farm near the city. Mildred was recently from an eastern city; the couple had met at Commonwealth College. As for the rest of us, we worked at various types of jobs; some were job hunting during the daytime hours.

Doria took care of rehearsals and theater paraphernalia, which amounted to a few costumes, a makeup kit, and sets painted on window shades. She both directed and took acting parts; she was busy all the time, and I don't think she ever got more than three hours sleep at night. She was always disappearing during the day, and we'd learn that she'd driven fifty or sixty miles off somewhere out in the sticks to see that our performance was being publicized.

"They knew about it! They all knew about it," she would exclaim with a lively, rippling chuckle, almost a laugh. She had been reassured. But before the next booking, off she'd go again. "Just checking," she'd say. We thought that to be UCAPAWA's job. But who was to do it? Only Otis Nation, who did help to get the bookings initially. I wanted very much to go on those trips with Doria, but I worked days. Not that I considered the publicizing necessary. There had never been anything like this for these back-country folks. An occasional medicine show came through; Toby shows and soot-faced minstrel troupes hit the larger towns, but people couldn't afford them or couldn't get to them. A family night at the movies was out of the question. The teenage daughter sometimes got to taste this much-coveted treat if pretty and able to attract a town boy with spending cash in his pocket.

Our first booking in the cotton country was southwest of Oklahoma City, about fifty miles into the outback—that vast area where the land is so flat that the horizon fits the earth like the rim of a gigantic inverted bowl. As we moved along, the rim was rarely broken, and then only by the blur of a blackjack thicket or the dry brush marking a creek bed. We traveled in two cars, Doria's and one belonging to Otis Nation. (But no organization was paying for our gas; *we* were.) The performance was to be in a schoolhouse, one of those little wooden rectangles where one teacher taught eight grades. This schoolhouse had been opened especially for us; school in cotton country was closed for picking. Since she lived in the neighborhood, the teacher was there to greet us with a word or two and, happily, a couple of Coleman lanterns. The troupe was all agog, not knowing exactly what was in store. Of them all, I was probably easiest in mind; I had worked among tenant farmers in '36 and '37, and I came from a poor farm family in the first place, as Jelly also had, but I was ten years older.

We tacked up our set, which in this case was a kitchen stove and cabinet painted on window shades. We had two short plays, the first entitled "Tillie," Dan Garrison's adaptation of an old melodrama, "Tillie the Toiler." "Tillie" was about how a farm family lost their farm to a mortgage company—and it was only with the help of the good old union that it could be gotten back. We had a good-sized audience; the little school was full. And in their quiet way, they seemed to accept us.

Our characters were drawn in archetypal form, as is done in the teatro of the California farm workers. The old work-weary farmer and wife; the beautiful young daughter, Tillie, representing the land; and the thoroughly hateable villain, Mortgage Company, with long curling mustaches, top hat, and black cape. Mortgage carries a cane that he brandishes as he slinks, and—you know it—Mortgage is after Tillie and keeps pounding on the farmhouse door with the fancy handle of his cane. (Since there was no set, Mortgage pounds on a board labeled DOOR held up by Bozo the Clown, always on hand to take care of such matters.) Again and again Mortgage slinks away, muttering between clenched teeth, "Bah, foiled again!" while Bozo, at the side, leads the audience in boos and hisses. Finally the door and Bozo are knocked aside, the hiding place of the much-coveted Tillie discovered, and she is chased around the stage by Mortgage, with Bozo behind pulling at the long black cape while the old farmer and wife wring their hands helplessly. Just as Mortgage grabs the screaming Tillie, handsome Union appears and rescues her from a fate worse than death. In the final scene, Mortgage is driven howling from the stage by Mom with her broom and Pop with the stove poker, and Union and Tillie stand centerstage holding hands. Then CURTAIN—a big sign held up by Bozo.

The cast put on a spirited performance. But Dan, our Bozo, all five-foot-five of him in his orange wig and a clown outfit that made him appear as wide as he was high, was the catalyst for communication between audience and players. He was the focal point. The tenant farmers and sharecroppers sitting cramped in school desks were worn out from their long busy-season day, and would most likely have remained unresponsive as they had during the opening speech if it had not been for Dan's Bozo characterization. He got them to respond. And by responding, some of them—the young at least— would remember what they saw and heard. After the play, Milton and I sang our solos, usually "Joe Hill" and "The Boll Weevil," and we ended with a lively sketch made up mostly of songs that we got some of the folks to sing with us: "Strange Things Happening In This Land"—the verses my father and I made up—"It's Me, Oh Lord, Standin' In the Need of Land," and "We Shall Not Be Moved."

The members of our troupe had varied backgrounds and occupations. Doria was from a well-to-do family of shopkeepers and was married to Paul, a young college instructor. Virginia's husband, Milton, was the letter carrier. Don, our villain, the gentlest guy imaginable, was an unemployed railroad telegrapher with a wife and two children to worry about. Jelly and Mildred were husband and wife who lived and worked for Jelly's folks on their small farm just outside Oklahoma City and in early fall kept us in watermelons up to our ears—literally, since on the road we ate the watermelons by digging our teeth into a slice.

Norman was a refugee from the circus—a real pro, and the only pro we had. He knew more about show business than all the rest of us put together; not that a know-how of showbiz was of any particular advantage to us. But in Norman's case it helped, since he easily memorized a whole play, could make quick changes of makeup and costume, and play two or three parts when one or several of us had to be absent from a performance. He was in his twenties, but give him three minutes and he could change into a sixty-year-old man— or woman—and then back again without a ripple. Sometimes I felt that it was Norman primarily who kept our performances from being a bit on the sloppy side, the rest of us being rank amateurs.

Dan Garrison came from a really wealthy family. He was a direct descendant of the great abolitionist leader William Lloyd Garrison. Educated at Annapolis and St. John's, he cut his social teeth in the best drawing rooms of Maryland. He began to be at odds with his family and what they stood for when they tried to make him into a Naval Officer and then to fit him into a managerial position in the oil business, with which they were connected. He did come to Oklahoma at their instigation—he was in his early twenties—but it took him one month to decide against a leather chair in a plush executive suite; he stayed in the oil business, but as a pipeline cat. He worked at this job for five years, keeping copious notes on his experiences and on the lives of the people he met, then writing all this up in the form of articles, short stories, novels, and plays. Unfortunately, very little he wrote was ever published in books and magazines. He was about thirty-two when I met him in the Red Dust Players, and he'd already worked at more different kinds of manual labor jobs than most folks do in a lifetime. Besides pipeline cat and roughneck in the oil fields, he had been a fruit picker, cotton picker, cotton chopper, had followed the wheat harvest from Texas to Canada, and had shipped out on a tramp freighter.

Dan had just landed a job on the WPA Writers' Project when I met him. But he'd be with us two or three evenings a week and on weekends. I don't know how he found the time and energy to do what he did; he was suffering from arteriosclerosis and took aspirins all the time, about five at one taking. Besides being Bozo, he was our script writer and adapter, and the dynamo of the group. Nobody got the blues around Dan—he'd snap you out of it quick with a funny story. He'd write skits on assignment, though I never thought he needed anyone to assign him anything.

One Saturday morning a few of us were at Doria's apartment, and Otis Nation of UCAPAWA called to ask Dan to put together a skit that would rally the sharecroppers around the question of medical care. No federal program had yet been set in motion, and as a short-cut to meet a most urgent need, the county relief setup was to be approached by the union with a follow-up demonstration if necessary. At the same time Congress had to be petitioned to implement the federal program already incorporated into the law of the land. Otis was briefing Dan on this over the phone; Dan was responding. "You say there's to be a meetin'—yeah, a countywide powwow— next Saturday and you need . . ." There was a pause and we could almost make out what Otis was saying. Dan picked up the conversation again with "*This* Saturday? You horse's ass, *this* is this Saturday! You want a skit—a new skit and a song tonight?" Poor Otis, he had too much to do; he'd forgotten what day it was. There was another quite lengthy pause and then Dan said, "Well, maybe I can. That is if you'll stop takin' up my time flappin' your mouth." Dan put the receiver on its hook, gulped a small handful of aspirins, turned to us and said, "Loop your tails, cats. We gonna have a new skit by tonight." He was always using expressions he'd picked up on the pipeline.

I was already looked upon as song maker of the bunch. "Sis, you get busy on a new tenant-farmer song, one about doing something to get a doctor, or a set of choppers, or some eyeglasses—get that all in." I had him give me a few more details.

"You mean something like no more store-bought teeth, nor more dizzy spells, no more spots before the eyes."

"That's it! You write a song like that—we need two songs."

"*Two* songs?" I said.

"Yeah. Dredge them up out of your past—pull them out of the air. And don't stand there useless as the tits on a boar hog. We'll need, let's see, we'll need about five songs."

"*Five* songs!"

"Yeah, at least five songs. And I'll knock together some dialogue.

That fart Otis said something about petitioning Congress, too. Hey, that would go in a song—that would make a song. Get in the broader political approach. Better than puttin' it in a long-winded speech. Get the folks singin' a demand to their congressmen." I took up my little accordion and started fooling around with tunes. He told me to go in the kitchen—he had to think. I went in the kitchen, but I came right back out, singing to the tune of "Little Brown Jug":

> Congressman, Mr. Congressman, sittin' up there in Washington
> If you don't listen to our song, you aint-a goin' to be in Congress long.
> No, no, no-o, no-sir-ee! In Washington you will not be
> If you don't listen to our song, you aint-a goin' to be in Congress long.

In almost no time I had a whole song put together, and in a couple of hours I had four more ready. Our skit took shape. We called Otis and told him we wouldn't be trying to cut his speech time on this occasion, because we'd be late getting to the meeting—we had to rehearse. I never memorized so fast in my life. Needless to say, there was a lot of ad-libbing on the part of those with lines to say that night. But you had to get the songs pretty much in your head before a performance. I had to do my memorizing while washing and ironing the week's working duds, since my meal-ticket job at this time was in an office, and I had to try to look fairly presentable.

When the weather was mild we had performances outdoors. Our stage on more than one of these occasions was the sagging front porch of a tenant farmer's shack or, if no porch, the side of the shack was our backdrop. We were going out into some of the same territory where I had tried to do some organizing in '36, but I could not find any of the people I had known before, nor any trace of them.

I remember one of these times quite vividly. Our lighting was provided by the headlights of the two cars we came in. The audience sat on the ground for the most part, with a bench or two dragged out of the shack for grandmas and any women pregnant or with a tiny baby to hold. A few sat on our car seats, which we put on the ground. There were black folks at these performances, but it was hard to get them to come up close. You could sure hear them singing though. For variation we now added a square dance at the end, for which I had made up a special "call." I was playing "Turkey In the Straw." Dan had changed from his clown outfit to work clothes and was calling the dance:

> First couple balance and swing
> Down the center and divide the ring
> Down the center and cast off six
> The tenant farmer's in an awful fix
> Swing at the head and the foot couple too
> Side four go right and left through
> Beans all gone, there ain't no more
> Down the center and cast off four.

There was a creaking sound, and the porch rocked a bit. But Dan went on:

> Home you are and everybody swing
> Allemande left and go round the ring
> Half the land is all dried out
> The rest is up the landhog's snout.

With another creak and a groan, the thin supports started to pull loose from the lean-to roof of the porch. A little girl in the audience dashed forward crying, "My kitties, my kitties!" We stopped the show and all stepped down off the porch while the little girl crawled under and hauled out a bent old enamel dishpan. Her kittens were in it, a litter not more than a few days old. The mother cat appeared, her big terrified eyes flashing in the headlights, grabbed a tiny gray bundle, and headed for the barn, followed by the child clutching the dishpan. We finished the finale out in the yard amongst the trampled weeds and the dust:

> Swing at the head and the foot couple too
> Side four go right and left through
> Cast off two and before we're through
> We're gonna cast off the landhog too
> Home you are and everybody swing
> Allemande left, go round the ring
> Billions of dollars the oil man's makin'
> While the tax is added to the price of bacon
> This sorta thing has got to stop
> Grab your partner and hippity-hop
> Grab your partner, promenade
> Everybody here is union made.

We stayed around, and our five menfolks helped the farmer fix his pitiful porch. We thought the folks might hold such a thing against us, but if they did they didn't show it. They asked us to be sure and come back—which we did, but we performed in the yard next time.

We were not always able to get a schoolhouse opened for our use, so we performed outdoors as long as the weather permitted. Then we discovered that a country church house was a good place to put on a show. Normally they had a kind of platform in one end, and when the box of a pulpit was moved to one side, we had a little makeshift stage. The church houses stood in treeless, weed-grown yards, forlorn little wooden frame buildings with a bit of a belfry, but usually no bell. The land surrounding them was flat or slightly rolling with a blackjack thicket visible somewhere off toward the upside-down-bowl horizon. On our way to a performance, after turning off the main highway, we'd find ourselves on a dusty, rutty, back-country road, and our drivers had to be on the lookout for "high center." The team and wagon was still used for Saturday town trips, and the roads were not yet adapted to the automobile; it was the custom to have a shovel along in case the car got stuck on the ridge between the wagon ruts.

Bumping along, we'd scare up a jackrabbit who'd go bounding off, his long ears and alert head appearing well above the cotton stalks with each jump, as though he needed to make sure he was going away from what was threatening him. Often a lazy bull snake, center section bulging with field mice, crossed the road in front of us, causing a slow-down from the slow-down the ruts were deviling us with. Garter snakes were a different matter. They were lightning-quick and slithered out of sight through the tall weeds before you could count their stripes. When we stopped along the road for any reason—a flat tire or to answer nature's demand in amongst the withering sunflower stalks—a cricket was often our unseen host, offering up its restful serenade. The sound of a cricket affected me in a certain way—it took my thought away from whatever was causing me to hurry. I wanted to stay there a while, walk over to the fence, and look out across the fields.

A short distance away a creek meandered through the cotton, a brown tangle of low bushes, cattails, and a few stunted trees marking its banks. Some pickers were out there still at work, catching the last bit of daylight. The evening hush was beginning to descend, and for a time the land seemed good, peaceful; I wanted to forget its ambivalence, its fickleness, its generosity to the powerful who owned it, its miserliness to those who slaved on it. And what about us—all our efforts to bring a message to those dispossessed of land? Was now the time? Were we telling the folks anything they didn't already know? Very little. But there were the kids, those in their teens and even younger, with ideas just forming in their heads. They would benefit—if they managed to survive.

The cricket was there still chirping away, but its magic was suddenly gone; they were calling me from the car. I could hear Dan, pitching his voice high so I would hear: "Those watermelons she ate last summer must have caught up with her." As I climbed in, he was getting his corncob pipe lit up before the car started. He snuffed out the match with his thumb and forefinger and, still looking at his pipe, said, "What took you so long? We were about to head back to Konawa to get them to send out flash-flood warnings along Muddy Boggy."

I didn't say anything about what I had been thinking. Dan Garrison didn't need to be lectured on such matters; he knew about them. There was a logic to his thinking that awed me sometimes—the economy of his thought processes! He didn't waste his mental energy on detours, as I frequently did; he'd cut straight through and get at the guts of the matter at hand. I believe he knew then that he didn't have long to live and had to make what time he had left count. The fourteen-year-olds, the twelve-year-olds, the nine-year-olds—it was in their minds that the future strained and fought to take shape. Even though many were denied the chance to become literate, they could be reached through the traveling theater. What we were doing was only a tiny beginning. Dan's dream was of hundreds of troupes like ours on the highways and byways, threading the land, putting live pictures in front of people's eyes—especially the eyes of the young. This, Dan believed, was the only real way to organize.

We got to the church house. There was no one there. We figured the farmers, just now struggling home from the cotton fields, would, of course, be late. The church was open; we went inside and got ready. Still no one. Around 8:30 the preacher came walking up with his wife and seven kids. Said they'd just come from picking. It was almost dark, and we had no lights inside. Doria and the preacher took one car, Otis and one of the preacher's boys took the other, and they drove around collecting up lanterns and families. The reverend apologized, "I didn't think you folks'd really come. Never had nothin' like this afore; hits kindy outa the way out cher."

We had an audience—more kids than grown-ups, but that was

fine with us. Doria told us later about the place where she'd picked up a family—a shotgun shack put together so shoddily that she wondered how it had stood long enough to get so weather-beaten; an Oklahoma straight wind should have blown it down long ago. The wife had been ironing their freshly washed clothes; this was what had delayed them. After our performance I struck up a conversation with a gaunt, toothless farmer who said he had participated in the Green Corn Rebellion. This was quite interesting, because there were members of our troupe who hadn't even heard of it. The very next day back in Oklahoma City, a dog-eared copy of my brother's book started circulating among them—that's how I lost my copy and didn't get hold of another for many years.

I always took the accordion along; even if assured that a piano was available, it was nearly always in the last stages of out-of-tuneness. This was not the case when we performed in the high school at Boley, an all-black town. (Boley, like Langston and several other nearby towns, was established by blacks who had been given their freedom in the Oklahoma Indian Nations at least ten years before the Civil War.) The piano in the school was fine, and I played the accordion only to accompany myself when doing my solo (my own song "Sundown" on this occasion). The audience was all black, mostly young people, and the students had organized a quartette that sang during intermission. It wasn't just intermission—it was the show that night, as far as *we* were concerned. Their singing made ours sound thin and pale. Several times at our back-country performances (as distinguished from those in the towns), we had audiences that were mostly black. In some localities the folks had not seen a movie or a show of any kind. We saw for ourselves that the blacks among the sharecroppers were the worst-off.

We gave quite a number of performances for the oil workers (Oil Field, Gas Well and Refinery Workers of America), a CIO union that was struggling to get a start against a tremendous upsurge of vigilante-type antiunionism. The union was throwing all the support it could muster behind a strike at the Mid-Continent Refinery of the Diamond-X Oil Company in West Tulsa, called on December 22, 1938. This strike was to last thirteen months and was finally lost; but like strikes in many industries during the early years of the CIO, it was a proving ground, a rehearsal for a most successful organizing drive throughout the oil industry.

In the UCAPAWA we had Otis Nation to do some of the spade

work, but in the case of the oil workers, Doria went herself to the towns and communities where there were locals needing the kind of morale building the Red Dust Players could help bring about. She would stay a day or so, feel out just what was needed, and make necessary arrangements. Here, too, we often worked by assignment—*self*-assignment. I recall writing a song during my Friday lunch hour at my place of work and singing it that night at a performance. The song was titled "The Oil Derrick Out By West Tulsa."

Dan would sit at his portable and type up a hailstorm, getting dialogue ready from that day's news stories—the D-X strike was making headlines in the local papers and in the *Daily Oklahoman*. What the Red Dust Players lacked in theatricality we made up for by being "hot off the press," and our audiences responded in a way that was rewarding, to put it mildly.

The strikers had a headquarters in an old, bare warehouse kind of place a half a block long. It also served as strike kitchen and mess hall, and we all ate together there with the strikers and their families, chipping in with whatever food we brought along. A couple of times we gave the show in a huge abandoned opera house in West Tulsa, which had more recently been a movie theater. On the first night we had to put up our set by the light of Coleman lanterns and flashlights. The seats were broken and the ceiling was gone, exposing rafters, and when you beamed a flashlight high up there it made you think of the gaunt ribs of some prehistoric monster, into the belly of which streamed a great tribe of primitive people to carry out rituals. But these men, women, and children were not primitive people, and our show was no ritual; the illusion was because of the ruins around us. It was shattered completely when, just at curtain time—not a minute sooner—electric lights flashed on. We had footlights! The workers themselves saw to that.

These performances were greeted by a standing-room crowd of over two thousand cheering, roaring strikers and their families and friends. My solo at all oil worker appearances was the "Derrick" song I had written, about the hanging of the injunction-serving, scab-herding judge. To the tune of "The Old Apple Tree," part of it goes:

> Say good-bye, say good-bye
> Say good-bye to the Judge and his gang

When the workers started chasin'
The Judge he started racin'
'Cause he knew if they caught him he would hang.

So the strikers climbed up on the crow's nest
And they captured that crafty old bird
Then they took a rope and strung him
By the neck and then they hung him
And now no more scabs does he herd.

There were a number of verses and different choruses to the song, and I had to wait a while between lines for the yelling and stomping and cheering to subside. Hatred for the judge had built up over a period of months since the strike had begun. At the end of the show, we got the loudest and longest ovation I have ever experienced. We felt good to see Dan so happy there among his loved oil workers. He was very ill. He died of his artery disease a year or two later, in his mid-thirties.

In performing for the sharecroppers, we faced a problem that continues today. Writing for the oil workers had been comparatively easy—you just took the day's headlines as the base for your material. But with the tenant farmers—facing not an immediate issue like a strike but an age-old oppression where the goal was not a foreseeable one like signing a contract—the task proved much harder. It is a problem, and I think a basic one, that challenges people's song writers of the present period. I don't know whether the approach decided on by the Red Dust Players was a correct one; it was more of a compromise. We sang of and acted out all of the things closest to sharecroppers' hearts, from their long-range hunger to own their land to their immediate needs—such as medical care, glasses, and false teeth.

The effectiveness of the Red Dust Players—especially our work with the oil union—was borne out by the reaction that came with suddenness and cut off our activities entirely. We came back from a strenuous weekend late one night in April or May of 1940 to find the homes of some of our members broken into, their letters and papers strewn about, household stuff in a shambles, and books missing. Actually this should not have taken us by surprise. A few months before, hell had broken loose in Oklahoma County, with raids on the homes and businesses of activists. Eight were arrested, jailed, and held incommunicado. Now the reign of terror was beginning to affect us, and a few of our members felt sure they were scheduled for arrest. They left Oklahoma never to return.

As for me, it was my long-time home; I did not want to leave, so I hid out for a while. That was a pretty hard time, and I kind of blacked it out. I don't recall much of anything that happened. My sister and I were holed up with a destitute farm family, and none of us had money to buy ammunition for the .22, so we couldn't bag any rabbits. We starved. For several days we all existed on a small quantity of milk from a bony old cow, a loaf of stale, homemade bread, and a single solitary egg, which we beat up into the milk and made fried bread. The setting for this hazy episode was stark; we were in the midst of eroded badlands. All around us was nothing but scrub oaks, jackrabbits, and the low, gypsum-streaked red hills.

After the Diamond-X strike was lost, I kept thinking about our experience. I couldn't forget it, especially the West Tulsa performances in the old opera house. No one had been calm or comfortable there in that powdery ruin; those whose aim it was to crush out the lives of the strikers were the comfortable ones, comfortably fixed in their fine mansions within the city limits of Tulsa.

I was living with my folks again. I borrowed their old car and drove east, through the area where the Red Dust Players had stopped many a time, until I reached Tulsa, where I drove through the fancy suburbs. I hated what I saw, hated the wealth that gleamed and glistened, immovably perched on the backs of oil workers and sharecropper families. When I hated like this, I thought of one of my favorite authors, Agnes Smedley, who wrote in *Daughter of Earth:* "I do not write mere words. I write of human flesh and blood. There is a hatred and a bitterness with roots in experience and conviction. Words cannot erase that experience." And, "That any living man or woman could demand less for another than he demanded for himself aroused not only my hatred, but my fear. When I faced such things, I saw that human beings are wolves. That frightened me and erased from my mind all hope of convincing people by argument that such things should not be. The enslaved must be strong enough to destroy such things—until then they must suffer and go to the ground." This aroused fear in her—it arouses fear in me. I never did believe that "we have nothing to fear but fear itself."

I went to West Tulsa to see if I could locate some of those wonderful people who held up under thirteen months of a bitterly fought strike. I wanted to find out what had become of them. Plenty of scabs had taken over jobs on a permanent basis (permanent, that is, until the union really got on its feet—which it did, but some time later). The strike leaders and any worker who played an active role were blacklisted for the time being.

I finally located the Beckers. Harley Becker had been a "Jimmie Higgins" during the strike, and like the character immortalized by Upton Sinclair in his book of that title, Harley Becker was always on hand to perform those myriad tedious jobs, unrewarded and unsung. He was the one who had gotten the little crew together to fix up lights for us in the old opera house. His wife Martha spent twelve hours a day in the strike kitchen, and she went from meal planning to potato peeling to dish washing in the flick of an eye. It took some doing to find them. They were out on a twenty-acre patch of rented ground, living in a propped-up box shack—they'd become tenant farmers. The soil there wasn't much good; any kind of crop had to be coaxed out of it.

"We're both pushin' fifty," Martha said. "What can we do?" She seemed very tired and looked years older than when I had last seen her—only months before.

"I'm goin' to get my old job back, that's what *I* can do. You'll see," Harley said. He got up from the bench he was sitting on, walked over to the sagging door frame, and stared out over the pitiful acres. He looked worn, but he was in better physical shape than Martha. He went on, "The oil workers is an up-and-comin' union and not on its way out like STFU, UCAPAWA, or whatever they call themselves. The oil workers is a newer union, but they know they're CIO—they got their feet on solid ground. I'm keepin' up my membership in the oil workers if I have to chop cotton all night to pay my dues."

I agreed with him that the Tenant Farmers' Union was shaky—the leadership squabbles had been a source of confusion to the membership. But I was not going to come out and say anything that would be critical of UCAPAWA.

"Harley came near to goin' back east to look for work," Martha said. "Then we talked of goin' to California. But we didn't do any of them things, we just come here."

Harley sat down again. "If I had me a case of 3.2 beer I could get ready for choppin'." Chopping season was coming up soon.

"You chop," Martha said. "I'm getting me a job as fry cook over at the Crossroads Diner." She rolled herself a Bugler cigarette and handed me the makings. "And I'll join UCAPAWA. They take women as full members, not just auxiliaries." She gave her cigarette a few vigorous puffs, reducing it to a butt, which she stuck through a crack in the floor. She took up the makings to roll another.

Harley was right about the Oil Workers' Union—it was here to stay. But unless Martha had in mind a packing or cannery job, it wouldn't do much good to join UCAPAWA. It was fading out of the picture as far as sharecroppers were concerned, and also those who had become field hands. This was not their time.

Had there been a time, which was missed because of opportunism, divisiveness, and downright clumsiness on the part of the top STFU leadership? There was one good leader, the black preacher Owen Whitfield, who had led his Missouri boot heel locals in one of the most astounding demonstrations the country had ever seen. That was in January of 1939, when two thousand evicted sharecroppers, mostly black, greeted the dawn of a bitter-cold day from the shoulders of Highway 61, their little encampments spaced so as to stretch for one hundred miles. They were also along fifty miles of Highway 60, which intersected 61. They had no tents except what they'd made themselves from pick-sacks and ragged quilts. A few truck beds with makeshift tarpaulins housed the old and the very young. Though the planters were out to get Whitfield—he needed all the help he could get—he could not stomach Butler, and he could not stomach Mitchell, so he sent them telegrams to stay away. The Socialist Party bigwigs, some of whom had been trying to corner the sharecropper cause as a juicy fundraising plum for various activities, were scared at the idea of having anything to do with the boot-heel show of strength. Whitfield was forced to go into hiding up north, and his wife and children were harassed out of their home on the La Forge Farm Security Administration cooperative farm. Captain Sheppard of the highway patrol told the feds on the scene that they wouldn't understand what might be necessary in the "handling of niggers." Landowners screamed "Sedition!" A St. Louis newspaper editorialized: "These people actually expect to get white houses with porches, dug wells, cars that run, a team of mules, gardens, chickens and hogs and cash money for clothes." God a'mighty, what were they going to want next?!

It snowed the second night. No tents. Still just pick-sacks and old quilts, mush and beans to eat, and not much of that. On the fourth day the state police came with trucks and piled the folks into them, hauling them to various locations back out of sight of the highways. The biggest contingent was taken to a small church, where many stayed in the yard, not being able to crowd inside where there was a potbellied stove. Most of the children were ill.

Meanwhile, Whitfield was behind the scenes working like mad. He raised money and bought a hundred acres of land close by, where he got his people settled down as best he could. A small percentage of them had drifted back to chicken coops on plantations when offered any menial work. But most took up permanent residence on the land Whitfield got for them; it came to be called Cropperville, and Zella Whitfield, after being kicked around from place to place, finally brought the children to live there.

The loophole in the AAA farm program was never closed; the committees were representatives of landlord interests. The Farm Security Administration, whose initial purpose had been to put into action a plan of home ownership for millions of tenant farmers and sharecroppers, never functioned in this direction. A measly half-million in grants went for tenant-farm projects, and hundreds of millions were showered on the landowners in the name of "cotton control" while a few white men calling themselves presidents and executive secretaries of a couple of unions indulged in leadership for leadership's sake. Neither the top men of the STFU nor UCAPAWA were able to subsume their leadership skills into what was without question the ultimate goal of rural unionization—land to those who work it. The rank and file had been right when at the beginning of the reign of terror they'd besieged the union's Memphis office for the go-ahead to take up arms in defense against the planters' night riders, who were firing machine guns into their shacks. Simultaneously, in the Powder River range war of 1892 in northeastern Wyoming, the homesteaders armed themselves against the hordes of gunmen hired by the cattle barons. The homesteaders won, driving the invaders out of Wyoming and holding the big ranchers in check with a minimal shedding of blood.

One cannot say with certainty that during the '30s there was a time ripe for achieving socialism in the United States. To come to such a conclusion would require thorough familiarity with the temper of the entire working class of that period. But it can be said that there was a time when the rural poor were ready to fight to the death to maintain their foothold on the land, and the fact that they were held back by their leaders was the prime tragedy of the decade.

At its height, the STFU had an active membership of thirty-five thousand. I saw blacks and whites working in closest unity. I saw the very men who set together the framework of this unique organization idiotically allow the efforts of all concerned, including their own, to go swirling away like so much flotsam on the floodwaters of the Mississippi.

If you take a trip through the delta lands of Arkansas, into those localities where union meetings were once so regularly held, and you hear voices and bursts of laughter by that deserted cabin over there in the sycamore trees, it will probably be the echoing voices and laughter of blacks telling the "dozens" and making references to the gross stupidity and ineptitude of the white leaders of the Southern Tenant Farmers' Union.

During my involvement in these various cause-related activities, my parents were barely surviving on the farm. Both were in their sixties, but I knew their age was not the main factor behind their continuing failure. My brother Jim—young, strong, hardworking— had been living at home for the last two years. But not even with his steady help were they able to keep up the mortgage payments out of the income from the wheat crop. There were payments on the principal plus a high interest. The grocery bill was not just the grocery bill—interest was added on. People like my parents were being systematically "robbed blind with a fountain pen." I had not removed myself from the home situation, and though I was away for long stretches of time, the very activities I was engaged in gave me an understanding of what Mama and Dad were facing and how matters were getting worse for them.

Nearly every penny from everything went to the bank. The folks denied themselves butter, cream, and eggs in order to have more to sell. Same with the pigs and chickens. The old sow's litter was sold as shoats down to the last runt, not one raised for home butchering as in the old days. Mama kept one incubator going during springtime and sold all her fryers. Dad had sold his younger horses and now had three, a team and a spare; the cows were all gone but two. This cutting-down had been necessary not because Mama and Dad worked less, but because debts were closing in on them more than ever before—and debts had always been pressing, unless my memory has failed me.

A qualitative change had taken place on the land in the '30s, an industrial revolution in agriculture extending over most of the U.S. Farming was no longer a way of life, it was a *business*; the time of the dirt farmer on his 160 acres was over, and the last vestige of the original Homestead Act of 1862 was erased. The land the homesteaders had meant to pass on to their children, the improvements they made with their own hands—none of this belonged to them; they must go elsewhere. My parents had to go elsewhere. Even if my brother and I both had decided to stay home and work hard and long, it wouldn't have mattered; it was no longer the work on a farm that saved it, it was capital. If years before I had decided to go on with my teaching in Watonga so that the farm operation would have steady money from the outside, that wouldn't have mattered either. It might have made things a little easier on the folks, but it couldn't have forestalled the inevitable. You needed capital enough for expansion, the acquiring of more land, up-to-the-minute modern farm machinery, and skilled business management. Profit-reaping had gained such momentum on the land that I was sure only the strongest unionization of dirt farmers could reverse the onslaught. (I know now that only socialism could have—and can—reverse it.)

In the spring of 1940, Dad's wheat not nearly ready to harvest, he decided to quit the farm. Jim had been home, and he came to the city to give me the news. Would I help him try to find a suitable acreage for them? I thought so, but I needed to know more. For example, did they have a buyer?

"Yes, the Matli family—you remember, those tractor farmers who've been buyin' up quarter sections all around us."

"Have they made Dad a deal?" I asked.

"They been talkin' to Dad. The equity sure won't be a hell of a lot. But Dad said he'd be satisfied with fifteen acres. Enough so that come spring he could plant a little corn and kaffir."

"What about Mama? Will that be what she wants?"

"She wants to raise chickens and sell eggs and fryers. She wants just enough room for that. Well, they want to keep a cow and a couple a pigs."

"And raise a garden," I said.

"No. They say that'll be your job. They count on both of us to live with them." Just as I figured.

We decided to go looking for a place right away. We could skip a couple of dance-band bookings—an activity both Jim and I were engaged in temporarily—and I could call in sick on my dinky job. We got the local papers and read the "Real Estate For Sale" sections. Nothing in the way of fifteen acres could be had that the folks could afford. We finally found two ten-acres plots with livable houses on them. We gave up on fifteen acres and drove home to give Mama and Dad the layouts and perhaps induce them to look at the parcels before any final decision was made. I dreaded facing the folks with less than good news, much as I wanted to see them.

I was not quite prepared for the emotional impact of coming home after such a degree of deterioration had taken place. As we approached along the road from the south, the garden patch was the first thing I noticed. It was completely weed-grown; how could anything edible grow there? Everything about the place had that old, tired look. Even the chickens seemed listless, not wanting to get out of the way of the car as we drove in the driveway, still washed-out from early spring rains. "Been meanin' to fill in those ruts," Jim said, and we bumped to a stop.

The steps to the back stoop were gone, replaced by cement blocks. The bottom pane of the kitchen window was half broken away, mended by a piece of gray cardboard. The little old house drooped. I pressed my eyelids tight to keep back tears.

Mama and Dad, of course, were glad to see me, but it was obvious they had lost their old resiliency. Mama's eyes had an unnatural brightness, and Dad's had a driven look to them. The worry of foreclosure had eaten away their energy, and they seemed to be going on sheer nervous tension. I started talking as fast as I could to try to hide my feelings. "Oh, Dad, we found two good places. And, Mama, you'll like the houses. We could never decide ourselves so we want you both to come tomorrow and look them over. They may be snapped up by somebody, so we have to act kind of fast." I felt like a fool. Worse than that, I felt like a traitor. After all, this occasion was more of a funeral than something to get bubbly about. But I fizzed on—I couldn't help it. I described the place I thought to be the more acceptable of the two, and Jim drew a layout of it, indicating where the improvements were. There was a pause as Dad and Mama put on their glasses and examined the sketch.

"Is this here one twenty acres?" That was Dad asking; so it was twenty acres he'd expected, not fifteen. It wasn't that we didn't mean to tell them right away about the size; that was the hard part, and you put something like that off as long as you could. Jim and I looked at each other, each hoping not to be the one breaking the news.

"Ten acres," Jim said.

"The other one ten acres?" a question more stated than asked. I think Dad was resigned by this time; Mama just looked at the sketch.

Next day we took Mama and Dad in the car to look at the acreages. They looked; their silence was loaded. I wanted to say perhaps we should spend some more time trying to locate a fifteen-acre plot; we hadn't looked east or south of the city. But they came suddenly to a decision. Mama said: "The one with the two houses on it, that's the one we want. That doctor is anxious to leave and go somewhere that he can get a better practice; he'll make us a good deal." The place was owned and occupied by a doctor and his wife; living on it also was an elderly couple who rented the second house, a one-room cabin. The main house had five rooms, and there was a long shed closed in at one end, a good place to keep chickens. There was no cellar; that we would have to build.

"Guess we can do with it," Dad said. So the deal was closed and we girded ourselves for the big job of moving. The Red Dust Players were in the process of disbanding. Since I had returned from my days in hiding, we had held a meeting or two and canceled a couple of scheduled performances. Our denouement almost coincided with my folks' quitting the farm.

Dad sold one horse and one cow and got rid of his main farm implements with no trouble, keeping one plow. Mama sold her straggly Rhode Island Reds; after thirty years of the same, she wanted to try a new breed of chicken. I had a feeling that Mama, unlike Dad, was looking forward just a little bit to a new lease on life. When the sow was sold, Mama said: "We must get a couple of pigs when we get settled; you need them to use up the slop or else it's wasted." She never could stand any kind of waste; she suffered deeply when something was not thoroughly used up.

Our furniture was good-for-nothing junk, except the piano and an oak table. But we agreed with Mama that we ought to move it anyway and get replacements gradually as we could. Naturally we couldn't agree on everything. Mama held out against parting with the boxes of things she'd been saving—at least a dozen packing boxes full, nothing among which had been usable in years. We promised her that we'd all pitch in and see that she got some new things to use in the new life she was going to. She finally gave in, not without tears, and in order not to leave the old house knee-deep in Cunningham leftovers from thirty years of living, we kept a pile of the stuff burning in the empty chicken yard for several days. We found we had a dismal conglomeration of odds and ends to move in spite of our efforts to eliminate used-up, worn-out, broke-down trivia. We argued about this and that as we endlessly sorted. I found myself nervously putting milk crocks into a tub of wadded-up newspapers and taking them out again. Dad stayed out of the way. Jim was the one who took hold. He got one of his musician friends to help. They borrowed a medium-sized truck and loaded it with just about everything from the house except one bed and the stove. They headed for the acreage, Jim shouting at me to keep the burning trash pile replenished till he got back, which would probably be noon the next day.

The old house really looked desolate now—and the barnyard, the poor garden, everything. A farmyard without the sound of chickens is too sad for words, and I wanted to get this over with and get away from there. Forget, forget. But of course, you couldn't forget.

We were halfway through the moving and Dad had not yet sold his team of horses. We felt he should because he might not be able to once we got located outside farm country. We talked about this between us, Jim and I, but neither of us could bring ourselves to say anything to Dad about it. We had been able to reason with Mama about her boxes. But this business of Dad and his horses was quite another matter; we couldn't figure out what to do about it. I believe Dad became aware of our concern; he finally broke his silence. "A man ought to be able to get a haulin' job now 'n' then. After all, it ain't like we was goin' to live in the middle a the city."

Hauling jobs with horses? In the age of trucks? Thinking this over I realized it was a necessary rationalization on Dad's part. His sense of his own worth was tied inseparably to this team of horses. If the horses went, so went the solidity of his last stance in this life. We decided to go ahead and move everything else but the team and wagon. Maybe Dad would think it over and decide to part with them if we kept our mouths shut. Again I began to feel like a Judas.

We got on with it. When the truck was ready to go, I was to follow in the car with Dad and Mama, the cats, and Jim's dog Tippy. Then Jim and his friend were to come back for the horses, and once more for the wagon, which they were going to take apart. That was the plan. But it didn't happen that way. I had Mama, the dog, and one of the cats packed in the car with the dishes, pots, clothes, etcetera, but Dad wasn't around. We hollered to him in the direction of the barn. He appeared in the barn door, his big frame almost filling it, though he was somewhat stooped now. He came slowly up the hill and announced he was going to hitch up and drive to the new place, and Jim could return the borrowed truck. Nobody said anything for a time. Then I blurted out:

"Oh, no, Dad, you can't . . . it's sixty miles. It'll take you a day and a half . . . you'll be all night."

"So . . . hell, it's the full o' the moon. Plenty light. Tain't like I was goin' to have a load; I can trot 'em most o' the way. Shit, it ain't nothin'. You all go ahead. I'll come along and haul ya if ya break down." He grinned. Damned if he didn't look pleased for the first time since the farm was sold. There was no use to argue; we knew that. Mama started to worry about Dad, of course, but she also had to worry about her cat Goldie, who was missing. "I'll find yer cat," Dad said. "She's with kitten. Couldn't stand the ruckus goin' on around here, so she hightailed it for some quiet. I'll smoke her out . . . fetch her in the wagon. An' the wheelbarrow you all forgot." He pulled his wide shoulders as straight as they would go, turned and walked back down toward the barn. We stood watching him; he looked back once and waved us to get going.

As I was driving away, I surmised that Dad wanted to be alone. He needed a few hours on the old place by himself to say good-bye to his land, walk once more out across it, sift a handful of it through his fingers without anyone watching. He most likely wouldn't start out until daylight the next day. I was right. Two days later he came driving in at the new place—Dad behind his horses, with Goldie and the wheelbarrow in the wagon.

The new place fronted on the south and extended acre behind acre northward to form a narrow strip. Two-thirds of the way back it started to slope quite sharply down to a shallow pond, which spread out into a swampy area covering the back acre. We thought this bit of swamp could be drained and filled in so that melons or maybe sweet corn could be raised on it. But this was never done.

The only good we got from the back part of our place was purely recreational. We could sit under the big tree at the bottom of the slope and fish. Once in a while somebody caught an eight- or ten-inch mud cat out of our pond or the muddy stream trickling from the west that fed it. We tried once to cook and eat these fish, but it was like eating a handful of mud.

We had brought a quantity of books from the farm, Dad's set of Dickens, the classics Bill had abandoned, and my accumulation of Marxist literature—books, pamphlets, magazines. About the time we got good and settled in at the acreage, the Oklahoma City raids took place. We had no way of knowing just how far this outrage would be carried, and I couldn't stand the thought of my family suffering because of something that was my affair alone. Since the vigilante minds were bent on using books as evidence of criminality, I put my Little Lenin Library, my three-volume set of *Das Kapital*, and copies of *New Masses* into a five-gallon lard can and some gallon syrup buckets and buried them a foot or so down next to the cement walls of our new cellar. (I have no memory of retrieving these books; I believe they were still there years later when the area was developed into a fancy residential suburb—shopping center and all.)

We were well into fall. There was no more Red Dust Players. I was back from hiding and had begun to look hard for a job. Mama raised her chickens—Plymouth Rocks now—and kept increasing her flock. Jim had gone to California, Carl fixed people's cars, Madge was having a baby. We were all fairly occupied except Dad. He worked on repairing the shed, mending fence and the like after the cellar was finished. But it was plain to see he felt he had become a putterer. Of course, no hauling jobs materialized; the horses were "eating their heads off," and after a month or two they had to go. Next spring, Dad would have to borrow a couple of nags for the plowing and cultivating.

We were near the city, but there were real farms not too far away to the north and west of us. And where there are farms there are sales. Late in November notices of a farm sale appeared on telephone poles around us, and Dad announced he was taking the car and going. For the first time since we moved he seemed like his old self as he started out for this little trip. When he came back he had a bunch of stuff he'd bought at the sale—two dozen jars of home-canned cucumber pickles, some chipped dishes, and, strangely, several big pieces of bright patchwork (some poor farm wife had started a quilt she hadn't been able to finish). He seemed cheerful unloading these things and bringing them in the house. It was as though he felt in some way useful again, and he was unusually talkative.

"You can use all them things, can't ya? Things was cheap. That'll make ya a good quilt, won't it, Sis? Only two dollars. Cheap, wasn't they?"

I managed to say yes, they were; I thought sure I was going to cry. I couldn't say anything else, and Dad went on talking about the dishes and the pickles and how cheap things were. He seemed at that moment to have a terrible need for a few words of praise from some of us, and here I was, tongue-tied. I'd never seen Dad like this before; his whole being seemed to beg for some kind of approval. I didn't dare open my mouth for fear I'd run out and start raging at the sky. The system had broken Dad; his farm was gone, his horses were gone, his reason for living was gone. Pitifully he had tried to break away from the helplessness that was strangling him by bringing the family a few worthless things from a farm sale. When my anger subsided I was left with an ugly, gnawing ache that keeps returning to me whenever I'm in the country and encounter a Mason jar, the kind used in home canning. The pickles Dad brought home that day turned out to be so embedded with sand they were inedible. I hurried to buy store pickles to put on the table, and Dad was not to be told by anyone that they weren't the sale ones. As for the patchwork pieces, they faded to a dirty gray when I washed them. I bought cloth of a better quality and was secretly patching a quilt to show Dad. But he died before I finished it.

Chapter 7

Gordon—The Almanac Singers and After

If one thousand men leave a thousand jobs to go and fight the foe
Our factory wheels would slacken their speed and the belts would move
    too slow
But when a thousand hard workin' girls step in and take a hand
Out roll the tanks and planes and guns and there's freedom in the land.

("The Belt Line Girl," words by Sis Cunningham, 1942, ©1989)

From Gordon's FBI file, the first released entry, June 9, 1941:

> [Deleted] advised that GORDON FRIESEN had attended Weatherford schools and graduated from Weatherford Normal, and that thereafter he worked for a newspaper several years. [Deleted] noted that many people recall radical stories of his which aroused many of the fair minded citizens in and around Weatherford.
>
> After working with the newspaper, [deleted] continued, FRIESEN lived in the home of his father, J. E. Friesen, about two miles southwest of Weatherford. He stated that while FRIESEN was on his father's farm he wrote for numerous magazines and several radical books of his were published, the names of which [deleted] was unable to obtain. [Deleted] further related that FRIESEN has never been known to do any work, other than writing for newspapers and magazines.
>
> [Deleted] continued that the description of Subject which [deleted] was able to obtain is very meager since Subject rarely ever associated with anyone, but he is described as about thirty-five years of age, of medium height and build.
>
> July 26, 1941: [Deleted] described the Subject as being an individual of quiet disposition, whom [deleted] does not consider a Communist. [Deleted] stated that Subject has written a few questionable articles, but that his articles are written along the sensational vein in an attempt to attain publicity for himself. [Deleted] mentioned that the

Subject has written several articles putting the Police Department and the Fire Department on the pan, and even though [deleted] disliked the Subject it is hardly possible that the Subject is a Communist. [Deleted] stated that the Subject keeps to himself pretty much.

[Deleted] that the Subject is generally reputed as being quiet, studious, and a thinker.

The trials of the four communist defendants—Bob and Ina Wood, Alan Shaw, and Eli Jaffe—had ended in swift convictions. Each was sentenced to ten years in McAlester Penitentiary, the state prison. They had appealed and were out on bail (the Oklahoma Court of Appeals later threw out the convictions). The Red Dust Players had been scattered to the winds, and we were pretty well blacklisted throughout the state. Sis and I had since met and married and there was really nothing to keep us in Oklahoma. So we started out in a rickety bus in early October 1941 for New York City. Our luggage consisted of two suitcases, Sis's accordion, and my portable typewriter. I had the manuscript of a second novel, for which I hoped to find a publisher.

We did not come with the Almanacs in mind. Sis was going to find a job to keep things going for a while in hopes the novel would be accepted—it never was. At any rate Sis did work for several months while I negotiated about rewriting the book. A friend of hers had been going to the Almanac hootenannies and at one mentioned to Pete Seeger that she was in New York and Pete responded by saying the friend should ask Sis to visit the Almanacs. So we took the bus down to the Village one afternoon and did so. It was the first time I had ever seen Woody Guthrie, although I had followed his career from Oklahoma and had a deep feeling for him as a fellow Oklahoman and, more important, a fellow dust-bowl refugee. He looked almost exactly like I had pictured him; he just looked like a dust-bowl refugee from Oklahoma: scrawny, underfed, uncut brambly hair, thin-faced, eyes that had learned to stay out of trouble, or at least not push trouble too far.

Lee Hays was still there that afternoon; he was sitting on a little bench in the tiny Almanac "office" making music with a pair of big spoons. Woody was standing in front of him, either with a guitar or mandolin, participating in making the music. Pete was at the desk messing with some file cards or other small bits of paperwork. He jumped up to greet Sis, whom he had met in Oklahoma, with the boyish enthusiasm he still has plenty of in these days of a receding hairline. He introduced us as just being in from Oklahoma, and Woody asked me, "Has the dust stopped blowing yet?" and I answered something like, "Yeah, yesterday afternoon at three o'clock." Lee and Sis talked about Commonwealth, remembering the buildings as they had been before the vigilantes burned them down.

We went to several hootenannies after that, but I don't remember, somehow, Lee appearing in any of them. Around the time of Pearl Harbor we moved into Almanac House, and by that time Lee was gone.

We decided to go to New York right away because a friend in Oklahoma said I could get some decent medical care there for my heart condition, so Sis borrowed thirty-five dollars from her mother, and we headed east. While Red Dust Players activity was still going on, Pete and Woody had come through Oklahoma City, and Sis had met them there. She was terribly interested in what they were doing. When we decided that there was just not very much we could do in Oklahoma, she kept thinking about the Almanacs. I suppose there was a little bit of cowardice in our decision to leave. We didn't want to get jailed or anything like that if we could help it. But there just didn't seem to be very much that we could do in Oklahoma. So we came to New York.

We were on the road for four days. We lived for a while in New York with the late Sid Grossman, a documentary photographer who died of kidney disease in the early '50s. Sis had met him in Oklahoma when he was traveling around the country taking pictures; he had made a few photographs of the Red Dust Players in action. His excellence as a documentary photographer is slowly being recognized. His subjects were naturalistic: people in the streets, rural poverty, and the like. Sid had in his possession some five thousand glass negatives taken by Lewis Hine, whose photos from the early twentieth century of immigrants, child labor, and workers in sweatshop factories have appeared in countless books and magazines. We often wonder what became of all those negatives.

The Almanac Singers first came to our attention when one of our friends in Oklahoma City bought a copy of their first album, which has become known as the "John Doe Ballads." Soon after we got to New York City, they asked Sis to join them.

After we got to New York, Sis said, "Let's go. I want to be auditioned for the Almanacs." So we went down to their West Tenth

Street headquarters in the Village. And she sang a few of her songs, songs that she had written and been singing in the Red Dust Players. And so they took her in. They also had a new bass singer, Arthur Stern. They had bookings going on all the time, very poorly paid ones, of course.

Early in the fall of 1941 the Almanac Singers rented a three-story house at 130 West Tenth Street in New York's Greenwich Village with the idea not only of making it the living quarters of some of the group and a working place for all the Almanacs, but also a gathering place for other singers and song writers and creative people in general. They dubbed it Almanac House, and it was a perpetual open house in the fullest meaning of the phrase. It was soon a bustling place. The door was open to everybody; you just walked in. Big names with ideas and projects dropped by, and there were always young people, students and such, coming around with their instruments to pick up pointers from Woody Guthrie and Pete Seeger. Some of these kids were very serious about learning and grew up to have good careers of their own.

The Almanac Singers had been organized earlier that year, in the very early spring of 1941. Pete Seeger got together with Lee Hays in New York City, and the two started singing around. This was the beginning. They were joined by Lee's roommate Mill Lampell. Mill played no instrument, never pretended he could sing, but he fitted in with his ability to think up good lyrics and played a key part in the creating of quite a few Almanac songs. Along about June, Woody Guthrie, who had given big-time commercial radio a whirl and found it extremely distasteful—in fact unendurable—joined the group. There were also generally some eight or ten other persons, not always the same, whom one might, I suppose, call second-team Almanacs; their voices were in the background, and in some instances in the leads of the Almanac recordings.

Almanac House was one of those quite narrow places with a sub-basement; like other houses of this sort, it had originally been a one-family residence. Pete had a little room on the top floor. There was also a room up there for guests, visitors who stayed on too late to go home or had some reason for not wanting to go home, or who simply had no home as yet and needed a place to sleep for a night or two (or longer). Mill had a small apartment of his own over on Horatio Street but would come around every evening. Woody had a room similar to Pete's, but on the second floor of Almanac House. On the ground floor, the front room was an office, with a desk and tele-phone. Pete, who was about twenty-one or so and very determined to keep the group together, did most of the office work. The back room was a combined kitchen and dining room. The evening meal (often lamb chops with candied sweet potatoes and a huge wooden bowl of green salad) was a big event. A friend who knew carpentry had built out of ordinary boards a long dining table seating fourteen, and more people if they squeezed in. He had also put together a matching pair of old-fashioned wooden benches the length of the table. It was a setup like you see in the movies where knights gather for a hearty meal in some old castle, although of course not nearly on so large a scale.

There was hardly an evening, at least at the beginning, when the benches weren't crowded with Almanacs and guests. There was gay and lively conversation, with all kinds of ideas flying back and forth. The guests changed from night to night, most of them at least, and sometimes you weren't sure as to who was who. Total strangers would come in off the street to squeeze in somewhere and silently eat a meal and be on their way, never to be seen again.

The idea was that the Almanacs would earn a living from book-ings. Bookings there were, but the pay was meager. Generally the performances were for young, struggling trade unions or house par-ties. Sometimes on Saturday nights the Almanacs would knock themselves completely out by giving five or six shows, racing from place to place, and come home at three or four in the morning blue from exhaustion with eighteen or twenty dollars to divide up among six or eight people. The effects of hard times on the Almanac Singers began to be evident as winter came on. Woody, for instance, had only about one set of clothes left: a red plaid flannel shirt, faded and thin; wrinkled pants; a skimpy jacket; worn, working-man's shoes; and an old army overcoat two or three sizes too large for him (it was probably from World War I but it could have been from an even ear-lier war). The rent (ninety-five dollars) was mainly to come from holding hootenannies in the basement every Sunday afternoon (ad-mission was thirty-five cents). This plan worked fairly well so long as the weather was warmish. Along about noon on Sunday, all the mattresses were gathered up, forced down a narrow stairway leading from the kitchen into the basement, and spread around on the con-crete floor. Early-comers dove for these mattresses and packed them-selves aboard. Later arrivals had to stand up or sit on newspapers;

some regulars learned to come in old coats that could be sat on without further damage.

The word *hootenanny* had been picked up that summer by Pete and Woody in the Pacific Northwest. Originally all four of the Almanacs started this tour, but Lee Hays became ill when they reached Salt Lake City and Mill brought him back to New York. *Hootenanny* had been in use in rural America from way back to designate something you didn't know the exact name of. Say, for example, a couple of farm boys in Oklahoma might be overhauling a "T-bone Ford" out behind the barn with pieces spread all around, and in fitting them back together one might say to the other, "that thing-a-ma-jig goes here and that hootenanny goes there." Anyway, the Almanac affair, with mass singing by the guests, some of them taking a turn at the mike, seemed like something new that didn't quite have a name of its own yet, and so it was called a hootenanny.

There was an exciting freshness about these Sunday-afternoon affairs. High points were many. There was Woody, head thrown back (his black, curly hair always seemed in need of cutting), singing "Worried Man" or the talking blues about the hens upstairs, "East Texas Red," and so on. Other hootenanny high spots were Bess Lomax doing "Another Man Done Gone" in her sweet and quivery voice, Arthur Stern booming out with "I'm On My Way," Pete singing "The Golden Vanity," and visitors like Leadbelly doing "Pick a Bale of Cotton" or "Rock Island Line," or Earl Robinson playing the "Tarrier Song" while his little boy Perry stole the show by doing a heel dance around his daddy.

In the office of Almanac House was a fairly large bulletin board. An examination of the items thumb-tacked onto it gave one a pretty good conception of the life being led there. Announcements of upcoming bookings and directions how to get there, messages, newspaper clippings with possible song ideas underscored, beginnings of songs, whole songs produced by one or more Almanacs and tacked up for the others to pass judgment on, slogans to keep up morale ("Take it easy—but take it"). Later on, as the world moved deeper into World War II, notices appeared containing appeals to join civilian defense or gather scrap and old tires for the war effort (Pete Seeger, always conscientious, did look around for, find, and roll home a number of discarded tires). Next door to Almanac House was a firehouse, and one evening a delegation of firemen going about the neighborhood in the interests of defense preparations dropped in to invite the Almanacs to come over and be taught how to put out fires, which might result if there were air raids. The Almanac menfolk kept this appointment, but found out quickly that the kind of lives they were being forced to live, with resultant nutritional insufficiency, was not conducive to physical fitness. About all they learned was to distinguish between the male and female couplings of a fire hose (the one goes into the other, but it doesn't work vice versa). Woody Guthrie, by grim determination, did manage to drag his section of hose up a practice fire escape. None of the others made it.

It is well known, of course, that America produced no really great and lasting war songs out of the agony of World War II, at least nothing to compare with the songs of the Revolution and Civil War, nor the somewhat lighter songs emerging from the First World War. Various reasons for this have been put forward; the most likely being that the commercialization of songs in America had tended to sterilize and flatten song writers and force song writing itself steadily downward to its lowest possible, most meaningless level. (When TV quickly developed itself into a vast wasteland, it was only following a trail broken earlier by radio.) Be that as it may, there were still some left who tried very seriously to create good songs to aid in the war against fascism, and among these were the Almanac Singers.

Their first war song followed the sinking of the U.S. destroyer *Reuben James* in late October 1941 by a Nazi U-boat with the loss of all hands. This song was written mainly by Woody Guthrie. He wrote all the verses but was stumped for a chorus. The other Almanacs felt the song was a very good one and kept steady pressure on Woody to finish it. For a while Woody tried to build a chorus around representative names taken from the casualty list appearing in the *New York Times.* He wanted to convey the idea that the crew of the *Reuben James* symbolized the fighting unity of melting-pot America. His aim was basically sound; the casualty list of the *Reuben James* was indeed a cross section of America and fairly begged for some such treatment. On it were Scandinavian, Irish, Anglo-Saxon, Jewish, and Spanish names—Ghetzler, Evans, Ortizuela, Johnston, Polizzi. But the idea was too broad for condensation into short poetry. Finally, at an Almanac session on the problem someone suggested the line "What were their names." Woody took it from there and finished the song.

It has been said somewhere that CBS opened and closed the war with the Almanac Singers' "'Round and 'Round Hitler's Grave." It would probably be more precise to give credit to Norman Corwin, the CBS writer and producer; it was he who created the shows spoken of and who sought out the Almanacs. This particular song was a real product of cooperative effort; it was a flowering of the idea behind the formation of the Almanac Singers, namely that a group of people would get together and each contribute whatever talent he or she possessed toward a joint artistic creation. One of the verses turned out to be quite prophetic—the one about Mussolini: "We'll salt his beef and hang it up to dry." Mussolini, as we know, was hung by his heels in the public square at Milan, although, of course, unsalted. The title and chorus were somewhat off, because Hitler never even earned a grave. Woody Guthrie came a little closer in his "Biggest Thing" when he wrote, "We'll burn his soul in hell," but this too was an underestimation, for Hitler didn't even make it to hell before he was burned. Leadbelly's very stirring twelve-string-guitar song about the war perhaps presented the best image: "We're gonna tear Hitler down . . . Bring him to the ground—some day." All of these songs shared a common belief, a deep faith that the good people of this earth are never going to let a monster like Hitler get away with his crimes against humanity.

The Almanacs went on to write a dozen or more songs about World War II—"Taking It Easy," "Sally, Don't You Grieve," "Deliver the Goods," and so on. The best of them were published in the summer of 1942 by Bob Miller. Tin-pan alley could certainly use another publisher like Bob Miller. He knew his commercial market, but at the same time was always ready to use some of his money to bring out material he thought was good, but which he knew would never make much, if any, profit. His own song about the war, "There's a Star Spangled Banner Waving Somewhere," sold a million copies. ("Somewhere," naturally, was heaven.) At the same time, he remained in touch with reality and life here on earth. It was Bob Miller who published "Joe Hill." It's an oft-repeated story of how Alfred Hayes and Earl Robinson went fruitlessly from publisher to publisher until they came to Miller's office. "Joe Hill" will be remembered a long time, while most of the real money-making stuff published around that time is long since forgotten. A topical song written by Bob Miller, "Eleven Cent Cotton, Forty Cent Meat (How in the World Can a Poor Man Eat)" was a big hit among the farmers in the South and Southwest during the depression days.

It might be a digression, but at the same time somewhat illuminating, to mention something about the man probably most responsible for popularizing "Eleven Cent Cotton." He was W. K. Henderson, a wealthy lumberman in Shreveport, Louisiana, who had his own personal—and quite powerful—radio station, KWKH, in the days when there was still some tolerance for American individuality. He was his own announcer, disc jockey, etcetera, and would play "Eleven Cent Cotton" over and over again, occasionally alternating it with "Oh, Dem Golden Slippers." In between he would give his opinions on things, set forth his likes and dislikes, in very earthy language; when a Texas oil magnate tried to finagle his wavelength away from him, he unleashed salty diatribes against that whole state, beginning his comments with the salutation: "Hello out there, you li'l ol' Tex-Ass." Henderson's enemies combined with Washington bureaucrats, and he was finally stripped of his license, despite his bringing a railway mail car crammed with thousands of letters from his supporters to the nation's capital.

Henderson, incidentally, was the reason why announcers for years now have been required to say: "You have been listening to a recording" or "to an electrical transcription." He used to pretend that the singers or bands on the records were actually appearing live in his studio. Say he was about to play a Guy Lombardo record. He would begin with: "Hey, there's somebody at the door. Why, it's Guy Lombardo. Hello, Guy. I see you brought your boys with you. Come on in, find some seats. What are you going to play for us?" And then put on the record. Of course, Washington's pretense that it had been to protect those of us listening to KWKH was only a gratuitous insult—as if we didn't know that Guy Lombardo and his band weren't *really* in the studio. Henderson was one of the first victims of the drive to put the stamp of conformity on Americans, a drive that has proceeded steadily since then, sometimes subtly and sometimes not at all subtly, and by now had come a long way down the road. It has affected all aspects of American life, including song writing.

The Almanac Singers labored on their songs in the winter of 1941–42 under steadily worsening economic conditions. When the really cold weather set in, it brought what turned out to be the fatal strain on the budget: the heating of Almanac House. Pete Seeger, the diligent fire builder and stoker, finally had no fuel left to feed the furnace. All efforts to keep the house heated on weekdays were abandoned. Frigid temperatures took over, windows frosted, pipes froze, icicles grew like stalactites in the bathroom. The only source of heat (really quite feeble) was the gas oven in the kitchen, lit and turned up full-force. Those huddled around the open stove door could hear upstairs the chattering teeth of guests fool enough to decide to stay overnight. Bess Lomax broke open her hope chest and passed out all her blankets to keep Almanacs and semi-Almanacs from freezing to death. Woody, always ready to record in song what went on around him, wrote a blues song, one verse of which went: "I went into the bathroom and I pulled upon the chain / Polar bears on icebergs came floating down the drain, / Hey, Pretty Mama, I got those Arctic Circle blues." Only for the Sunday afternoon hootenannies was there any serious attempt made to provide heat. For a time there was money enough for a Sunday basket of coal. But even that gave out. Arthur Stern would lead a band of young early-comers out into the streets ahead of time to scrounge for anything burnable. Sometimes they would return elatedly with a busted, discarded table or some other good-sized something that would burn. But Greenwich Village was full of cold people that winter, and there were a lot of other scroungers in the field. Arthur and his faithful foragers would come back mostly with slats from broken orange crates. Warmth for the last hootenanny ever held in Almanac House was provided mainly by accumulated copies of the good-old *New York Times.*

Failure to make any financial progress, despite the active help of sympathetic friends, led, more than anything else, to a feeling of discouragement and a resultant slackening of joint song producing efforts by Almanac Singers in early 1942. Perhaps the most concerned about this development was the youngest Almanac—Pete Seeger. Several of the others began to turn back to individual projects. Mill Lampell wrote the beautiful poem that later—set to Earl Robinson's fine music—became "The Lonesome Train."

Most of the time all the Almanacs went to the bookings—Pete, Mill, Arthur, Sis, Bess, Woody. Once in a while one of them would have a bad cold or a toothache or something, and then the rest would go. They all knew all the material, so sometimes as few as two went on bookings. But usually it was at least four and most of the time five, six, or all. It was very exciting; they wrote their own songs. They wrote quite a few songs together. They would just sit around and somebody would have an idea for a song. And everyone would throw in suggestions, whatever changes they wanted, whatever improvements they could suggest, until finally they felt like they had the song completed. They wrote a lot of songs that way.

We had supper, and we'd clear out the young guests—we always had some guests for supper—clear them out and just sit there and talk about song ideas. Somebody would say, "Hey, I've got an idea for a song." And, of course, there were some songs that were written out by one or the other of us, like Sis's song, "The Beltline Girl." She wrote that completely herself. And Pete did "Deliver the Goods."

Sometimes the band was invited to parties, late-night parties, mostly parties by left-wing groups. They'd have a Saturday night party. And then they would always sing something topical, whatever was really fresh in the news. Afterward they would sing things like "On Top of Old Smoky" and "Four Nights Drunk," songs like that, just for pure entertainment. But at the other functions, the union functions, they always sang almost altogether topical material. And they usually decided after they got there what they were going to do. They'd size up the situation and just decide then at the time. Sometimes, right in the middle of a program, Pete might say, "OK, Sis, OK. You sing your song." Or, "Woody. Hey, next song's gonna be Woody. Get up here Woody." Pete basically would decide. Woody left it up to Pete pretty much what they were doing on a given program.

Once they were engaged to sing at one of those out-of-town places. It was in the middle of winter, around Christmas time or New Years', at Chesters' Zunbarg, a winter resort. They got up there—Pete, Woody, and Sis, as well as myself. Mill was going to come, but for some reason or other he couldn't. So when they got up there, the manager said, "But there's only three of you!" He said, "What are we going to do? There's only three of you, and we booked four Almanacs." And the publicity leaflets that they had gotten out, the programs that they had printed up, had four Almanacs. So I, who can't carry a tune, stood up there. I knew all the words so I just lip-synched. And we got by with it. The audience didn't seem to know the difference at all.

Woody Guthrie returned to his autobiography, *Bound for Glory*, and began to pound away on it with a concentration that has always remained enviable. He took over the long wooden table in the kitchen (nobody was using it to eat on anymore anyway), establishing himself there with an ancient, beat-up typewriter that had been donated to the Almanacs. Alone on the long matching bench, his back to the warmth from the open oven door, he would type away at a fast hunt-and-peck pace all night, hour after hour. You could wake up almost any hour of the night and hear his machine going. When it got too cold, he would draw an old army blanket around his hunched shoulders. From time to time he would brew himself a pot of Oklahoma-style coffee (you just added new water to old grounds). When morning came he would either fall asleep beside his type-writer or stumble to his feet and disappear into one of the Almanac House rooms, leaving as many as twenty-five or thirty pages of new manuscript on yellow-pad paper, single-spaced with no measurable margins. Toward evening he would wake up and go out somewhere to find some food (the Almanac cupboard was bare), although God knows if he found very much (he was so skinny you couldn't tell by looking at him if he'd had anything to eat in weeks). Then back to the typewriter.

Bound for Glory and the persistent, disciplined way Woody worked on it under the adverse conditions that existed provide a key as to what it was that spurred Woody Guthrie's creativity. The story he tells in the book is, of course, a very tragic one: a picture of life (at least in the first two-thirds of the volume) almost unbearable. Many modern American writers have produced, and are writing, books with, shall one say, an extremely bleak outlook on life. They show you a fearful picture, saying in effect, Look how horrible and terrifying is man's existence. But there they stop, with the implica-tion that the situation is unalterable, that's the way things are, noth-ing can be done about it, and if you can't take it, then die. But the author of *Bound for Glory* says in his book and in many of his songs, Read and listen, and then for God's sake do something to change things so that human beings won't have to go through the same suf-fering over and over again. There is everywhere in his message a deep and unshakable conviction that man can change things—dras-tically—for the better, once he decides to do so. And he says further-more, I'm going to keep on telling you this no matter how tough you make it for me. The late William Faulkner could have been speaking of Woody Guthrie, both as an individual and a symbol, when in his Nobel acceptance speech he declared: "Man will not only endure, but will prevail."

In his writings and in his songs, you can see his deep understand-ing of how this new world, this, as he likes to call it, one big world "union," must come into being. It will not arrive automatically while you patiently wait for it at the station. First there is going to have to be considerable sacrifice and struggle. You do not wait for ideal conditions in which to work for it; you work wherever you are and struggle with whatever weapons you have; Woody's were his songs and writings and music. And Woody also had no illusions concerning on whose shoulders rests the main burden of bringing the better world about—it's going to have to be the ordinary guys, the workers in mines and mills and fields, the dispossessed, the unemployed, the racially persecuted—the "humble people," as Fidel Castro calls them.

In the Almanac days Woody was a thin, starved-looking guy, but fairly wiry. His black hair was like a bramble bush, full of tight kinks that somebody described as "the bobs from bobwire." He was quick to smile, but sometimes that smile hid seething emotions, although actual explosions of temper were rare. Among his mannerisms was a sort of disarming jauntiness; starting out on a booking he would sling his guitar across his back and stride along the street bent forward at the waist pretending that the instrument was a heavy load.

An old-timer from the New York Unemployed Councils remembers a night in 1939 or 1940 when Woody came up on the West Side of Manhattan to sing for his local. With Woody was a buddy, Mike Quin, the California writer who died of cancer in 1947. Woody sang and played for an hour or so, then collected his agreed-upon fee—seventy-five cents. He and Mike bought a bottle of wine and had enough money left for the subway (those were the days of the nickel fare). On the way downtown, Woody began singing and playing for the riders. Mike, who didn't have a bad voice, joined in, and from among the passengers they picked up another singer. The trio wound up performing the whole night through, riding the subway out to the end of the line, New Lots Avenue, and back, out and back, until past dawn.

It was only among the common people that Woody was really at home—among the unemployed, among subway riders, in union halls, in saloons across the land patronized by workers and drifters, in the camps of the migratory workers, on the Staten Island ferry, on merchant ships in World War II. There was little money to be found here; it was a world of nickels and dimes. The big money was in the world of commercial entertainment, but in order to share the loot, you first had to sell your soul, and this Woody refused to do. The commercializers recognized his talent early and would undoubtedly have rewarded him liberally had he submitted to their wishes, broken his alliance with the people from whence he came, toned down and sugar-coated his criticism of society. There was a time when they saw him as potentially a second Will Rogers and launched a serious effort to shape him into one. But Woody, for much clearer reasons than motivated Holden Caulfield, walked out on the phonies. He found himself unable to endure, and finally rejected altogether the world of American big-time entertainment, populated, as he saw it, by wheelers and dealers, shifty-eyed, hypocritical, glib, fast-talking, sex-excited men and women who could not wake without benzedrine or go to sleep without barbiturates. Woody went instinctively back to the little people, who, although tainted by the corrupted, decaying society in which they live, do manage to hang on to an inner core of decency. He would leave a fruitless conference in some Rockefeller Center office where talk of fantastic sums of money flew all around, have a few beers, and go down with a buddy like Cisco Houston to sing and play on the Staten Island ferry, returning at 2 A.M. proud of his pocketful of coins with which the passengers had rewarded him.

Much as he despised those in control of the entertainment field, Woody had an even greater hatred for the phonies in the progressive movement who mouthed radicalism as they compromised, adjusted, and readjusted to the demands of Madison Avenue. As time went on, it became increasingly more difficult for Woody to hide his true feelings. During the Almanac period, some well-meaning friend with connections tried to steer a few dollars their way by getting them an occasional booking at high-class society affairs. Woody would go along, and mink-coated, bejeweled women would surround him, insulting him with every unwitting remark: "Look, it's a real cowboy! Isn't he just darling—so picturesque." One night at a high-powered affair in New York's Westin Hotel he shocked a penthouse full of cocktail-drinking party-goers by abruptly ripping down an expensive twenty-foot brocaded drape, wrapping it around himself like an Indian, and stalking out. (A diplomatic emissary from the hotel recovered the drape the next day.)

On another occasion a friend—probably the same misguided one—got Woody, Pete, and Sis a booking to sing in the Waldorf-Astoria for a national convention of big-business moguls of some kind or other—executives, managers, bosses. It was the summer of 1942, and America was at war with the Hitler-Tojo fascists and fighting desperately to gain a toehold in the Pacific. Pete was getting ready to leave for the army in a few weeks.

The hour was fairly well along when the three Almanacs stepped up to the microphone to entertain their hosts. Much whiskey had already flowed down the throats of the four or five hundred conventioneers, who were eating hurriedly, impatient for the next promised round of pleasure—the girls. From some tables the cry was beginning to rise:

"Bring on the girls!"

The Almanacs sang a few of their new antifascist songs, but no one really listened; the drunken hubbub drowned out their efforts. This time it was Pete's temper that exploded. He grabbed the mike and delivered a furious lecture, which went something like this: "What are you, human beings or a bunch of pigs? Here you sit slobbering whiskey, stuffing your fat bellies and hollerin' for whores. Don't you care that American boys are dying tonight to save your country for you, and many more thousands will die before this is over? Great God Almighty, haven't you got any shame?" Frankly, it was like shouting against the wind; a drunk millionaire at one of the front tables bawled: "Aw, shut up and play some music. How about 'She'll Be Comin' Around the Mountain'?"

Woody's guitar and Sis's accordion took up the song, and Pete cooled off by concentrating on the strings of his long-necked banjo. After a few minutes, Woody said, "Let me take the next verse." Stepping real close to the microphone so that the room was filled with the sound of his voice, he sang to the bosses:

> She'll be wearin' a union button when she comes,
> She'll be wearin' a union button when she comes,
> She'll be wearin' a union button,
> She'll be wearin' a union button,
> She'll be wearin' a union button when she comes.

When he finished there was a moment of hush, in which Woody, Pete, and Sis packed up their instruments and walked off the stage; but as they left, the drunken cry rose again, louder than ever: "Bring on the girls! Bring on the girls!"

One morning in the middle of the winter of 1941–42, Pete Seeger tacked up a new notice on the bulletin board. It was a friendly message from the sheriff of New York County announcing the date of a forthcoming eviction for nonpayment of rent. Woody Guthrie stood studying it for a while, then rejected it as a possible inspiration for a new song; after all, he had covered the eviction of millions of Americans in his dust-bowl ballads. He went back to work on *Bound for Glory.* Some of the other Almanacs began to hustle around looking for another place to live, and found an apartment on Sixth Avenue near Ninth Street, up above Luigi's and a dancehall called The Dome.

There was no thought of hiring a professional mover, or even of renting a horse and wagon. The moving had to be done afoot with the help of volunteers. Arthur Stern rounded up his loyal little band of wood gatherers. Since the huskiest of this bunch wasn't free until around midnight, the migration didn't really get under full steam before that hour. It was like ants moving from an old colony to a new one. In one direction proceeded a file of Almanacs and supporters, lamp shades on their heads, boxes of books and papers or articles of furniture in their arms; some were pushing beds (the old-fashioned kind with casters) piled high with clothes, bedding, etcetera. As this line pressed more or less steadily forward, it was passed by a silent file of empty-handed ants returning to Almanac House for fresh loads.

Woody remained oblivious to what was happening around him (that's one way to get a book written). He kept typing away in the kitchen while stuff was being moved out from all around him. The house grew extra cold because the front door was propped open for the convenience of the movers going in and out. Several times the burdened file was stopped by suspicious police, whose questions indicated they feared a gang of brazen looters had descended on Greenwich Village. Not until they backtracked to verify the movers' story were they satisfied. The cops in one squad car, learning they had stopped the same people for a second time, begged: "Please, if you ever move again, do it in the daytime."

It was sunup before the end of the operation came into sight. The last items to go were the typewriter and the kitchen table on which Woody was working. Later in the day, when a couple of Almanacs returned for a last check, they found Woody curled up on the cold linoleum kitchen floor in front of the feebly hissing oven. He was sound asleep, hunched up tight as a ball under a spread-out copy of the *New York Journal American*, his manuscript beside him. They went away and left him in peace. (He showed up at the new Almanac residence a few days later, found a corner to work in, and it was back to *Bound for Glory.*)

"The Sun's Gonna Shine in My Backyard—Someday." A month or two after this move, things took a turn indicating that Horatio Alger might not have been kidding the public after all; it seemed that all the perseverance and struggle under mounting difficulties were about to pay off for the Almanac Singers. Suddenly, within the space of a few days, all these things happened: they were signed by the William Morris agency for a nationwide tour; signed by Decca Records to record their own songs; booked into the Rainbow Room at Rockefeller Center; and hired by a radio network to do a daily show consisting of topical songs they were to write on the happenings of each day.

Just as suddenly, all these arrangements were abrogated. The ink on the contracts wasn't even dry when a front-page story appeared in a "liberal" New York City newspaper attacking the Almanacs. The article saw something strange, in that "Peace Singers" had become "War Minstrels," the peace part referring to the *Songs For John Doe* album—as though millions of other Americans hadn't undergone the same change as fascism advanced. But to shorten a story meriting greater length, the news story resulted in the cancellation of all the contracts. For the Almanac Singers, it was the beginning of the end.

What can one say except to note that the blacklist is not a new thing in America, that we had McCarthyism long before Joe McCarthy. Certain historical facts, however, should be kept straight. There was nothing alien about the *John Doe* songs. They were a purely American phenomenon, no more and no less. The album was an expression of the feeling and thinking of much of a whole generation of American youth. This was the generation that had been bluntly informed that World War I was not the noble crusade portrayed by the propagandists, but a ghastly slaughter of tens of millions of human beings in order to enrich a handful of profiteers led by the munition makers. It was a young generation affected deeply by that great touchstone of the twentieth century: Spain. It was a generation profoundly (even permanently) shaken, disillusioned, and angered to see its government reject the Spanish Republic's perfectly legitimate appeal for arms and stand piously aside while Mussolini's legions and Hitler's Luftwaffe smashed Spanish democracy and placed the fascist butcher Franco in power. It is against this background that the *John Doe* songs must be judged. Change a line or two and some of the songs could apply today. Who wants to die in Cuba so that the gangsters can return to reopen their whorehouses in Havana?

One thing about the Almanacs as a whole was their basic instinct for down-to-earth, no-fancy-stuff folk music. They held the likes of John Jacob Niles in utter contempt, and used to go around mockingly imitating him. Richard Dyer-Bennet was acceptable only for "Waltzing Matilda." The Almanacs grew more and more disenchanted with Burl Ives and made up this parody about him:

> Burl Ives is so folky
> With sobs and with tears
> He's been cashing in on Old Smoky
> For the last fifteen years.
>
> On top of Old Smoky
> All covered with snow
> Burl Ives keeps on singing
> At forty below.

(I wonder if the former Almanacs in the Weavers remembered this when *they* cashed in on "Old Smoky.")

After Pete went into the army, Woody moved into the now extra room in our new Hudson Street apartment. He was working on the final draft of his autobiography. The young-woman editor Dutton had assigned to him came by frequently as they refurbished the final paragraphs. Sometimes Woody and I would lie on the floor at night with a couple of quart bottles of beer and talk about the inevitable coming of socialism to America. Woody, Sis, and Cisco Houston became the new Almanac Singers and got a few bookings and radio appearances.

While Woody lived with us, there was one incident that showed his fierce antiestablishmentarianism. He came rushing in furiously one late afternoon and asked Sis and me to lend him seven dollars. He wanted it so that he could go over to New Jersey and buy a gun with which to shoot Mill Lampell. It seemed that Mill had taken him to some producer's plush office to discuss some kind of deal involving Woody's music. While Mill was fast-talking the producer, Woody sat on a couch over in a corner playing softly on his harmonica. Mill asked him to stop, telling Woody, "We're talking big money here." Woody stopped for a short period and then began playing his harmonica louder than before. This time Mill snatched the instrument out of his hands. It was too much for Woody. He left precipitously and hurried home to ask us for the gun money. We did not have seven dollars either. So Woody took out his rage by half-wrecking the apartment. A few days previously he had bought a mandolin in a pawn shop. Now he jerked it off the wall, smashed it on the floor, and jumped up and down on the pieces. In the commotion two yellow vases that Sis had picked up somewhere were jarred off the mantle and shattered into bits. I went out and bought several Shaefers; we drank them, and Woody finally cooled down.

Once I went with Woody to a bar on the Hudson River frequented by longshoremen. He tried to play and sing for them, but they told us to get the hell out of there. This experience led me to doubt the Guthrie legend that he had played his guitar and sung in bars all over the United States, with the working-class people crowding around him and soaking in his every word along with their boilermakers.

Several times a week a bunch of our musical friends would come over for a jam session. There was Leadbelly with his twelve-string guitar, Sonny Terry with his mouth harp, Brownie McGhee with his six-stringer, and Sis would play her accordion, all joining in with Woody to sing hard-travelin' songs. At one point Leadbelly announced, "I am king of the twelve-string guitar, Sonny is king of the harmonica, and Sis is queen of the accordion." These sessions would last until two or three in the morning, getting louder and louder, accompanied by more and more forceful stamping of the feet. We finally got into trouble with the landlord. He explained that ours was one of three duplicate tenements built side-by-side and that the central wooden beams ran through all three. So not only were complaints about the noise and shaking coming from the tenants in our building but those in the other two as well.

We occasionally went to hear Leadbelly perform at the Village Vanguard. Working extremely hard, sweat rolling from his face, he did three sets a night—ten o'clock, midnight, and two o'clock—six nights a week. All this for a weekly stipend of sixty dollars. He put every ounce of himself into such songs as "Take This Hammer" and "Gallus Pole." He put such intensity and meaning into "Gallus Pole" that one was almost ready to cry when in the final verse he asks his best friend if he has brought any silver and gold to save him, and the friend replies, "No, I came to see you hang from the Gallus Pole." His theme song in opening and closing the sets was "Goodnight Irene." When his stint at the Village Vanguard ended, he had to apply for welfare.

Sis and I visited him and his wife Martha in the rotting tenement where they lived just east of Tompkins Square Park. The place stank, it was overrun by cockroaches, and you had to watch where you stepped to keep your feet from going through ratholes in the floor. But Leadbelly always tried to keep himself neat and presentable— shaved, hair slicked down, and wearing a white shirt and a necktie with his always-pressed double-breasted blue suit. He was always a gentleman, and at his best singing for children. But neither he nor Woody (during Woody's active career) ever "made it." It is ironical that films have now been made about them. The world owes everlasting gratitude to Moses Asch of Folkways for recording Huddie Ledbetter and Woody Guthrie when they were at their best.

Who can tell what further songs the Almanacs might have produced had they not been cut down in their prime. After all, it was not until five or six months later that the younger Almanacs went into the armed forces, Woody into the merchant marine, and the others their separate ways.

When Sis and I arrived in Detroit in the latter part of December 1942, it was an extremely cold day. The sky was overcast, low, gray clouds, below freezing—it must have been around zero as I remember it, a bitter wind blowing. I don't ever remember being in such a cold day in my life. It was snowing and the wind was driving the snow along the streets, piling it up among the garbage that hadn't been collected for some days; and the weather remained like that for at least two weeks. During all that time, I never saw the sun, and as a result I lost my sense of direction; I was turned around. Not completely turned around; about 180 degrees. All the while I was in Detroit, I never did get my directions straightened out, and it bothered me a lot. Afterward, when I became a reporter and I had to know which was east and which was west, I always had to stop and straighten out in my mind which was which. In my mind, Woodward Avenue ran east and west, when actually it ran north and south. Anyway, I always had to carry a little map in my pocket, and when I got an assignment to go to East Jefferson or West Forest, I had to get the damn thing out and study it and square things around in my head as to which way to go.

We both got jobs in war plants just a few days after getting to Detroit. They had tooled over to making implements of war machinery, and they were looking for workers. You could walk into almost any plant and they'd sign you right up, ask you if you had any experience, and if you did, you got a little higher-paying job than if you didn't, but even if you didn't have any experience you went on the payroll right away. I became what they called the "stock chaser," which was the lowest category of work—well, maybe it was one degree above a sweeper—in a Chevrolet plant that was making parts for machine guns. They were making the sights and the cooling jacket round the barrel, but they weren't making the barrels or the stocks or the triggers or anything like that; that was subcontracted elsewhere. These parts were being made in six different plants, and they were shipped to Flint, as I remember it, where the machine guns were put together and shipped out to the war fronts.

In this plant they also made the shells for 75 mm cannon. Again, the complete product wasn't made there, just parts, which were shipped elsewhere. Each stock chaser had a wagon, a flat-bottom wagon about four feet long, and when a certain operation was completed on one floor, I went around from machine to machine and loaded the parts onto this wagon—it wasn't a cart, it was a four-wheel thing—and took them down the freight elevator to the next floor, where a certain other operation was done. Then finally when they were completed, I dragged them down onto the ground floor to the shipping department, where they were boxed up and shipped out. I worked there at least three or four months, walking to work ten to twelve blocks. It was snow and ice all through that period, through the middle of the winter. I'd leave before dawn; in fact, to get from where we were living to the war plant I was working in, I walked through the black ghetto, which ironically was called Paradise Valley. I had to transverse right through the heart of the black section.

Sis, in the meantime, got a job much closer to home, just two or three blocks. Her job was as an inspector where they made pneumatic tools, especially riveting guns—machines that were used to drive rivets into airplanes. They were shipped out to wherever the warplanes factories were. It was a more skilled job; it was a higher-paid job. She had to use a micrometer and get the clearance within

.004 to .016 of an inch. Later on, in the place I was working in, I was offered a job as an inspector. They trained me for it; when I wasn't chasing stock I helped inspectors on the benches who taught me the rudiments and all that. But it was easier being a stock chaser. You just wheeled the stuff from floor to floor on the freight elevator and took it down from floor to floor. It was a fairly large building, four stories high, all plate glass—all you saw from the outside was glass, not windows, but the shell of the structure itself was largely glass. One of the advantages of being a stock chaser was when you got caught up, when there was a half-hour or an hour in which there was nothing to do, you could take it easy while the guys on the machines were grinding away. They had to work steadily; every hour or so they got off five minutes to go to the toilet and then they had to get right back on the job. But the stock chaser, he had a chance to goof off from time to time. There were a couple of other guys around there that had similar jobs, not requiring them actually to be chained to the machines. We used to gather—three or four or five of us—up on the top floor, where there was no machinery. The top floor was full of bins of parts, mainly nuts and bolts and screws; each had its marked bin. So it was my job occasionally to go up there and drag some of these boxes down to the machine where they were needed. Hid-away and stuck at the back end of the top floor was an enclosed room taking up maybe about one-fifth of the space on that floor, and in this area some of the wheels of the Chevrolet top brass were hidden away—five or six brand-new Chevies. Of course, this was wartime, and the purchase of new cars was rationed; anybody couldn't just go out and buy a new car. So they had kept these back from the inventory and had hidden them up there in case the opportunity came to drive the things out and use them for their own purposes. We used to hide away and sit in these cars, take along a bottle of whiskey—couple of bottles—sit in there and put our feet up on the back seat, and get pretty well stoned, telling jokes and laughing and keeping an eye out in case some supervisor or foreman or higher wheels of any kind might come up there to check whether his car was still there or whether somebody might have carried it off. We did this quite a bit; it was a nice, comfortable hiding place.

I remember one young guy who was part of this little group; he was about twenty-two and cocky. He hated the Chevrolet Motor Company; he'd been working for them ever since he was eighteen or so. And his draft papers came. This was after I'd been there three or four months. He was being drafted into the navy, and on his last day on the job he took out a lot of his animosity. We were up on the top floor, and he got roaring drunk. He got another guy into a contest with him to see who could break out more of these window panes. They were three by five feet, with a little strip holding them together. These two guys spent a good deal of the afternoon taking these boxes of bolts and nuts and breaking out these windows. I didn't take part in that because I wasn't part of the contest; besides, I was going to have to stay there—I wasn't going into the navy the next morning like this cat was. This was on the fourth floor, pretty damn high up, and there must have just been a shower of glass going down the outside of the building onto the ground. I was surprised somebody didn't come up there and check into it—see what the hell was going on—because they broke out literally hundreds of these windows. The next morning when I came to work, I looked up there and it looked like three-fourths of them were gone, just one intact pane here and there. Anyhow, there was some inquiry into it; nobody knew anything about it, I didn't know anything about it, and they finally connected it to this young guy who had gone into the navy, but by this time he was on a troop train going to California to be put on some battleship to go attack the Japanese.

It was only a few days after that that I finished my job at this war plant, because several months earlier—in fact, within a few days after we'd gotten to Detroit—I had put in an application to the *Detroit Times*, and it was just about this time that the *Times* called me up and asked me to work. My supervisor, foreman, or whatever he was at the war plant, begged me to stay on and they would make me an inspector and I would get maybe ten or fifteen dollars a week more than I was getting as a stock chaser, but I had a background of sorts as a newspaperman, and I thought I would rather do this. So I went to work for the *Times*; I guess it was early spring of 1943.

Where Sis worked there were a lot of women; in fact, there were whole families. This was the period when they were bringing in thousands of workers into the war plants. They had recruiting agents down in Alabama, Ohio, Tennessee, Arkansas, Oklahoma, bringing in these thousands of people to staff the "arsenal of democracy," which Detroit was then becoming, providing not only our armies but the British, the Russians—whatever ships could make it through to Murmansk. It was what they called the "hotbed period." Hotbeds were rooming houses where the bed was rented out for only eight hours. You worked an eight-hour shift, you slept in one of these beds for eight hours, and then you left and the next guy—or the next woman—crawled in while the bed was still hot from the body heat of who'd been sleeping there before; and then came the third shift, so the beds never really had a chance to cool off.

In Sis's plant there were whole families—father, son, children—they had to be old enough to work; they weren't kids. She met one family from Arkansas—father, mother, five children—and they had come to Detroit once before in the '30s. Their farm had been foreclosed, so they became Arkies, but instead of going to California, they came to Detroit. These people worked two shifts; they had two different jobs, not in the same factory. They would work eight hours and then go to another plant and work another eight hours, then they would sleep eight hours. And then during the next twenty-four hours they would repeat the process. Anyhow, they had been to Detroit earlier and had accumulated, by working their asses off in this fashion, enough money to go back to Arkansas and buy their farm back. But in the five or six years after that, they again lost their farm. So here they were back in Detroit again, trying once more to earn enough money so they could carry it all back and get their farm back for the second time, and whether they ever did, I don't know.

On the *Times* I was a general reporter. I wrote a lot of features, but in the main I was the guy they sent out when some news break occurred. I covered murders, suicides, fires; I went along with the brass sent from Washington to visit and inspect the war plants. Just the general run of things that were going on. One of my jobs for a while was to look up and interview family members of war dead. They gave me a mimeographed list of material put out by the War Department—the marines, the army, the navy. (At this time it was mainly soldiers who were being killed.) These lists were made up and sent to areas wherever the killed-in-action or missing-in-action soldiers lived. They made up a list to be sent to Detroit, or to Chicago, or to New York; in other words, you didn't get a mass file of everybody in the United States who had been declared officially dead. Your list generally had on it five to seven names (after a major battle somewhere, maybe a couple dozen), and you had the name of the next of kin—father and mother usually—and their address.

So I would take this list from the *Times* (the other papers, the *Free Press* and the *News*, had them too) and go from address to address, getting little background stories—where they had gone to high school, what special things their parents remembered about them, and so on. Before you got hardened to it, it was a sensitive thing to do. The family was sad, people were crying; they would show you the toys these boys had played with as kids. In some instances the parents were Polish, maybe, and didn't know too much English; they couldn't express themselves so you could understand, and then you couldn't really get a story. Sometimes the best stories were from the younger brothers and sisters who remembered a great deal about their dead brother, had grown up with him—he had read or told them stories, had played games with them. They'd tell of his having been on the school football team and having scored a touchdown at such-and-such a crucial game.

The one incident that was the most tragic was when I went to one of these families one morning to get the story, only to find that the army had fucked up somewhere and the folks hadn't received their notice of the death of their son. Generally these lists were not sent out until the War Department, or the public relations people for the War Department, had first notified the next of kin—had sent a telegram three or four days or a week before they sent the list out to the newspapers. But somehow this family had not received its notification. I walked in. They asked me what I had in mind writing; everybody seemed happy and things were in their normal condition. Then they offered me coffee, and didn't seem to know what I wanted. I assumed the normal procedure had taken place and that they had received their notification; I just assumed that. So I blurted out something to the effect that I just wanted to get a story of the background of Roger, who had been killed. At that time the main battle casualties were coming from North Africa, as I remember, so the whole family went into shock—the father and the mother, a daughter of about eighteen, and some young kids. The mother became absolutely hysterical, this being their first word that their son had lost his life. She started screaming and weeping, and the father sat off in one corner, his head in his hands, and here I was embarrassed as hell, wishing I could just jump out the nearest window. But the oldest daughter sort of took over, she tried to calm them down, hugged and kissed her mother and put her arms around her father—she really got a grip on herself and told me the story of her brother.

The one thing I remember about that was her taking me upstairs to the room that had been his and showing me his things. His most prized possession had been his suits of clothes; he had about twenty or thirty suits in his closet, most of them nearly brand-new, just bought before he went into the army. When he got back, he was going to be one of the best-dressed boys in Detroit, I suppose. I was never able to get over that. I was cursing the goddamn fucked-up army; cursing myself for not having felt them out beforehand. But there hadn't really been any reason to; here I'd been carrying on this routine for months without ever running into anything like this. As I remember, the family was Polish; there were a lot of Polish boys from Detroit in the army.

I remember getting hell from the city editor once. Somebody had called up the *Times* and given them the name of a young person who was working in a garage and had just come back from Guadalcanal as a war hero, full of decorations and full of exploits; he had killed—Christ—thirty, forty, or fifty Japanese single-handed, a real 100-percent genuine hero. They sent me out on that story, and I met the guy; he talked and talked about all his exploits, and I wrote them down. I wrote a big long story, which was printed. We even had a photographer along at the time, and had a picture of this great hero in the paper, and I had a byline on it. Two or three days later somebody called up the paper and said the whole thing was a hoax; the guy had never been in the army, in fact he'd never been out of Detroit as far as anybody knew. His friends were laughing about it; they really hoaxed me. So the city editor sure ate my ass out. But I reflected on it awhile. It really didn't make that much difference to me, it was a great story and the purpose was to build up patriotism: fight for your country, go out there and duplicate this cat. Kill off half the Japanese army and we'd be that much further ahead, and if the hoax served that purpose, I don't see that there was too much wrong with it. I don't know about a lot of these other stories I wrote, whether they were 100-percent factual or not. To me it didn't seem to make that much difference, but there was shame at the *Times*, all through the city room, and the blame was on me for having been such a stupid idiot as to fall for such a hoax.

A little more background on the *Times:* The *Detroit Times*, which is now long defunct—they went out of business in the middle '50s—was a Hearst paper. I don't know whether it was a typical Hearst paper or not, but old man Hearst was still alive in those days. On the city editor's desk they had a spike; they spiked various kinds of news, but they had a special spike from Hearst, who always signed his telegrams "Chief." And whatever came in there from the Chief, everybody had to get out onto it. There was a lot of bigotry on the *Times*. The city editor, for instance, never used the word "Negro"—it was "nigger." When he spoke of Italians it was "the guineas." When he spoke of Jews it was "the Hebes." And "Polacks," of course, for Polish people. It permeated the staff.

One of the photographers, in fact probably the best photographer they had on the paper, was a Jewish guy, Arnold Freeman, and the others on the staff continually harassed him. They'd make swastikas or signs calling him a "Jewboy" and paste them where he couldn't miss them, above the developing tank in the darkroom where he used to get his pictures ready for the paper. I remember once they had tacked up a poem that was being widely circulated in the war plants in Detroit by fascist elements. And there were plenty of them there; Detroit was the gathering point, simply because it *was* the arsenal of democracy. This poem, as I remember, was mimeographed and spread around to try to hurt the morale of the workers, and they posted a copy of it up at the *Times* for the benefit of this Jewish photographer. It objected to the way in which the workers were urged to stay on the job, "don't slow up the job, keep steadily on the job, the war effort needs every ounce of your time and strength." And it went something like this: "Shit in your pants and piss in your shoes, and win the war for the Goddamn Jews."

The practice in covering stories was that the photographers had cars, and in almost every instance covering a story, they would send out a photographer and a reporter as a team; the two would go together, and the photographer got a certain fee for the use of his car—so many cents a mile. Sometimes Freeman and I would go out on stories, and I had expressed my opposition to anti-Semitism; he knew I was against it and considered it an abomination and a weapon of the fascist enemy. He used to cry about these things when he and I were out in the car driving to cover some story. I used to try to buck him up, telling him, "Just do your job—look, it's everywhere, I don't know how the hell you can stop it. You might wreck the fucking *Times*, but I don't see what purpose it would serve—you'd be out of a job." I tried to buck him up with some ridiculous ideas of my own, because I didn't have any really effective ones.

I didn't like the *Times*. I didn't like the atmosphere in which I was working. But it was the old story: you have to pay the rent, buy enough groceries to keep going, gotta have shoes on your feet, especially in Detroit in wintertime because it gets colder than hell there. It did in those days—maybe it's warmed up now. Just keep working, plugging away. Freeman shared my contempt for the *Times*, so we didn't hesitate to fuck off on a story. Once we were assigned to go out in a snowstorm way up north into Michigan—into the thumb, as I remember it. The job was supposed to take all day, to drive up there and get a story. But it was snowing, one of those freezing winds blowing. So we started out, and then we stopped in at a bar about three blocks from the *Times* to sort of think it over, and I told him, "Look, let me call up this guy on the phone we're supposed to interview three hundred miles away. Let me call him up and see if I can get a story from him on the phone, a passable story." So I put a call through and managed to get ahold of this guy, and I talked quite a while with him, took a lot of notes, and got a good story out of him on the phone. I went back and told Arnold, "Look, I got a story that'll hold up, and I got a lot of dialogue, me talking to him, right on the scene, so what we got to do is figure out about photographs." So we figured out we would tell the picture editor that it was snowing so hard up there that the camera froze up and that the pictures were no good.

We spent the whole day in the bar drinking up; I got pretty stoned on boilermakers. We waited till after dark and then reported back to the *Times*. The city editor had gone home; the night editor was in charge, and he wasn't such a bad guy. I typed out my story and we told him about how awful the trip had been—icy roads, we almost cracked up several times, had a hell of a time making it, and we went into this rigmarole about how Arnold was afraid his pictures were no good but he would go in to develop them. So he went in the darkroom, stayed in there about a half-hour, came out and said, "Nothing." There was absolutely nothing. So Scott said, "Okay, we'll use the story without the pictures." So we did that, and I don't think anybody was ever the wiser that we'd spent a warm afternoon in that bar. Stayed out of the freezing cold, that much we did.

I was kind of outspoken in my liberal—I considered them radical—views. In the *Times* city room I went too far, and at one point one of the older reporters, Ed Brand, told me that the city editor had offered him a tidy bonus if he'd beat the shit out of "that nigger lover Friesen." That's what he called me, "nigger lover." It so happened that Brand and I—I don't think he could have done it, he was twice as old as I was—were in a bar and had quite a few drinks, ate a lot of those boiled eggs they gave away, and he finally broke down and confessed that he had been asked to do this to me, and that he'd considered doing it for a while but finally decided that maybe he better not, so he told me about it. The editor had said, "Take a sock full o' shit and beat him to death." I don't know if you can beat anybody to death with a sock of full of shit—unless you add a rock or two to it.

The Chief (Hearst) had decided years before, I guess when he started his first newspaper, that stories about animals would sell. People love animals, they're sympathetic to animals—they see a newspaper with a story about an animal in it, they'll buy it, and circulation will shoot up. So we had this special thing going on with animals. I was sent out on a story about a dog. Somebody's dog had got out on a board floating in the river, and people were trying to save him, and there was no way to save him, he was in a raging current or some goddamn thing carrying him farther and farther from shore. This was also some distance from Detroit, and again, a snowstorm was blowing, and it was probably a couple of hundred miles we had to go, so we stopped in at that same bar, as I remember, to think it out.

The photographer remembered a friend of his who lived only two or three miles outside Detroit—maybe ten miles out—and had a dog, and there was a pond on this guy's place, so we figured well, maybe we could go out there and do something—we didn't think we could get by twice without pictures, so we drove out there. He was a good old buddy. We told him what we had in mind and he agreed to it. There was a broken-up door lying there that had been taken out of the house and replaced and wasn't fit for any other purpose, so it had been thrown in the weeds. We got his dog and put it in the middle of the door and tied him to it (tied a string around his neck and what was left of the doorknob) so that he wouldn't fall off and drown. And then we tied quite a long piece of cord to the door, and with the dog on this door we pushed it out into the pond, holding onto the string so it wouldn't get away. The snow was coming down pretty heavy. We floated him out twelve or fifteen feet from shore while Arnold shot some photographs of him, making sure that he got him in the middle of the snow flurries. He got some good photographs this way. So then we pulled the dog back to shore and turned him loose, thanked the friend, had a few drinks together, warmed up and had some coffee. By this time the dog was in the kitchen with us nice and warm; he'd been a little scared, puzzled about what the hell we were trying to do with him. Maybe he thought he was going to float away forever. The dog was happy, we were happy, Arnold was sure his pictures would come out.

So then we went back to our favorite bar, and I wrote up a story. I made it quite brief: the project had been a failure. Tragedy had terminated the whole pitiful incident; raging water had carried the dog off beyond all hope of rescue—carried him off into the dim distance where we couldn't see him any longer, but Arnold had managed to snap a few pictures of him just before the current carried him off into oblivion. It was a very sad story. The dog was gone. Of course, there wasn't much else to write about, except that the expedition had been a failure and one of the animals William Randolph Hearst loved so much had been lost. I imagine even that sold newspapers, because tragedies always sell newspapers, and here we had a double feature: man's best friend ending up in a tragedy. Incidentally, we never did learn what happened to the *real* dog. We didn't fake things too often—and anyway, there were much more serious examples of journalistic faking going on.

The United Auto Workers (UAW) were news; they couldn't be avoided. They had a lot of conventions, meetings, dinners, and luncheons where some union leader would address them. And the photographers assigned to these stories were instructed to line up the delegates or the committee members, whoever was in top echelons—to rearrange them quite innocently, not to let anybody get wise. Line them up and tell them that this would make a better story or picture: "*You* stand there, *you* stand there, *you* stand there, move up a little bit, move a little bit closer." And they would always arrange it in such a way that the black delegates were on the ends of the lines. Then when they developed and printed the picture, they would crop them off and have the lily-white group standing in the middle. So if there are any black leaders in Detroit who wondered why they never appeared in any pictures taken by the *Times*, this is the explanation for it.

Photographers are always trying to get action into a story. During the Detroit race riots, a few minutes before midnight on Sunday, June 21, 1943, I checked into the city room. I was assigned to the police beat, covering the midnight shift, and it was routine to stop by and consult with the night editor before continuing on to the central police headquarters, which was within walking distance of the *Times* building in downtown Detroit. Sometimes reporters on the day side sent in stuff that needed following up.

That night the day side had left nothing of consequence. As I was about to leave, Jack Manning, publisher of the *Times*, came into the newsroom. It was a rare thing to see him there at that time of the night. "What have you got from Belle Isle?" he asked the night editor.

"Nothing, not a thing. What's up?"

Manning had visited friends in Grosse Pointe, and returning had just driven by the mainland terminus of the bridge leading to Belle Isle, a public park and recreation center in the Detroit River. "Something's happening out there," Manning said. "Police cars all over the place. A big crowd milling around. I stopped to ask a policeman. It's some kind of race trouble. It could be big."

"We'll get right on it," the night editor said, motioning with a jerk of his head for me to get started.

Early that morning my photographer friend and I were out covering the situation on Cass Avenue, outside the black ghetto, only a block or two from Woodward Avenue. We were there when smallish white mobs were beginning to roam the streets on the fringes of the ghetto. That's not too far from the main street, which is Hastings Street, and there were a dozen or so white boys, eighteen or twenty, bunched up on the sidewalk near a car with five or six black workers in it on their way to their jobs in the war plant. This was happening all over Detroit that morning to black workers who hadn't had time to listen to the radio, who'd had to hurry and get breakfast, get together in their car pool and start to work, and who were completely unaware that this so-called race riot was going on and had been going on since one or two o'clock in the morning. Well, a photographer told these boys, "Look, here comes some niggers. Stop 'em." And so they ran out in the street holding up their hands for the car to stop. They began to tear at the doors; the blacks, although they didn't exactly know why, sensed they were in danger; they were being attacked for some reason. They jumped out and got away, ran away as fast they could, back towards the black ghetto from where they had come. So the photographer didn't get a good picture.

Here he was, camera all ready, and all there was was an abandoned car sitting in the street. He wanted action, so he told his boys, "Let's get some action in the picture; tip the damn thing over." So they all got on one side and heaved, and tipped it over on its side; he took a picture of that, but he still wasn't satisfied. When they turned the car over, the cap on the gas tank jarred loose and gasoline ran out under the car on the pavement. Another bright idea occurred to this photographer. He told the boys, "Put a match to it." So the boys put a match to it, and the whole thing was in flames, black smoke rolling up—it could be seen for blocks. So he got real action pictures out of this burning car. This was the first car set afire during those riots, and within an hour there were cars burning all up and down Woodward Avenue, set afire obviously by people who got the idea from seeing this one burning, the black smoke billowing up. Many blacks escaped from these burning cars on Woodward. Some of them didn't; they were dragged out and either beaten mercilessly or actually killed.

There was the case of a man with an ice truck on Woodward Avenue, and he handed out three or four hundred ice picks to whites, encouraging them to "kill niggers." One young black man was dragged out of his car and pulled behind a beer sign on Woodward Avenue and stabbed to death with these ice picks. They said he had 250 ice pick holes in him. It was an indication of the frenzy of the white mobs. This victim, too, was innocent. He had driven innocently into what turned out to be a trap without being fully aware of what was going on and how serious the rioting had become.

The day of June 22, 1943, lengthened, and there was no abatement of the violence. It became obvious that federal troops would have to be sent into Detroit. President Roosevelt then signed, and Secretary of War Henry L. Stimson issued, a proclamation placing the city of Detroit under the jurisdiction of the United States Army. At the sight of jeeploads of steel-helmeted federal troops with bayoneted rifles beside them rolling down Woodward Avenue, the white mobs melted away and disappeared. In Paradise Valley, Roosevelt's soldiers were greeted by the black people as liberators. I rode with a small convoy of federal troops on an inspection tour along Hastings Street the next day. The convoy stopped several times, and the soldiers got out of their trucks to stand in line on the curb, rifles down at their sides, while the commanding officer inspected the ravaged stores. I'll never forget the black crowds who gathered to greet these white soldiers at every stop—men, women, and children, many of the women with tears of relief on their cheeks.

Chapter 8

Sis and Gordon Following World War II

Oh, the people of Greece,
 they only wanted peace
And a chance to build their lives in their own way
But the Wall Street bankers said,
 "We'd rather see them dead"
And so the Truman Doctrine was born that evil day.
 Oh, we don't want that Truman Doctrine;
 take it away, take it away

("That Truman Doctrine, Take It Away," words by Sis Cunningham,
late 1940s, ©1990)

Gordon applied for a job with the Office of War Information, and
we came back to New York in May 1944. I had our first kid very
quickly after that. Aggie was born the next January.

I was happy that we were going to have a baby, but I got restless
by the fourth month of the pregnancy and decided I had to do something besides housework. I got a part-time job stuffing envelopes in
an office down near Canal Street and rode the subway to work all
the way from East Eighty-fourth, where we lived. I worked for two
months, and one night on the way home I nearly collapsed on the
subway and was barely able to drag myself home from the station. I
was hemorrhaging by the time I got there. The doctor ordered me to
bed, where I stayed for two months; I couldn't even get up to go to
the bathroom. A friend helped with the bedpan and bringing me
food until my mother arrived from Oklahoma. We had no medical
insurance and could not think of hospitalization; home nursing care
was also out of the question.

While I was laid up I had spells of drifting quite far away from
reality. I guess you could call what I had a daydream repeater, but it

wasn't in the day, it was at night while Gordon was slogging away on the graveyard shift at the OWI. At these times it seemed to me we were doing very well financially and we had a house out in the country. Gordon was writing novels again, he had found a steady publisher, his books were selling, and he would climb right on up, there was no doubt about that. We'd have this baby and one or two more. My dream was of these children playing happily with their sleds in the woodsy space around our house. It was always winter in this dream, with snow on the ground and the sound of the wind in the trees, and there was a delicious warmth inside the very large beam-ceilinged room that was the main room of the house. Halfway up along one side, there was a balcony with two or three bedrooms opening off of it, and underneath these a big old country kitchen with a wood-burning range in the middle of one wall. I don't recall any visions of this house in a summer setting, which is rather funny—strange, I should say—since I have no love for northern winters when I am in control of my likes and dislikes and not fantasizing. It could be that the winter of the fantasy was the cold, hard world that I had finally managed to overcome—my children were safe, and all they had to do was open the door and they'd be inside in that all-enveloping warmth of the big, homey room. That is just a guess at the meaning of the fantasy, if indeed it had any special hidden meaning, which I doubt. But while I stayed in bed I indulged in it many times, and all I have to do now is close my eyes and I can see that house and feel the warmth of it.

The really funny thing about this experience is that I actually had myself fooled. I remember feeling pretty certain that we would be able to move up into such a cushiony life. The pregnancy was doing strange things to my brain. The aberration could have been the workings of body chemistry; or it may simply have grown from a strong reach toward a secure life for the child I was going to have. I had gone through a checkerboard existence myself for thirty-five years; now I was having a baby—that is if I could tough out the rest of the pregnancy—and things had changed.

They hadn't, of course. True, we were going through a period of feeling good about our prospects; at least, I was. I really felt that Gordon was doing something he liked to do, and he fitted into the job well—it suited him and he suited it. And we *were* glad to be having a kid. But I didn't discuss my middle-class vision with Gordon. There was something that caused me to hold back on that, an inkling of just how maudlin it would seem to him; so I kept it to myself. Maybe the thing that put a break on my dream more than anything else was the loud singing and heiling of Hitler in the German beer garden across the fence from our yard. We lived in the ground-floor apartment of a building in Yorkville, then the Germantown of New York City. Our neighbors were mostly of Nazi orientation, and come evening they pulled out all the stops. Their fanatical vociferations kept me fully aware that a world war was still going on. Gordon slept in the daytime, since he worked nights. And after I was put to bed, most of my sleeping was done in the daytime also. And though they closed the beer garden quite early on week nights, I lay listening to all that racket as long as it lasted. Gordon would be home Saturday nights, and we both listened to it, feeling kind of like two people marooned on an island in shark-infested waters. "Sieg Heil! Sieg Heil! Sieg Heil!" At about two in the morning it got really bad.

I was allowed to get out of bed during my ninth month. The condition causing the threat of miscarriage had stabilized, but I could barely creep around. Mama did most of the housework. I walked to the store a few times for groceries, mainly for some air, but that's about all.

Aggie was born healthy, but she was the sleepiest baby they'd ever had, the nurses said. The doctor said that was because I had been so inactive during the last lap of the pregnancy. The war was just about over. The people in the neighborhood were bitter and moody over how bad things were going for their side. Some of them got a lift in April when Roosevelt died; there was a short spurt of noticeable increase in the commotion in the beer garden back of us.

There were still a lot of job openings for women in offices, and by the time the baby was two months old I got restless and took a full-time job. Mama agreed to stay, and she kept one eye open on the baby night and day. I went to work but wasn't strong enough to stick it out; I had to quit after a few weeks. So Mama went back to Oklahoma and I became a full-time housewife.

We began to try to get out of that crazy neighborhood. V-E Day came in May, and the war was the next thing to being over as far as the people around us were concerned—they were subdued now—but we hated the place. I spent all the time I could looking for an apartment. Gordon got up around noon and took over the baby, and I would start out, picking a different neighborhood every day. I went all over Manhattan; I saw a nice place once in a while, but all were too expensive. I saw horrible places, couldn't think of taking a baby into them. We answered dozens of ads by telephone—already taken.

In the fall the people who owned the old house we lived in wanted it back in a hurry so they could live there. The man was an army captain, and there was a ruling that if an army man owned a house and had rented it out for the duration, he could have it back for the asking. We thought something was up; he had not renewed our lease when it expired in September, right after V-J Day. We got a warning to vacate and then an official eviction notice, the first of three we were to get in New York. Gordon and I took the baby and went to city court to try to get a stay of eviction, but we couldn't swing it. So Gordon's coworker at the OWI vacated his one-room kitchenette apartment in the Village to make way for us. We hadn't known this fellow very long, and looking back over our experience in New York City, it seems nothing short of amazing what he was willing to do for us; he had to move into a rooming house.

Gordon was still working at the OWI, but he had only a short time left in which to submit a reply to the Civil Service loyalty rating questionnaire he'd received. The thing couldn't be replied to, of course; it was never meant to be replied to. Those things were drawn up as ultimatums; they've got you, so get lost. Disappear. Go up with the smoke. And they meant the family along with the breadwinner. However, it turned out that our time had not yet come, although HUAC (House Un-American Activities Committee) had been in action since 1938. Gordon was able, after a short delay, to go right on with what he had been doing, only this time at a CBS office. The government had subcontracted CBS to do some of the same short-wave radio broadcasting in which OWI was engaged. (The principle target here was South America, though there were certain European desks translating into French and other languages).

FBI Interview with Gordon Friesen, March 27, 1945, in New York Field Division Office:

Mr. Friesen, we have requested your voluntary appearance here today, not for the purpose of conducting a hearing but in order that you may answer questions concerning an investigation currently being made by the Federal Bureau of Investigation and to enable you to make such comments as you might wish concerning this inquiry. You may decline to answer any of the questions propounded to you. As you may be aware, the Federal Bureau of Investigation is required by Presidential Directive to investigate matters coming within the purview of Public Law No. 252, 76th Congress. This law prohibits membership on the part of any Federal employee in a political party or organization which advocates the overthrow of our constitutional form of government in the United States. A copy of the report of this investigation, which will include your statement, will be furnished the Interdepartmental Committee on Employee Investigations and the agency by which you are employed. After the notes of this interview have been transcribed, you will be given an opportunity to read them making such changes as you may desire. In order that the statements made by you may have particular credence, you will be placed under oath if you have no objection.

Q. What is your full name?

A. GORDON ELMER FRIESEN.

Q. What is your present title and position?

A. Well, my present title is Script Editor with the Master Radio Desk in the Office of War Information.

Q. What is your local address?

A. 353 East 84th Street, New York City.

Q. Are you at the present time a member of the Communist Political Association?

A. I am not.

Q. Have you ever been a member of the Communist Political Association?

A. I have not.

Q. Have you ever been a member of the Communist Party?

A. No.

Q. Have you ever attended meetings of the Communist Political Association or Communist Party?

A. I have attended several meetings of the Communist—I have never attended any meetings of the Communist Political Association. I have attended several meetings of the Communist Party. Yes, Sir.

Q. Can you tell us the date of the last meeting of the Communist Party you attended?

A. I don't recall exactly the date. I once attended the Communist Party meeting at Madison Square Garden. I think it was the—I'm sure it was the fall of 1942. I remember there was snow falling so it must have been late in 1942. I don't recall, but I think Mr. BROWDER spoke, but I don't remember exactly if he did.

Q. How many meetings of the Communist Party have you attended?

A. Well, I attended a meeting. I don't recall whether it was a Communist Party meeting or an event staged by the "Daily Worker," in

Detroit in the summer or fall of 1942, at a place called Graystone Gardens, I think. It was around the corner from where I lived at the time. In both instances they were open meetings and I was, I wanted to see what was going on.

Q. Are those the only two occasions at which you attended any Communist Party meetings?

A. They are the only occasions I can recall offhand. In the spring of 1941, I think it was the latter part of March, I went to Oklahoma City from my hometown in Weatherford, Oklahoma, in the western part of the state, to become chairman of what is known as the Political Prisoners Committee in order to do publicity work and help in the defense of, well they were, I think there were nine people charged with their criminal syndicalism. Four of them were tried. In each instance each either admitted or it was fairly well proved that they were members of the Communist Party. One of them was openly the State Secretary of the Communist Party in Oklahoma.

But the charge was, well the principle for which I came to their defense, there were very few people in Oklahoma who would do it, was that of selling books. They sold MARXIST literature, as well as a lot of other stuff. The Oklahoma County Police, if I remember right, confiscated—the Oklahoma County Sheriff confiscated some ten thousand books, and I went to their defense and became Chairman of the Political Prisoners Committee.

Q. What was the entire name of that committee?

A. I think that is the entire name of it, the Oklahoma Political Prisoners Committee.

Q. Was that connected with the National Committee for the Defense of Political Prisoners?

A. No, it was purely a local committee.

Q. What was your interest in this committee, Mr. FRIESEN?

A. Well I had what I considered more or less of a liberal background, and before I assumed this position, which took me before the public eye as chairman of this committee, I went into it rather thoroughly and the issue to me did not seem to be one of Communism at all. The people who were prosecuting this case there had a book burning in which a certain Dr. WEBER of Oklahoma City, a radio preacher, conducted a book burning. I forget where in the hell it was, but it was out on Eastern Avenue in Oklahoma City in rodeo grounds or something, and his forces raided this book store which the Communists ran on East Grand Avenue and piled his books up and set fire to them. Well, in my mind it was exactly and precisely the same damn thing that was happening in Berlin. The books which were burnt, were burned, were by the same authors and same titles, and I looked further into it and this Dr. WEBER who was conducting the G—— d—— thing had the background of the Silver Shirts in California, had been associated with the Party, and the guy who was pressing the charges was an Assistant County Attorney by the name of JOHN GIBBERLY, who was connected with the Coughlinites, who in my mind along with Dr. WEBER were trying to institute Fascism into countries which were interrelated, and not a question of Communism at all but a question of Fascism.

Q. Were you compensated for your activity in that committee?

A. I was not compensated to any great degree, no.

Q. By whom were you paid for the compensation you did receive?

A. The committee appealed for funds in order to carry on the defense, and from these funds I received enough to just keep alive. There was no set sum whatsoever. I wrote a pamphlet for them.

Q. What was the title of this pamphlet?

A. The name was "Oklahoma Witch Hunt."

Q. Did you receive any payment resulting from the sale of that pamphlet?

A. Well, I received a certain sum for writing it. It was considered more or less freelance work on my part.

Q. By whom were you reimbursed?

A. I was reimbursed from funds taken in by the Oklahoma Political Prisoners Committee. We had a number of contributors in the bulk of the state of Oklahoma. People who were afraid to get out in the public eye and make their names known, but were prepared to contribute funds in order to carry on the work we were doing, which they were convinced was a defense of the American Bill of Rights, the violation of which in this case might ultimately lead to Fascism.

Q. Have you ever registered to vote as a member of the Communist Party?

A. No, I have not.

Q. Did you ever sign a petition for Communist Party candidates?

A. I don't recall that I ever did. During that time in Oklahoma, I was answering your question, I did attend a number of Communist Party meetings because people we were fighting for were Communists and I wanted to find out what in the h—— they were up to and so forth. I don't recall where, but I did attend several of them.

Q. Did you distribute any Communist literature?

A. No, I never did.

Q. Have you ever written any Communist literature?

A. No, I never have. However, I wrote this pamphlet called the "Oklahoma Witch Hunt" to which I signed my name, and which I was thoroughly convinced was the right thing to do at the time, and which I am still convinced was right.

Q. Do you have anything further to say concerning the questions I put to you? Any statement you would like to put on record?

A. Well, I think I pretty well stated my position, at least during that particular period, and it is added because of the convictions I held before I went to Oklahoma City to take up the defense of the Communists, and convictions which I maintained ever since. In fact, I quit a secure job in Detroit and turned down more money in order to come to New York City and work for the Office of War Information for basically the same convictions. The whole thing is a fight against Fascism, and somebody's got to do it.

I would like to add, the Oklahoma fight was all four of these people were convicted in very short order. However, the Oklahoma State Court of Criminal Appeals reversed these convictions on virtually the same grounds on which we fought for them. I think they were exactly or more or less the same. All four of them are free at the time. Two of them are in the Army, one of them in France, and the third one, there were three men and one woman, Mr. and Mrs. ROBERT WOOD, ELI JAFFEY and ALAN SHAW. JAFFEY and WOOD are both in the Army. WOOD is in France. SHAW was registered as a psycho-neurotic 4-F because he made the mistake of taking his examination in Oklahoma where the old prejudices still apparently played a dominant part in his case. Otherwise, I think he would have been in the Army for the past sixteen months. The point I was trying to make was that the Oklahoma Court of Appeals upheld the same things I was in their employment for.

April 10, 1945—I have never in my life advocated the overthrow of the U.S. Government by force and violence nor have I ever belonged to any organization advocating such.—Gordon Friesen.

Selections from Gordon's United States Civil Service Commission Interrogatory, August 14, 1945 (unanswered):

Q. If you were employed by the Oklahoma Committee to Defend Political Prisoners, please explain why this employment was not included on your civil service application, Form 57.

Q. The Commission has received information to the effect that in September 1941 a student at Central High School, Oklahoma City, was apprehended distributing to students of said school copies of the "Oklahoma Story," and the "Sunday Worker"; that upon being questioned, said student admitted having received this literature for distribution from one Gordon E. Friesen of Room 300, Saving Building, Oklahoma City; and that said student admitted further that said Gordon E. Friesen had instructed him at length in the doctrine of Communism. Since you were reported to have been employed, or actively engaged in the activities which emanated from Room 300 (formerly Room 600), Saving Building, Oklahoma City, what comment do you care to make regarding this information received by the Commission?

Q. The Commission has received information to the effect that in August 1941 you held yourself out to be Secretary of the American People's Mobilization. Please state the dates of your membership in the American People's Mobilization; the dates of your office as Secretary of this organization, as well as any other offices held by you therein; and your understanding of the aims and purposes of the American People's Mobilization.

Q. The Commission has received information to the effect that various of your residences at New York City were used as the headquarters of the Almanac Singers; that you were a member of the Almanac Singers, and occasionally appeared with this group as a singer; that the activities of the Almanac Singers were lauded highly on numerous occasions by the Daily Worker, official Communist Party newspaper; and that during your residence at 647 Hudson Street, New York City, from June to December 1942, the Almanac Singers, with headquarters at this address, received occasional checks from the Daily Worker, which checks were endorsed by you prior to having been cashed or negotiated. Please explain the arrangements under which your various residences at New York City were used as a headquarters for the Almanac Singers.

Q. In an article in the Daily Worker of March 28, 1942, there appeared an advance notice of a "Kansas Barn Dance for Earl Browder" which was to be held the following evening at 430 Sixth Avenue, New York City. Since this was your residence at that time, please state whether or not you attended this barn dance, either as a paying guest, or as a member of the Almanac Singers; and what connection, if any, was the location of said barn dance with your apartment at 430 Sixth Avenue.

Q. The Commission has received information to the effect that on August 20, 1943, you were in attendance at a meeting of the Midtown Communist Club, held in your apartment at 460 Prentiss Street, Detroit, Michigan; that on September 3, 1943, you were present at a functionaries meeting of the Communist Party held at Schiller Hall, Detroit, at which meeting prominent Communists, including Patrick Toohey, Secretary of the Communist Party of District No. 7 for the State of Michigan, were principal speakers; and that on September 5, 1943, you attended the Annual Communist Picnic held at Horvath Park, near Detroit, at which picnic William Z. Foster, then Chairman of the National Committee of the Communist Party, United States of America, and recently chosen new head of the Communist Party of the United States, was the principal speaker. What comment do you care to make?

Q. The Commission has received information to the effect that there exists a copy of a "Branch Transfer into the Community Club," Number 716, reflecting that Gordon Friesen, then residing at 460 Prentiss, Detroit, Michigan, was being transferred into the Midtown Communist Club; that said transfer indicated further that Gordon Friesen formerly had been a member of Branch 5, Section 9, of District 7, of the Communist Party; and that said Gordon Friesen had joined the Communist Party in 1941.

What comment do you care to make concerning the allegation that Gordon Friesen, formerly at 460 Prentiss, Detroit, Michigan, had joined the Communist Party in 1941?

Q. The Commission has received information to the effect that on November 14, 1943, you were observed selling the "Worker" and "The Soviet Power" in front of the premises wherein the American-Soviet Friendship Rally was in progress. Please state your interest in, or activities in behalf of the American-Soviet Friendship Rally, if any.

Q. The Commission has received information to the effect that on January 9, 1944, you attended a meeting of the Midtown Communist Club, held at the Twelve Horseman Civic Center, which meeting was called for the purpose of nominating officers for the ensuing year; that you were nominated to the War Activities and the Legislative Committees; that on January 23, 1944, you attended another meeting of the Midtown Communist Club, held at the Twelve Horseman Civic Center, which meeting was for the purpose of electing officers to serve during the ensuing year; and that you were elected as Chairman of the Legislative Committee of the Midtown Communist Club, as well as to membership of the Executive Committee at Large of said Club.

Please state the dates of your offices as Chairman of the Legislative Committee and as member of the Executive Committee at Large of the Midtown Communist Club.

Please explain in detail the duties involved in connection with your offices as Chairman of the Legislative Committee and as member of the Executive Committee at Large of the Midtown Communist Club, as well as the extent of your activities in connection with said offices.

Q. The Commission has received information to the effect that on

May 4, 1944, at the State Convention of the Communist Party, District 7, held at Jericho Temple, Detroit, Michigan, one Gordon Friesen, as a representative of the Midtown Communist Club of Detroit, was in possession of regular delegate's credentials signed by one Agnes Cunningham as Executive Secretary of the Midtown Communist Club; and that said credentials indicated that Gordon Friesen, 35 years of age, and a newspaperman by occupation, then had been a member of the Communist Party for three years.

Were you an official delegate from the Midtown Communist Club to the State Convention of the Communist Party, District 7, held at the Jericho Temple, Detroit, Michigan, on May 4, 1944? If so, please explain in detail the extent of your participation in said convention, whether or not you were appointed to any committee, the nature of your services thereon, etc.

What relation to you, if any, is the Agnes Cunningham, referred to above, who, as Executive Secretary of the Midtown Communist Club, signed the delegate's credentials issued to Gordon Friesen on the occasion of the State Convention of the Communist Party, District 7, held at Jericho Temple, Detroit, on May 4, 1944?

Q. Have you been a member of the Communist Political Association of the Communist Party at New York City since your return from Detroit in May 1944? If so, please state the dates of such membership, the dates and titles of any offices held by you therein, and the extent of your activities therewith.

Q. Are you now, or have you ever been a member of any group, organization, or association which has had affiliation with any Communist, Fascist, or Nazi organizations, or of any group or organization whatsoever which advocated the overthrow of the constitutional form of government in the United States? If your answer is in the affirmative, please state the name or names of the organization or organizations, the dates of your membership therein, and the extent of your association therewith.

Please note hereon any comments you desire to make regarding your loyalty to the United States of America which you feel would aid the Commission in determining your suitability for Federal employment.

NOTE: THIS INSTRUMENT MUST BE NOTARIZED.

We now lived on the Upper West Side in a three-room furnished apartment. We had gotten no furniture of our own except a crib for Aggie, which we brought into the new place. When we got settled a friend gave us an old piano—which was a damn good thing, because the old restlessness at not having a job where I could earn some money was creeping up on me again, and to ease it I would sit down at that old piano and pound away. The upper two octaves were untuneable, and several keys stuck, but I was happy to have it. I knew it would be foolish to try to do anything but babysit; I wouldn't be able to stay with a regular job. I had to be satisfied that Gordon had a steady job.

The Communist Party was trying hard to regenerate itself after being knocked to pieces by Browderism during the war. It wasn't a political association any more, it was the Communist Party again, and a system of street branches had been resumed. I went to some of the branch meetings, but I took on no special tasks except to lead a discussion now and then. Old Sol Devine was out there selling *Daily Workers*, or *Weekly Workers*, or whatever the paper happened to be at any given time; he would be given a fountain pen or some such reward now and then for selling more papers than everybody else put together. As I remember, Gordon helped with leaflets, both the writing and the distribution of them, and it was around this time that he first got into American Labor Party work—not a chance of our dropping out altogether. Not a chance, even though I remember suffering from chronic stomach trouble that took my weight down to around one hundred pounds again, and on doctor's orders I had to give up coffee—didn't drink a drop for three years. I hated that. Coffee was a mainstay and a fortifier of us old activists and Almanacs. Very few of us drank anything stronger. Now I couldn't even drink that.

I mainly functioned as a housewife during this time, but I did try to keep in touch with the topical-song movement, led by People's Songs, and then a little later on, People's Artists. Between babies I had tried to get back to writing songs and singing, and I managed to get three paid bookings through People's Songs and People's Artists, plus a couple on my own. As for the money, I took in around one hundred dollars over a period of three years. I played at benefits for small struggling unions, Labor Party affairs, fund-raising for this and that radical organization. The ones that paid were with Pete Seeger and Bernie Asbell in Atlantic City at a Fur and Leather Workers convention, and two concerts upstate with Cisco Houston, Bernie, Betty Sanders, and Charlotte Anthony. I sang gratis at Henry Wallace rallies in the months before the 1948 presidential election. Nobody saw much of Woody. He was on the drift, and later we knew that the symptoms of his disease, Huntington's Chorea, had already set in.

He tried to settle down from time to time, and we received a mimeographed songbook autographed for us, which he had put together all by himself, music notes written out and everything. This was around the time he wrote "This Land Is Your Land," and that was one of the songs in the book. I saw Woody at a couple of People's Artists hoots; he was performing, but he kept his large, black loose-leaf notebook in front of him on a music stand, constantly referring to it as though he wasn't able to memorize any of his lyrics.

I remember one of those programs especially. I'd been asked to sing, and I waited backstage till 1 A.M. before I came on, and then I was told to sing only one song—make it short. I had a feeling that they were doing to me what they'd done to Aunt Molly Jackson a few years earlier. The city folk singers took over, especially if we country singers specialized in content rather than in performing technique. Let me put it this way: the city folk singers were going in for showmanship, a lot of them. City audiences liked that and responded to it. It began to be more important *how* you sang than *what* you sang about. Lyrics weren't noticed as much as the skill with which a performer accompanied himself. (Political movements of the 1960s snapped folk audiences back to listening to lyrics—for a time.)

The singing phase of my life came to a slow, painful end during this period—I mean singing on bookings. The best-paid bookings were taken by those who could stay with the work steadily and make a sort of career out of it. I was one of those who could not make steady work of it. So during the peak period of People's Artists I was seldom called on for anything except benefits. I gradually fell out of touch. My accordion got heavier and heavier. I wasn't getting paid. Besides, I didn't like some of the folks around People's Artists; they were overbearing and pushy, and I got the idea that just about everybody was trying to grab off the good bookings instead of following the stated policy of giving all the members a chance. I didn't like them, and they didn't even like each other; groups seemed to hang together only because they thought they stood a better chance of making it that way.

One of the groups with roots in the Almanacs and People's Songs did make it pretty big until the members' backgrounds finally caught up with them, and that group was the Weavers. But to gain success they built their repertoire mostly from traditional folk songs and shied away from current topical songs. They reworked a few topical songs to make them more acceptable to audiences who would be apt to attend their concerts. They did some great things, the Weavers. Some of them appeared with Paul Robeson in '49 at his Peeksill concert and got their heads pelted with rocks; they appeared as a group on the sound truck in the Vito Marcantonio mayoral campaign of the same year and got pelted with overripe tomatoes. But they did one thing they should never have done; they changed and twisted one of our most loved songs of all time, Woody Guthrie's "So Long, It's Been Good To Know You," just so some money-minded producer would accept it for recording purposes. (The version of this song most widely sung now is Woody's original one.)

About my sinking into silence, to say that it was painful is an understatement. I suffered deeply; I couldn't stop blaming myself. I felt I had failed. I went on for years under the cloud of failure, unable to sing, unable to write. My silence was total.

I got really stuck with housework for a while, so much so that to keep from going balmy I had to plan my days, the first time in my life I had ever done that with housework. I had to set up a weekly schedule for washing, cleaning, cooking, shopping, and caring for Aggie, who started walking before she was a year old and got increasingly demanding of my time and energy from then on. There were no laundromats at that time, and I had to wash our clothes in our tiny kitchen with its combination sink/washtub. Gordon's brother Ollie and his youngest sister Ruth came to live with us. We had two beds in the living room that they slept in, while Gordon and I and Aggie had the bedroom. Ollie was getting his "52–50" (fifty dollars a week for fifty-two weeks) after his discharge from the army. Ruthie worked first as an usherette in a neighborhood movie house and then as a salesgirl at Gimbels, both low-paid jobs. They gave me grocery money, and I shopped and cooked dinner for them. I had the baby full time, not knowing the women in the neighborhood well enough to arrange a baby exchange.

I was tired all the time, but I'll admit there was a kind of security to being nothing but a housewife, stultifying as it was, and I began to think seriously of trying to have another child. After all, it was no good to raise an only child, so I'd been led to believe. And I was stuck anyway. Ruth left, then Ollie left after about a year of being with us, and the schedule of housework loosened considerably. In the period of comparative relaxation I got pregnant again.

In the fall of 1948, a month after discovering I was pregnant, Gordon got screened out of his job at CBS. This turned out to be his denouement in the field of work he liked and was best qualified for. He was blacklisted when the CBS thing became final, and I think he knew it at the time he was fired, but I didn't fully grasp it right then. I can remember feeling bad but not especially scared; I thought Gordon would find another job quickly and we'd go on as we had been. But soon I could see he was very worried. Staying on top of the news had been his job for quite some time; he was more aware than I was of the rotten political climate, or, I should say, of how much more rotten it had gotten with the onset of the cold war. He read the newspapers more carefully than I did; he was out there associating with people while I had been isolated in the house.

I could sense that Gordon was getting more tense as the time drew near for me to have the baby. But I refused to get that worried. Maybe nature was protecting me. I've read somewhere that a pregnant woman is to a degree isolated from emotional shock, not for her sake but for the purpose of getting her child gestated through its nine-month period. I can't quite go along with that theory though; I believe environmental conditioning is more likely to be the principal tranquilizing factor—at least, I think it was in my case. I was lulled into a false sense of security by the novels and magazine stories I had read and the movies I had seen, and I was happily forgetting my previous pregnancy and also what my mother and my grandmother had gone through.

I didn't go into shock until after the baby was born. Gordon and I both went very close to the brink then. Gordon got very sick; he was vomiting continuously for days. He would try to sip a little water, but that made it worse, and he was getting badly dehydrated. We'd managed to hang on to the telephone, and I called my brother Bill to come and take Gordon to the hospital. Bill was a busy fellow, and he said: "Why don't you get an ambulance?"

"They take people to city hospitals. I want Gordon taken to St. Luke's."

St. Luke's was in our area. I'd have taken Gordon myself, but I was barely in shape to drag myself out of bed, and we didn't have neighbors we could call on for that kind of help. Bill came. The doctor at emergency gave Gordon some phenobarb tablets and told him to stay in bed. He lay down and was in a coma for several days, and I just had to let him lie there. We had no money; our savings were gone, and we had no Blue Cross. And to top things off, I was so weak after the birth that I thought I'd faint every step I took. I had a steady flow of blood. I got my doctor on the phone, the one who had delivered the baby, and he said I must stay in bed. When I told him about Gordon, he suggested a family service who sent housekeepers to families in an emergency situation.

I had reservations about this—it wouldn't work out for us. I was recalling a story I'd been told by a black woman named Emory who came to the American Labor Party headquarters a year or so before. She had been in the hospital to have a breast removed, and because she was a widow with no relatives, she had been sent to a convalescent home for a few months. Upon being released, she applied for two weeks of home care through a hospital social worker. On top of her other trouble, she had arthritis. She was told a nurse would come to her apartment, and indeed a nurse did put in an appearance two days later, for which Mrs. Emory lost no time in expressing her gratitude. Now everything would be all right. The nurse sat down and opened a hospital chart, as Mrs. Emory crept back into bed.

"Mrs. Emory, you are taking one of your pills each morning, and a half a pill each night, right?"

"Right," Mrs. Emory replied.

"Well, now," the nurse said, "you are to take one pill in the morning as usual, and then at night you are to take a whole pill instead of a half. Understand?"

With that the nurse put the chart in her bag and left. She did not return.

Thinking of Mrs. Emory's experience, I wondered how a home service could work out for us. But when I saw little Aggie, only four years old, trying to fix herself something to eat and "some for Daddy too" from the next-to-zero amount of food we had in the house, I grabbed the telephone book and started looking for numbers. My eyes were so clouded over from weakness that I could hardly see the numbers, but I managed to call a family aid agency only to be told they operated by appointment only and I'd have to come into their office. I called other numbers and finally got a woman to listen to me; I was desperate, and I guess I sounded like it. I can remember the conversation almost word for word. I begged her to tell me what to do. And I was crying into the phone, sobbing and crying. "What can we do, what can we do? Please, please help me!"

"Get ahold of yourself, that's the first thing you can do," she said.

"You aren't standing up and facing your situation. Your main trouble is self-pity—you're wallowing in it." I recall this very distinctly.

"But my baby is ten days old. I can't take care of her—and our other child. I just can't . . . without help. Can't anyone help us?"

The woman's breath kind of exploded into the phone. "The baby, the baby! Why people like you have babies I'll never understand!"

Would it have done any good to explain that we were in good shape when I got pregnant and that none of this crazy mess was mine or my husband's fault? But this was no time to think about that—I was just begging for help, immediate help, and I wasn't going to let the woman off the phone. Finally she interrupted my pleas.

"But we do recognize that a baby is a baby, and when I've checked with your doctor, I'll try to arrange with the visiting nurse service for one of their nurses to come in for an hour a day. But only for the baby and only if we have the word of a physician, you understand."

So the visiting nurse came—why hadn't I known about this service in the first place? She bustled around, bringing the first faint glimmer of hope the place had seen in days. She made formula and bathed the baby, even bounced her over her shoulder for a time on each of her visits. The poor little mite had wailed feebly but continuously in her carriage for days before this vigorous female shook a little life into her. At the end of the hour she plumped Jane back into the carriage and ran.

I don't remember clearly what else happened during this very bad time. I know I stayed in bed as much as possible. Gordon told me later about how he snapped out of it, and I don't recall any of that at all. The kids in the building, helped by other kids in the neighborhood no doubt, had thrown a lot of debris on the stairs that led to the basement in front of our apartment house, then they set the stuff on fire. The front of our building was burning; people were yelling. Gordon said he leaped up from his coma and was completely cured. All I can say is it was a good thing he got cured when he did, because Aggie came down with one of her upper-respiratory infections and an attack of asthma. With these attacks she had terrible stomach upsets and vomiting fits. She would vomit every twenty minutes; you could almost set your watch by it. She was a brave kid, never did cry. And we had no doctor, no medicine—she just had to tough it out. Gordon made us soup and pulled Aggie and me through while the visiting nurse saw that Jane got fed. After about three weeks my hemorrhaging stopped, and we were like a family who had come through a tornado.

Our blacklisting was absolute now; we had to face that fact. It was another one of those solid walls—I can't think of better words to describe it. We couldn't figure out what to do about it, but we knew that with the two babies, we had to do something. Both of us had faced solid walls before, but not with kids in our arms.

We had nowhere to turn, no one to borrow from. I got five dollars from my brother Bill, who came one day to check on us after that experience with Gordon. With the money we bought a gallon of milk, a chicken, and potatoes to make soup, and I paid back two dollars I had borrowed from the woman across the hall. Gordon's unemployment benefits either had run out or were just about to; they only lasted twenty-six weeks back then. The American Labor Party paid him a little for running the sound truck in our area for the Marcantonio mayoral campaign. But the amount he got for that through the whole campaign was hardly enough to pay one month's rent. So we were down to nothing and scrimping on what we ate so the kids could have enough food to stay healthy.

There was a seventy-five-dollar camera in the house that had belonged to Gordon's brother, and I pawned that together with its leather case and got fifteen dollars. My birthday watch got us three dollars. That was all we had to pawn. I couldn't have gotten fifty cents for my accordion, it was so old and out of tune. I tried to pawn Gordon's overcoat, but the man put the collar under a strong light and shook his head. "Worn slick," he said. He pushed the coat at me and motioned me toward the door. I felt numb about that and went home to go through the house once more for some misplaced bills or coins. Bitterness set in and swelled until the pain of it began to rival the buried pain of my lost writing, and a snatch of song grabbed me, stuck in my memory. Not written down until recently; never sung:

> Have you ever dug around in your old coat pockets
> In your old coat pockets for a dime!
> You're plain flat broke and it ain't no joke
> And you dig around one last time.
>
> You've done it before but you do it once more
> Keep pokin' your fingers through the holes,

And from a fuzzy corner if you dig out a quarter
It shines in your hand like gold.

There was some book I had read—a book they made a movie from—that told how a mama went to a lot of trouble pulling all kinds of ruses to keep her kids from knowing the family didn't have a dime in the house. She managed to do it. That was bunk to me. You can't keep kids from knowing something like that. You can try your damnedest, you can go to all kinds of lengths, but you can't do it. Even the baby took on the tensions from us and was a little bundle of nerves. We put on pretenses of glee, romped around and acted like clowns; we grinned and sashayed all over the place. But those kids knew things were wrong. They showed it in different ways, of course, one being a baby and the other big enough to put things into words. We could not keep our deep worries from them, but somehow we had to keep them from going hungry. Kids couldn't be let to go hungry—that would be really crazy. Every once in a while, not very often, we got ahold of a bunch of free food. There'd be a food drive usually by the American Labor Party, and since Gordon was still keeping up some activities there and they knew at the headquarters something of our situation, we'd get things like bricks of yellow cheese, cans of pork and beans, boxes of oatmeal, peanut butter, and so on.

Some friends, a middle-aged couple we'd known for some time, invited us to their place for supper. They listened to a more-or-less detailed account of what we'd been going through, and they advised us to apply for relief. I nearly choked on my food. We'd been on demonstrations and hunger marches and all that in the '30s, and belonged to organizations that did nothing else but fight to make relief and unemployment insurance a part of the laws of the land. But I couldn't see *us* going on relief! Where we lived on West 106th Street in Manhattan, we could look across the alley and into the back windows where there were families we surmised to be on relief. There were kids of all sizes cowering in corners while their parents slugged and clawed it out with fists and fingernails and crashing furniture and dishes. A man picked up a screaming baby and threw it at a woman—she almost didn't catch it. When things got like that I shut the window and pulled the shade down. How could these friends of ours suggest we go on relief?

I was still having spells of weakness from the birth. I figured I must have been too old to have a baby, not being too strong anyway. At any rate, going out and trying to get a job was unthinkable at that time. And Gordon had almost given up looking. We went to the relief office, waited in the crowd from morning through most of the day with the kids on our laps, and finally got to fill out an application. We went home and waited. Nothing happened. Our old communist friend, Sol Devine, who came once a week or so to talk and drink coffee, told us we wouldn't get on relief that way.

"Well, how do we?" I asked.

"You've got to go for emergency cash," he said. And he stopped there.

"How?" I said.

"Just go and sit there. And have a sandwich with you. When they call your number say you got no money, not a dime, you spent your last one for carfare getting down there. Don't let them see you eating your sandwich. You'll most likely be there all day. You'll have plenty of company."

"I know *that*," I said.

The next day I went. I left the kids with Gordon. It was like Sol said, and just as crowded as before. A young woman was screaming for emergency cash, said she'd been there all day the day before. "Emergency cash!" she screeched. "Emergency cash! It's the law. I was promised. I can't eat yer damn promises!"

Something like this would set off babies who might otherwise have remained comparatively quiet, and there would be a din till the kids got worn out yelling and went to sleep on laps—there was no room on benches. Most grown-ups sat quietly through this. An old man vomited, a woman fainted, and an enormously fat young man snored loudly with his chins on his chest—someone had to shake him awake when his number was called. People were good about helping each other that way.

Shortly before four o'clock my number was called, and a short, stocky woman with tiny sharp eyes motioned me behind a semipartition where there were some desks and chairs. She had our application in her hand and questioned me about this and that for fifteen or twenty minutes. She asked what we'd been living on for the past two months. I said we'd borrowed money from Gordon's brother, just like it said on our application.

"Why don't you keep on borrowing money from him?" she said, and she kind of snapped her words out.

I told her, "He's gone; he gave us all he had."

"How much did you borrow from him?" she asked.

"Two hundred seventy-five dollars," I said.

"That should have lasted you longer."

I opened my mouth to explain that $160 had to go for two month's rent, but she rushed on, "Besides, there's a discrepancy here, there's a discrepancy."

"A discrepancy?" I said. My heart sank—we must have goofed badly.

"It says here, Mrs. Frycin, that you borrowed *$280* from your husband's brother!" And she shriveled me with a look from those pinpoints of eyes.

I couldn't say anything for a while. The discrepancy had me licked temporarily. Miss Sharpeyes sat there darting her glance from me to the application papers and back again. She thumped her pencil on the desk while I silently grappled with the discrepancy, trying for vantage ground. The problem began to simplify itself in my mind.

"Well now," I said, "it must have been $280 if that's what it says on there."

"You ought to know what it says," she snapped. "You wrote it!"

I told her, "Well, I think my husband wrote that. Yes, he filled in those blanks."

"Now, Mrs. Frycin, I don't think you'll qualify. My supervisor must be told about this discrepancy. I must discuss the matter of the discrepancy with her." God, how she loved that word.

She got up from her chair and disappeared. In about fifteen minutes she came back with an envelope and, after explaining with sanctimonious overtones that I was getting this emergency cash only because of the children, she handed me the envelope. There was seven dollars and some cents in it, which she said was a food budget for four people for three and a half days or until she could make her home visit and report back to the office. She wouldn't say just when she was going to make her visit—they never told you that. (It was many years later, after welfare mothers organized, that an appointment was required for home visits, and a family no longer had to go through the agony of not knowing when a caseworker would appear.)

I went home at five o'clock with my seven dollars and some cents. I picked up a few groceries on the corner, and old Sol was there when I got back to the apartment. He was curious. He didn't usually come to our place two days in a row.

"How'd you do?" he asked.

"I don't know, but I got a little over seven dollars cash."

"Then you're on," he said. "They don't give out emergency cash unless they've put you on the rolls."

Immediately I felt good. It was good to be on relief.

Miss Sharpeyes came. She said we'd have to move; they wouldn't pay the eighty-dollars-a-month rent for the furnished apartment we lived in. She said she'd take care of us; she'd find us a place to move to and told me to call her on the phone when our check arrived. She told us we barely made it onto the rolls and said we were the first white-collar family her unit had had. "There'll be more, though," she predicted. I wondered about her last remark. She may have been aware of the growing climate of thought control in the country and known the blacklist had just begun to take its toll.

This snappish woman was to be our caseworker for some time to come. Her name was Mrs. Samuels. I went to a phone booth and called her when the check arrived, and she said she had a place for us to move, a nice big room with a kitchen used by only three other families and a better-than-average bathroom in the hall. The check we had just gotten covered fifteen dollars in moving expenses and the new rent of twenty-two dollars a week, including utilities. When I got away from the phone, I multiplied twenty-two dollars by four, and it came to a monthly rent of eighty-eight dollars, just about exactly what we were already paying counting gas and lights. And with the extra two or three days in the average month, it actually came to more than they would be paying.

We didn't move to the room. We paid no rent where we were because we knew we'd have to move. We got an eviction notice. It was an official one from the city marshal's office and came in an envelope with a slogan printed in the lower left-hand corner: WHEN FAMILY LIFE STOPS — DELINQUENCY STARTS! One of the supreme ironies of the age, we thought. This was the packaging in which poor families now received their eviction notices. What better stopper of family life was there than an eviction?

Sol Devine offered to share his fifth-floor walk-up with us, and we took him up on the proposition. We would be cramped, but it wouldn't be like trying to live in a welfare hotel. It was some time later that we found out why it was that they wanted us out of our apartment and were willing to pay more for us in a rooming house. People going on relief were to be turned into transients if they were not transients already. We must not be allowed to feel settled in. This was policy. By law we could not be sent packing. But by policy we could be made so miserable that we'd be apt to get lost of our own accord, and that way we'd be quickly off the rolls. Getting people off the rolls must have been second only to keeping them off in the first place.

Our Mrs. Samuels did, however, write out a recommendation that we be allowed to remain in Sol's place. Our share of the rent was about twenty-eight dollars plus gas and lights, bringing the total to less than thirty-five dollars a month. That much of a saving was enough to make the situation acceptable. Or was it the fact that in no way could Sol's place be considered comfortable for the four of us? This our caseworker must have seen at first glance—she paid us a visit right away. She knew the city better than we did at that time. We had to wait till winter to find out that the heating in such a slum just about didn't exist, even though there were radiators. And even if we'd known this, we wouldn't have realized how our two tiny children would suffer in a heatless New York apartment. Sol didn't warn us about this—he didn't seem to be aware of it. He spent most of his time away from home and came back at night to visit for a few minutes, crawl into his tiny hall bedroom, and go to bed. We froze that winter. The kitchen was down a long hall from our little rooms, so we could get no heat from the gas oven. Jane was an infant, and Aggie was five. I kept them zipped in snowsuits all the time, unzipping the baby only for diaper changes, Aggie for the toilet. Fortunately I had been able to get them snowsuits by spending a lot of time combing the streets for storefront rummage sales; the snowsuits saved us that winter.

There was not much playing that the kids could do. Aggie tried to play, but for the most part she sat and drew pictures, colored in her coloring books, and read Bugs Bunny and Porky Pig comic books. She learned to read very young and went on to books like *Heidi* and *Little Women*. The baby didn't learn to crawl until she was a year old; I'm sure the tension of our lives had a lot to do with this.

Since coming north I had always liked spring. But I never welcomed one like I did the spring that came after that first cold winter.

We began to spend sunny days in the park, which, lucky for us, was only a short distance away. All four of us would set out with a bag of sandwiches and a bottle for the baby. I took along my shorthand notebook and a pocket full of sharpened pencils and practiced Greg shorthand.

Just before Aggie was to start school I realized she had no suitable clothes. I hunted rummage sales again for things to fit her, but nearly everything had to be cut down and made over. I was thinking that even my mother on the farm had a treadle sewing machine. But there was no way I could get one, no way. I felt wasted, more wasted than I had ever felt in my life. I remember crying a lot and hating myself for it. I ought to be stronger—had to grow stronger. Jane was getting bigger; she was weaned off the bottle and toilet-trained. It was necessary now that I take on some activity or other else I would have to admit to myself that I'd become a nonentity.

Gordon was keeping up his membership in the American Labor Party. He spent quite a bit of time at their headquarters helping people with all kinds of problems, and mainly going on committees to help families get on welfare who couldn't get on by themselves— the red tape at the relief office increased by the week. He also helped out with rallies, mimeographing leaflets, and making an occasional speech—various things.

Aggie was in the hospital for a few weeks with an active infection of the joints. They thought it might be rheumatic fever because I had had it and the tendency to get such diseases was inherited. So they kept her for three more months in a convalescent home in Connecticut. Speaking of crying, I really cried the day they sent her off— but only *after* she left; I wasn't going to let her see me cry. She was happy that day. They had built this up to her as a sort of joyous camping trip, and she was beaming all over the place waiting for the car that was to take her and three old grannies to the home. I had brought her best set of clothes to the hospital and dressed her; she sat there, her little face all lit up, eyes sparkling—and her running a fever at the time. I didn't know what to say or do. I didn't want to spoil this moment for her, but still I couldn't just sit and watch her there in her child's innocence thinking everything was coming up roses. Why had the doctors and nurses bunked her about this? Parents couldn't fool kids, but these doctors could. I doped it out that they didn't want trouble with her as they must have had with lots of kids in this situation. I suppose some kicked and screamed. There was Aggie, happy, holding her two little plastic dolls—twin dolls, she called them—one in each hand. She was so small and so trusting. I wanted to scream and claw somebody, whoever had put her so in a state of mind to be hurt. I hated the thought of that moment of let-down that surely would come before this day was over. She might not be able to cope with it; I wouldn't be there. It turned out that she was strong, and she did cope very well, as I learned talking with nurses later. But on that day I foresaw the worst. And I was helpless to do anything about it. I couldn't tell my little girl that what she was going to was just an extension of the hospital existence she'd known for the past weeks, confinement in an iron crib and loneliness and pain.

I went to visit Aggie every week on Sunday, going to Connecticut on the train and taking a bus from the station to the home. Once Gordon and I took the baby and all went up in someone's car. We couldn't both go up to the ward together; one of us had to stay down with Janie. Aggie seemed to have forgotten the baby when I said we brought her with us. She held up during the visits—I mean she didn't cry. I almost wished she would. Her little face was drawn and her eyes had a film over them as though she had gone into a never-never land she couldn't get back out of. She had lost her little twin dolls, but she didn't ask me to bring a replacement. She was very thin. But while there I saw other children, and I observed that our little girl was well-off compared to some of those others; many of them would never get well. I got a grip on myself.

The day came when we got a telegram from the hospital in New York saying Aggie was there and we could come get her. I unwound half a roll of toilet paper and soaked it with tears before I could get dressed and out of the house. Our kid was well again! The first happiness on such an occasion is almost frightening in its intensity; it's not just happiness, it's something beyond. I had agonizing doubts about being able to stay in control when I got to the hospital ward and saw her. I kept counting slowly, slowly—one, two, three—in an attempt to calm myself down on the way there.

We had Aggie home—if the place where we lived could be called home. After a day or two of the heaven of simply having her with us, we began to face the terror of winter in that cold, rotting hellhole. We knew we couldn't keep her there in her present state of health; she'd have a relapse if we went on as we were. We had to do something, so as soon as we could collect our senses we applied for an apartment in a low-income housing project and began our long battle for a decent place to live. It was seven years before we got placed.

Aggie was to go back to school in a week, and I made up my mind to try for some clothing money from welfare. A caseworker was never easy to reach by phone—or any other way for that matter. On certain days and at certain times they were supposed to be reachable, but that didn't mean they were. When I got Mrs. Samuels she said I had to come to the office, but she doubted if there'd be any clothing allowance for us. We had never received anything for clothes though we were entitled to this by law once a year.

I went to the office. I sat in the crowded room as usual. My number was called. Mrs. Samuels took me to a desk and immediately began to yak at me. Our checks would be smaller because they must subtract food allowance for one child for three and a half months. This should, she said, have been subtracted from each of the seven checks we'd received since Aggie had been hospitalized. But the case loads were so great that this had been overlooked. Now it must be done on future checks, but they wouldn't do it all at once—they were kind and considerate. It was going to be taken off a little at a time; we'd starve only a little bit faster than usual. I got sick right then. But luckily, out of my mental confusion and anger, I thought of something to hit back with. I said that I'd spent more than the equivalent of the child's food allowance getting to Connecticut to see her once a week. I said the hospital had insisted that I do that. She snapped back at me with something to the effect that I had no right to spend welfare money in such a careless way. "No welfare budget ever covers such an unnecessary expenditure, Mrs. Frycin." (Why couldn't the bitch learn how to say our name?)

I felt my voice box tightening, and the next thing I said came out at a considerably higher pitch. "It was *not* unnecessary; it was necessary!"

I believe I must have sounded definite. Mrs. Samuels's neck reddened for just a second, then her face took on the hardest look I had ever seen on a human countenance. She was building up to a supreme moment of some sort. She hesitated a few seconds more and then out it came. "You don't love your children, Mrs. Frycin!" Her pinpoints shot right at me to note the effect of her words.

Was I hearing her right? Did she really say what I heard her say? I couldn't be sure until she repeated it, word for word. I didn't know it then, of course, but she was giving me the "Routine for Breaking Down Mothers." I found out that it was routine when it was tried on me by other subsequent caseworkers.

Mrs. Samuels went on, "If you loved your children you'd have a job! You would be supporting your children and you'd be doing it gladly and you would never stoop to ask for welfare for them and for yourself!" (They left husbands out of this routine.) There was more, but my ears closed about that time, and I just watched the woman's lips moving and twisting around some quite ugly words that must have been coming out. She got up finally and flipped out of the cubicle. I followed. She didn't see me, and I got into the back office behind her. Once in the door I darted past her. I knew who the unit supervisor was, and I went straight to her and talked so fast she just sat there with her mouth open. When I paused for breath she asked what was I doing there in her office. "Talking," I said. Mrs. Samuels stood there looking funny; her eyes had gotten bigger than the black specks they usually were. The supervisor looked at her and then at me.

"Well," she said, "this is a bit unusual, considering that you have no appointment." (Since when did anyone ever manage an appointment with a unit supervisor?) I opened my mouth to start talking again, but she made a quick, up-and-outward gesture with her arm and said: "Don't bring all that up again; your checks won't be reduced. We've reconsidered your case."

I was baffled by how easy this had been. I stared at her for a minute, then turned and left. I was crying, of course. And I'd completely forgotten to ask for our pitiful clothing allotment. It came to me on the way home that I'd been tricked. I figured that giving me the routine at this time was deliberate to make me forget what I came for. Caseworkers got merit marks on their records when they managed to steer clients away from asking for something extra that they were entitled to. Samuels probably got a merit mark for making me forget what I came for. But, poor thing, she may have gotten a demerit for letting me into the back office.

We spent a ridiculous amount of time and energy trying to get a decent apartment in which to raise our kids. We went through the business of applying for public housing, and after waiting a year we were advised by a doctor at St. Luke's Hospital to work through one of their social workers. We did that. The social worker assured me that she was really going to bat for us, and within a month she said she had gotten us on the emergency list by sending a series of regis-tered, return-receipt-requested letters to the housing office down-town on LaFayette Street. She said this was all she was in a position to do; she couldn't personally go with me herself. We waited; noth-ing happened. I made a couple of trips down to the office myself, only to be told both times that the worker handling our area was not in that day. On the third visit I got there when the office opened at 9:30 and announced right off that I was going to wait until some-one would see me. So I waited along with other harried folks.

It was nearly four o'clock in the afternoon when I was beckoned through a door and down a corridor, on one side of which were acres of tall file cabinets back to back in rows appearing to stretch end-lessly into the bowels of the building. On the other side was a row of desks spaced some ten feet apart. Soon I was seated across a desk from a thin, sad-faced woman with huge, thyroid eyes, which she lifted toward me for a split second and then kept riveted on an open folder in front of her. She pronounced the usual salutatory "What can *we* do for *you?*" without looking in my direction—indeed, I never saw her eyes again, just the enormous tremulous lids as she moved her face ever so slightly from side to side while perusing the papers on the desk.

I got straight to the matter of our family being on the housing emergency list. She turned a page over; her fingers were incredibly long, and she moved her hands in little nervous jerks. "Yes, I see here your family is on one emergency list. Our record indicates the health problem of a child."

I asked, "*One* emergency list? There are more emergency lists?"

"Oh yes, certainly. There are emergencies and then there are emergencies. Yours is just an emergency."

I had to wait a moment to let this sink in. "Well, I have to know something," I said. "What is an emergency, the kind with the 'just' in front of it, which ours is or what you have it down there as?"

"Well, that emergency is one which should be taken care of within two years. Yes, within two years."

Again, like at the welfare office, I wondered if I was hearing the woman correctly. If so, I didn't need to read any more Kafka—I was living it. In spite of my strenuous efforts to get it deemed otherwise, the Friesen family's emergency remained the kind with the "just" in front. We had a year and eleven months to wait according to their schedule, and I couldn't budge them with all the accounts of my child turning blue repeatedly with asthma attacks and pronounce-ments that her death would be on their hands if they didn't place us right away. Our child couldn't live two more years freezing the whole winter.

Of course, I didn't know the half of it at the time. As things worked out, we did not get placed until six more years had passed, the period reckoned from that day when for me the dictionary defi-nition of the word *emergency* became obsolete. Fortunately, by keeping up a constant hunt, we found a slightly better place in which to spend the last four years of our waiting period. I remember observing that New York City was made up of those financially well-enough-off to live there and those who were too poor to leave. We were among the latter.

I had it figured out that going on relief kept us from being sepa-rated and put in the various city shelters. But if we didn't get a break soon, this terrifying thing might still happen. So I began to feel around for work I could do to ease myself into some kind of regular job. A friend asked me to take on a temporary typing job with her; we'd work together evenings for about three weeks or until the job was finished. The job was for a man connected with the Marshall Plan who had set up office in a midtown hotel to work out arrange-ments for some foreign mine operators to tour the mining areas of the United States. Visitors from all fields of mining and from coun-tries far and near had been invited. The function of the office at that time was to make final preparations—work out an itinerary, set up dates for visiting the areas, and reserve accommodations. Rose and I were the only typists, but several men—bigshot types—were around to do leg work for the boss and collect paychecks. Every gov-ernment program had its hangers-on; the Marshall Plan was no ex-ception.

After the Communists won out in China and the Chinese Peoples' Republic was set up, the Marshall Plan operations were broadened. The project Rose and I worked on in 1951 was to include more than just European countries. South Korea was on the list (the Korean War was going on, but it had not yet reached its peak). It turned out that there were no mine operators in South Korea who were Korean; what mining there was had been taken over by U.S. capitalism. It was deemed absolutely necessary by our boss that there be a South Korean representative on this tour. So he got on the phone to theatrical agencies in New York to try to find a Korean actor who could pretend to be this mine owner. They had no Korean actor—there was none to be found. But there were plenty of Chinese actors, would one of them do? It was decided that this was okay, and they hired a Chinese actor; who'd know a Chinese from a Korean? The ruse seemed to have worked out—I never heard anything to the contrary.

This business with the Korean caused me to think of the story of an earlier difficulty this country had with its South Korean machinations. When our government was looking around for a puppet to carry out U.S. control of South Korea in 1947, our agents there picked out the perfect man. Just one thing was a little off-key—his name happened to be Wun Bum Suk. They mulled this over and decided he wouldn't do. We couldn't have anybody named Wun Bum Suk carrying out our dictations, even though in Korea the name could have meant something very noble. So a second choice, Syngman Rhee, got the job.

It had been fairly simple to solve the problem of there being no South Korean mine owner. But another more serious problem plagued the planners of the tour—accommodations for a bunch of foreigners of mixed color. They would stay out of the South, of course. But that didn't completely solve things. Rose and I were typing away one evening when the boss was on the phone in the adjoining room making hotel reservations for the visitors. He'd been making these long distance calls, but something in his tone caused us to listen to this particular conversation. "I tell you, they will cause you no trouble." (Pause) "What do you mean, your regulars will vanish? Surely not in Detroit; I thought Detroit was a midwestern city! You sound like you're in Shreveport." (Pause) "Yes, yes, some of their skins will be dark. But their hair will be straight!"

Rose and I were really listening now. It's a wonder the boss didn't notice the typewriters had stopped clicking. "I guarantee you that their hair will be straight!" He was fairly shouting now. He didn't seem to be getting anywhere; the conversation stopped with the slam of the receiver. He had to settle for a cheaper hotel in Detroit.

The Marshall Plan stint didn't lead to a regular job for me; in fact, I felt that if I had to work for an outfit like that I'd rather be on relief. But I got to practice typing, which was good, and I thought we could live for a while longer as we were. That wasn't to be, though. About this time the welfare folks put Gordon into their rehabilitation division; seems we had been on home relief as long as was allowed without someone in the family going on a work program. You get soft and lazy, you know, lolling around on relief. Of course, we'd still be on welfare, but in a different phase of it—the phase where folks worked and got paid way below minimum wage.

They put Gordon in the office of the children's shelter at 104th Street and Fifth Avenue, and he walked to work—it was right across Central Park from where we lived. But soon it would be getting cold, and Gordon had no overcoat. The old one I'd tried to pawn a couple of years before was completely shot, gone to threads. And the money I'd earned from the typing job all went for food, a few school clothes for Aggie, a doll, a kiddie car, and shoes for all of us.

Winter was coming, and Gordon had to walk across the park. I hit Samuels up for an okay on a clothing allotment for an overcoat. I thought if I limited the request to this one item I would be more apt to get it. I was still smarting from the way I had been tricked out of a clothing allotment before, and I decided now was my chance to even up the score. Not that you could do that, but you could at least try a trick that you had up your sleeve. I appealed to some ALP friends of mine, some of the women who were making a clothing drive for their annual rummage sale. Would they try to save out a large-sized overcoat for Gordon? They would, and they did.

Caseworker home visits came about once a month in those days, but you couldn't guess within ten days when you'd have to put up with one of these hateable intrusions. I got ready for Samuels, and when she came I told her I would be forced to take my problem right over her head to the unit supervisor if she didn't come through with money to get Gordon's overcoat. I said she had forced Gordon into the rehab program, had done a hatchet job on us. I said if Gordon went to his job in rags, the rehab thing would backfire, wouldn't it now? Wasn't it a program to get families off relief? They'd kill a very good thing, nip it in the bud, if they demanded that folks go to jobs in rags. What boss would put up with this—he'd send the guy home, wouldn't he now? I remember yanking my own seedy old winter coat off its hook and asking Samuels would she like to show up at her unit in something like that. She kept opening her mouth to speak, but I beat her to it each time. I showed her a drawer full of ragged shirts, underwear, and socks, talking all the while. "Gordon is not going to go to that job once the cold sets in," I said.

"He has to go." Samuels managed to get in a word or two. "You will be cut off welfare if he doesn't."

"He won't go," I said. "We'll take the kids and a committee from the American Labor Party and we'll sit in at the welfare office."

She said, "You are making a threat, Mrs. Friesen! We do not listen to threats!" (She at least had finally learned to say our name.)

I said, "Maybe you don't listen to threats, but I've heard that the supervisors often listen to committees down there at the office. I believe it might be better all around if Gordon got an overcoat." Well, I got a check for twenty-five dollars. The overcoat from the ALP had been stuck away in Sol Devine's room for several weeks—now I could get it out. It was a very big one—it had belonged to Paul Robeson. Samuels would ask to see it next time she came. Twenty-five dollars was more than a little bit back then. We spent the money on food—beef for several stews, chickens for baking, some jars of jam and peanut butter, ice cream and cake. Triumph!

And Gordon, in his heavy coat, was warm walking across Central Park and back every day. But his need for the coat was soon to end. Funding for the care of lost kids was slashed and he was let off the job with a formal letter commending him for excellent work in putting out a news-letter for the shelter. Now he was stuck in the house taking care of the girls while I looked for—and found—a full time job. It was as a typist in the headquarters of the I.W.O. (International Workers Order).

There were five other women, two of them black, in the division where I worked. My job was to type benefit checks (the I.W.O. was sort of an insurance company for low-income families). I thought I wouldn't mind doing this kind of work, but I discovered I needed glasses; I began to suffer from eyestrain.

The head of the division, a white woman, was not the type of person I could take a liking to. I thought her a wee bit giddy. Every once in a while she'd spend a half hour or so in the morning telling the office staff what happened on the *I Love Lucy* show the night before. She had one of the old black-and-white TV sets, the others did not. The women seemed to enjoy her enthusiastic renditions; I did not. Most of the others kowtowed to her; I did not. Soon I began to realize that this was a mistake on my part, that is, if I wanted to keep my job. And God, did I! So I tried pretending to listen to Fanny—I'll call her that—and laughing along with the others at her impersonations of Lucy. But it was too late. There was nothing I could do now to keep Fanny from hating me.

One of the black women—I'll call her Nadine—had a desk

straight across from me with a large unshaded window beside it. Years before I had worked at a job disassembling type which had caused the same kind of eyestrain I was feeling at this time. A doctor had told me then to stop work for a moment and look out the nearest window; focusing on something at a distance would rest my eyes. I remembered doing this and it had worked. So now I tried this when I felt the strain coming on. The office was quite narrow, so I would sit at my desk and look out the window by Nadine. One day I noticed Nadine going over to Fanny's desk and whispering something to her. Both of them kept glancing at me while whispering.

The next day I was told to report to the main office; there was some kind of complaint. What could it be? The big boss's secretary had told me they liked my work, said I could type checks faster than anyone they'd had before. In a state of puzzlement I went to the main office. The big boss, a white man, told me to sit down; I did. He said I was being charged with racial harassment by the head of my division, what did I have to say? I couldn't say anything. I felt like I was being asphyxiated. The big boss just stared at me. Finally I laboriously stuttered out—in what way had I racially harassed anyone? He said Nadine had told Fanny I was in the habit of sitting at my desk and glaring at her. Again I was struck dumb by what I was hearing. How? When? Had I slipped over into another dimension?

I was told not to come to work the next day. If I wanted to appeal, I should come back on a specified day and I would be allowed a hearing. Well, certainly I wanted a hearing. I was still in a state of agonized puzzlement. It finally dawned on me that it was my looking out that damned window by Nadine's desk that had triggered the thing. Fanny had seized on Nadine's complaint as a way of getting rid of me. Me, a racial harasser? Me, who had been the first white woman member of the Oklahoma chapter of the NAACP— me, who had been on the committee to meet the Scotsboro Boys coming into the city and who worked with Negro tenant farmers in the STFU?

A day was designated for the hearing. I went and sat before a group of office big shots. There's not much more to this story. After my first shock I had felt like fighting. But upon fully realizing the situation, I didn't have much fight left. I explained about the eyestrain and focusing on some rooftops out the window to relieve it. I don't know whether or not my inquisitors believed me; it didn't matter. My goose was cooked. Fanny hated me. And she had been head of that division for eons. I had a feeling Nadine believed me. But she, perhaps more than I, needed to keep her job; she had to stick to her story. She had to do what Fanny wanted her to do. I wanted to speak to her alone to find out whether or not she believed the eye story. But I didn't. I wished later that I had—just to *know*. Because nothing could have kept me from being fired.

So. We were back on welfare.

There's a song we printed in *Broadside* in 1969 called the "Welfare Song," written by Mike Millius. One of the lines is "Not enough to live on, but a little too much to die." We came to the conclusion that there was little or no difference between killing people and not allowing them to live. We were not being allowed to live. We were a man, a woman, and two children—a family in the good-old American sense—condemned not to live. Multiply the four of us by hundreds of thousands and you get a picture of the McCarthy period. It was a horrible national catastrophe stretching out over a decade, involving millions of people and with an aftermath still taking a toll in the wasted lives of the children born during the period. The fire is out, but the smoke remains, and young folks come into adulthood in a lost world they had no part in making.

I will not say I have no bitterness about what happened to us; I would be lying if I said that. The blacklist was a death that we lived through only because we had a pretty good idea of what was happening in the country and in the world; we knew what the cold war was. Our predicament was not our fault. I wish I had been this clear-headed about my inability to continue singing. My talent in music had already started to die of neglect some years before Gordon was blacklisted, and I saw the trouble as stemming from something within me instead of two primary outside forces: working-class oppression and women's oppression, both killers. The circumstances of the blacklist was for me only the final pull into silence.

Out of the hundreds of thousands blacklisted during the late '40s and throughout the '50s, there were many who didn't see clearly what was happening—thought it was in some way or another their own fault—and they went crazy, committed suicide, killed themselves with alcohol, or literally starved to death from not being able to face what they had to face to get on relief. It was a desperate time, and though my reasoning told me one thing, my emotional reaction was hard to hold down; I could only do it by building up the defense that by giving up and going under we'd be doing exactly what the enemy wanted us to do, and that we must exert every effort to keep from obliging the twisted criminal minds that were shaping things during what Lillian Hellman understatedly called "scoundrel time." They would have folks like us die without a fuss; just break down and dissolve. We didn't oblige.

Cover of pamphlet, *Oklahoma Witch Hunt*, by Gordon Friessen [sic], published
October 1941. (Collection of Ronald D. Cohen)

A selection of Gordon Friesen's drawings from the 1930s and 1940s.
(Cunningham/Friesen Family Collection)

"Evolution," 1938

"The Last Loaf," 1939

[untitled figure with flag], 1940

THIS WAS DRAWN 30 YEARS BEFORE THE UNITED STATES OF AMERICA
MADE MY LAI A HOUSEHOLD WORD AROUND THE WORLD.

[untitled figure with rifle], 1940. Published in 1976 with new caption.

"The Spellbinder," 1940

"Sin," 1940

"The Long Journey," 1940

"Terror," 1941

"The Book Burners," 1941

"The Folk Singers," c. 1942

CALIFORNIA to the NEW YORK ISLAND

C A L I F O R N I A

San Francisco <u>Chronicle</u> 1/22/65

Broadside---
Topical Song Bible

Ralph J. Gleason

THE BIBLE OF THE TOPICAL song world, which is the truly vital part of folk music, is a mimeographed monthly newsletter and magazine from New York called Broadside. . . . .

BROADSIDE got its name from the practice of printing songs and statements on single sheets of paper which was prevalent in England for hundreds of years. The British Museum has thousands of samples of old broadsides in its collection and the practice was common in this country too in the early years. Among those who published their writing via broadsides was Benjamin Franklin. More recently, Woody Guthrie, the folk singer and composer mimeographed his compositions himself when they were turned down by commercial publishing houses. . . . . .

By the end of 1962 Broadside was struggling along with only 60 subscribers but has had a steady growth since then. The magazine now prints over 1200 and has an international circulation.

Topical songwriting, which was all but a lost art a few years ago, has prospered to the point where dozens of songs come unsolicited in the mails to Broadside on almost any event or newsstory of significance in any month.

Agnes Cunningham and her volunteers regard all this as a most happy development even if it does threaten to drown them in a sea of manuscripts. There's the joy of discovery. "Little Boxes," Sis Sunningham recalls, was printed in Broadside over a year before it was a popular hit and more than 50 of the songs Broadside has first published have been recorded and made available on the general market. And that's no small achievement.

N E W   Y O R K

the village VOICE, *January* 14, 1965

Most afficionados mark the birth of the topical song movement with the publication in February, 1962, in New York of the magazine Broadside (though the seeds of the movement go far back into the '50s), put together by Pete Seeger, the selfless patron of the movement, Sis Cunningham, its chronicler, and Gil Turner, its talent scout. The first issue contained five songs, including "Talking John Birch Blues" by a 20-year-old named Bob Dylan Fifty-five issues and 500 songs later, Broadside is the mimeographed bible of the topical song apostles and their disciples, stretching from the redwood forests to the Gulf Stream waters.

And after those three years the new-wave song writers are on the verge of dominating folk music.

Drawing by
Agnes
Friesen

Keep up with this new song movement (and Freedom Songs from the South). Subscribe to:

BROADSIDE MAGAZINE
Editor: Sis Cunningham;Advisory:Pete Seeger. Monthly. Topical songs by Len Chandler,Phil Ochs,Peter La Farge,Buffy Sainte-Marie,Eric Andersen,etc. Art: Agnes Friesen. Articles:Josh Dunson,Julius Lester,etc. BROADSIDE has put out 4 LP records with FOLKWAYS (165 W. 46 St,New York) & a songbook (OAK Publ.,165 W.46,NYC)

- -

S U B S C R I P T I O N   B L A N K
BROADSIDE, 215 West 98 St.,New York,N.Y. 10025: Enclosed find _____ for (check below)

[ ] 1 year subs. to Broadside (12 issues) - $5.   [ ] Set of first 50 issues - $12

(Please print) NAME _____ ADDRESS _____

CITY _____ STATE _____ ZIP _____

(If you are already a subscriber,please pass this blank on to a friend)

Broadside subscription form, mid-1960s. (*Broadside* Collection)

Introducing...

BROADSIDE #1   Feb., 1962
Box 193 Cathedral Sta. NYC 25
Price . . . . . . 35¢

BROADSIDE

a handful of songs about our times

guilty of a "betrayal of public trust" when he steered the measure through the Assembly while he was a board member of a shelter firm.

For 45 minutes last night, Carlino answered questions from about 100 of the estimated 3,000 persons who came to the capital to demand the repeal of the shelter law.

The demonstrators carried placards reading: "Peace on Earth—Not Under It" and "Holes Are for Moles, Not for People."

"The John Birch Society hurts terribly . . . we lost him because of John Birch attacks made upon him."

When a doorkeeper at the entrance to the gallery refused to admit some Negroes, they began singing a "freedom" song and were ordered out.

Have we come to this as a society? Is it true that we care more for our dogs than for our brothers?
PEARL DAVID.

New York, Feb. 1, 1962.

LEGION'S HEAD SAYS WAR IS JUSTIFIABLE

a shortage of linen . . . I saw one woman, who was wet up to her neck and took a chill, give the aid a dollar and beg her not to forget to come back to take the bedpan from under her . . . I went downstairs to get a cup of tea during the night. Couldn't find a tea bag, only cockroaches running over the table."

Topical songs have been an important part of America's music since early Colonial days. Many people throughout the country today are writing topical songs, and the only way to find out if a song is good is to give it wide circulation and let the singers and listeners decide for themselves. BROADSIDE'S aim is not so much to select and decide as to circulate as many songs as possible and get them out as quickly as possible. Our schedule calls for twice-a-month publication -- this will depend mainly on the contributing songwriters. BROADSIDE may never publish a song that could be called a "folk song." But let us remember that many of our best folk songs were topical songs at their inception. Few would deny the beauty and lasting value of some of Woody Guthrie's songs. Old or new, "a good song can only do good."

Hassayampa Creek flows into the Gila River near Palo Verde west of Phoenix; one who drinks of it is said thereafter never to be able to tell the truth, unless he drinks above the trail when the reverse is true and he cannot tell a lie. The "Arizona nightingale" is the hardy burro of prospecting days, with a terrifying bray, but who nevertheless has been im-

Today's greatest social problem is the weakening of moral and spiritual values which results in family disintegration and an in-

this marked the mid-point in the decade of tinsel prosperity; 1929, because this marked the collapse of the stock market; 1933, because this marked the bottom of the great depression; 1939, because this marked the last year before World War II; 1948, because this marked the close of the violent inflation of World War II and the postwar period; 1955 and 1958, because these

enemies from within. Hence the idiot bombings of Protestant ministers in Los Angeles. Hence the paranoid charge that Eisenhower and Allen Dulles were conscious agents of communism. Hence the current talk not only of impeaching Chief Justice Warren but even of lynching him.

Number 1, February 1962

Broadside # 47

THE NATIONAL TOPICAL SONG MAGAZINE

JUNE 30, 1964   PRICE — 35¢

LOVE

one another
the time is
at hand

CONTENTS

S O N G S   B Y
ALFRED ALBERTI
DON & HEDY WEST
MATT McGINN
ERIC ANDERSEN
BUD FOOTE
TOM PAXTON
DAVE ARKIN &
WALLY HILLE

ALSO: "DEATH COMES TO
ABC-TV HOOTENANNY"; "PHIL
OCHS ON RECORD"; PETE
SEEGER SETS RECORD STRAIGHT
ON WOODY'S SO LONG; "DE"
GREENWAY UNDER MICROSCOPE.

"The kitchen sink at O'Farrell
Street." A. Friesen 2/64

Number 47, June 1964

BROADSIDE

"THE NATIONAL
TOPICAL SONG MAGAZINE"
JANUARY 20, 1964
Price — 35¢

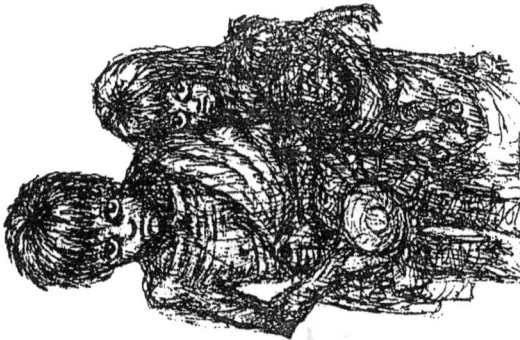

#38

IN THIS ISSUE:

"TIME of the
TIGER"

BY
LEN CHANDLER

also Songs by:
PHIL OCHS
ERNIE MARRS
TOM PAXTON
MALVINA REYNOLDS
WOODY GUTHRIE

and an article by — BOB DYLAN

NEW YORK TIMES. Seldom have the vicious effects of
poverty on the richest city in the world been
better illuminated. A quarter of the families in
the city live in grinding, abject, hopeless circumstance. They provide most of the grist for
the juvenile courts, the family courts, the jails.
They swell the relief rolls. They provide an
element of social dynamite in the existing order.

JANUARY
1964

Number 38, January 1964

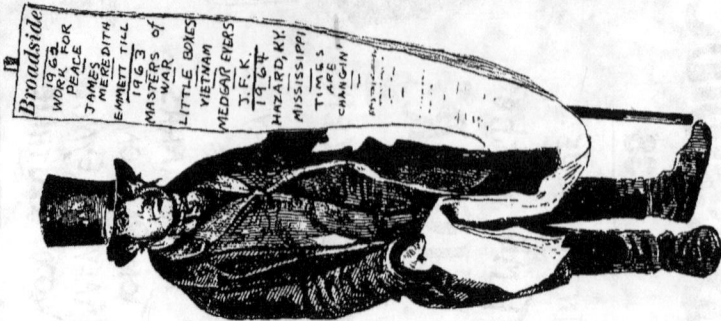

Broadside #52

THE NATIONAL TOPICAL SONG MAGAZINE   NOV. 20, 1964   PRICE — 50¢

THIS OLD WORLD IS CHANGIN' HANDS

by PHIL OCHS

© Copyright 1964 APPLESEED MUSIC, INC.

VERSE D MODERATELY

1. Oh, a thousand marching armies and a million marching men Have won the wide world o-ver and lost it back a-gain. But now the word has gone to ev'ry fallen land, That this old world is changin' hands. CHORUS: to the servant, from the master the servant, from the owner to the slave, Co-lonial days are buried in a deep & dirty grave; It's so ea-sy to see and well under-stand That this old world is changin' hands.

(continued→)

"West 104th St., Manhattan." By Agnes Friesen

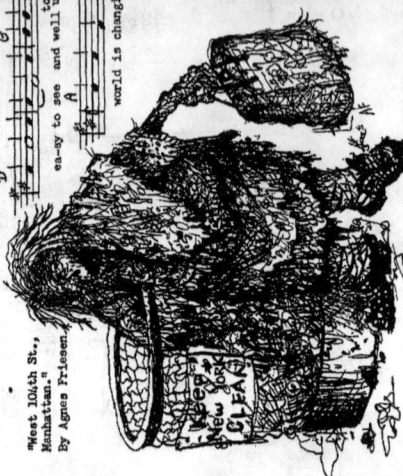

ALSO IN THIS ISSUE:
Songs by: Carolyn Hester, Matthew Jones, Jo Mapes, Malvina Reynolds, Tom Paxton, Buffy Sainte-Marie, Matt McGinn, Patrick Sky, Peter La Forge, others. Article "The Freedom Singers" by Julius Lester.

BROADSIDE #48

JULY 20 1964 Price 50¢

THE NATIONAL TOPICAL SONG MAGAZINE

IN THIS ISSUE

SONGS BY

RICHARD FARIÑA
LEN CHANDLER
PHIL OCHS
MALVINA REYNOLDS
ROGER K. LEIB
PEGGY SEEGER
JOHN BRUNNER
JENES COTTRELL

ARTICLES

THE ART OF BOB DYLAN'S "HATTIE CARROLL" --- BY PHIL OCHS

TOPICAL SONGS IN THE STREETS OF NEW YORK -- BY JULIUS LESTER

HOMAGE TO ERIC ANDERSEN

U.C. FOLK FESTIVAL

Broadside
1962 WORK FOR PEACE, JAMES MEREDITH, EMMETT TILL
1963 MASTERS OF WAR, LITTLE BOXES, VIETNAM, MEDGAR EVERS
1964 J.F.K., HAZARD, KY., MISSISSIPPI, TIMES ARE CHANGIN'

Broadside #67

THE NATIONAL TOPICAL SONG MAGAZINE   FEBRUARY 1966   PRICE — .50¢

Len Chandler

IN THIS ISSUE

"IS THERE ANYBODY HERE?"
Phil Ochs

"BABY, I'VE BEEN THINKING"
Janis Fink

Also:

RICHARD KAMPF
AGNES MARTIN
PATRICK SKY &
 ERNIE MARRS
MALVINA REYNOLDS
ALEX COMFORT
FRED HARDEN
LEN CHANDLER
CARL WATANABE
TOM PAXTON
JANE ROSENBERG

Poem:
"THE NEW DYLAN"
Other poems by
MIKE ROCOSM
CAROL RACZ

CAN GOOD PRO-
TEST SONGS
MAKE THE
MASS MEDIA?
"NO!"
says
Tom Paxton
In an inter-
view with:
Steve Mayer

Article:
"FOLK SONGS"
ON THE RIGHT

Number 67, February 1966

Broadside #92

Sculpture by Jane Friesen   Photographed by Erik Falkensteen

in this issue

"Let Us Wrap You In Our Warm And Freedom Love" by FREDERICK
DOUGLASS KIRKPATRICK. "Help Your Brother's Beat Across" by
JOAN COSMAN. "Sixteen Year Grudge" by ERIC ANDERSEN. Also:
LARRY HANKS, PATTY ZEITLIN, DOTTIE GITTELSON and EDWARD
LIPTON...JAC HOLZMAN replies to PHIL OCHS. TOSHI SEEGER and
the "star system."

JUNE, 1968   50¢

Number 92, June 1968

Broadside #90

Jimmy **Collier**   Frederick Douglass **Kirkpatrick**

The CITIES ARE BURNING

A L S O   I N   T H I S   I S S U E

"Joaquin Murieta" by R.C.GREENFIELD. MALVINA REYNOLDS, PETER
IRSAY, JONATHAN KWITNY, EDWARD DI GANGI, SUE SCHWARTZ. Part 2
of an interview with PHIL OCHS. Cuba visit by IRWIN SILBER.

April- 1968   50¢

Number 90, April 1968

Broadside #100

NINA SIMONE'S REVOLUTION!

MIKE MILLIUS' the pusher

also

JIMMY COLLIER

PETE SEEGER

IRWIN HEILNER
&
AARON KRAMER

NINA SIMONE

"We will not tolerate violence.
Reason must prevail!"

JULY 1969

75¢

Number 100, July 1969

A selection of *Broadside* benefit concert posters. (*Broadside* Collection)

October 24, [1973], Columbia University, New York City

WBAI CLUB & BROADSIDE magazine present "CITY SINGERS in CONCERT" with PHIL OCHS, JOHN HAMMOND, MARK SPOELSTRA

FRIDAY, MARCH 8   8:30 PM
AT THE C.C.N.Y.
FINLEY STUDENT CENTER
(GRAND BALLROOM - 133rd and Convent)

TICKETS: ALL SEATS $1.25 at FOLKLORE CENTER 110 McDOUGAL GR 7-5987

SUBWAY: B'way, 7th Ave. IRT to 137th

March 8, [1968], City College of New York, New York City

BROADSIDE Magazine presents a folk-topical CONCERT

WITH

Rev. Frederick Douglass KIRKPATRICK
Ric MASTEN (Big Sur Poet-Singer)
MIKE MILLIUS
PETER SEEGER
ELAINE WHITE
others

at the UNIVERSALIST CHURCH
4 W. 76th St. NYC (corner C.P.W.)
SUNDAY, APR 27, at 5 P.M.

DONATION: $2.50 - CHILDREN: $1.

April 27, [1969], Universalist Church, New York City

BROADSIDE MAGAZINE

PRESENTS THE FIRST-OF ITS SERIES

BENEFIT CONCERTS '88

Featuring:

MATT JONES, LUCI MURPHY, TOM PAXTON,

PETE SEEGER

Host: **SIS CUNNINGHAM**

SUNDAY, SEPTEMBER 11, 1988
AT 4 P.M.

FOURTH UNIVERSAL SOCIETY

Corner 76 St. & Central Park West, New York

ADMISSION: $12.50 ADVANCE $15.00 DOOR

Tickets Info: Mail Order: (Checks Payable)
Broadside Magazine P.O. Box 670
Cathedral Station, N.Y., N.Y. 10025
(212) 874-3423   (718) 774-8244

Apostrophies Bookstore	212-877-6940
Matt Umanoff Guitars	212-675-2157
Music Inn	212-243-5715
Corner Stop Mini Mart	718-646-1192
Mayfair Photo	718-743-5400

FOLK SONGS OF FREEDOM AND STRUGGLE

STRICTLY FOR THE PURPOSES AND PUBLICATIONS OF BROADSIDE MAGAZINE

Printed By The Progressof, Inc., 885 Rogers Ave., Brooklyn, N.Y. — 774-0830

September 11, 1988, Fourth Universal Society, New York City

---

mary ann pollar presents

benefit for
broadside

(the topical song magazine)

Malvina Reynolds
Rosalie Sorrels
Mark Spoelstra
Gil Turner
Will Geer

*

SATURDAY, April 13

8:30 p.m. garfield jr. high school
rose at grant streets . berkeley

admission: $ 2.00, 3.00

tickets: record city, 2340
telegraph, berkeley (th 1 - 4652)

information 836 - 0584

* courtesy ACT

April 13, [1968], Garfield High School, Berkeley, California

Chapter 9

The *Broadside* Years

Yesterday is gone, today is racing on and tomorrow rolls towards us like a
  wave upon the shore;
And new generations will hold in their hands
A Freedom only dreamed of before.
For the Age of Space will be the Age of Peace
Dreams now unfettered flying free.
Men and women of all races working hand in hand to witness the dawn
  of history.

("An Anthem for the Space Age," words and music by Sis Cunningham, ©1962)

Sis

In 1969 or 1970, on an autumn night in New York City, I was walking the dog in front of our apartment building when I heard the
ruckus of merry-making up the block. A group of five or six young
people were coming in my direction, laughing, pushing each other
around, walking backward one foot in the gutter, goofing off in general. When they got in front of our building, one of the young men
sat smack down in a broken chair that was there awaiting disposal
by the city's sanitation engineers. It so happened that it was a chair
we had thrown out, an old maple chair with its arm broken off. The
kid just sat there with a discarded lamp shade on his head, pretending to be king-on-a-throne or something, while the others were
expostulating, "Come on, come on, man. Let's get on!" They
seemed to be going partying.

The situation interested me, and I got an idea. The dog and I made
our way to the center of the little group, and I said, "Young man, do
you know who else sat in that chair besides you?" Silence.

Then with a note of sarcasm he asked, "No, who?"

"Bob Dylan sat in that chair many times," I said. The group tit-
tered, and one of them put a hand to the side of his head and made

a circular motion with his finger. So for a moment I was a fruitcake. Then I pointed up and said, "See that window up there? That's the office of *Broadside Magazine*, and I'm the editor. Dylan used to come to our audition meetings and sing his songs onto our tape recorder; I transcribed them, and we put them in our magazine. We printed twenty-eight of his earliest songs. 'Blowin' in the Wind' was one."

Then one of the fellows, after somewhat of a pause, said, "Hey, man, she's cool. I think she's tellin' the truth." The group mulled this over. Then the kid in the chair said, "Who else sat in this chair?" I said that was a big order, and I reeled off a bunch of names: Phil Ochs, Tom Paxton, the Seegers, Malvina Reynolds, Janis Ian, Peter La Farge, Len Chandler, Reverend Frederick Kirkpatrick, Moe Asch, and so on.

"Did Woody Guthrie sit in that chair?" one of the young women asked. I paused a moment to catch a thought. "No," I said. "Woody Guthrie didn't. But, I have sat in the same chair Woody has. And you can touch me." The kid in the chair got up; I stuck out my arm and they all touched it. Then two of the fellows swung the chair up to their shoulders, a girl picked up the broken arm, and they all pranced off toward Broadway. Resuming their merriment with even more hilarity then before, they disappeared around the corner of the building.

It was years later that I got to thinking about this little experience. These young people, just any group that one might meet on the street at any time, had brought up the name of Woody Guthrie; I hadn't. They saw the connection between Dylan and Woody and *Broadside*. And there is a connection. If Gordon and I hadn't met Woody in the Almanac Singers and got to know him well, it's more than possible that *Broadside* would not have come into existence back in 1962. This may be looked upon as speculation, but I believe that if Woody hadn't died tragically in 1967 at the young age of fifty-five, *Broadside Magazine* would have achieved a far greater level of appreciation and consequently a more far-reaching circulation. As it happened, we remained small. It was the great movements of the '60s and our focus upon them that enabled the magazine to survive at all. It's true that *Broadside* saw its first light of day in 1962, five years before Woody's death. But though he was always with us in spirit, he was too sick to take an active part in what we were endeavoring to do, which was to get down in print and on records as many of the great body of topical protest songs as possible. These songs were springing from the Civil Rights movement and from the burgeoning opposition to the Vietnam War. There was a veritable outpouring. Let's not lose them, we thought. Let's spread them around if we can. Woody would have gone along with that—that's what he had been doing during his active years. And did he crowd a lot into those short years! Yes, if Woody had lived, the story of *Broadside* would be easier to tell. In fact it would tell itself.

There's a little story that illustrates how some of the *Broadside* memorabilia got lost. A lot of the leftover *Broadside* papers, even quite a few of the letters, never were filed properly. Every once in a while the accumulation would be dumped in a packing box and the box placed on top of a cabinet in our cramped little office room, presumably to be taken care of later. We had a big neutered tomcat, Acie Boy, who, as he got along in years, made a home in one of the boxes way up next to the ceiling. There was room in this particular box for him to bed down, so that only once in a while did we see his two ears above the rim. The cat got old and finally he got sick. He was quite weak, and we wondered how he made the jump from the lower cabinet to his home. One day we found him dead. We closed the top flaps of the box, and out went the papers, letters, and the poor old dead cat.

For years *Broadside* operated on a shoestring. The people who helped us financially were the Seegers, Pete and Toshi. They contributed thirty-five dollars weekly to cover the cost of paper, envelopes, cans of mimeograph ink, and, in the very beginning, postage. Subscription money, which began to come in after the first several issues, soon covered postage costs. We had no telephone during the first six or eight months of our operation. Our office was the small front room of the low-income project apartment in which we lived—the four of us: Gordon, myself, a middle-sized daughter, Aggie, and a small daughter, Jane. This room was also where we ate our meals; we cleared the dirty dishes off the table and went to work cutting stencils on a manual Underwood typewriter, or I would set up the scope and do the music. When the time came, we set up the mimeo machine, a hand-cranked one we had inherited when the American Labor Party branch closed in our neighborhood. (A friend coming back from Cuba said this machine was exactly the same model as the one Castro had in the Sierra Maestra.)

Broadside was a rag at first. Or considered as such by some who regarded our skinny issues with distaste because of their appearance. I say "appearance" because some of the very people who didn't like the looks of *Broadside* became everlasting subscribers; a number of them later became enthusiastic volunteers. We could never have operated without our volunteers. The very first thin issue contained six songs, words and music; one had been written by Malvina Reynolds and one by Bob Dylan. The date was February 1962. We attempted to put it out twice a month, but managed to do so only for a short time, becoming monthly before the year was out. By the fall Phil Ochs became a contributor, and throughout most of 1963 we hardly put out an issue that didn't contain one or two Ochs songs. There was a Reynolds and a Dylan in nearly all of those early issues. Tom Paxton, Len Chandler, and Peter La Farge came aboard, and many more of those fine '60s song writers became what we called *Broadsiders*. We had writers sending songs from foreign countries; we printed letters and articles from all over. We were kept busy.

Though we did get some songs through the mails—mostly on tape, a few lead sheets—we got much of our material by setting up monthly meetings and encouraging writers to come to our little apartment with their guitars and sing into our big old reel-to-reel recorder. I transcribed the music and insisted on being supplied with a copy of the lyrics so that every word would be correct in the magazine. Bob Dylan came to these monthly meetings for well over a year. Gil Turner, emcee at Gerde's Folk City, brought him to the first one. Dylan was quite shy and would often sing just a verse or two of a song and instruct his companion, Suze, to send us a copy of the lyrics the following day—which she would do.

Phil Ochs started coming within a few months and continued to come long after we discontinued the monthly meetings. He always visited us when in New York after his move to California; he still put his songs on tape for us, and Gordon and I taped long interviews with him, which we transcribed and printed in *Broadside*. We later recorded some of the conversations on L-P albums through Folkways Records. He spent a lot of time with us during the summer and into the winter of 1975, talking hour after hour about being under the surveillance of the FBI. Phil was quite ill, so we taped none of this. But later we confirmed what he said by sending to the Freedom of Information Act for a report on him and receiving over four hundred pages. In a letter we were informed that some material on Phil remained classified and unobtainable. Phil died April 9, 1976; we believe he was harassed to death by crazy circumstances.

We never could decide which was the more prolific song writer, Phil Ochs or Malvina Reynolds. We had sixty-nine of Phil's songs in *Broadside,* seventy of Malvina's. And left over in our files is a fat folder of her lead sheets and a collection of her small reel-to-reel tapes. Putting all these songs in, much as we wanted to, would have meant leaving out some of the newer writers, which we were trying not to do. I have never known anyone who resembles Malvina Reynolds in the least. There may have been women like her, but they lived before my time. Her uniqueness stood out like a trumpet beacon; it shone with the undeniable brightness of a lodestar, yet she never considered herself to be a star of any kind. She was down here with the rest of us all the time. The hundreds of songs she wrote and performed were of a kind to make each of us feel somehow important in the scheme of things; that was the essence of Malvina's genius. To have her as a staunch supporter gave us assurance that *Broadside* would continue. Her home was in California, and the most money the magazine ever received in one wad was when Malvina arranged a benefit concert for us in the San Francisco area. She gave two smaller benefits when visiting here.

At one of these benefits, Janis Ian joined Malvina; Janis was sixteen, Malvina was in her sixties. Janis first came to our apartment/office when she was thirteen and sang her first little song for *Broadside.* She became one of our volunteers; she typed, collated, and stapled. Before age fourteen she had written a song, "Baby, I've Been Thinking," which we printed and which became a national hit under the title "Society's Child." It was a song about a white girl being attracted to a black boy and being very much frowned upon for straying from the norm. Fabulous little Janis; she was very soon to become a recording star and give a one-woman concert in Avery Fisher Hall—before her seventeenth birthday. For that event she ordered a big black limousine to take her parents and Gordon and me to the hall.

In going through a stack of *Broadside* back issues, you would find the names of other song writers who have achieved varied degrees of fame, or *well-knowness,* a term I prefer. Some of these persons come to mind as I write: Buffy Sainte-Marie, Peggy Seeger, Vanessa Redgrave, Billy Edd Wheeler, Julius Lester, Johnny Cash, Nina Simone, Leon Rosselson, Eric Andersen, Steve Forbert, Carolyn Hester, Kristin Lems, Les Rice, Pete Seeger, John Brunner, Lucinda Williams, Sammy Walker, Bev Grant, Alex Comfort, Henry Foner, Matt Jones, Pat Sky, Hedy West, Frederick Douglass Kirkpatrick, Lewis Allen, Jonathan Kwitny, Bernice Reagon.

Keeping *Broadside* alive was never easy. We both, Gordon and I, had to do other work to pay rent and keep food on the table. I had an outside, part-time job for several years, and we both did typing at home, paid by the page or by the reel-to-reel tape we were transcribing. Toshi Seeger gave me part-time work at the office of Pete's manager, Harold Leventhal. When I wrote that we started out on a shoestring, I should have admitted that the shoestring was a long one that stretched over the entire expanse of *Broadside*'s existence. Once it broke. In the early '80s we found it necessary to turn the operation over to someone else. Both Gordon and I were troubled by various illnesses, Gordon's being a series of little strokes and an ulcer he developed during the time of Phil's sickness and death (he was very close to Phil). My trouble, as I later realized, was burnout. We had difficulty resuming the *Broadside* work in '85 but managed by setting up a collective of eight interested people to keep the magazine going for three more years. Some very good issues came out of this period. For their efforts at this time, Julius Gordon and Carol Hanisch belong in the *Broadside* Hall of Fame—if anyone ever decides to set one up.

We decided to fold after the November–December 1988 issue. We accepted the fact that being in one's late seventies was too far along in years to undergo the stress of holding things together in such an enterprise without adequate resources. Time only will tell whether our efforts through the years served to bring about a modicum of change.

During the 1950s my accordion was stuck in the back of the closet, moldering back there. I didn't do anything for about fifteen years, not very much of anything in the way of music. Gordon and I handled Pete Seeger's correspondence. That was one of our jobs. Seeger dictated his letters onto reel-to-reel tapes, then he'd send the tapes and I would type them. I did most of the typing. Gordon did some of it. And there was a correspondence between Malvina Reynolds and Seeger about this idea of having a topical song magazine that would be specifically devoted to the printing of new, topical, protest/political music.

I don't know who first had the idea, but I believe Malvina did. Malvina had said in the letter that she was considering starting a magazine because she felt there was a great need for it. She didn't think *Sing Out!* was printing enough topical material. They were going back and printing up a lot of old folk songs and things. So she thought there was a need for a magazine that devoted itself specifically to topical protest. Finally she decided and said, "I don't think I want to spend my time and energy to put out a magazine. I want to just go on writing and singing wherever I can and devoting myself exclusively to that, to writing and performing my own songs and recording them and putting them in song books and stuff."

Well, when I realized that she was not going to do it, I spoke to Pete. I said, "Well, you have this idea of a topical song magazine. I think I can do it because I can transcribe. I think Gordon and I can do it. Gordon's a good writer." So Pete said, "Oh sure, hey, that's a good idea." We didn't have any money at all. We just had nothing. But we worked. We sent out a kind of a feeler letter to fifty or one hundred people to see what they thought about it. And some of them came back saying, "Yeah, that's a good idea," and "Why don't you do it?" We got a few contributions—not a lot. But Pete and Toshi said they would sort of pay expenses, they would pay for a telephone, for materials we were going to need. With the American Labor Party mimeograph machine, we decided we could do it, although we weren't allowed to have any kind of business in our low-income project apartment. But we did it for two years and got by with it.

Pete and Toshi came to the monthly meetings. At first Gil Turner would bring singers to us, Bob Dylan, Phil Ochs, Tom Paxton, Len Chandler, because Gordon and I didn't go out a lot to the clubs. We had a Revere reel-to-reel tape recorder from Pete, and it really taped the stuff so you could understand every word, and then I would transcribe the songs. After the magazine got circulated, we started to find singers ourselves—topical-song writers started coming from nowhere; they were dropping out of the sky. At first we mimeographed all the pages, then we had the song pages printed but still mimeographed the editorial pages and just stuck them in. We'd have some young volunteers come around to help with all the collating and stapling. We worked pretty hard. I can remember sometimes setting a deadline for ourselves to get an issue out, to get all the material together, and I can remember lots of times working all night. It wasn't easy.

Gordon and I would listen to all the stuff, and we would pick out what we thought was good. We were also getting in the mail a lot of songs on these little reel-to-reel tapes, and we would listen to them. Then if Phil Ochs or someone—Peter La Farge, Tom Paxton, or Len Chandler—happened to drop in right around the time that we were deciding, we would play the tapes for them and let them help us decide. Of course, Gordon and I did the initial weeding out of material that we didn't think belonged in the magazine. When Malvina Reynolds came to New York from California, she'd visit us and give advice. In every issue we wanted to get some absolutely brand-new, utterly unknown people, and there were an awful lot of real good songs starting to come out at the time. Gordon and I usually decided what to put on the front cover, but we also let whoever came around give their advice. Phil would come around and say, "I got seven new songs." We'd say, "What! Seven new songs?" So he said, "Yeah." And Gordon would ask him, "Well, where do you get all your material?" He'd say, "Well, I get it out of the newspapers and out of *Newsweek*. I wrote two of them on my way up here on the subway from the Village." And almost every day we'd get something from Malvina Reynolds on a little reel-to-reel tape, or she would send the lead sheets. But we had a lot of songs by absolute unknowns, and sometimes they would just hit it and come up with a very good song. And if they did, we'd put in it, no matter if anybody had ever heard of them. Then they sort of dropped out of sight, a lot of them.

By the mid-'60s we had a circulation of about a thousand, and then it grew to around twenty-five hundred—that's about as big as it ever got. Of course, when we sent out our advertising cards we said three thousand. We got quite a few ads: a few from Columbia Records because we didn't charge too much for them—seventy-five dollars for a full page—and some from Vanguard and Elektra Records. Moe Asch had this standing thing. He said, "Don't waste a whole page. I'll pay for a whole page, but just put a notice at the bottom of the page." And Seeger did that a few times too, put a little notice at the bottom of the page saying, "This page paid for by Pete and Toshi Seeger." And then a few other people did that too.

In 1964 we moved to a seven-room apartment on the Upper West Side. Gordon's brother Ollie was without a place to live and was on a veteran's pension, so he helped pay the rent. This was a semiprofessional apartment; you couldn't live in the building unless you ran a business. The rent jumped five times from what we had been paying in our little low-income housing apartment—sixty dollars a month with gas and lights included. Gordon didn't want to do it. He said, "Oh no, that's terrible. We can't even think about anything like that." And I said, "Well, that's the only way *Broadside* is going to grow. And what the heck else are we going to do with our lives? There's just nothing else." I would be slaving away at some kind of terribly low-income job, and Gordon would also be slaving away part of the time on a barely-above-minimum-wage job. He couldn't get a job in journalism. So I said, "How in the world is *Broadside* going to grow? We've got to figure out some way to do it." So we took all the money we had, absolutely all the money, and we paid the deposit and one month's rent and just moved in. We had nothing, nothing. I was still working in a day-care center taking care of three-year-olds; Gordon was doing a lot of typing at home. I was also going to Harold Leventhal's office, Pete's manager, to do some bookwork for Pete and Toshi. And *Broadside* was growing. So, with Ollie paying half the rent, we jumped in and took the risk.

First of all, we had to prove we were going to run a business in the apartment. The landlord could not charge such rents unless the residents were making money on the premises. There were doctors, lawyers, graphic artists, and even a small theater in the building we were trying to get into. People like Joseph Papp and Alan Lomax had offices in it. You had to show items you produced and letters from clients or customers. I gathered my stuff and went to a downtown office to meet with the landlord, Mr. Wald, in the presence of a city official. I took out my stuff for both of them to peruse, among which was the latest issue of *Broadside*. When Mr. Wald looked at it, he studied it awhile and got a scowling look on his face. "Wait a minute," he exclaimed. "This is an antilandlord song you got right here on the cover of this magazine." My breath went out of me. What had I done now to foul things up? I looked over at the magazine. Jesus H. Christ, I could just as well have brought the next-to-the-last issue! There on the cover was Malvina Reynolds' song "The Faucets Are Dripping":

> The faucets are dripping in old New York City
> The faucets are dripping and oh what a pity

The reservoir's drying because it's supplying
The faucets that drip in New York.

I collected my thoughts quickly and decided the only thing to do
was to laugh. So I laughed. And I said, "Mr. Wald, that's not an antilandlord song, it's just a funny—a very funny—song." I knew that
wasn't enough; my thoughts were racing. I hesitated a moment or
two, then said, "If you are going to feel bad about antilandlord stuff,
just don't read the newspapers and newsmags that are coming out
now. But a funny song like this, how can you feel bad about that?"
I let go with a hearty chuckle.

Well, it worked; we got accepted.

II: Gordon

In the fall of 1961 Pete Seeger and his wife, Toshi, taking along their
smallest daughter, Tinya, made a tour of the British Isles. Almost
everywhere they went they were invited to gatherings where people
sang songs for them, old and new.

Pete was impressed with both, but especially so by the extent and
quality of the new song writing. These songs were what are called—
for lack of a better name—topical songs. Unlike the vaporizings of
tin-pan alley, which go on whining about love, love, love year after
year, decade after decade like a stuck needle, they deal with the un-
limited range of topics of the day. One might call them singing commentaries on the times, mixing satire, humor, and often deep, probing insight. In England and Scotland Pete heard songs demanding an
end to atom-bomb insanity, songs scandalizing corrupt politicians,
songs frankly telling Uncle Sam to take his nuclear submarines out
of the Clyde and stick 'em. A whole album of songs about the housing plight had been recorded under the intriguing title of "Songs to
Swing Landlords By."

Shortly after returning to the United States, Pete was talking
about his trip to Sis. "They're writing an awful lot of new songs over
there. About everything under the sun," he said, adding, "and many
of them are damn good songs, too." He wondered aloud at why
something similar was not happening in America, and he and Sis
discussed the situation back and forth. For one thing, freedom of
expression had never been curtailed in Britain to the magnitude that
it had in America during the tragic 1950s; there was never an un-

British Activities Committee prowling the land. Here in the United States, the Weavers had been blacklisted at the height of their popularity; the Pentagon itself reportedly ordered the banning of Vern Partlow's song "Talking Atom" from the radio waves. Seeger had been sentenced to prison (the sentence later was reversed).

True, a handful of American song writers—Malvina Reynolds, Ernie Marrs, Pete himself—had kept stubbornly on, putting the things they felt needed saying into their songs. The flame was kept alive in the "Folk Process" column in *Sing Out!* magazine and by such recording companies as Folkways, with its "Gazette" series. But the dark hand of McCarthyism had lifted, and Sis felt that the changed conditions must inevitably bring with them more creative activity in the United States and that the country's song writers would be sharing this. She argued her point something along these lines: "How do we know that young people all over America may not be writing topical songs right now? It's just that we're not hearing about it. The big commercial music publishers and recording companies aren't interested in this sort of material. We may just be assuming that songs like this aren't being written and sung. God knows there isn't much of an outlet for them."

Out of this conversation emerged *Broadside*, which was to try and serve as an outlet for topical songs, a place where writers of such songs could exhibit their wares to performers looking for such material. Physically, it wasn't a fancy showcase. There was no modern printing press available, only an ancient mimeograph machine. There was no slick paper; only sixteen-pound mimeo at eighty cents a ream. But though the magazine in appearance was lowly, its aims were lofty. As Sis said, "We want to give some sort of hearing to exactly those songs in which the 'commercial music world' has little or no interest." (She could have added "at the present time," for within less than two years, topical songs were being sung, published, and recorded all over the United States.)

Among those turning thumbs down on the idea was Lee Hays, who argued that no good songs would be written because it was impossible for anyone to write a worthwhile song about something outside his or her personal experience. This was the same point Woody Guthrie used to maintain when the Almanacs would debate song writing theory. "You can't write a good song about a dust storm unless you been in one," Woody would argue. "You can't write a good song about a whorehouse unless you been in one." However,

Woody would sit down, maybe that same night, and write a song about a mine disaster he never was closer to than the story he read about it in the *New York Times*. There was also the fine song he wrote during World War II about the Soviet girl partisan, Ludmilla Pavlichenko, who killed three hundred Nazis—with its rousing chorus, it was one of the most popular songs the Almanacs ever performed. Woody, of course, had never been in the Soviet Union, never slew a Nazi, and never was a girl.

Sis, in considering Lee Hays's opinion, pointed out that in today's shrinking world many issues have become so vast as to affect almost everybody. "The threat of an atomic holocaust, for example, directly and personally involves every single human being in the world. There are probably few people who haven't vividly imagined what will happen to them individually in an atomic explosion." The struggle of the millions of American blacks for their freedom makes itself personally felt throughout the nation, in the North as well as the South.

Pete and Sis decided to go ahead and launch *Broadside* as best they could. Issue no. 1 came out in February of 1962. It had five songs in it, including Bob Dylan's "Talking John Birch Society Blues" (it was Bob's first appearance in print, if you can call what a mimeograph machine does *printing*). On its cover was a brief statement, drafted mainly by the third key figure in the birth of *Broadside*, Gil Turner. He was instrumental in seeing that the magazine got not only songs from the northern group but also those created virtually in the streets during black demonstrations in southern towns and cities. He returned from a 1962 tour of Mississippi (with the New World Singers) with the first of the latter songs to appear in *Broadside*: "Ain't Gonna Let Segregation Turn Me Around," "Oh, Pritchett, Oh, Kelly," and others. Later Pete Seeger brought back the songs "Back of the Bus," "I Ain't Scared of Your Jail," "Never Turn Back," and others.

It should be mentioned that other key persons were Josh Dunson and Julius Lester, who wrote articles on the new songs, their use and significance; also the magazine's artist, our daughter Agnes, whose drawings occasionally bring the comment that they are as good as the songs they are illustrating. The main contributors, however, were the song writers themselves, known and unknown, who flooded *Broadside* with their creations and then waited more or less patiently to see what would happen to them.

Some of the songs became national hits and even made their way overseas. "Blowin' in the Wind" was in *Broadside* fully a year before it soared to wide popularity; Malvina Reynolds's "Little Boxes" almost as long. Established folk singers like Carolyn Hester, Barbara Dane, and the like learned to follow its pages for new material. (Nina Simone, asked where she got some of the songs on her program, answered: "From *Broadside,* of course. Where else?") One thing that made getting a hearing tough for those topical-song writers who did not themselves perform was that quite a few of the top performers—Dylan, Ochs, Paxton—used little or no material that was not their own. Pete Seeger was one person making it a regular practice to sing new songs by unknown writers.

The times, "they were a-changin'," and topical songs had an audience never reached before in the United States (Joe Hill was born too soon). The Chad Mitchell group packed Carnegie Hall with a program "so filled with social commentary that it almost seemed more a topical review with music than a concert" (*New York Times*). Commercial folk-singing groups who once strictly shunned songs with a message were now putting out record albums with such titles as *Time to Think* and *Songs of Our Times* in an effort to hang on to their slipping popularity. (A reason this effort seemed not to be meeting with any great success may have been that these groups still couldn't quite bring themselves to sing the blunt, straightforward, hard-hitting material of the Mitchell Trio, Dylan, and Ochs.)

Why were so many young Americans writing and singing these songs called *topical?* And why were so many other Americans listening, and demanding more of them? These related questions did not have simple answers. Phil Ochs said of the song writers: "We're trying to crystallize the thoughts of young people who have stopped accepting things the way they are." Bob Dylan was described as a spokesman for American youth who were fed up with warmongering, corruption, race hatred, hypocrisy, injustice—the list of social flaws is long. Phil Ochs was one convinced that topical songs were not just another fad. "This is a solid thing," he said.

One reason for what Pete Seeger had called this "virtual explosion of topical-song writing in America" may be described as technical—the availability of a means of expression. Pete wrote in a *Broadside* article: "People have discovered that this short form known as a 'song' is ideal for saying some of the things they want to say." It is ideal because, among other things, it bypasses those who own and monopolize the multimillion-dollar means for communication in America. Creative artists in other media—plays, books, paintings—must meet the approval of the investors with money and access to theaters, printing presses, galleries, etcetera. To present a song all you need is to own a guitar (a conveniently transportable piece of equipment) or to know a guitar picker willing to sing it for you.

Then there was another peculiar thing that happened: the discovery (or rediscovery, if you will) that if you have a poem and put it to music it will take on an entirely new dimension—sprout wings and really fly. Poets with much to say and relying solely on the printed page to get their messages across often spend their whole lives without reaching more than a few thousand contemporaries. But set music to the poem and there's no limit to the number who may hear you. Bob Dylan typified this fact. Most publishers know beforehand that a book of poetry by a new author will definitely lose money and not sell to more than maybe five hundred people. Much of Dylan's work is sheer poetry ("Hard Rain," for example). If he had found a publisher disposed to put out a Dylan book of poems, how many Americans would ever have heard of Bob? Certainly only a minute fraction of the millions who buy records with Dylan songs on them.

Phil Ochs quite consciously reached the conclusion that wrapping your ideas in music might be the best way to get them heard. He studied journalism for three years at Ohio State, and the main lesson he learned was that it would be extremely difficult, if not impossible, to find freedom of expression in the journalistic field, with things the way they are. So he got himself a guitar, learned to play it, started writing his thoughts into songs, and at twenty-three was probably far more widely known than any journalist in the country twice his age.

But a song and a guitar make up only two sides of the triangle; essential also is somebody to listen to you. Where did the audience for topical songs come from? Most of it was made up of youth, mainly college students (with a surprisingly large number of high school students also). This was as it should be, since many observers noted that university campuses were one of the few places in America still open to new and nonconformist ideas. And there is the significant fact, too, that some of the best-known topical-song writer/singers were themselves from the campus: Phil Ochs was at Ohio State; Bob Dylan at the University of Minnesota; Buffy Sainte-

Marie was educated at the University of Massachusetts; Tom Paxton is a graduate of the University of Oklahoma; Len Chandler holds a master's degree from Columbia.

These modern-day writer/performers, however, are anything but academicians. With few exceptions they heed Woody Guthrie's oft-quoted advice: "The worst thing that can happen to you is to cut yourself loose from people. And the best thing is to sort of vaccinate yourself right into the big streams and blood of the people." Some of the song writers in *Broadside* probably spent as much time on picket lines and at civil-rights demonstrations as they did performing in coffee houses, night clubs, and college auditoriums. Malvina Reynolds canceled a trip to Europe to keep on doing what she had been doing for years: writing songs and singing them to California peace and civil-rights demonstrations and union rallies. Phil Ochs and Tom Paxton lived with and sang for the impoverished miners' families around Hazard, Kentucky; Gil Turner and Len Chandler were acquainted with the insides of jails (Len's civil-rights activities led to his being jailed in both the North and the South).

A long list of names in *Broadside* participated in the Caravan of Music in Mississippi during the summer of 1964, helping COFO (Council for Federated Organizations) in the black voter-registration drive. We published the accounts of several of these participants, notably Bob Cohen's "Mississippi Caravan of Music," Len Chandler's long poem "Random Thoughts on a Mississippi Muddle," plus his introduction to his beautiful and memorable song, "I'm Goin' to Get My Baby Outa Jail," all in issue no. 51. In earlier issues we had printed "Oh, Pritchett, Oh, Kelly" by Bertha Gober, a black teenager, written while she was in jail in Albany, Georgia, for her fourth arrest, and "If You Miss Me at the Back of the Bus." One of the most moving songs we printed during this period was another by Bertha Gober, "Never Turn Back." Bob Dylan's early "Balad of Emmett Till," about the brutal murder of a fourteen-year-old black youth, and "The Lonesome Death of Hattie Carroll" are examples of great writing on events preceding what became known as Mississippi Freedom Summer. Phil Ochs went south that summer and wrote us moving letters from there; his "Here's to the State of Mississippi" was one of the strongest songs ever to scorch the pages of our magazine. We also received a jolting song from Nina Simone, "Mississippi Goddam." We received some letters from Broadsiders while they were down south, but for the most part they were too involved in the activities to do much writing; we listened to their reports when they returned. Nearly all were enthralled by their first experience in political action—and greatly stimulated.

Tom Paxton once observed in talking about the debt the new song writers owed his fellow Oklahoman Woody Guthrie, "The most important thing Woody gave us was courage, the courage to stand up and say the things we believe." This same courage comes to many folks from the example of black people fighting for their freedom. It could be the decisive inspiration behind the whole topical-song-writing development in America. *Newsweek* has said: "History has never known a protest movement so rich in song as the Civil Rights movement." And whatever troubles the northern song writers had pale to insignificance when they saw a whole people go right on singing and making up new songs in the face of police dogs, fire hoses, electric cattle prods, jailings, beating, dynamiting, and murder and assassination—when they saw Mrs. Fanny Lou Hamer, a black citizen of Mississippi beaten almost to death when she tried to register to vote, in the midst of death and murder make up a new verse to the song "Back of the Bus":

> If you miss me in the freedom fight,
> And you can't find me nowhere
> Come on over to the graveyard,
> I'll be buried over there.

There were great changes after *Broadside* first started publishing, although some things remained the same. The British became envious of American topical-song writing. It was hardly credible that such savagely biting songs as Dylan's "Masters of War" and "God on Our Side" would ever be recorded by a major company, but they were—by one of the biggest: Columbia. Recognition of topical-song writers was widespread in the press, with even the *New York Times* printing a two-page article about "the angry young men of song." The word *broadside* came back into popular usage (the 1963 Newport Folk Festival called its topical-song workshop Broadsides). Topical songs replaced traditional folk material in the repertoires of many performers, including Joan Baez and Peter, Paul and Mary. *Broadside* got a number of letters from singers over the country saying: "I used to sing only traditional folk songs. Now I sing only songs from *Broadside*." Others letters told how these songs penetrated the farthest reaches; a subscriber from a small town in the Canadian hinterlands wrote: "You might be interested to know that Nina Simone's 'Mississippi Goddam' is very popular here."

Changes in some other areas were hardly noticeable. While one arm of the giant Columbia corporation recorded Dylan and Pete Seeger, another barred them from CBS Television. ABC-TV presented a show called "Hootenanny," but from it blacklisted the man who, with Woody Guthrie, assigned such events that very name. In the winter of 1964 the vaunted leader of the "free world" forbad Ewan MacColl to come to its shores. In its strongholds of southern California and Dallas, Texas, the John Birch Society succeeded in driving Malvina Reynolds's "Little Boxes" from the radio waves.

The question of whether the songs in *Broadside* were folk songs remains unresolved. Pete Seeger is willing to leave the final decision to the distant future: "If some folklorist a hundred years from now wants to call them folk songs let him go ahead—our dust will not object." And when Malvina Reynolds was described in the press as a "folk singer" she replied with a song: "I don't care what you call me, just so you sing my songs."

When we started *Broadside* we had two main purposes in mind. One, the most important, was to encourage young topical-song writers, and two was to keep as best we could a record of this kind of song, often in no broader form than clues for future researchers. We possessed no illusions that any great number of these songs would be picked up and popularized by the big commercial recording companies. In most instances they were written not for a mass audience but only spontaneously for local purposes. For example, the songs for civil-rights marchers and demonstrators or for those among them who were arrested and jailed (to keep up their morale while in prison—for instance, Bertha Gober's "Never Turn Back," which she wrote for her fellow black inmates). We were acquainted with the role topical, "homemade" songs had played in American history, beginning with the Revolution—in "The Bennington Rifles," the Green Mountain Boys warn the British that their rifles "will prove no trifles" and predict that the British will run home much faster than they came. Of course we all know the history of how our national anthem "The Star Spangled Banner" came to be written in one night by Francis Scott Key. At least a half-dozen songs made up by marching Union soldiers still survive from the Civil War.

Less remembered are the songs of the Hutchinson family. They wrote at least two hundred songs, which they sang at abolitionist meetings. They traveled extensively with the fiery speaker for abolition, Frederick Douglass, himself an escaped slave. Douglass lectured for the end of slavery while the Hutchinsons, who were white, presented the same message in songs. Often they were attacked by proslavery mobs. They protected themselves by tearing apart the speakers' platform and using the two-by-fours to beat back their attackers. Of all the songs the Hutchinsons composed, frequently for a purely local situation, only one is remembered well enough to be sung, and that by only a few people.

The innumerable songs of the American socialist movement that grew quite broad in the latter half of the nineteenth century have either been forgotten or remain in yellowing newspapers and leaflets in a few archives. Yet they served their contemporary purpose in socialist rallies and demonstrations. In our times the works of the Wobbly song writer Joe Hill are better remembered. It is ironical, however, that a song not *by* him but *about* him is the most widely popularized. This song by Alfred Hayes and Earl Robinson, "I Dreamed I Saw Joe Hill Last Night," was sung by Joan Baez to the hippies at Woodstock and has been recorded by her. She still performs it at many of her concerts.

The songs of the Great Depression were really the first protest music to be recognized by the big commercial recording companies. This was because the depression was so deep that all their song writers were making up music about it, and so many people were affected that the market was as plain as the nose on your face. The number-one song hit, at least outside the big cities of the North, "Seven-Cent Cotton, Forty-Cent Meat (How in the World Can a Poor Man Eat)," was written by a New York commercial composer, Bob Miller. Outside the rural areas, the big hit was "Brother Can You Spare a Dime" by E. Y. "Yip" Harburg, also of New York and a lyric writer for stage musicals.

Black folk singers were putting their protests in personalized blues. They had been widely exploited by the big record companies in the late 1920s and early 1930s, but their chief market, made up of the poorest of the poor, the black strata of our society, disappeared for the simple economic reason that their listeners hardly had money to buy food, let alone records. These composers of black folk blues were dropped like hot potatoes. They were left to shift on their own for the next forty years, when they were "rediscovered" during the folk revival of the 1960s. This pattern was exemplified by the case of Mississippi John Hurt. A master musician, he had made scores of records from 1927 to 1929. Then he was assigned to oblivion. The prime of his life was spent as a menial laborer, working on crews constructing gravel roads or dragging fallen trees from the Mississippi River. It was not until he was in his seventies that he was brought back from his obscurity. A series of Hurt recordings was produced, and he was invited to appear at folk festivals and to give concerts. His traveling to these concerts was the first time he had ever ridden in an airplane. But he was already an old man; he died in the middle of his new existence. He was one of perhaps a half-dozen such rediscoveries. Many of the black folk/blues musicians who had been recording stars in their youth vanished without a trace during this interim. Their names are known only from the labels on rare records that have survived and have become collector's items.

The main inspiration for the founding of *Broadside* was Woody Guthrie. Here was a man who wrote over two thousand songs. None of these songs became a national hit during his active career. Yet each served a purpose, sometimes regionally but more often only locally. He wrote about the dust bowl and about the refugees from this disaster and sang the songs at rallies in California, where attempts were being made to organize migratory workers. He composed songs about the building of the Grand Coulee Dam. He put together an album on the Sacco-Vanzetti miscarriage of justice. He wrote of miners dying in explosions, of the hard life of workers; he wrote about hobos and outlaws. Many of his songs are about the impoverished and the dispossessed. He traveled widely helping to organize the CIO. Yet from all these efforts he earned less in the way of finances before he was hospitalized and his creativity paralyzed than his son Arlo, who is a pop star, earns from one concert. Woody had a radio program in California for a year, and his income therefrom consisted solely of pennies his listeners would send in for copies of his songs, which he mimeographed himself.

It was only after he was hospitalized with dread Huntington's chorea that Woody's songs started earning money. Thousands of dollars started rolling in from such songs as "This Land Is Your Land." Total irony is the only way to describe the fact that the financial recompense for his life's work should start piling up when he could no longer enjoy it. The ironical ending of Woody's career, and finally of his life, had actually begun earlier. The beginning symptoms of

Huntington's disease frequently resemble drunkenness: loss of muscular coordination, slurring of speech, and so on. So it was with Woody Guthrie. His friends in New York put him down as an alcoholic, kicked him out, and deserted him. He was allowed to exist for a year in the gutters of the Bowery. He wandered over into New Jersey and was picked up by the police and thrown into the drunk tank. He continued to lie there for five days while his fellow inmates dried out and were released. It finally occurred to the jailers that this case was something more serious than simply a man on a binge. Only then did they call in a medical advisor who diagnosed—in reality, misdiagnosed—Woody's trouble as mental and had him placed in an institution for the insane. Months passed before it flashed into one of the doctor's minds that this might be a case of Huntington's chorea. By this time royalties from his songs were coming in, and those formerly close to Woody reappeared and had him transferred to New York City. Twelve long years of slow and painful deterioration were to follow before Woody finally died in 1967. An employee of the hospital told a friend of ours that when he carried Woody down to the morgue, his wasted body was light as a feather.

So we began *Broadside* for the purpose of providing an outlet for song writers deeply motivated by local struggles rather than aiming at becoming "stars." Some of the songs we printed did happen to become commercially profitable nationwide, such as Bob Dylan's "Blowin' in the Wind" and Malvina Reynolds's "Little Boxes," mentioned earlier. Pete Seeger's "The Big Muddy," which dealt allegorically with President Lyndon Johnson's stupidity in becoming ever more deeply enmeshed in the Vietnam War, found its way into the American language; a *New York Times* writer began his column with, "Before we got involved in the big muddy . . .". This Seeger song, incidentally, destroyed the Smothers Brothers' CBS network television show. When the Smothers Brothers invited Seeger to sing it, the big wheels at CBS bore down with the heavy hand of censorship. The Smothers Brothers fought back stubbornly. Seeger sang "The Big Muddy" on their show, which was canceled shortly afterward. They found only sporadic work on TV thereafter. Janis Ian's "Society's Child," which became number one or two on the national charts, was another song first published in *Broadside*.

These were exceptions. Mostly we had such songs as "Talking Crystal City," which told of the majority Chicanos fighting to take political control from the Anglos in city government. (Crystal City is a town in Texas that calls itself "the spinach capital of the world" and has a huge statue of Popeye in the middle of town.) Another song from Texas involved a university student named Roger whose "straight" parents had him placed in a mental institution when he refused to accompany them in killing deer and stayed in his dorm room reading socialist books instead of going to Longhorn football games.

We, of course, printed scores of civil-rights songs, ending with the "Ballad of Martin Luther King" by Mike Millius, which describes the murder of Dr. King in Memphis. It has been sung widely by black audiences but recorded only on a *Broadside* LP. Our anti–Vietnam War songs are almost too many to count. We believe the best song to come out of that conflict is "Pinkville Helicopter" by Tom Parrott. It is an ode to the only two true American heroes of that whole obscene U.S. aggression against the people of Vietnam. They were the pilot and copilot of a helicopter at the My Lai massacre of helpless children, women, and old men by American troops. (My Lai was called Pinkville by Lieutenant Calley's soldiers because the area was colored pink on their battle map.) The two men operating this particular helicopter picked up a wounded Vietnamese child to fly it to a medical station. Troops on the ground demanded it be thrown out so they could finish the job of killing it. The pilot and copilot refused, confronted the murderers with their own guns, drove them back, and flew the wounded child to safety. "Pinkville Helicopter" was reprinted in *I Hear America Singing*, compiled by Hazel Arnett.

We received numerous songs about Watergate. The best of them was written by a young Texan, Ron Turner, who chose as his hero Frank Wills, the alert black security guard who exposed the whole criminal plot by his discovery that a lock had been taped back. Turner took the necessary liberties to make it into a true folk song. "The Ballad of Frank Wills" was performed nationwide by the black singer/song writer Frederick Kirkpatrick. Almost invariably his black audiences gave him a standing ovation for his rendition of this song.

The folk process generally concentrates on one central point of an incident and excludes aspects considered not pertinent to the story being told. Take, for example, Woody Guthrie's "Pretty Boy Floyd." He portrays Floyd as a rural outlaw robbing Oklahoma banks and sharing his loot with the poor, à la Jesse James. In actuality,

Floyd was an enforcer for the Kansas City mafia. His assignment was to visit gambling dens and whorehouses that fell behind in their payments to the mob. He broke arms and legs and killed whenever the delinquency was too extreme to satisfy the gangster hierarchy. There is no hint of this in Guthrie's song; the song is essentially about the starving Oklahoma farmers rather than about the outlaw Floyd. Folk singers also often borrow from other sources. The key line in Woody's song, "Some will rob you with a six-gun, some with a fountain pen," was taken from a letter O. Henry wrote to Al Jennings, an Oklahoma bandit. They both served time together in an Ohio penitentiary, Jennings for trying to rob a train near Oklahoma City, O. Henry for embezzling from a Texas bank where he worked as a teller. They kept up a correspondence after being released from prison.

America's topical-song movement of the 1960s also had an international impact on song writing. Followers—in content and singing style—of Bob Dylan's protest songs appeared in England, France, West Germany, and elsewhere. In the Soviet Union, tapes of local performers singing Dylan songs were passed around among the youth. A Japanese group calling itself "The Broadside Four" was formed to sing songs from the magazine.

The question was frequently asked as to why so many *Broadside* writers concerned themselves with topics like wars; why didn't they write more often about love, flowers, winds upon the hills? Well, the magazine did print such songs (such as Rich Astle's "The Autumn Winds"). But topical-song writers, as distinct from other creators of music (which is often commercialized escapism), have always tended to deal with reality. And there was nothing more real than the U.S. war against the Vietnamese and the war's dehumanizing effect on Americans both in Vietnam and here at home.

It would not be fair to imply that the topical-song movement in the U.S. during the 1960s moved forward in a straight line, from mainly pro–civil rights to mainly anti–Vietnam War songs. The tempest was not without its turbulence. British critic Ewan MacColl, in a *Sing Out!* symposium, described the American topical/folk music scene as having become "a bewildering spectacle." One of the storm centers was Bob Dylan. He had been a key figure in the revival of folk-oriented topical songs in the early '60s. Acknowledging that his model was Woody Guthrie, Dylan wrote in 1962 and 1963 such songs as "Blowin' in The Wind," "Masters of War," "With God on

Our Side," and "Hattie Carroll." These songs constituted the blunt-est kind of political commentary, in the Guthrie manner; and, like the work of the Oklahoma balladeer, they were couched in near folk idiom and accompanied by folk-style tunes often borrowed from the past. There is no doubt that the success of these early Dylan songs was a main source of inspiration for the whole topical-song movement.

But then Dylan, almost suddenly, repudiated this kind of song and turned toward introspection, to probing his own soul, as it were, rather than looking outward to examine the flaws of the society in which he found himself. In a sense, the new product remained pro-test songs in that the selfsame society had helped create the inner soul he now held up for popular inspection. But when Dylan accom-panied the change in lyrical content by simultaneously abandoning that traditional folk instrument, the acoustical guitar, and switching to electric folk-rock, the result was shattering. He lost most of his original audience. He picked up a brand-new, vastly larger following, the young lovers of folk-rock. Some followed Dylan in his transition, others gave up in confusion. Much of the criticism leveled against Dylan accused him of "selling out," of surrendering his ideals in exchange for commercial gain. This has always been difficult to un-derstand, since the purely topical songs of his first phase, exempli-fied by those on the tracks of his L-P *Free Wheelin'*, were quite suc-cessful as commercialized products. His defenders, like Phil Ochs, maintained that there had been no real change, that Dylan was only developing his immense artistic talents to new poetic heights.

Whatever really happened, it did have a definite effect on topical-song writing. It caused scores of young song writers to abandon their original direction (toward ballads, political commentaries, etc.) in order to try and become new Bob Dylans. They began writing in-volved, personal, introspective poetry and then attempting to set the result to guitar music with mouth harp interludes. It looked so de-ceptively simple at first, but it turned out to be extremely difficult. It was as though a generation of young artists looked at Picasso and said to themselves, "that's easy." But like Picasso, Dylan proved to be unique. Most of his imitators were unable to match Dylan's elo-quent poetry or to master his musical technique (where Dylan's gui-tar chords unfailingly complimented his lyrics, theirs often became crashing intrusions). In trying to follow Dylan down his newfound road, many a young song writer was unhorsed. Literally hundreds of songs imitating Dylan were submitted to *Broadside*. Of them all, Chris Gaylord's "Daisy Queen" probably came the closest to the level of the master.

The preceding, of course, applies to only one facet of Dylan's complex career: its influence in the field of what might be termed social realism in topical-song writing. In the pop field, the results of Dylan's presence were also on the positive side at the beginning. Popular song, which had existed for decades on almost the sole subject of love—an empty, banal, peripheral love at that—acquired from Dylan's example the courage to introduce broader themes. He broke trail, as it were, for the meaningful early songs of The Beatles, Simon and Garfunkel, Donovan, and the like. This also seems to have been only a transient phenomenon, which apparently peaked and then vanished with the success and then suppression of the antiwar song "Eve of Destruction." The song-writing newcomers retreated from the harsh face of reality and—shades of tin-pan alley—began writing about love again, albeit with more shading and deeper probing than had been prevalent in the earlier, popular torch ballads. Another favorite theme offering escapism was that of the new drug taking among youth. Here again they took their cue from Dylan, some of whose songs of the new period were deemed to be talking, symbolically at least, about drugs ("Mr. Tambourine Man" was interpreted, for instance, as being a salesman of marijuana). In fact, Dylan's L-Ps were accepted by many acid heads as background music for taking a psychedelic trip and, in the process, dropping out of society. Like Dylan's songs of this kind, the work of his imitators was deeply shrouded in symbolism, obviously to confound the censors.

With a few remarkable exceptions, the topical-song writers aimed for the national popularity charts. There is absolutely nothing wrong in this; the composer should try to reach his or her maximum audience—and besides, the money comes in handy. But in striving to shape songs acceptable to the establishment—which, after all, owns the bulk of the nation's media for communication—and bring the author fame and fortune, there is an inexorable pressure to make songs more and more general in content. The end result can be a song so generalized that it may actually come to mean to many the exact opposite of what the author originally intended. The most reactionary elements can then press it to their bosom as their own. I found it necessary to argue with a young person who insisted

"Blowin' in The Wind" was all about Hungary. A letter in Bill Buckley's conservative journal, *National Review*, maintained that Malvina Reynolds's "Little Boxes" should be welcomed because "it described life under Communism." Peter Yarrow of Peter, Paul and Mary noted in a television interview that the group was astonished by the enthusiasm with which an all-white Mississippi university audience greeted "The Hammer Song." It turned out that the students interpreted the song as hammering out a warning against the danger to their freedom from encroaching desegregation. The "hammer of justice" to them meant white justice, the justice of the Ku Klux Klan. Along the same lines, Birchite delegates to the Republican convention joined in singing, with great gusto and conviction, "This Land Is My Land." Obviously, their interpretation was that America belonged only to the super-patriotic reactionaries. This is at least 100 percent the opposite of what Woody Guthrie had in mind when he wrote "This Land."

There is a certain kind of traditional topical song that makes an unequivocal statement that generally cannot be misinterpreted. These are the songs written to accompany direct action in people's movements. The historical use of such songs might be described as purely utilitarian. They are created for—and not infrequently at—peace demonstrations, political meetings, sit-ins, student strikes, freedom marches, rallies in support of the War on Poverty, demands for better housing, and so on. So long as people have problems, they write songs about them. Even though the Civil Rights movement, which witnessed an immense outpouring of such songs, had waned, songs continued to flow from other specific, down-to-earth social struggles in the United States. One can think of the students' songs of the free-speech movement on the Berkeley campus, the fight for better living conditions in the city slums (for example, the songs of Jimmy Collier in Chicago and Fran Goldin in New York), the satirical ditties about the War on Poverty composed by the impoverished people of Appalachia (there have always been great song makers in those mountains). But the strongest example of the continuing tradition was the creative song writing emerging from the *huelga* (strike) movements of the mainly Mexican American farm workers (*campesinos*) in California and Texas.

In California a theater company, El Teatro Campesino, was formed to tell the story of the *huelgaistas* through songs and skits. Made up mainly of the workers themselves, this company appeared at the Newport Folk Festival, in New York City, and in Washington, D.C., in support of a nationwide boycott of grapes produced by non-union growers. And during a Texas pilgrimage from the Rio Grande valley to the state capital, Austin, the marchers made up so many new songs that a whole afternoon was set aside on the return march to present them in a concert. There are also the *corridos* (traditionally styled Mexican ballads) written by the Mexican Americans involved in the land-grant struggle led by Reies Tijerina in New Mexico. In contrast to the folk style used in the above songs is the antiwar "Hell No I Ain't Gonna Go" by Matt Jones and Elaine Laron, which might be described as the first Black Power song. It deliberately uses the instruments and the beat of modern folk-rock music in order to better reach the young audience for which the message of the lyrics is intended.

Indicative of the steady, continuing flow of folk songs and folk artists from among the people during the late 1960s was the emergence of Jimmy Collier and the Reverend Frederick Douglass Kirkpatrick, a singing team of the poor people's campaign for jobs or income. Both came from the impoverished areas of the rural South, Collier from Arkansas and Kirkpatrick from Louisiana, and they wrote and sang with deep conviction about the miseries and hopes of the poor. "Kirk," an imposing six-foot-four, was sent to Grambling College, the mill that turned out black products for the professional football leagues (he was good quarterback material). Instead of following the routine, he began leading civil-rights demonstrations, was expelled, and went on to Texas Southern to do the same. Kirk was the closest artist to Huddie Ledbetter to come along; his physical stature combined with a deep voice of great range reminded old-timers not only of Leadbelly but of Paul Robeson, too.

The last thing on the minds of these song creators was whether they stood a chance of making the top forty. Nor was their aim that of scaling the heights of poetic artistry (though some songs turned out to be fine poetry nevertheless). The artistic quality of the songs needed to be no better than that of the homemade picket signs the singing demonstrators held aloft. They served their purpose just the same. These songs should probably be judged on the same utilitarian level as one judges the durability of the shoes on the marchers' feet. Both shoes and songs shared the same basic purpose: to help the marchers reach their destination. The songs provided strengthened morale and bolstered determination to keep the shoes moving. This has always been and remains the classic use of topical song.

A hiatus followed the appearance of the school of gifted song writers in the early '60s—Phil Ochs, Bob Dylan, Len Chandler, Peter La Farge, Buffy Sainte-Marie, Mark Spoelstra, Richard Fariña, Tom Paxton, Julius Lester, Carolyn Hester, Patrick Sky, Eric Andersen, Debby Lewis, and others. The untimely deaths of Peter La Farge in 1965 and Richard Fariña in 1966 were made all the more tragic by the fact that Fariña had just entered the threshold of what promised to be a very fruitful career, and La Farge was just beginning to realize his deepest talent, as in one of his last songs, "Drums." There were still some hopefuls, among them Ochs, who felt that Dylan would yet return to the scene of his greatest triumphs, the political song. Ochs himself was experimenting with new forms of lyrics and music, but said he was determined not to make the same mistakes Dylan made. Paxton had shown that a song writer could stick firmly with social satire and still turn out songs increasingly better melodically and lyrically. Buffy Sainte-Marie decried the label "protest singer," as applied to her, pointing out that she had written some two hundred songs, of which only a mere five could be classified as "protest." She seemed baffled by the fact that her songs that had achieved the greatest popularity—"Universal Soldier," "Now That the Buffalo's Gone," "My Country 'Tis of Thy People You're Dying"—had come from this handful.

By 1968 there was considerable evidence that the hiatus had ended; new faces and new voices were appearing. There was Janis Ian, who was discovered at a *Broadside* Village Gate hootenanny when she was thirteen. She appeared in concert at New York's Philharmonic at the age of sixteen. (Julius Lester and Patrick Sky also got their first record contracts out of appearances at *Broadside* hoots.) There was also Arlo Guthrie, who can factually be called one of "Woody's Children." His satirical song series "Alice's Restaurant" had already swept college and high-school ranks throughout the country before his first record was released. There were other young song writer/performers on the horizon: Elaine White, Chris Gaylord, Lucinda Williams, Bruce Murdoch, Kristin Lems, Carol Hanisch, Tom Parrott, Bruce Phillips, Ronnie Peterson, Ricardo Gautreau, Charyn Sutton, Sammy Walker, and Alex Cohen, to name a few. The field of song writing in the U.S. was widening all the time, and *Broadside* admittedly was able to cover only a certain area of it.

During *Broadside*'s existence, each of our daughters spent some years in California, Aggie for health reasons—she still suffered from asthma—and Jane mostly to be with her sister. However, for a good deal of time one or the other of them—or both—lived here and worked along with us on the magazine. They were both gifted in graphic design; they put together many of *Broadside*'s covers and laid out our ad pages, those not sent in camera-ready. While still in her early teens, Jane became a great paster-upper, once we began to do less mimeographing and took our mock-ups to a photo-offset shop. She wielded a mean T square, something we were never good at. She also sprinkled our pages with her funny little cartoons. She did fine miniature clay sculptures, which we once had photographed and used on a cover. Aggie did literally hundreds of ink drawings, both humorous and serious, without which the magazine would have had little visual appeal. She also did some writing, two or three songs and a couple of articles.

When we did benefits the girls not only put together the flyers, but they'd go out and spread them around, stick them up in stores and on lampposts throughout the neighborhoods where the benefits were held. They manned literature tables where our issues were sold. They did menial work such as collating, stapling, stamping, and stuffing. They did mailings. How could *Broadside* have gone on without Jane and Aggie?

In the early days Israel Young was the person who did the most in New York City to get the magazine circulating among the people who appreciated folk music of the sort we printed. He had a small establishment, a kind of storefront, in Greenwich Village, which he called the Folklore Center. It had a back room in which many a newcomer to the city's folk/topical scene was welcome to crash for a night or two—perhaps a week of nights. We wouldn't care to guess how many good protest songs were composed in this back room. Informal concerts, hoots, or jam sessions were constantly in progress at the Folklore Center; Izzy liked to round up talented unknowns, give them a chance to be heard, encourage them, and bring them in contact with one or two of the better-knowns in the field. His tiny hall would hold fifty people at most, and at performances the listeners sat on hard benches—no chairs with back rests—or stood against the walls of shelves and magazine racks. They were cramped—hot in summer and chilled in winter. But who among them noticed the discomforts when they could be carried into another dimension by the likes of Bob Dylan or Matt McGinn?

Izzy had his shelves and racks stocked with folk-music books, old issues of *People's Songs*, the latest *Sing Out!*s, and great stacks of *Broadside*s, along with leaflets announcing our hoots at the Village Gate or wherever. When Israel Young left the country in 1973 to live in Sweden and establish his new Folklore Centrum, we lost a staunch supporter in our efforts to keep *Broadside* alive and kicking. Of course, we never lost touch, and he kept up his interest in *Broadside* and got us some subscribers across the waters.

Epilogue

Growing Old in New York

I: Gordon*

New Yorkers, when young and even in their middle years, move around a lot. Since Sis and I came to New York City in 1941 we have lived at ten different addresses, at least. We never heard the word fear. Sometimes we walked the streets all night—Harlem, Chinatown, the bridges, Times Square—talking, experiencing the pleasure of seeing different places, feeling free, no apprehension.

For some years we lived on the West Side a block from Central Park. Each weekend we took our two children on long rambles through the park. We especially liked to explore what the kids called "the wild part of the park," that area lying north of 103rd Street where so few people came that it still retained many features of the wilderness.

In 1964 we moved to Ninety-eighth Street, still on the West Side but right next to Broadway. The twelve-story building had originally been built for upper-middle-class families. The apartments then had dining rooms, sitting rooms, galleries, and even a diminutive maid's room with a tiny bathtub. The maids must have come awful small in those days. By the time we moved in, the designations had long been forgotten; the rooms now were simply rooms.

We were already putting out our little protest magazine *Broadside*, printing songs based on the folk idiom Guthrie used. When protest music turned to rock, what little success *Broadside* had began to fade away. Even though much of the music hitting the charts was definitely topical, it was the rock idiom that was beyond us. At the same time, we discovered we were growing old; illness was overtaking us. We had left only one-fourth of the energy we once knew; we had become immobile.

It was about this time that the rent-control law was changed, so

*Drafted by Gordon Friesen in the late 1970s.—Ed.

that when a controlled apartment became vacant, the landlord could charge what the traffic would bear. What the traffic would bear was a doubling of the rent. The landlord boasted that for an apartment like ours—the D apartments—he could easily get, and did get, five hundred dollars a month. This was possible because when a family moved out, the new tenants were young people—students, part-time workers, clerks, and so on—who moved in as a group of five or six and shared the rent. He began a program of gradual harassment to drive out the families still under rent control. There was a clause in the law exempting the poor elderly from rent increases, which became known as SCRIE (Senior Citizens Rent Increase Exemption). We applied for this exemption, but the landlord fought us tooth and nail, using fabrications and cutting off services. We turned to various sources for help. Influenced by Governor Carey's inauguration speech, in which he expressed great concern for the elderly, we wrote his office; we got back a curt note saying ours was the city's problem, not the state's. A similar request to our assemblyman, Al Blumenthal, brought us a sheaf of documents upholding the landlord's position. Representative Bella Abzug also upheld the landlord's position and told us not to bother her anymore. A minor politician finally got us a partial exemption, far less than what we were legally entitled to. Our little magazine had to be virtually forgotten, at least as far as building it up was concerned. It took all the money we could beg and borrow plus our Social Security just to pay the rent. Our issues got thinner and thinner. But after a number of years we did get on SCRIE.

Meanwhile, our apartment continued steadily to deteriorate. Danger from the streets invaded the building. Decreased security permitted a robber to come into our apartment. After terrorizing us he took Sis's purse and hurried out. The purse contained only sixteen dollars, but more important, our keys and telephone number were in it. One of the keys was to the outside door. We immediately told the landlord he should have a new lock installed downstairs. He steadfastly refused. For several weeks after the robbery, we received threatening phone calls. And some time later I saw this same thief in the building. So we continued to live in what amounted to a kind of terror. There were a number of robberies in the building, and a near murder shortly after our experience. Two elderly men were murdered in their own apartment a block from us. A next-door neighbor, also an elderly man, was robbed of his Social Security money—also in his own apartment—and beaten so savagely one eye protruded from its socket.

We filed a number of formal complaints against our landlord regarding the apartment's deterioration, but very little was done; Sis's foot went through the floor in one of the bedrooms. That floor was replaced, but the splintery floors in the rest of the seven rooms remained as they were. Twice we took grandchildren to the emergency room with splinters so large and deeply embedded that a surgeon had to be called down to remove them. The Department of Rent and Housing accepted as valid the landlord's insolent rebuttal that the splintery-floor problem could be solved by us wearing shoes continuously. When we asked the inspector why nothing was done, he replied that the department was so chaotic that incredible inefficiency reigned.

Rat holes in the walls remained; the windows remained stuck, their frames rotting away; a fire hazard due to a rusty, defective stove continued. An appeal to the main office of the Mayor's Committee for the Aging brought this reply from a spokesman: "Don't you people know that the landlords run New York City? You might as well quit this useless fight." But we were not ready to give up the fight, although our health problems were growing worse and we had less energy with which to carry on. At age sixty-seven I spent a month in St. Luke's Hospital having a major stomach operation. The following year I spent another month in the hospital having half of my stomach removed. Even after a period of recuperation, I could only hobble a few blocks. But we lived for several years near Rabbi Bergman's Towers and saw firsthand what a hellhole some of the nursing homes can be. I didn't want to think of that possibility, even though it was about this time that I started having what they call "little strokes."

Growing old in New York has been for us a terrible experience. We bought no clothes; Sis went to rummage sales and kept mending our old stuff. As for food, we ate mostly bean soup, and kept an eye out for food lines in the neighborhood. Elderly people leave their apartments to get food usually around 10:30 A.M. That seems to be the least dangerous time of the day; they do not go out at night at all, but huddle behind doors with three and sometimes four locks. The neighborhood becomes increasingly dangerous. Broadway between Ninety-fourth and 100th Streets swarms with more and more junkies, muggers, winos, pimps, and prostitutes. The reduction of the police force and firemen has made things worse. Recently, ten people perished in a fire six blocks from here; eight of those who died were children. I sometimes imagine New York City becoming a second Calcutta. If the firing of teachers, policemen, firemen, city workers and the closing of hospitals and schools continue—if more and more of the city's children, and even adult workers, become victims of ruthless sweatshop operators—who can say what the city will become? A big change must take place; the people must come first, not the profits of bankers and landlords. The welfare of our citizens from childcare centers to old age so that they can live, work, and retire in dignity must be protected and diligently expanded or New York City will perish.

II: Sis

While growing old in New York I have had the time to come up with a few generalizations on the outcome of the long life I've had the good fortune—or the misfortune—to live.

My ancestors, to my knowledge, were from way back and for the most part a restless, itchy-footed, frontier-seeking lot who just couldn't manage to stay put anywhere. This was true on both my mother's and my father's side. I have earlier described some of their experiences: their escapades, their sojourns to get away from their environments or to get out of what they considered to be their entrapments. I might describe them flatteringly as born pioneers. They had an unquenchable thirst for something better: "the grass looks greener on the other side of the fence." And I have to admit that this feeling was all mixed up with the need to settle down. After sojourning during the prime of their lives, most of them did finally sort of settle down. But by that time they were in poverty. And they stayed in poverty till they died.

My main generalization is this: quite a few of the families with whom I've come in contact while growing old in New York, whose ancestors stayed more or less in one place generation after generation, are a good deal better off than I and my progeny are; they enjoy a condition of life that we cannot.

As I have indicated, I believe the above to be only *generally* true. In this country's great migration westward during the eighteenth and nineteenth centuries—and into the twentieth—there were business-minded individuals, groups, companies, or what have you, who unhesitatingly took advantage of families and persons of little means. Agribusiness is a notable example of this. The participants did well for themselves; they thrived. But the great masses on the move did not thrive. My ancestors were among these.

If Gordon cared to look into this matter, I'm sure he'd come to the same conclusion. His ancestors were just like mine. Do we bemoan this situation? Well, not exactly. As for me, I'll admit I wish it were not the case. Struggling against it is perhaps what has kept me from bemoaning it to an excessive degree.

Appendix

"Oklahoma Witch Hunt"

I. Oklahoma

Now Oklahoma is a state of many fine men and women. It produced one of the kindliest and most warm-hearted of men, one of whose famous sayings was:

"I never met a man I didn't like."

The average Oklahoman feels that Will Rogers spoke for him. He does not want to hate anybody; he would rather shake hands, squat down in the shade, roll a Bull Durham cigarette and ask: "How's things going at your house?"

You know some of these folks. You met them when you met the Joads in *The Grapes of Wrath*.

But against their desire to be decent and human are set a number of forces. The economic system is painfully out of order. A few oil millionaires and utility tycoons on one hand, unspeakable destitution for thousands of the common people on the other. In the shadow of Oklahoma City's skyscrapers lies Community Camp, the worst human scrapheap of its kind. Its 3,000-odd inhabitants, living under rusty scraps of tin, in disease-infested filth, forced to carry their water from one common drinking tap, and forced to pay rent for this misery—are perhaps one of the worst examples in all America of how greedy men treat their brothers.

This text was published as a pamphlet by the Oklahoma Committee to Defend Political Prisoners in October 1941. The following note appeared on the verso of the title page:

"The author of this pamphlet, Gordon Friessen [sic], was born in Weatherford, Oklahoma, in March, 1909, his parents having migrated to Oklahoma from Kansas in the early 1890s. In his early youth he worked as a farmhand and cotton chopper, later becoming a reporter for the Associated Press, United Press, and several Oklahoma dailies. He is the author of the novel, *Flamethrowers*, published in 1935, and an artist of striking originality."

For more information on the committee and the occasion for this pamphlet, see the editor's afterword below.

You know the story of the dust bowl refugees and their exodus on Highway 66.

You don't know the story of Oklahoma's K.K.K., of the armed vigilantism, of the anti-Semitism, the public book burnings, the fascist ranting about the danger of reading books—or of people sent to jail for ten years each because of what is in those books.

Americans have never been afraid of books.

Americans have always been afraid of men trying to choose their books for them.

With the firm conviction that the American people will never accept Hitler's way—so long as, in the words of Thomas Jefferson, "reason remains free to combat error"—we give you our story.

•   •   •

In the Oklahoma County Court House, in the middle of June, 1941, a trial is in progress.

In the defendant's chair sits an attractive young woman. You ask about her, and learn that she is Ina Wood, one of a family of nine children in New England, that her family was poor, that she went to work at the age of 15 and she contributed regularly from her pay check to the support of the family. With what was left she paid her way through high school, college and law school. The story of a typical American.

Why is Ina Wood being tried?

Did she commit a murder? Did she steal, kidnap somebody? Did she break *any* law of the land?

You learn from the prosecution itself that she did not. She only read books which some people in Oklahoma don't like. She only stuck by her anti-fascist husband.

At the table beside her are two lawyers: One is George Croom, born and raised on a farm in Izzard County, Arkansas, educated in Oklahoma schools. Lean of body, slow of speech but quick-witted, a true son of the Southwest. The other is Samuel A. Neuburger, out of the labyrinth of New York, sent to Oklahoma by the International Labor Defense. It is of the old American tradition that an Arkansas Methodist and a New York Jew should meet in Oklahoma paired in the defense of a Boston Catholic girl.

The "evidence" against Ina Wood, who is charged with criminal syndicalism on the basis of "membership in the Communist Party," consists of thousands of books. Some 10,000 of them (taken out of a public book-store and five private homes) stacked in pasteboard boxes and piled on the floor of the courtroom. They cover about one third of the floor space.

The Judge displays a Chamber of Commerce smile at intervals. The rest of the time he automatically overrules every defense motion, automatically upholds every prosecution motion. Monotonously and stolidly he personifies the wheels of a well-oiled frame-up machinery grinding through the days, in a stacked courtroom.

It is the chief prosecutor, John Eberle, assistant county attorney, who draws your fascinated attention.

The fact that his victim is a woman makes no impression on him. There is no trace of chivalry in him. Very little evidence of human feeling.

Picking up book after book, reading half-sentences from them, piling insinuation on insinuation, he builds his false, ugly picture with crafty persistency. John Eberle is a coward. Shifty-eyed, he plainly avoids looking his woman victim or her attorneys in the face. He stalks back and forth in front of the jury snarling at them—your job is not to grant justice—your job is to convict—to send this woman to jail.

Out of Ina Wood's application for a job under an assumed name he paints a slinking female saboteur. The job was in a packing plant and she worked only three days—wrapping hams!

Out of a schoolgirl trip abroad, recorded in a naively enthusiastic diary, Eberle tries to paint for the jury a female master conspirator going to Moscow for instructions. He reads from the diary:

"Glasgow, Scotland. The temperature is 92 here today."

He gives even this a conspiratorial ring.

Then he walks to the rear of the courtroom—turns around and stares fixedly at the defendant and her lawyers. At these moments you are struck by the expression in his eyes. You feel a creeping sense of apprehension that this man, or men like him, have the power to decide whether freedom-loving Americans should continue free or be sent to prison.

You feel, watching him and listening to his song of hate, that this is a man dangerous to everything America stands for. More than that, you feel you are watching an example of fascist mentality and method at work. And it is not a pleasant thing to behold.

Behind it are images engraven in the memory of every liberty-loving American—a Berlin street where a pile of books is afire. Into the light limps a small man: "We consign these books to the flames in order that a greater, holier Germany may arise." America, with its deep historical consciousness of the treasure of human freedom, shuddered when Dr. Goebbels turned the clock back five centuries and retreated from reason into the arms of barbarism and folly.

"But what did Ina Wood do?" The voices of attorneys Croom and Neuburger, echoed by defense supporters all over the country, bring you back to Oklahoma as over and over they repeat the question:

"What did Ina Wood do?"

John Eberle does not answer. He doesn't want to answer that question. His jury brings in a verdict of ten years in McAlester Prison, a fine of $5,000 for Ina Wood, the Boston Catholic girl who believes that in America you can read what you please and think with freedom.

II. How Did It Happen?

The answer to that question must be traced to its beginnings in Oklahoma, the 46th state of the union, in our time.

Land in Oklahoma, which was free to the first comers only a generation ago, is concentrated in fewer and fewer hands. The census figures show that at least 62,000 Oklahoma farmers were forced off the land in the past five years, good men and women and helpless children stripped of their homes and driven onto the roads to drift aimlessly about the nation.

Adequate relief is denied able-bodied men and women. Two dollars per month per person in the families of the unemployed sends them to live in the indescribable huddle of shacks that form Community Camps. Even this pittance has been fought tooth and nail by the very men whose greed and savagery created their misery. Each recent legislature has further crippled education. Health conditions are intolerable. Repeatedly the University Hospital has pleaded for expanded facilities, pointing out that men and women with curable diseases are dying before a bed can be found for them. These patients are largely farming people, the finest people in the state, the backbone of Oklahoma economy, impoverished by droughts and low prices and exploitation. They are proud people.

It is not good to see them sentenced to death by neglect.

In 1940 much of the bad in Oklahoma came to the surface. The K.K.K. came back into the open, preaching its un-American poison of race hate, violence and terror. Anti-Semites began secret meetings and spread their vile philosophy. Gangs of hoodlums began to beat up members of Jehovah's Witnesses. Vigilante bands were organized.

A college professor, Streeter Stuart, was dismissed with the approval of Governor Phillips, front man for the gas and utility interests of the state. Stuart had written a letter to his Congressman opposing the then pending conscription bill.

In Oklahoma County, Sheriff George Goff, preparing for an election campaign, mailed thousands of membership cards to thousands of Oklahomans urging them to join his semiprivate army, the "Civil Guards." He followed this with a letter asking all recipients to "register" their firearms.

A similar organization, the "Emergency Defense Battalion," sprang up, headed by another politician, Sam Sullivan, a protege of Phillips. It is significant that the members of these secretive private armies were over-eagerly sought after as jurymen by the Oklahoma county attorney's office in the "criminal syndicalism" cases.

The Rev. E. Nick Comfort, who is also Dean of the School of Religion at Norman, was chaplain at the state asylum in Norman. Nick Comfort is loved all over the state for his courageous championing of the poor and oppressed. Certain of the American Legion leadership did not like it. They asked for Comfort's discharge. Phillips fired him.

At Hugo officers of the "law" brutally blackjacked a Negro named Lyons into confessing a murder. Testimony in the trial revealed that Lyons was beaten steadily from six in the evening until half past four in the morning, until, unable to endure any more, he answered the officers' question the way they wanted it answered. "They beat me, they beat me, they beat me, . . ." Lyons said in court.

When he withdrew his "confession" he was taken to the state prison at McAlester, beaten again. So convinced were many people that he was being framed, even the parents of one of the murder victims collected funds for Lyons' defense.

This was a partial picture of Oklahoma in 1940; these incidents were straws on the surface, indicating the stirrings in the murky depths below.

III. Dr. Goebbels Comes to Oklahoma City

Over Radio Station KOMA in Oklahoma City comes the voice of a "preacher" ranting against "Communists." You feel like checking your radio set, to see if something has gone wrong and this is Berlin coming in. But it is "Dr." Webber of Oklahoma City and not "Dr." Goebbels of the Nazi Reich.

On Grand Avenue in Oklahoma City, upstairs at 129½, Robert Wood, Communist State Secretary, has for a number of years had a bookstore, the Progressive Bookstore. One night a muttering gang appears at the foot of the stairs leading in from the street. For some time they mill around, about a dozen men, gathering courage to commit a crime. Finally they advance up the stairs. Ina Wood, Robert Wood's young wife, blocks their path with her body by grasping the railings on each side. They surge against her, she holds tight bravely, but at last her hands are torn loose and she is thrown roughly to one side. But the men go away.

On another night they return. The bookstore is broken into and wrecked. The marauders cram books and literature into gunnysacks and flee with their loot.

Over the radio the triumphant voice of "Doctor" Webber announces a "special treat" for his listeners. Communist literature has come into his possession, no matter how. There will be a public book burning.

On a night in June, 1940, in Oklahoma City, a match was applied to a heap of books in an Oklahoma City stadium. In the fire were consumed thirty-one copies of the Constitution of the United States, stolen from the Progressive Bookstore.

IV. Reign of Terror

August 17, 1940. On this day a storm against the liberties of Oklahoma's people, a storm that had been brewing for months, broke into full fury.

It was a day of terror. It struck directly at some thirty-five persons, women and men and children, in Oklahoma City.

So shrouded in secrecy was the sudden storm-trooper-like procedure that only the Oklahoma county attorney's office knows to this date the exact number.

On this day the Oklahoma County attorney's office ordered a raid. The police went forth bearing illegal search warrants to which had been added the words: "and books, papers and other records which are evidence of the crime of Criminal Syndicalism or any other crime against the State of Oklahoma or the laws of the United States."

They burst into the Progressive Bookstore, and without discrimination arrested everyone present, and visitors who came in later. They pillaged the store and carted away some 10,000 books, papers and pamphlets. It was perhaps the first time in American jurisprudence that completely unrestricted police power was used to confiscate an entire, legal, going business concern.

Five homes were invaded, and all present, whether they resided at these homes or were merely casual visitors, were arrested. Private libraries and files in the homes were looted, books and papers and letters taken.

The victims were spirited away to the county jail and hidden from their friends and relatives by aliases given them by the police. They were held incommunicado. Inquiries seeking to learn why they were being held were answered with coarse threats and such statements as:

"We could kill you like we would rattlesnakes."

At least two of the smaller men were mercilessly beaten by other prisoners, fed rubbing alcohol by guards. The women were thrown into the "tank" with prostitutes.

Not until almost a week had passed did attorneys succeed in establishing contact with the political prisoners. And then only after the attorneys, Stanley Belden and George Croom, circumventing threat and attempted intimidation, obtained court writs to pass the hostile jailers.

The prisoners were finally brought before a justice of the peace. It was only then that they and their attorneys learned that they were being held under a law passed in 1919 to deal with striking coal miners at Wilburton, the Criminal Syndicalism law.

All faced two charges under this law: possession and sale of books, and membership in the Communist Party.

The attorneys forced the bail issue. Bail was set—at $100,000 for each of six of the defendants, $840,000 for all!

These were very poor people.

Eight hundred and forty thousand dollars!

They returned to jail.

It was not until four months later, just before Christmas, after the International Labor Defense had entered the fight and succeeded in getting the bail reduced, and put up most of the bail, that the last of the victims, Eli Jaffe, finally came out of the Oklahoma County jail.

But what of the Bill of Rights?

"The right of the people to be secure in their persons, houses, papers, and effects, against unreasonable searches and seizures, . . .

"The accused shall enjoy the right . . . to be informed of the nature and cause of the accusation; . . .

"The accused shall enjoy the right . . . to have the assistance of counsel for his defense. . . .

"Excessive bail shall not be required."

The answer is simple. On August 17, 1940, the Bill of Rights in Oklahoma County was blacked out.

V. The Trial of the Books

As the story of the terroristic raids slowly emerged from the secrecy with which they had been deliberately shrouded, the people of Oklahoma waited to learn why. An amazing truth became apparent.

There was no real evidence against a single one of the accused!

Not then, or ever later, did John Eberle, or County Attorney Lewis Morris, accuse even a single one of the defendants of ever using or personally advocating the use of force and violence.

Who then, or what then, was accused?

Books!

Books, and the right to own them, read them, sell them.

Robert Wood was tried first—in October. The specific charge was that the possession and selling of certain books was a violation of the criminal syndicalism law. What books did Robert Wood have in his bookstore? Books by Marx, Engels, Lenin, Browder, Foster. And books by Thomas Jefferson, Abraham Lincoln, Thomas Paine, Jack London, copies of the United States Constitution. The very same books burned by "Doctors" Goebbels and Webber.

For hours Eberle read from the books. He read only carefully chosen sentences, phrases out of sentences, separating them from their context, distorting and perverting their meaning. John Eberle could have made a stronger case, in this fashion, against the possessor of a Bible. The rulers of old Salem hung and crushed under stones their neighbors because of an isolated passage in the Bible calling for the destruction of witches.

The books were found guilty. The jury stated in effect that possession and sale of any books which the assistant county attorney did not like was criminal syndicalism. The conviction carried the maximum sentence of ten years in the state penitentiary and a fine of

$5,000—for Wood. For the books? The jail furnace when the prosecution finishes with them. But it is not yet finished.

Next came Alan Shaw. The charge in his case was that membership in the Communist Party violated the criminal syndicalism law. But the "evidence" was the same as in the Wood case—the same books.

As Eberle harangued the jury and court it became obvious that not the Communist Party but the rights of all Americans to join any minority political party, political freedom, were under attack.

A change of venue to Canadian County was denied. There was no prejudice against the defendants in Oklahoma County—swore Goff, Sullivan, *and* "Doctor" Webber!

Eberle, as in the first trial, eliminated all Negroes as prospective jurymen.

For nine hours in his closing summation Eberle read from the books. Always isolating phrases, twisting them maliciously, interpreting them to appeal to prejudice and hatred.

Again the defense pointed out that in America, after the Constitution was adopted, an individual must be tried for a specific crime, not for the books he happens to own, or his friends happen to own, books which he may not even have read.

The jury came back with a maximum conviction—10 years and $5,000.

Alan Shaw, 22 years old—a brilliant student, said to the court:

"Over the entrance of this courthouse there is an inscription with a quotation from Thomas Jefferson: 'Equal and exact justice for all, regardless of state or persuasion, religious or political.' That inscription and these words have been disregarded in my case. It has been a mockery from the beginning."

In April, 1941, the third victim, Eli Jaffe, 27-year-old writer, playwright and worker among the youth and unemployed, went on trial. The charge—membership.

One prospective juror said:

"I believe in a fair trial, even if the defendant is found to be a Communist." Eberle took him off the jury.

Another said:

"I will convict Jaffe, *even if the evidence shows he is not guilty.*" John Eberle tried to keep him on the jury.

This time Eberle read from the books for fourteen hours.

Defense Attorney Neuburger addressed the jury:

"It will take courage to come out with a verdict of not guilty in the face of the pressure being brought to bear on you. But you have taken an oath to try this case on the facts and there is not one scrap of evidence to show that Eli Jaffe advocated violence, sabotage or revolution.

"You cannot convict a man for what he thinks. You cannot try a party." The verdict was—guilty. Ten years in the state penitentiary. A fine of $5,000. Jaffe told the judge just before he was sentenced:

"I have held for freedom and justice for all—and I have tried to the best of my ability to live by these words. In this court I have been charged with no specific act; I have been convicted on generalities. Nowhere was it shown I advocated or committed an act of violence—nor have I ever in my life done so."

"Opinion is free, only conduct is amenable to law," said John Erskine in his court defense of Tom Paine, one of the greatest of the founders of American freedom.

Now came the woman. Mrs. Ina Wood was to be tried on June 2. On the afternoon of May 30 the defendants' local attorney, George Croom, was arrested on the highway, the defense files in his possession seized. He was transported, in violation of the state law which says the arrested person must be taken before the nearest magistrate in the county wherein seized, from Creek County to Oklahoma County, a distance of some ninety miles. He was placed in John Eberle's county jail and held incommunicado for twenty hours. During this time his files were gone over, he was questioned.

The attempt to intimidate George Croom failed.

He was freed the next day, his files returned in disordered condition.

The Tulsa *Tribune* put it into one editorial sentence, asking:

"What kind of insanity is this?"

On June 9, the trial of Ina Wood began. The real issue behind the Oklahoma County "criminal syndicalism" drive came forward more sharply than in any of the other trials.

"An anti-fascist is a Communist," Eberle sneered during his fourteen-hour harangue of the jury. *John Eberle and his kind were making their own definitions.*

You had to be for him and what he stood for, or against him and what he stood for.

John Eberle made no simple address to the jury; *he placed before the people a program for a fascist America!*

He attacked, for hours, the rights of Americans to read, write, think, discuss, speak, as their consciences guided them.

He upheld racial hatreds, branding anyone against Jim Crow lynch terror as a criminal and a traitor.

He branded everyone who disagreed with John Eberle a traitor to his country, just as Hitler brands everyone disagreeing with him personally a traitor to Germany.

He defended his use of illegal search warrants, his holding of Americans incommunicado, his brutal disregard of the entire Bill of Rights. It is noteworthy that the "evidence" on which he based his speech included such things as seventeen blank cards of paper and a pencil held together with a rubber band, and a broken doorbell set.

The defense met the attack squarely.

ATTORNEY CROOM: "Books! Books! Books! When has it ever been a crime for an American to read a book! Some of my own relatives fought and died on Bunker Hill to establish the rights of Americans to read what they please—yes, and to write what they please, think what they please, say what they please. These are sacred rights, the rights which this pro-fascist county attorney's office now wishes to destroy. . . ."

ATTORNEY NEUBURGER: "Democracy can survive only by expanding, by digesting every shade of opinion, assimilating the good and spewing out the evil. Democracy cannot survive by contracting the rights of the people. America will perish as a democracy when it can no longer permit men and women to read freely, write freely, assemble and discuss."

County Attorney Lewis Morris closed for the prosecution. A professional jury addresser, "When I die, may the government wrap me in an American flag . . ." he squats on his heels like a college cheer leader as he delivers his summation.

The verdict: ten years in the state penitentiary and a fine of $5,000.

Ina Wood says:

"I say to the people of Oklahoma: Read—*read*—READ! *Find out what these pygmy minds have forbidden you to know.*

"Read! Find out what is the specter that so haunts Mr. Eberle and Mr. Morris and the men they stand for. Haunts them so much they are willing to take ten years from the life of one woman to keep it from you!

"Women in Oklahoma now know that native fascists have the same stripes as fascists everywhere."

VI. Who Are the Remaining Defendants?

J. M. Gillespie was a 72-year-old pioneer Oklahoma farmer. He had come into the city on Aug. 17, 1940, to sell vegetables. Before starting home he stepped into the bookstore to buy a daily newspaper. He was seized and jailed. After two weeks, friends succeeded in getting him out on bail. For trying to buy a paper! The shock of imprisonment was so great he has not been able to return to his farmwork, has become a trembling, infirm old man.

Gillespie still faces ten years in prison for trying to buy a daily paper!

C. A. Lewis, too, was a pioneer Oklahoma homesteader. He is a descendant of Thomas Jefferson. His wife is a graduate of a state teachers' college and taught school for years. Both have worked hard in recent years making a living raising rabbits and milking several cows. They were in jail for months, with no one to see after their affairs. As a result they face the loss of their small home. Both have been bound over for district court trial.

Their son, Orval Lewis, 17, was thrown into jail with them, kept several weeks, released, then jailed again. At his first release, a gang of young men, apparently with knowledge beforehand of his release, followed Orval home from the county jail and beat him up.

Herb Brausch has a wife and six children, five of them girls; the oldest child is only eleven. Herb Brausch has earned a living for his family by working with his hands, and working hard. He is a hodcarrier, and a good union man. In his youth he was a divinity student. He came into the bookstore to do some carpenter work and was arrested.

His family suffered greatly during the months he was in jail. Since coming out on bail he has been hounded from job after job by slanderers who follow him about, putting pressure on his employers. On his last job, at the new city airport, his foreman resisted this shameful pressure for weeks, and during that time Herb Brausch worked his way to the top and most responsible work in his department. But pressure forced even this decent and sensible foreman to give way. Since that time Brausch and his wife and children have suffered intensely. Their only regular help comes from the I.L.D. Prisoners Relief. None of his babies has sufficient food; they live in an extremely wretched shack.

Herb Brausch still faces trial and the county attorney's office has repeatedly expressed its ambition to put Herb Brausch behind penitentiary walls.

Elizabeth Zeleny Green is the daughter of a D.A.R. Her father is a famous scientist, for many years on the faculty at Yale. As a social worker she saw little babies dead of rat bites in unspeakable slums. She felt she must devote her life to the remedying of such inhuman conditions. She is not very well: to sentence her to a long prison term will perhaps sentence her to death. Why? America has retrogressed a long way if it is now ready to send a girl to prison for believing that it is wrong in a land of tremendous potential production that babies should live and die in slums with rats.

Assistant County Attorney John Eberle has attacked Elizabeth Green viciously in the course of the previous four trials, uttering malicious and shameless insinuations. He has built up a systematic structure of slanderous innuendoes against her, preparatory to her trial.

VII. The Meaning of the Trials

In all the trials nothing was so obvious as the fact that not the defendants present, or the Communist Party, was the real objective of the prosecution. All of us who believe in the freedom and liberty which George Washington, Thomas Jefferson, Franklin and Paine established here, and Lincoln preserved in a great crisis, were under attack.

Four people, three men and a woman, were convicted because John Eberle said they belonged to a political party John Eberle and Lewis Morris did not happen to like.

The danger threatens all of us who believe in political freedom.

One man was sentenced to ten years in prison for having and selling books John Eberle and Lewis Morris did not like. This is a direct and immediate threat to all Americans who believe in intellectual freedom, in the right of men and women to choose their own books to read, or to write the books they please.

VIII. The Prairie Fire Spreads

In Germany the destruction of civil liberties was carried out under the guise of combating "Communism." In Oklahoma the violent suspension of the Bill of Rights and the first "criminal syndicalism" convictions were followed by an all-out assault upon the civil rights of the whole people.

Reaction launched a veritable barrage against organized labor. Speakers, from Governor Phillips down, slandered the working men and women of Oklahoma either as traitors or dupes. A flood of bills to paralyze labor, one of which would outlaw strikes, was introduced into the spring legislature.

Ministers came under wide-scale attack. In Germany Martin Niemoeller still rots in a Nazi dungeon because he would not desert Christ.

Martin Dies sent, or was invited to send, a "subcommittee" of doubtful legal status to Oklahoma to "investigate" Nick Comfort, the Rev. John B. Thompson of the First Presbyterian church at Norman, and the Rev. Paul Wright of the First Presbyterian Church in Oklahoma City. A subpoena ordered the three to bring "all financial and membership records of the Communist Party."

Thompson, Wright and Comfort, as well as other ministers and liberals, who had formed the Oklahoma Federation for Constitutional Rights, which included in its sweeping defense of all civil liberties the violated rights of the Oklahoma City victims, shortly came under fire again, this time at the hands of a state senate investigating committee quickly dubbed "Little Dies."

Ostensibly, Little Dies was set up to ferret out subversive activities. Within a few days the hearings degenerated into an unrestricted assault upon the Federation. A dead giveaway to the whole shameless circus came when Little Dies permitted the Ku Klux Klan to distribute its literature—*in the committee hearing room!*

The hearing became ridiculous. A sample:

An august legislative inquisitor, who admits he never got past the third grade, demands to know what Professor W. C. Randels (on the Federation Council) teaches at the University of Oklahoma.

Randels teaches higher mathematics; he produces several weighty papers on integral calculus.

The investigator stares confusedly at the pages, mutters that he never saw anything like this before, that it looks like "Communist code" to him.

The Oklahoma of Will Rogers roars with laughter.

Another inquisitor demands of Roscoe Dunjee, Negro newspaper editor, what he knows about the Bill of Rights.

"I know my people are not getting them," Dunjee answers simply. Several students in the audience applaud. Immediately, five of them are subpoenaed for investigation on the spot.

Oklahoma, seeing an ugliness, does not laugh.

Public reaction forced suspension of the hearing. "Little Dies" recommended the state enact a law barring the Communist Party from the ballot. Such a bill has since become law.

Another law makes it compulsory for political officeholders to swear that they are not Communists. Still another forbids Communists from running for office. Or "sympathizers."

On a national scale the action in Oklahoma made itself rapidly felt.

IX. The People Resist Aggression

If the enemies of freedom saw the "criminal syndicalism" prosecutions as a green signal to go ahead, all-out, the believers in liberty were awakened to the peril which threatened. They rallied to its defense.

A few days after the raids the Oklahoma Committee to Defend Political Prisoners was formed. It appealed to the International Labor Defense for legal assistance, for aid to the victims' families, and got it. It began to publicize the cases.

"Not a handful of people—but the Bill of Rights—our constitutional guarantees—are on trial," said its first bulletin. Events have more than proved this first interpretation.

The I.L.D. has labored valiantly from the start to provide the best legal assistance possible, has put up most of the bonds, and, if supporting funds are forthcoming, will carry the appeals, if necessary, to the United States Supreme Court.

Many individuals and groups have answered the I.L.D.'s plea for contributions, and many persons over the nation have come to the committee's support.

Not only has the Oklahoma Federation vigorously defended the victims' civil liberties, as well as their own, but the National Federation for Constitutional Liberties early plunged into the struggle and has fought hard for the restoration of freedom to the people of Oklahoma, pointing out the danger to America as a whole if the forces of reaction and un-Americanism win in Oklahoma.

Protests from individuals over the state and nation have risen to such a flood that the Oklahoma county attorney's office has felt forced to threaten, in the local newspaper, "contempt of court" citations.

The National Lawyers Guild, in its national convention at Detroit, passed resolutions condemning the Oklahoma prosecutions, and sent protests against the arrest and holding incommunicado of Attorney Croom to Governor Phillips, and the Attorney-Generals of Oklahoma and of the United States.

Letters of protest drafted at the American Writers Congress and signed by over 200 of the most famous authors in America were sent to Phillips and Morris.

In sharp contrast to Oklahoma, the St. Louis *Star-Times* said editorially: "This country is a democracy, and in this city the constitutional guarantees of free speech, free press and free assembly are respected . . . and cherished."

And the Kansas City *Journal*:

"American democracy will cease the very moment dictator methods are used to defend it."

Said the Tulsa *Tribune*, June 6, 1941:

"The hysterical anti-Communist trials in Oklahoma City are no longer humorous. Men have been sentenced to the penitentiary and fined $5,000 for no other crime than being members of the Communist Party and having in their possession ordinary run-of-the-mill Communist literature. . . . *Now a woman is to be thrown to the lions.* [Their] attorney was himself clapped into jail and held incommunicado.

"What kind of insanity is this?"

The St. Louis *Post-Dispatch*:

"Now Oklahoma is a Democratic state and most of her Democrats pride themselves on being Jeffersonian Democrats. Before they passed their law barring free speech, did they take the trouble to read Thomas Jefferson? It would seem they didn't."

Then the *Post-Dispatch*, on June 20, 1941, devoted half of its editorial page to an editorial and a cartoon on Ina Wood.

"Mrs. Wood, of course, is a woman of no importance. In the eyes of some Americans, particularly of the Ku Klux type which they breed in Oklahoma—and this goes for some of their judges, prosecutors, sheriffs and other public officials—the fact that Mrs. Wood is a Communist places her beyond the pale . . . of the law, of justice, of the fundamental rights for which Americans have died and for which they may soon die again. . . . Mrs. Wood is nothing. . . . Let us not deceive ourselves.

"Mrs. Wood . . . is everything. Because once [she] is persecuted with impunity, the whole philosophy of American freedom and justice is turned to dust, ashes and blood. . . ."

The "spread" carried a cartoon by Fitzpatrick depicting the Statue of Liberty with the torch of freedom covered by a K.K.K. hood bearing the inscription: "Oklahoma Criminal Syndicalism Prosecutions." Its title: "Start of the American Black-out."

But still more understanding, more help, are needed.

Out-of-the-way Oklahoma is the experimental ground on which are being developed the weapons easily applicable on a nation-wide scale to destroy the Constitution and the liberties of the whole American people.

If the battle of Oklahoma is lost, if nazism is not stopped here, America and the great American dream of total human freedom will have suffered a grievous blow.

If the battle of Oklahoma is won, then a decisive victory for the cause of American freedom will have been achieved.

We have shown you how it happens. By telling you the story of Oklahoma we hope that we have aided in tearing aside this artificial fog behind which fascism attempts to advance, and we hope that we have won you as a friend and supporter of our fight for freedom.

Afterword

Ronald D. Cohen

In the early chapters Gordon and Sis, both born in 1909, root their lives in the soil of their youth in rural Oklahoma and Kansas during the early decades of the century.[1] Place, time, family, friends, natural disasters, hardships, happy memories—all are remembered, and all have a place in their lives.[2] Although they moved to New York in 1941, their permanent residence thereafter, they never shook the dust of Oklahoma from their clothes, speech, and memories; they always identified with their past. Their experiences also shaped and molded their radical politics. Of course, most of their family and neighbors, sharing the same hardships and grievances, did not become members of the Communist Party or lifelong rebels against the political and cultural status quo. Economic suffering can produce all sorts of responses. But for Sis and Gordon, experiences certainly molded their future beliefs. We learn about their schooling, games, pranks, family relationships, music, chores, illnesses—the minutia of growing up in rural Oklahoma and Kansas, in that place at that time.

Most important were family and friends. White settlement opened in Oklahoma in 1889 with the first land rush; Kansas had a much longer white presence. Neither proved particularly hospitable to the Friesen and Cunningham families; both clung to their hardscrabble farm life, continually on the edge. As both vividly recall, the dust storms, pests, droughts, and other problems hardly started in the late 1920s—they had been there all along, both natural and manmade. "In subduing and arranging the land, the pioneer did untold harm to the natural order," H. Wayne Morgan and Anne Hodges Morgan wrote.

> His first act was usually to plow a fireguard around his claim, then burn off the grass surrounding his dwelling. To ease the task of planting, he often burned off whole fields before plowing. Those burrowing

creatures and other wildlife who survived this fiery carnage soon fled before the cutting, probing plow. Determined to mine the prairie environment with habits of farming learned in other climates, the first settlers turned the light, rich soils, then exhausted them with too many crops. The soil that did not blow away in dry times washed off in rainy seasons. Human energy, self-deception based on the desire for security and gain, and mechanical inventions broke the balance of nature that had sustained the complex ecology of plains life.

For many, hard times were the rule rather than the exception.[3]

They both connected with Weatherford, Oklahoma—Gordon first, Sis later. "Weatherford . . . is a neat college town in the center of a fertile farming area," according to *Oklahoma: A Guide to the Sooner State,* compiled by the Writers' Project of the Work Progress Administration and published in 1941. "It was named for William J. Weatherford, a United States marshal stationed here in Territorial days. On a hill at the northern edge of town is SOUTHWESTERN STATE COLLEGE, established in 1901. . . . Here also is located the SOUTHWESTERN OKLAHOMA MUSEUM." As for Watonga, Sis's birthplace, the guide notes: "Named for an Arapaho chief, WA-TONGA . . . is the seat of Blaine County. It was settled in 1892, the year the Cheyenne and Arapaho reservation was opened to settlement, and many Indians still live in or near the town. Until recently the streets of Watonga . . . were brightened by the older tribal members who still retain their traditional dress, the women in colorful blankets and moccasins, the men with their long black braids interwoven with gay ribbons. . . . The grain elevators beside the highway symbolize the town's principal economic asset, the fertile farmlands, which comprise the Watonga trade area."[4] The Cunninghams had lost their farm a few years before this passage was written.

Sis's and Gordon's rural experiences also shaped their musical tastes, their love for folk music—the music of the people. Thus, while their story takes awhile to unfold, presenting details of their formative years, this information is vitally necessary in understanding their later political and musical commitments. Moreover, while sharing the same locale and experiences, their lives were vastly different because of gender differences. So we see an interesting contrast between growing up male and female in rural Oklahoma, a valuable juxtaposition of memories that merge with marriage and more than a half-century of shared life. For example, when they were young their attitudes towards sex were quite different: Gordon, innocent and confused, yet welcomed contact with a little girl; Sis fled in shame when attacked by an older boy, then marveled at her girlfriend's sexual talk.

While Sis is quite explicit in discussing her family's lack of religious observance or belief, Gordon is proud (and knowledgeable) of his Mennonite heritage and upbringing, though he did not remain a believer.[5] They were certainly both influenced by their "religious" backgrounds, which shaped their political sentiments. Gordon identified with the sufferings and survival of the Mennonites in Europe; Sis traced her ancestry back to medieval Scotland and the exploits of Sir William Wallace and Molly Haney, her family role models for bravery and dedication to a cause, particularly against exploitation. They connected the past to their present as children and throughout their lives.

Both tell similar stories of sorrows and happiness, like the possible death lurking behind a cloudburst filling the dry creek beds with raging waters then just as quickly subsiding. Life was dangerous and fragile in rural Kansas and Oklahoma. Sis and Gordon were both steeped in local history, which they absorbed in school and from local lore and which shaped their sensitivities in various ways, not always officially intended. Western stories of cowboys and Indians were fresh, with living examples still around. They identified with the past sufferings and futile struggles of the natives—for example, Chief Roman Nose's death during the Battle of the Arikaree—whose stark reminders were all around. In their isolation, they also lived in a vivid imaginary world peopled by exotic characters that took them out of their temporal surroundings, at least for brief moments. Dreams and fantasies are a normal part of growing up, but were perhaps more necessary among children on the lonely, windswept plains and in the runty towns of Oklahoma and Kansas. Part of this escape took the form of reading—books, magazines, newspapers, anything available—the desire to learn about another world, the outside world. Their experiences with the emerging technology—autos, telephones, etcetera—were similar as these devices quickly lost their uniqueness and became indispensable aspects of everyday life, even for the poor.

During their early decades three issues dominated both their lives: poverty, sickness, and knowledge. They tried to overcome the first two and grab as much as possible of the latter. All three, plus the influence of local radical politics, influenced their easy turn to the left in the 1930s.

Gordon's life back in Oklahoma, his high-school years, and a bout of sickness are quite dim in the retelling though obviously influential in molding his life. Certainly his expansive reading during this time branded his intellectual development: H. L. Mencken, Sinclair Lewis, John Steinbeck. These were the transition years from poor farmer to budding journalist and political activist.

Sis rather quickly passes over her college and teaching experiences in early adulthood, from 1926 to 1932. Her brief classroom stint before returning to Southwestern and her three years teaching music after college are given short shrift, surely painful memories, taking place just as the depression rapidly gathered strength—although it seemed her family had always been in a depression. But her memories of the years at Commonwealth College are particularly sharp and colorful—a joyous, enriching time in the midst of the depression. Everything at Commonwealth was different—the beautiful mountain scenery (instead of the endless plains), friendships, communal lifestyle, the educational environment, radical politics, and labor songs. Commonwealth College opened in late 1923 in western Louisiana as part of the Newllano colony and settled near Mena, Arkansas, in 1925. Kate Richards O'Hare and William E. Zeuch, the original guiding lights, envisioned a resident labor college combining workers' education and a cooperative lifestyle and emphasizing social-class conflict and working-class solidarity, with socialist overtones.

"Commonwealth College is a few hundred acres of rocky plow land and timberland, with about twenty small buildings of pine lumber, ten miles west of Mena, Arkansas, in the heart of the Ouachita Mountains," Sis's brother Bill, a teacher at the college, wrote in *The World Tomorrow* in 1929. "It is also an experiment in workers' education, academic freedom, self-supporting education, and communal living." He also explained: "The teachers receive no salaries, therefore they are not hoping for increases or fearing reductions. They are not required to frighten adolescents into cultural pursuits nor keep them from wickedness and idleness, therefore they keep no attendance records, nor do they conduct final examinations. They are not inquisitors, disciplinarians, wardens, clerks, nor 'models for the young,' therefore they have opportunity to be teachers."[6]

Commonwealth weathered numerous difficulties, both internal and external, although the hardest blow came during Sis's stay, as she partially narrates. Richard Altenbaugh summarized the story:

> A major internal struggle at Commonwealth exploded on December 2, 1932, when several students struck for two days. According to the protesting students, the main issues centered on student representation and their right to control student discipline, the admission of black students, and the dismissal of certain teachers. Personality conflicts were important to that dispute. School administrators conceded on the issue of student discipline but refused to budge on the other demands and, further, suspended the two "communist" student leaders, Jack Copenhaver and Henry Forblade. Thirty-four students struck in protest. Seventeen other students chose not to participate in the protest and earned the label of "scabs." . . . Jane Addams volunteered to mediate the dispute, but it was in vain. Commonwealth's administrators had warrants issued for the arrest of the strike leaders, and the local sheriff removed them from the campus. As a result, thirty-four students abandoned the school in protest. In spite of the "communist-led insurrection," the school's administrators continued to welcome the enrollment of avowedly communist students.[7]

Commonwealth limped on for another few years, joining briefly with the Southern Tenant Farmers' Union (STFU) in 1937, with Claude Williams as the new director. But STFU soon withdrew its support, Williams resigned in 1939, and the next year the college permanently closed its doors. "Whether this tiny mutant in the Arkansas hills, struggling with its most unfriendly environment, perishes and leaves its skeleton among the rocks or survives and establishes a new species," Bill Cunningham recorded in 1929, "its life history must be of great interest to the historian of education."[8]

Commonwealth left its mark on educational history as well as on Sis, who was long gone when the school collapsed. While she was a student, however, the college published her first song book, *Six Labor Songs*—which she fails to mention—including "The Cry of the People" and "The March of the Hungry Men." She composed the music but not the lyrics; the cover noted, "Since enrolling as a student at Commonwealth College she has written music for a number of well-known revolutionary poems." Some years later Raymond and Charlotte Koch, in their autobiographical *Educational Commune: The Story of Commonwealth College*, gave a brief, flattering description of Sis's activities:

In no time at all she was training quartets, leading group sings, pounding the piano before meals and at dances, organizing stunt nights and coaching the participants. She wrote and produced musical dramas. We published the music she wrote to Chartist and modern protest poetry. While a student she was an unofficial teacher, a fact the school soon acknowledged by adding her to the faculty as dramatic director. She was driven by her creativity—writing, music, painting, drama. Was the drive inherited from her fiddler father who had helped open up the Oklahoma Territory? . . . Commonwealth had many cultural directors during its lifetime. But there was only one Sis.

Arriving at Commonwealth in 1937, a few years after Sis's departure, Lee Hays, a disciple of Claude Williams, also contributed his musical talent to the school. Within a few years he would be joined by Sis in the Almanac Singers.[9]

Sis's stay at Commonwealth was both exciting and troubling. She loved the natural setting and stimulating faculty and students but was bothered by a variety of issues, particularly the lack of black students. Her relationship with Hank Forblade was complicated, particularly during the debates leading to the upheaval of December 1932, when Hank and Jack Copenhaver were expelled and followed by most of the students. She also thought about the Green Corn Rebellion because of her brother Bill's novel on the subject. While largely unmentioned, Sis, indeed, was well acquainted with Oklahoma's rich radical heritage.

The Populist movement had swept Oklahoma (and Kansas) during the late nineteenth century, leaving a somewhat bitter legacy of activist politics. Early in the next century, however, socialism took root throughout the region, sparked by the *Appeal to Reason*, published in Girard, Kansas, with over twenty-two thousand paid subscribers in Oklahoma alone in 1907. Socialist Party candidate Eugene V. Debs pulled over forty-two thousand votes in Oklahoma in 1912, 16.6 percent of the state's total. A mounting tide of conservative reaction quickly developed, although economic difficulties boosted the party's support in 1914, and union leader Fred Holt's socialist campaign for governor drew 21 percent of the total vote that year. By 1916, however, the party was again on the defensive, attacked by the Right and also challenged by the militant Working Class Union (WCU), founded in late 1914 by Dr. Wells LeFevre.

Gaining particular support in eastern and southern Oklahoma, the WCU used strikes and boycotts, as well as barn burning, bank robbing, and night riding to further its ends—the abolition of rent, interest, and profit-taking, and, after the outbreak of war in 1917, draft resistance. Somewhat affiliated with the Industrial Workers of the World and led by former Wobbly H. H. "Rube" Munson, the WCU had perhaps twenty thousand or so supporters by the summer of 1917. The Green Corn Rebellion, an antidraft resistance, as partially described by Sis, was short-lived. Early on August 3 a group of protestors gathered on Spears Bluff and flew the "red flag of rebellion"; they also cut telegraph and telephone wires, burned railroad bridges, and blew up some oil pipelines. A mixed group of whites, blacks, and Indians, they were told by Munson and other leaders of simultaneous uprisings throughout the West and of a planned march on Washington. Within a day, however, a posse of seventy attacked the stronghold, quickly scattering the rebels. During the following week the posse used force to arrest 450 rebels, many Socialists uninvolved in the protest; 184 were indicted, 150 convicted, and about 80 sentenced to prison. The Green Corn rebels "were not ignorant night riders or religious fanatics," James Green argued, "and their rebellion was certainly not 'apolitical.' They followed Eugene Debs, Kate O'Hare, [Oscar] Ameringer, and the others because these popular propagandists talked about politics and economics in a simple, concrete way that tenants and workers could understand. The rebels also understood and accepted the Socialist party's analysis of the causes of World War I and its reasons for opposing intervention; they simply rejected its nonviolent tactics." War hysteria and mounting repression soon severely crippled the socialist movement in Oklahoma, which limped through the 1920s. Though only eight at the time of the Green Corn Rebellion, Sis was surely aware of these radical activities, yet barely mentions the *Appeal to Reason* or says much about her family's politics. Though not involved in the Green Corn Rebellion, Sis's father was a follower of Eugene V. Debs, the perennial Socialist Party candidate for president and eloquent spokesman for the party and its ideals.[10]

Gordon's memories of the 1930s are briefer than Sis's. He prefers to discuss his journalistic endeavors, particularly quirky stories that reveal his deep sense of humor. There is no mention of his writing for the Oklahoma Writers' Project, whose director was initially Bill Cunningham. Jim Thompson, even then developing a reputation as an imaginative writer (and later the author of numerous bleak, troubling, now celebrated novels), succeeded Cunningham in early 1938 and soon after hired Gordon as a staff writer for about a year. Their intellectual and political friendship weathered good times and bad until Thompson's death in 1977. Gordon also passes over his novel, *Flamethrowers*, published by Caxton Printers of Caldwell, Idaho, in January 1936. While generating small sales, it received numerous positive reviews.[11] The novel is heavily autobiographical: the story of a Mennonite boy searching for his identity. Gordon does not give a detailed sense of the depression's terrible hardships, either on himself, his community, or the country. While Weatherford was not located in the dust bowl proper, which only included the northwestern slice of Oklahoma, much of the western exodus came from the Cotton Belt of Texas, Oklahoma, Arkansas, and Missouri, which area included Weatherford.[12]

He also says little about his political odyssey, but by the decade's end his radical transformation was complete. Oklahoma's Communist Party had a membership of perhaps five hundred by 1938, attracting a plethora of writers and union activists, including Bill Cunningham, Jim Thompson, Gordon, and Sis—thus his work for the Oklahoma Committee to Defend Political Prisoners and his strong opposition to the antired policies of the Oklahoma government, detailed in his pamphlet *Oklahoma Witch Hunt*, published by the committee in October 1941. Oklahoma's criminal syndicalism act, passed during World War I, made it illegal to circulate or display subversive printed materials. Ina Wood, Robert Wood, Eli Jaffe, and Alan Shaw were Communists charged in September 1940 and subsequently convicted under that law. The Woods owned the Progressive Bookstore in Oklahoma City, and Robert, secretary of the Oklahoma City committee of the Communist Party, also supported local labor unions. The International Labor Defense provided legal counsel. Formed in 1925 and heavily Communist-dominated, the ILD had already defended Angelo Herndon and the Scottsboro boys, trade union members, and southern sharecroppers—always controversial cases. The four defendants received ten-year sentences and five-thousand-dollar fines, but the Oklahoma Criminal Court of Appeals finally overturned the convictions in February 1943. Gordon lashed back in *Oklahoma Witch Hunt*, where he predicted, "If the battle of Oklahoma is lost, if nazism is not stopped here, America and the great American dream of total human freedom will have suffered a grievous blow." Curiously, his short discussion in the autobiography of working with the committee includes anecdotes about two characters he met in the Travelers' Hotel, one a black veteran of World War I and the other an Indian con man. The first piqued Gordon's mounting hostility to racism while the second tickled his funny bone—he loved stories of fleecing gullible country rubes, something he had tried more than once—both reinforcing his hostility to capitalism's values and practices.[13] Eli Jaffe recently captured Gordon at the time:

> He had written an angry letter to the *Daily Oklahoman* strongly protesting the vigilantism and illegal prosecution against us in Oklahoma City so Gordon Friessen [sic] was invited to join Nena Beth in the leadership of the Oklahoma Committee to Defend Political Prisoners. He eagerly accepted. . . . It appeared inevitable that Gordon's political odyssey would join ours. "I was a radical since the age of 9 and running through everything I've done is the thread of my upbringing as a Mennonite—namely compassion for the oppressed," he said. Although he was a soft-spoken and witty man, *Oklahoma Witchhunt* [sic], the pamphlet he wrote for the defense committee, bristled with righteous indignation and stirring language. He was also a gifted artist whose specialty was monstrous figures. His artwork on the cover showed one of his brutish monsters putting a lighted torch to a pile of books, among them: the Constitution of the United States, Benjamin Franklin, Earl Browder, Tom Paine, and Karl Marx. Written after our trials took place, the booklet was a compelling appeal for justice composed in the finest spirit of the Oklahoma people.[14]

Jaffe's respect and gratitude has spanned more than fifty years.

The previous summer, Woody Guthrie and Pete Seeger had visited with Ina and Robert Wood in Oklahoma City, the local Communist Party organizers. "They spent the night with the Woods," Joe Klein wrote in his biography of Woody, "who were the sort of unassuming, devoted, and quietly brave people that radical organizers often turn out to be in isolated outposts like Oklahoma City. Although Woody later wrote that his song 'Union Maid' was inspired by the story of a southern Tenant Farmers' Union organizer who was 'stripped naked and beat up, and then hung to the rafters of a house till she was unconscious,' it's probably that Ina Wood was a more direct influence. A militant feminist, she criticized Pete and Woody for never singing any songs about the women in the labor movement, and Woody responded that night by writing a parody of 'Redwing.'"[15]

While Gordon practiced his journalistic skills and plunged into the local political caldron, Sis left Commonwealth and returned to Watonga. Eli Jaffe had recently moved to Oklahoma from New York, and while visiting with the Cunninghams in April 1938, during a freak blizzard, met Sis. He describes her in his autobiography:

> Sis, who had been sickly as a child, was not as pretty as her younger sister [Madge] but her thin face and sad eyes had an elusive appeal. In addition to the political education she obtained through her father's Socialist preachments, she was infuriated by the story of General MacArthur's attack on the Bonus Marchers told to her by a veteran who had been at Anacostia Flats in 1932. Her radicalization, she said, had been finalized by the fascist attack on the Spanish people and their elected government. When she told me that, I realized why I felt such a close kinship with Sis. . . .
>
> One morning Sis was playing her "squeeze box" and singing "Hungry, hungry, are we . . . just as hungry as hungry can be . . .". Her father looked up from his newspaper and growled, "Come on, Sis, you haven't missed a meal in your life." That may have been so, Sis said, but they had come "mighty close" any number of times.[16]

Sis identified closely with both black and white tenant farmers throughout the Cotton Belt, whose circumstances continued to deteriorate. She had a sharp grasp of the situation—the New Deal's agricultural failings, the mechanization of the cotton fields, the compounded plight of the black sharecroppers—in general, the political economy of the farm predicament. Her years at Commonwealth had well prepared her for involvement with the Southern Tenant Farmers Union and its radical approach to the emergency. The STFU in Oklahoma had more than eighty local chapters by 1935, then soon declined because of the mass exodus to California and numerous other problems.

The union was formed in Tyronza, a small town in northeastern Arkansas, by filling-station operator Clay East and dry cleaner H. L. Mitchell, who began discussing Socialism in the late 1920s. In 1931, they joined sharecropper Alvin Nunally and others to form a local Socialist Party. Three years later, following a return trip by national party leader Norman Thomas, they organized the racially integrated Southern Tenant Farmers' Union, including sharecroppers and agricultural wage laborers. Blending black and white southern religious revivalism and leftist politics, the STFU attracted radical religious leaders such as Howard Kester, Ward Rodgers, and Claude

Williams, who had run for governor of Arkansas in 1934 on the Socialist Party ticket. "Kester and Rodgers both threw themselves into the STFU's organizational work despite the risks they ran as 'outside agitators,'" wrote James Green. "Another radical Presbyterian, Claude Williams, set up a 'New School of Social Action' in Little Rock and there trained some of the STFU's black and white organizers. Williams continued organizing the unemployed through the Workers' Alliance and brought together old Socialists with young Communists from Commonwealth College who were now entering the Popular Front period." Using strikes and pressure tactics as they expanded into Oklahoma, STFU organizers faced constant violence from the establishment as well as competition from Communist Party leader Don Henderson, who first encouraged all farm tenants and owners to join the National Farmers' Union or the Farm Holiday Association, while wage workers should organize AFL unions.[17]

Oddly, in mid-1937 the STFU, now with over thirty thousand members in Arkansas, Missouri, and Oklahoma, joined the newly formed CIO-affiliated United Cannery, Agricultural, Packing and Allied Workers Union (UCAPAWA), led by none other than Don Henderson, whose politics had not changed. There was constant friction between Mitchell, Williams, black organizer E. B. McKinney, and now Henderson. After more squabbling, the STFU split from UCAPAWA in early 1939. While struggling along until 1946, when it became the National Farm Labor Union–AFL, the STFU never survived the fight with Henderson and the CIO. Simultaneously, the STFU first affiliated with Commonwealth College in August 1937, then expelled Claude Williams from the union's executive council the following year. Lee Hays, acolyte of Williams and short-lived supervisor of dramatics at Commonwealth College beginning in September 1937, wrote a play for the 1938 STFU convention in Little Rock, *One Bread, One Body*, urging union membership on sharecroppers. Despite the seeming Popular Front mentality of the time, Communists and Socialists, led by dominating personalities with conflicting agendas and ideas, found it difficult to cooperate in the STFU. Sis, identifying with the former, had a bird's-eye view of these events, as she demonstrates in this book.[18]

She also mentions working with the Veterans of Industry of America in Oklahoma, a little-known offshoot of depression organizing. Ira M. Findley, a former Socialist and confidant of Governor William H. Murray, founded the VIA (originally known as the

Veterans of Industry) in September 1932; he worked closely with the Farmer's Union in promoting government jobs for the unemployed, an old-age pension, and a graduated land tax to preserve small family farms. Having reached a peak membership of perhaps 125,000 in 1935, the VIA struggled through the latter 1930s, then finally affiliated with the General Welfare Federation of America in 1941.[19]

Her stay at the Southern Summer School for Women Workers, though brief, broadened her horizons and connections among labor and political activists. Founded by YWCA workers Louise Leonard McLaren and Lois MacDonald in 1927 at Sweet Briar College in Virginia and later moved near Asheville, North Carolina, the organizers envisioned a school along the lines of Brookwood Labor College or the Bryn Mawr Summer School. With initial support from radical organizer Elizabeth Gurley Flynn, among others, they recruited activist women educators and attracted white students between eighteen and twenty-five with at least six years of schooling and two years of industrial experience who were interested in labor organizing. Over three hundred women attended classes during the school's first fifteen years. "After 1935, the school abandoned its connections with women's groups and became more dependant on organized labor," Mary Frederickson wrote. "However, contrary to union priorities, the school's leaders continued to insist that workers' education and the organization of women workers were crucial to the movement. And they urged students to maintain an independent stance toward all institutions, including trade unions." Bending to union pressure, however, the school began admitting men in 1938. Under various guises, the school limped on until 1950.[20]

Returning to Oklahoma, Sis plunged into various radical activities, many associated with the Communist Party. Formed following World War I and quickly faced with organized and unorganized opposition, often violent and certainly crippling—although the public response would hardly have been positive at the time—the party limped through the Roaring Twenties. With the depression, however, many throughout the country turned to drastic answers to solve their economic and cultural hardships, and the party slowly revived, although temporarily retaining its aversion to coalition politics. In middecade, however, party leaders in Moscow and New York, reacting to the rise of fascism in Europe and continuing domestic difficulties, created the Popular Front, reaching out to link arms with fellow socialists and even the left wing of the Democratic

Party. This proved difficult to accomplish. Party members became instrumental in the labor movement, particularly the newly forming Congress of Industrial Organizations (CIO) and in numerous cultural organizations and activities now stimulated by the various New Deal alphabetical agencies. Centered in New York, the party yet reached into all sections and segments of the country, even the Great Plains states, where Sis and Gordon found a political home among fellow radicals. Their commitment to the party would cause problems throughout their lives. Historians are still wrangling over the party's structure and goals, its members' beliefs and actions—whether allegiance to Moscow triumphed over domestic policies and issues. Perhaps there is no answer, but surely for many (the bulk?) of the rank and file, their social, economic, racial, and other principles should be recognized, even lauded.[21]

Party members and political bedfellows used various methods to circulate their messages to the masses, including theatrical productions. Workers' theater with a radical slant—called agitprop (agitation propaganda)—following a century-long gestation period, emerged in Britain and the U.S. in the early 1930s. "An indigenous workers' theatre movement developed in the early 1930s," Daniel Friedman summarized the situation. "It was the only grass-roots amateur movement in U.S. history in which workers created theatre for their fellow laborers. At its height, the movement involved hundreds of troupes and tens of thousands of workers who wrote, directed, performed and attended their own theatrical pieces. They did so with the deliberate intent of helping to create a distinct working-class culture which they hoped would reflect and inspire their fellow workers in their economic and political struggles." While the bulk of these troupes performed in urban-industrial settings, others aimed their message at farm workers and others of the rural proletariat. Songs often appeared in the plays, and by middecade workers' musicals proliferated with the onset of the Popular Front.[22]

Following her musical work at Commonwealth College and the Southern Summer School for Women Workers, a well-seasoned Sis joined the Red Dust Players in Oklahoma. "Two conditions determined the organization and working methods of these [theatrical] groups," Douglas McDermott wrote: "the use of worker-actors and the desire to find a worker-audience. With few exceptions, these groups were composed of class-conscious workers, able to devote only evenings and weekends to theatrical activity. Consequently, almost all actors were untrained and under-rehearsed; and the production of a play, from selection of the script to staging of the business, had to accommodate these conditions." The Red Dust Players, organized in late 1939, certainly fit this description; composed of working people, as described by Sis, the troupe scurried around the countryside, entertaining and proselytizing rural audiences starved for any sort of entertainment. "Touring was the staple of each group," McDermott continued. "Most operated in a single city, but others ranged farther afield in search of an audience. The Red Dust Players toured all over Oklahoma, and the Labor Drama Group of Commonwealth College covered as much of the state of Arkansas as possible, playing to agricultural workers." Almost in the wink of an eye the Red Dust Players vanished, crushed not by audience apathy but political repression.[23]

"Six months later I was in Oklahoma City," Norris Houghton wrote in *Advance from Broadway: 19,000 Miles of American Theatre*, published in 1941:

> I tried to call on the Red Dust Players, but they were no more. I talked on the telephone to a young man who I was told had been connected with them, but Peter-like he thrice denied them. You see, Oklahoma's criminal syndicalism law has been freshly invoked; it has become a treasonous act to suggest to sharecroppers or tenant farmers that their lot may be bettered. The Red Dust Players' meager quarters were raided; all their scripts and material were seized; its leaders found it necessary to disband and abandon the theatrical work Miss Schmidt described in her letter.

Houghton referred to a letter written by Dorothy Schmidt to the New Theatre League, based in New York, far from the Oklahoma hills, in May 1940:

> I wish every one of you could have been with us on our last Tuesday's booking for the Oklahoma Tenant Farmers Union up in Creek County. It's sharecroppers part of the state, rolling hills covered with red sand. What hasn't been bled out by the oil wells has been blown away by the wind. We were off the highway, some ten miles from the nearest town, in a little Negro church, playing by light of five oil lanterns that the audience had brought with them. Our audience came from twenty miles away in all directions; some of them we had to fetch in ourselves. The admission was ten cents, children under six, free—but we felt we should have paid them for the pleasure of per-

forming. . . . One woman said she would've stayed up all night seeing it over and over, and one woman said it'd been ten years—maybe longer—she'd forgot just when—since she'd "clupped her hands together" last. But they clupped and they laughed way down deep, Negro and white together, and scraped their feet on the floor, and said, Yes, sir, that's the truth; that's the way it is; and sang "We Shall Not Be Moved."

This reinforces Sis's convinced memories of their difficulties as well as impact on the rural population.[24]

Sis and Gordon met in March 1941 during the political trials, married in July, and moved to New York City in November, just before Pearl Harbor. Certainly not a propitious time for Communists in Oklahoma; flight now seemed in order, the farther the better. "I bet you've forgot this: when you were getting ready to go East to join the Weavers (Almanacs?) you asked us what name you should use and we all chortled because we couldn't think of anything more genuinely folksy than Sis Cunningham," Dorothy Schmidt recalled over three decades later.[25]

Obviously, moving to the bustling New York, light years removed from rural Oklahoma, was a major change in their lives, but unfortunately they hardly discuss their adaptation to this fresh, alien environment. Instead, Gordon comments on the influential Almanac Singers—a valuable firsthand account giving much detail as well as humanizing this group of extraordinarily creative individuals—yet somewhat from a distance; we get little of Sis's views as she plunged into a continuous round of rallies, performances, and hootenannies, including a few recording sessions. They lived in Almanac House at 130 West Tenth Street from December 13 to January 26, then moved to 430 Sixth Avenue—the transfer vividly described by Gordon— where they remained until October 23, 1942. Next, until December 3, they resided at 647 Hudson Street. Before arriving in New York, the city's Left had already been introduced to Gordon, in Daniel Bowie's flattering *Daily Worker* article, datelined Oklahoma City: "An artist from among the people, Gordon Friesen, Oklahoma-born son of pioneers who homesteaded in the western part of the state, shows a deep hatred of Hitlerism and oppression abroad or at home, in simple, vigorous, pen-and-ink drawings." Accompanied by two of Gordon's drawings—"The Banker and His Wife" and "Nazism"— Bowie's article stresses Gordon's "almost savage hatred and contempt for fascism," foreign or domestic. The article quickly found its way into Gordon's slowly expanding FBI file. Also according to the file, during 1942 Gordon worked for the USO, Pathe News, and *Graphic Magazine* in New York.[26]

In late 1940, Pete Seeger, Lee Hays, and Millard Lampell formed the Almanac Singers. Soon joined by Pete Hawes and others, they moved into the first Almanac House on Thirteen Street in Greenwich Village and initiated a continuous round of rent parties and appearances at leftist meetings and labor rallies, composing their own topical songs. Joined by Josh White, they recorded their first album, *Songs for John Doe*, in March 1941, full of biting, highly controversial antiwar songs. In May, the same group recorded *Talking Union*, filled with clever, hard-hitting, prounion ditties, many of which have lasted to the present, followed by the more traditional *Deep Sea Chanties and Whaling Ballads* and *Sod Buster Ballads* in July. When Gordon and Sis arrived in New York the Almanacs had already moved into their new quarters on Tenth Street, now including Bess Lomax and Woody Guthrie, although soon enough Lee Hays would move out.[27]

Mill Lampell, the group's flamboyant wordsmith, later vividly captured Gordon and Sis, with his customary literary license:

A couple who knew Pete and Woody from the days when they were singing their way across Oklahoma turned up. Sis Cunningham was an angular, square-jawed woman who played the accordion and had a singing voice sharp as the wind whipping across the flatland. Her first name was Agnes, but no one ever called her that. She had sold her cow to pay for the trip to New York with her husband, Gordon Friesen. An ex-communicated Mennonite, big-shouldered and callused, Gordon had come of age on a hard-scrabble, Dust Bowl farm near the Red River. . . . Gordon didn't sing or play an instrument himself. Mostly he carried Sis's accordion and drew scraggly figures of monsters with floppy, nine-toed feet, claw hands, crossed eyes, and snaggle teeth to illustrate the postcards we had taken to sending out. Aside from the monster, who was likely to have the best features of Hitler, a razorback hog, an alligator, and our landlord, Gordon's drawings featured a twisted microphone and a lineup of banjo, guitar, and accordion players with faces like ducks, playing to a wildly cheering audience with faces like ducks. How he got all that on one little penny postcard was a mystery. It was also a mystery why he decided to make such a big play to the duck population. Very few of them turned up.[28]

In mid-December, a week after Pearl Harbor, Pete, Woody, Sis, Mill, and Arthur Stern auditioned for NBC radio, and soon performed prowar songs for the opening show of the widely broadcast *This Is War* series, CBS's *We the People, The Treasury Hour,* and assorted Office of War Information broadcasts heard overseas. They also had an awkward yet successful audition at the swank Rainbow Room atop Rockefeller Center, arranged by the William Morris agency, but they refused the job because they would not kowtow to the management's demand that they wear hillbilly outfits. And their possible recording contract with Decca remained stillborn due to mounting criticism in the mainstream press. Meanwhile, they put on benefit concerts for Aunt Molly Jackson (then ill and living in a slum), with such performers as Leadbelly, Burl Ives, Josh White, Earl Robinson, Will Geer, Tony Kraber, Richard Dyer-Bennet, and others. Gordon wrote a sketch at the time for the *Daily Worker:* "Aunt Molly's doctor has advised her she has a leaking heart and must restrict her activities, but her fighting spirit remains undampened."[29] In the spring of 1942 the Almanacs—now composed of Pete Seeger, Sis, Millard Lampell, Bess Lomax Hawes, and Arthur Stern—recorded "Dear Mr. President" for Keynote Records. During the summer Pete left for the army, and Stern as well as Bess and Butch Hawes moved to Detroit, forming a branch of the Almanacs. Sis continued with the rump New York Almanacs into the fall, appearing in *Its All Yours,* a musical drama written by Earl Robinson and Millard Lampell; she joined with Woody and Cisco Houston or Sonny Terry and Brownie McGhee for hastily arranged concerts.

Then Sis and Gordon moved to Detroit, first living at 5757 Second Boulevard from December 3, 1942 until May 14, when they moved to 460 Prentis, Apartment 11, just as Bess and Butch returned to New York, joining with Stern and Charlie Polacheck in the surviving remnant of the Detroit Almanacs. By the spring of 1943 their performing had ceased, although not before issuing a small song book, *Anti-Fascist Songs of the Almanac Singers,* including Sis's "Tehran and Roosevelt" and "The Rifles!" Sis has written to me, with characteristic modesty, "I don't think *I,* personally, contributed a whole lot to Almanac activities. I came into the group late, I wrote only a few songs, I had no great singing voice, and my accordion playing was secondary to the string accompaniment of guitars, banjos and mandolins. The fact that I was a woman member may have been of importance; I don't know. Gordon contributed nothing except to act as my accordion carrier and to boost morale occasionally with his sense of humor." Perhaps true, but she did perform extensively with the Almanacs and other friends in New York, surely a vital presence on the political folk scene; and Gordon kept everyone as cheery and honest as possible.[30]

In his discussion of Woody, Gordon expresses his own views of life, capitalism, the inherent goodness of the working class, the common people. He identified closely with Woody—certainly admired him—not only for his musical genius, but, perhaps more importantly, for his rock-ribbed commitment to basic human values stemming from their shared rural Oklahoma backgrounds and radical political beliefs. While respecting Woody's obvious talents, Gordon stood up to him when necessary. "Gordon Friesen had no musical ability whatever," commented Joe Klein in his biography of Woody;

> he was a writer, very witty in a countrified way, and an absolutely demonic cartoonist. His main function with the Almanacs, aside from carrying his wife's accordion case around, was keeping Woody in line. Gordon was uniquely qualified for the job, having grown up on a scraggly dirt farm in western Oklahoma, the heart of the dust bowl. Whenever Woody started flaunting his "authenticity" and going on about the migrants, Gordon would let him have it: "Woody, what on earth are you talking about? You never harvested a grape in your life. You're an intellectual, a poet—all this singin' about jackhammers, if you ever got within five feet of a jackhammer it'd knock you on your ass. You scrawny little bastard, you're shitting the public: You never did a day's work in your life."[31]

Despite natural friction, Gordon and Woody became close cronies, often walking the streets of Manhattan—the former's six-foot-three frame towering over his much shorter friend—and lunching on Mexican chili plus mug after mug of bock beer in some greasy spoon. Gordon also defends the Almanacs' anti-war songs, released on their *John Doe* album, putting their pacifism into the larger political, generational context.

Sis and Gordon's stay in Detroit, though brief, included various activities, among them Sis's work with the Almanacs and her stint in a war plant. Gordon, following an interlude working in a factory, returned to his favorite trade as a working journalist with the *Detroit Times* from February 8, 1943, to May 20, 1944. His survival mechanism was to mix serious with fanciful reporting, and he continued to identify with the underdog, like his colleague, the Jewish photographer Arnold Freeman, helping him cope with homegrown anti-Semitism. His most memorable story was covering the Detroit race riot in 1943, a searing experience later recorded in his story "Day of Infamy," published in *Mainstream*.[32]

Gordon quit the *Times* on May 20, and the couple immediately returned to New York, briefly living at 29 Bethune Street until their move to 353 East Eighty-fourth Street in late August; Gordon started working for the Office of War Information five days later as a script editor in the Overseas Operations Bureau, for thirty-two hundred dollars per year. Unfortunately, Gordon's experiences with the OWI and the war's end are not recorded. At the time, the government became increasingly concerned about his politics. He was first questioned by the FBI on March 27, 1945, followed by the Loyalty Rating Board of the U.S. Civil Service Commission's Interrogatory just as the war was ending, on V-J Day, August 14. Sis mentioned only the second incident, which included a detailed listing of Gordon's alleged political activities since the late 1930s, obviously furnished by the FBI. Caught in a classic Catch-22 situation, Gordon could hardly answer such detailed charges—to what purpose? The government had already made up its mind that membership or even affiliation with the legal Communist Party or Communist Political Association, its new identity for the war's duration, denoted subversion, even while the Soviet Union was a close ally.

These charges and inquiries, shortly leading to Gordon's blacklisting, are searing indications that the Red Scare antedated the war, particularly with the creation of the House Un-American Activities Committee in 1938, regularly fed information by its sidekick J. Edgar Hoover and the FBI, and quickly picked up following V-E Day. Long before Joe McCarthy hit the headlines, red hunting had become de rigueur in the nation's capital, with Sis and Gordon early caught in the net. He bravely stuck to his guns, but with little success. HUAC became a permanent standing committee in 1946, continually working to root out "subversives" and ruining many lives in the process.[33]

While Gordon worked for CBS until he was fired in late 1948, when the blacklist's yoke became firmly fastened around his neck, Sis continued singing at various progressive events. She performed some with People's Songs and its booking agency, People's Artists. Formed during the last days of 1945 by Pete Seeger, Lee Hays, and assorted others, People's Songs published a bulletin and encouraged

topical-song writing and performing. It reached its peak as the singing arm of the Henry Wallace presidential campaign in 1948, collapsing soon thereafter. Sis did a little recording—the unissued "Parnell Thomas Blues" and "Henry Wallace"—but, as she candidly
admits, for various reasons became increasingly estranged from folk
music at the time. Gordon summarized their involvement in a letter
to Richard Reuss in 1965: "We were not around at the organizational
meetings of P.S. or P.A. We did belong for a while to a branch of it
on the West Side of Manhattan (in 1946–47?). . . . There were a lot
of people in that chapter, lots of people, lots of talk at meetings, but
nothing ever came of it. . . . Sis did take some bookings from central
office downtown; her last appearance seems to have been in 1947
when she went with Pete and Bernie Asbel[l] to Atlantic City to sing
for the Fur & Leather Workers' convention." A photo in the *Daily
Worker* of Sis performing with Bob Claiborne, Charlotte Anthony,
Audrey Frost, and Betty Garrett in July 1946 accompanied an article
captioned "People's Songs for Political Action" describing a demonstration for "Buy Nothing Day": "It was hard singing in the rain. It
was also difficult for Sis Cunningham to lug her guitar [accordion]
through the heat, but the singers knew they were accomplishing
something and enjoyed it. Peter Seeger, Bob Claiborne and Sis composed 'The Black Market Blues' while they were on that march."[34]

Sis's heartrending tale of suffering through the Red Scare and
blacklist gives human form to what is usually an abstract account
of the anti-Communist crusade and its victims. Having grown up in
poverty perhaps prepared Sis and Gordon for further hardships, but
did not lessen the mind-numbing anguish of the experience, particularly with two little girls to provide for. Welfare allowed them to
survive, barely, but with little dignity as they scraped through the
1950s—constant sickness and the daily struggle taking their toll.
The FBI visited Gordon in 1954, who was then living at 74 West
103rd Street, but he "stated he had nothing to say to the inter-
viewing agents." Nonetheless, the local agent recommended to J.
Edgar Hoover that a Security Index Card be prepared for Gordon, in
addition to the ongoing file.[35]

They somehow outlasted the witch hunters and welfare department through the 1950s, and reemerged in the 1960s not exactly
part of the Kennedys' Camelot—Sis and Gordon were of another
generation—but certainly with spirits revived. They were prepared
musically, politically, even physically, if not economically, for a new

venture, the launching of *Broadside* magazine in early 1962. While Sis and Gordon had been on the periphery of People's Songs in the latter 1940s, they modeled *Broadside* after the *People's Song* bulletin, the topical-song magazine published from 1946 to 1949. Irwin Silber, editor of *Sing Out!* almost from its inception in 1950, had not abandoned topical songs, but could squeeze few contemporary compositions into each issue (five a year). With the enthusiastic support and counsel of Malvina Reynolds and Pete and Toshi Seeger, and added financial help from the latter, *Broadside* began its score and more years of publishing, quickly securing its preeminent role in the topical-song movement. They announced in the first issue: "*Broadside's* aim is not so much to select and decide as to circulate as many songs as possible and get them out as quickly as possible. Our schedule calls for a twice-a-month publication—this will depend mainly on the contributing songwriters." The first song was Aggie's "Will You Work for Peace or Wait for War." Sis was listed as the editor, with no word of Gordon, who always hovered in the background, seldom leaving the apartment, writing much, while keeping up the correspondence and the family's spirits. Their ambitious publishing schedule soon proved to be impossible, but not for lack of effort.[36]

Josh Dunson, closely involved with the magazine's success, wrote:

> During the second year of *Broadside's* publication, topical songs and a number of topical singers became tremendously popular. Peter, Paul and Mary's version of "Blowin' in the Wind" sold over one million records. Far more important, Bob Dylan's own album, consisting almost entirely of topical songs, made the top lists, selling over 150,000. *Broadside* itself more than tripled in circulation. . . . The outpouring of higher quality topical songs marked a turning point for *Broadside* that can be placed approximately at issue No. 20, February 1963. Bob Dylan's "Masters of War" and "It's All Right," Malvina Reynolds' "Little Boxes" and Phil Ochs' "Hazard Kentucky." . . . An important part of early publicity were *Broadside*-sponsored concerts in March and May 1963, which gave a topical singers like Phil Ochs and Mark Spoelstra a special chance to try their songs in a quiet concert atmosphere.[37]

Dunson failed to mention that he also appeared in no. 20, with an article on the "Birth of Broadside," describing a typical music session. "*Broadside's* home is a small little room that's got chairs and a sofa with a tape recorder finishing off the bottom wall space," he began. Gil Turner, Bob Dylan and his girlfriend Suze Rotolo, Phil Ochs, and Happy Traum soon crowded into the room. "Boy, this room was so jammed packed with people that there was real foot and banjo and guitar shifting necessary to get Phil Ochs close enough to the mike to record his three new songs." *New York Times* journalist Robert Shelton later asserted in his biography of Dylan, "Along with Paul Krassner's *The Realist* and *The Village Voice, Broadside* probably pioneered the 1960s underground press."[38]

Besides publishing the songs and promoting concerts, Sis and Gordon also began issuing records through Moe Asch's Folkways Records—over a dozen all told. "As you say," Gordon wrote to Richard Reuss in May 1963, "it is not enough to merely put a song into print. It's very hard to make it come alive. So, as you may know, we've issued an L-P, Broadside Ballads Vol. 1. We're not too satisfied with it, but actually had very little to say regarding its final content (it's produced by Folkways). . . . In addition, OAK Publications wants to do a 'Best of Broadside' song book. There's mountains of work here, and about all we can really do is get out our skimpy little magazine." Perhaps Bob Dylan and the topical song movement would have emerged without the boost from *Broadside*—certainly the times were changing in that direction—but the magazine played a central role in providing an outlet not only for those who scored some commercial success, but for hundreds of others from throughout the country who thrilled at seeing their songs in print.[39]

Soon *Broadside*s were springing up throughout the country. "I think one of the most charming things that has happened in many a year is the way three small magazines all started 19 months ago, each calling itself 'Broadside,'" Seeger wrote in his *Sing Out!* column in late 1963. "And today each continues to publish, under the same name, undoubtedly to the confusion of many potential readers. . . . All three have honestly individual characters and aims. The Boston B reports on coffee house doings and occasional record reviews and songs and singers in that area. The Los Angeles B has more theoretical articles. The New York B exists mainly to print up new topical songs, with editorial content at a minimum." As usual, Seeger ignored his ongoing role in the original *Broadside*'s creation and survival. Also, he never mentioned that Sis currently served as his paid secretary, for sixty dollars weekly, handling much correspondence and other matters, while the Seegers were on their year-long world tour that started the previous August. Pete maintained a steady stream of letters from various countries: "Hope you and Sis will be able to get something from Newport foundation soon," he wrote Gordon from Japan. "Broadside is too important for you to lose your health doing it all alone. It must gradually over the years continue to grow. And you get paid decently for it. I am depositing microfilm copies of it in library here, as everywhere."[40]

In addition to publishing so many songs, *Broadside* also featured numerous articles, including Gordon's series on the Almanacs, and scores of newspaper clippings, situating the songs in their temporal context. The magazine had its critics. The editors of *The Little Sandy Review*, Paul Nelson and Jon Pankake, self-styled defenders of "traditional" folk music, kept up their carping. "There are two *Broadside* magazines," they wrote, "plus a Boston-based pamphlet of the same name. Confusing? You bet, since the East Coast *Broadside* is one of those P-for-Protesty things featuring songs the level of most of the poorer material on Seeger's *Gazette*, Volume Two." Sis responded: "Thanks very much for your mention of *Broadside*. . . . But we are a little puzzled as to why you dismiss us as just 'one of those P-for-Protesty things,' especially when you use so many of your pages (see LSR #22) praising a number of the songwriters we publish: Bob Dylan, Woody Guthrie, Peter La Farge, etc. We would suggest that it reflects an unresolved contradiction in your own approach to so-called 'protest' songs." In a lengthy retort, the editors stuck to their guns. Our "argument against the Protesty song," they explained, "is, by and large, that it is neither true protest nor true song (one may also add that such noble topics as world peace, world war, and international brotherhood deserve far more artistry and effort than the hack, ritualized treatment they get from the writers of BROADSIDE; such roaring incompetence only cheapens and makes burlesques out of otherwise serious subjects)." This colorful exchange—bothersome, perhaps disturbing—did not sidetrack Sis and Gordon from continuing their efforts.[41]

Moe Asch, owner of Folkways Records, who had concluded a marketing deal with MGM/Verve Records, bristled at a review by Stu Cohen of a new Woody Guthrie record. The reviewer complained about the Verve record's sound quality. "I usually ignore criticism good or bad written about the records I produce," he bitterly complained to *Broadside* in October 1965. "But I thought that Broadside would have enough sense to understand its moral obligation to help

BIG COMPANIES whenever they go out on the limb and issue an unrealsed [*sic*] album such as the Woody Guthrie. . . . You have no right to judge being no God, of what is good folk or bad folk. Folk is people and all folk or people are good." Gordon responded to Moe, who was still issuing Broadside Records, with a defense of the review, only to hear again from Asch: "The only obligation I have to anybody including Woody or Broadside is to be true to them and not in the image of those who wishing to be liked by all become the mirror of all." And that ended that.[42]

David Nobel launched an attack from another direction. A Christian fundamentalist, Nobel wrote as a graduate paper at the University of Tulsa "A Historical Analysis of the Radical Folk Tradition as Presented in *Broadside* Magazine February, 1962–November, 1967." He had already connected popular music with the devil in *Communism, Hypnotism and the Beatles* (1965) and *Rhythm, Riots, and Revolution* (1966), both issued by Christian Crusade Publications. After a close reading of each issue and other sources, he concluded: "There is no doubt that the bible of the topical song world is *Broadside* magazine." Nobel was particularly galled by Pete Seeger's appearance on the *Smothers Brothers Comedy Hour* on September 12, 1967. "Never has a *Broadside* partisan reached such a pinnacle. From a mimeograph machine (hand pushed) in the front room of a single home to the front rooms of America through Columbia Records and the Columbia Broadcasting System who can dispute the fact that *Broadside* has come a long way in five and one-half meagre years!"[43]

Perhaps troubled by the diverse attacks from Nobel and *The Little Sandy Review*, Sis and Gordon were considerably more distracted by their ongoing economic problems. Mary Ann Pollar organized a successful benefit in Berkeley in 1963, featuring Malvina Reynolds, Rosalie Sorrels, Mark Spoelstra, Gil Turner, and actor Will Geer as emcee; unfortunately, there were no others as lucrative. In 1964, Sis and Gordon unsuccessfully applied to the Newport Folk Foundation for some support in order to go to photo-offset printing and hire a part-time clerical worker—hoping for one hundred dollars per issue for one year. Money dribbled in from subscriptions, sales of back issues and the OAK song books, and a series of *Broadside* musical programs at the Village Gate during the winter of 1964–65. *New York Times* music reporter Robert Shelton effusively greeted the first Village Gate Topical Song Workshop in November 1964, when

Barbara Dane, Phil Ochs, Tom Paxton, Bernice Reagon, Len Chandler, Pete Seeger, Buffy Sainte-Marie, Patrick Sky, Jack Elliott, and Julius Lester crowded the stage. "What is probably most important is that the topical-song movement writers as well as audience has grown so in the last few years that this is no longer an underground or narrowly partisan cultural phenomenon," Shelton argued, then concluded, "the degree of concern for the world irradiated an entertaining and instructive program."[44]

San Francisco music critic Ralph Gleason gave a needed boost in various articles. He mentioned *Broadside* in his *San Francisco Chronicle* column in early 1965 and informed Sis, "I've just done a long piece for Ramparts, which is a monthly magazine published out here which has a national distribution, on topical songs and I quoted you in there and ran some space on Broadside." Unfortunately, the reference somehow disappeared before the article was published in April. He also suggested to Barry Olivier that he include a topical-song panel during the next Berkeley Folk Festival, with Sis and Malvina Reynolds; the panel existed, but without Sis or Malvina. As late as 1973, Gleason did manage to do justice to *Broadside* in *Rolling Stone*, the rock bible: "There's a small mimeographed quarterly put out in New York called Broadside Magazine which is one of the most important publications in the world of music and deserves anybody's three bucks for a subscription. Not only does Broadside publish original topical songs in every issue, but it frequently publishes information ignored or forgotten by the mass media publications and which is invaluable."[45]

Compounding their financial problems, Moe Asch was predictably reluctant to report the sales or pay royalties on the records. While they had managed to sell *Broadside* copies at previous Newport Folk Festivals, in 1966 they could not afford to rent a booth for two hundred dollars plus the extra two hundred dollars for insurance, and no one offered to share their booth. "There was a point around #89 and #90 when we might have expanded and gone onto a firm footing if certain important things had not gone completely wrong," Gordon informed Richard Reuss in May 1968. "We've had to fall back into the position of simply providing a boost, quite limited to be exact—to new people who show up." Early the next year, Gordon forecast that "*Broadside* may now make it to the century mark since we have received a small but desperately needed stipend from the Newport people. We were down to the bare bones the last 3 or 4 months, in the worst plight, somehow, since we started." In 1969, the Newport Folk Festival Board invited Sis to lead the Topical Songs Workshop, with Len Chandler, Jean Ritchie, and Buffy Sainte-Marie.[46]

They continued to publish, with mounting difficulties. Sis wrote to Pete just after Christmas 1970: "I know the times we are going through now are not good for any of us. The alienation, or near-alienation, affects us all. With us the main problem as you know is complete lack of money. We have none, can't seem to raise any with the little affairs we were trying to give. Our children have none, can't get any, even though both of them possess a much more than usual amount of talent and, I believe, intelligence." Aggie's asthma was crippling; Sis and Gordon continually rushed her to the hospital. Gordon complained bitterly to Reuss seven months later: "Not only *Broadside* but we as a family are in a heluva shape since St. Peter [Pete Seeger] became God and withdrew his support, sentencing us to disintegration and death—we struggle daily for beans and rent, never mind the gas and lights bill, which has run up to 8 mths. again." A week later Pete promised that "he will raise money for us if we can come out in the form of cassettes. Well, I don't know whether we can do this—make such a radical adjustment in our operation. We are in our sixties, very worn out, our children are in bad shape. *But*—Seeger has offered." But this was simply not possible.[47]

About this time Robert Shelton, now living in England and working on his biography of Bob Dylan, whose career he had boosted in the *New York Times*, privately showered praise on *Broadside*. "Looking back over my file of Broadsides, which is big albeit not totally complete, I am struck by what a magnificent contribution Broadside has made to the topical song movement," he wrote Sis and Gordon in June 1970. And a year later: "It strikes me as cruel that you and Sis have had to struggle along while so many made so much money during the 1960s. . . . There is an imbalance, because you, more than Sing Out, did really help shape an era." In another letter, in commenting on their inability to raise money, he expressed outrage, but little surprise: "Somebody among your alumni—Janis Ian, Eric Anderson, Ochs, or whoever, ought to be able to organize a benefit concert if Dylan is either unwilling or unable. I supposed [*sic*] you've tried all these avenues before. The injustice of it all does really make one wonder about that marvelous 'folk movement' we had back in the early 1960s." They certainly agreed.[48]

Sis poured out her grief and feelings in a series of letters to her old friend Wally Hille, covering family matters, music, socialism, and much else. In early 1971 she wrote:

> Well, Wally, my personal philosophy is one of the reasons Broadside was ever started in the first place. No one else wanted to do this—I had to talk and talk to Gordon to go along with me. We were on relief at the time, and both of us were quite beaten down. I had tried to get jobs with Levanthal [*sic*], Sing Out and Moe Asch and failed. . . . Once I talked Gordon into this he leaped into the saddle and has done a hell of a lot more than I have, or ever could have, to shape Broadside and make it the really important project I believe it to be. . . . The girls, with their drawings and their layout work have also played an important part. Up until recently when things slacked off, we had like a continuous workshop going here in the Broadside office. As I said in my other letter, literally hundreds of young folks have come and gone, each picking up something they could take with them, and leaving something of themselves with us.[49]

By 1972 their troubles seemed to proliferate, a combination of various factors and forces. "Some of the decline of *Broadside* is plainly due to moves we deliberately decided upon a couple of years back," Gordon confided to Irwin Silber, now with the *Guardian* newspaper, with whom they had a prickly relationship. "We chose to become more radical. What resulted was that our liberal-minded support fell away like flies before a spray of flit, and, worse, no new audience appeared to fill the vacuum. . . . However, we were also sharply affected by general trends beyond our control. . . . Here is what I think occurred: the creation of protest song shifted, in the middle 60s—67, 68—from the 'folk' world, which had been the wellspring of this kind of material for so many years, to rock musicians. And we were not in a position to keep abreast of this transition." The times had changed, and so had *Broadside*'s audience. Yet Gordon managed some optimism: "Irwin, we're not really frustrated except by illness and lack of money. Protest songs continue to go down widely, specifically among the youth." Sis also became thwarted when she tried to collect royalties on her song "How Can

You Keep On Movin'," recorded by the New Lost City Ramblers, and most recently by Ry Cooder. "We are women—and therefore admittedly at a disadvantage in certain similar ways," she complained to Toshi Seeger. "Every one of the dozen or so persons involved in separating me from the songs I wrote in the thirties are men. Every last one of them! ... I am simply infuriated—repeat, *infuriated*—when I review in my mind the ways I have been pulverized—the fruits of my efforts syphoned off by a male oriented society, small as those fruits may seem." She finally collected royalties from Warner Bros.[50]

Pete and Toshi always remained *Broadside*'s salvation, although they never contributed as much as Sis and Gordon would have liked. "The main thing that is needed is money for promotion," they wrote to the Seegers in October 1972, following the magazine's tenth anniversary. "Pete said in a recent note to us something to the effect that he felt more like shedding tears over Broadside's failure to grow. Broadside was never meant to 'grow'; it has always had a built in limitation, namely, it has always since its inception held to the course of presenting new, young songwriters of whom no one had ever heard. 'Commercial' success cannot be built on such an ideal in this capitalistic system. We were never under the illusion that it could." They appreciated the $530 Pete had raised at a concert some months earlier, but still "right now Broadside is virtually at the end of its rope." Perhaps they could merge with *Sing Out!*, as Pete had already suggested. Despite their proliferating difficulties, *Broadside* continued to publish unknown songwriters as the 1970s unfolded.[51]

Gordon became more personal in describing to Silber their current plight: "Sis and I are in a sort of bind—we're getting old and are sick, and in our weakness are being consistently ripped off while struggling to dig up the bread for rent, gas & lights, and some bean soup to eat. We've backed ourselves into a corner where we have nothing left to hang onto but B'Side." Looking back at *Broadside*'s glory days of the mid-1960s, he sadly agreed with Silber, "The young songwriters who came around when B'Side was started were exclusively sons of the middle class—we've never been able to find a working class one. It wasn't hard to recognize that they were reformists, calling on the capitalistic structure to curb its crudities and make itself less hideous and more presentable." As lifelong radicals, Gordon as well as Sis accepted this situation, while continuing their struggle for revolutionary change and music, although such songs were few and far between. Issue no. 100 included two, Nina Simone's "Revolution" and Jimmy Collier's "Pickaxe & a Stone." [52]

Phil Ochs's suicide in 1976 deeply disturbed Sis and Gordon. Mark Eliot soon published a shaky biography, which Gordon panned—to Eliot's chagrin. "How unfortunate that you have let your criticisms become reduced to the level of tantrum ('non-book, piece of trash, unverified mish-mash, packed full of distortions, vague half truths, outright lies, twisted all out of shape,' etc.)," Eliot rejoined. But Sis and Gordon had nurtured Phil to the end, one of their cherished friends and song writers, and they had difficulty coping. "He would ring our doorbell at 7 o'clock in the morning after sleeping in a doorway or on a park bench," they related to Jacques Vassal, who had released Eliot's book in France. "We would feed him and get him to take a shower and give him clean underwear, shirt and socks and strings for his broken shoes. We tried to help him in our own ineffective way; we gave him money (he'd come without a dime in his pocket); we'd listen to him for hours and hours and Gordon would try over and over again to get him to write down the long rambling discourses." But nobody could help Ochs, his mind spiraling out of control, perhaps triggered by FBI and CIA harassment as Sis and Gordon believed. [53]

Jim Capaldi wrote a flattering portrait of Sis, Gordon, and *Broadside* in the February 1977 issue of *Folk Scene*, published in Los Angeles. "In the beginning, *Broadside* was issued semi-monthly, then monthly, and then bimonthly," he concluded. "At the close of the Sixties, with the decline of interest in protest songs and politics in general, the magazine lost many subscribers and was forced to publish semi-annually for several years. However, they have recently begun printing quarterly. . . . These days, they are supporting themselves mainly by selling complete sets of back issues of *Broadside*." Then Capaldi gave a plea for their continuing support, "After all of their struggle and sacrifice, it would be tragic to see them forgotten by those whom they assisted over the years and those who sing the songs that have appeared in *Broadside*. . . . If they have demonstrated one thing over the years, it is their faith in humanity and the durability of the radical movement. Gordon Friesen and Sis Cunningham know that a better world is coming, and therein lies their strength." Due to financial and other problems, they reluctantly agreed to give up on the magazine in 1980. In perhaps a last letter to Reuss, in February 1984, Sis complained, "The new publisher of *Broadside* is primarily a bustling business man with an office centrally located on Broadway where with a small staff he does microfilming, and only does Broadside as a secondary venture. . . . I don't know, but I believe he means to make money on Broadside. I hope I'm wrong, because if I'm not the content of the magazine will change—has already changed to some extent." Now in her seventies and still committed to topical music and radical politics, Sis had to confess that "Neither Gordon nor myself has the energy to keep tab on things any more; and both of our girls have children to raise."[54]

Surprisingly—even miraculously—a collective of eight people, including Sis, Gordon, and their daughter Jane, regained control of the magazine in the mid-'80s, and managed to produce issue no. 181 in June 1987. Other numbers appeared on a bimonthly basis for a year or so, finally ceasing in late 1988 with issue no. 187. *Broadside* had run its course—a brave, influential, feisty publication, survivor of feast and famine, good times and bad, topical music's waxing and waning, the loud and clear voice of Sis and Gordon for over twenty years.

For decades they had devoted their lives to organizing farmers and workers, attempting to bring about an economic and political revolution. This had not worked. In the 1960s they turned their attention to helping revitalize the topical-song movement while admitting that the audience for folk songs mainly existed on the college campuses and among the nation's young people. They had readjusted their sights, but not their dreams for a more equitable and just society. The Vietnam War also had become their concern. Gordon admitted to Irwin Silber in 1972, "We want the National Liberation Front to win; we have always wanted it to win. So what can we do besides sit and feel guilty that the Vietnamese are dying in a battle that rightly is our responsibility." Music had always been part and parcel of their lives, both as entertainment and a tool to promote social change. *Broadside* would be their monument.[55]

In 1998, in her late eighties and suffering from various illnesses, Sis could look back on a rich and fulfilling life, although certainly not without hardships, sacrifices, and much anguish. She and Gordon had survived poverty, sickness, political blacklisting, and welfare dependency. More important, they had fought the good fight as they saw the situation, struggling to defeat racism and discrimination, economic inequalities, union busting, political repression, fascism, and many other evils—Gordon through the pen and Sis through music and theater. Their long affiliation with the Communist Party marked not their enslavement to party regimentation and doctrine, but a commitment to equality and integration, however possible. The publication of *Broadside* was the culmination of their long struggle, deftly connecting music and political action. Their lives are a testament to their dogged perseverance despite all obstacles.

I continue to learn intriguing details about their lives. Only recently, Sis reminded me that Gordon also wrote songs, often under a variety of pen names—including "Mary Brooks" and "Martha Case." He wrote "Tehran and Roosevelt" (with Sis) and "Mister Hutcheson, Dubinsky and Woll," both part of the Detroit Almanacs' repertoire. Later, he penned "The Jack Ash Society," "Fayette County," "The Ballad of Billy Boggs," and others included in Sis's *Red Dust & Broadsides: A Piece of People's History in Songs, Poems & Prose*, which she published in 1990.

The past continues to intrude on the present. Pete included a previously unreleased version of Sis's "My Oklahoma Home Blowed Away" in his sparkling collection *A Link in the Chain* (Columbia/Legacy 1996), to her delight. On the other hand, she read with dread and fascination Greg Mitchell's detailed *Tricky Dick and the Pink Lady: Richard Nixon vs. Helen Gahagan Douglas—Sexual Politics and the Red Scare, 1950*, a chilling reminder of her and Gordon's personal tragedies and sorrows as casualties of that benighted era.[56]

I consider it an honor and pleasure to be able to call Sis a friend following our first meeting in 1992. Unfortunately, I never met Gordon, ensconced in a nursing home in 1989 because of complications from multiple brain infarcts. Gordon, increasingly incapacitated, died on October 15, 1996. But their daughter Jane, granddaughter Ellie, and great-grandson Nicholas have greeted me during my all-too-infrequent visits to the apartment. Their daughter Aggie also has two children, now grown. I have learned much from the correspondence between Richard A. Reuss and Sis and Gordon. Alas, Dick also died before we could meet; his expertise on all aspects of folk music and the folk revival, both firsthand and through his extensive scholarship, remains unsurpassed. Sis has given me Dick's letters, and I have obtained copies of their (mostly Gordon's) letters from the Reuss Collection in the University Archives at Indiana University, Bloomington. The archivists, starting with Bruce Con-forth, have been most cooperative. Others have also lent their assistance and support, including Wade Black, Eli Jaffe, Irwin Silber, and Guy Logsdon. I particularly want to thank my friend and folk colleague Dave Samuelson, whose knowledge of just about everything musical (and otherwise) always keeps me honest.

Dozens of Sis's friends joined her on the stage of the New York Society for Ethical Culture on November 2, 1997, for a long-deserved, thrilling tribute, "Topical Songs from A(lmanacs) to B(roadside)." With Izzy Young and Sonny Ochs as emcees, Pete Seeger, Len Chandler, Bev Grant, Sharleen Leahey, Matt Jones, Julius Lester, George Lorrie, Luci Murphy, Rik Palieri, Tom McClelland, Fred Stanton, Sammy Walker, Jon Kwitny, Bob Cohen, and others regaled the audience with songs and stories. "To celebrate the life of Sis Cunningham is to celebrate the triumph of courage and hope over fear and despair," Sharleen Leahey wrote soon after. "In a world filled with cynicism and resignation, it is an honor to participate in a tribute to a woman so deserving of our admiration. Thank you Sis, for staying true to your ideals!"[57]

Notes

1. See, in general, Jim Capaldi, "Broadside: The Struggle Continues," *Folk Scene* 4 (February 1977): 16–23. On Gordon, see Allan Teichroew, "Gordon Friesen: Writer, Radical and Ex-Mennonite," *Mennonite Life,* June 1983, 4–17. On Sis, see Suzanne H. Schrems, "Radicalism and Song," *Chronicles of Oklahoma* 62 (Summer 1984), 190–206; and Madeline B. Rose, "Sis Cunningham: Songs of Hard Times," *Ms. Magazine,* March 1974, 29–32.

2. On local history, see H. Wayne Morgan and Anne Hodges Morgan, *Oklahoma: A Bicentennial History* (New York: W. W. Norton & Co., 1977); Kenneth S. Davis, *Kansas: A History* (New York: W. W. Norton & Co., 1976); Donald E. Green, ed., *Rural Oklahoma* (Oklahoma City: Oklahoma Historical Society, 1977); Davis D. Joyce, ed., *"An Oklahoma I Had Never Seen Before": Alternative Views of Oklahoma History* (Norman: University of Oklahoma Press, 1994).

3. Morgan and Morgan, *Oklahoma,* 11–12.

4. Kent Ruth et al., *Oklahoma: A Guide to the Sooner State* (Norman: University of Oklahoma Press, 1957), 254, 365.

5. See Douglas Hale, *The Germans From Russia In Oklahoma* (Norman: University of Oklahoma Press, 1980).

6. William Cunningham, "Commonwealth College—An Educational Mutant," *The World Tomorrow* 12 (December 1929): 503; William Cunningham, "Commonwealth College, Learning and Earning," *American Association of University Presses Bulletin* 15 (February 1929): 158.

7. Richard J. Altenbaugh, *Education for Struggle: The American Labor Colleges of the 1920s and 1930s* (Philadelphia: Temple University Press, 1990), 219–20, and *passim* for the history of the college.

8. Cunningham, "Commonwealth College—An Educational Mutant," 505.

9. Agnes Cunningham, *Six Labor Songs* (Mena: Commonwealth College, n.d.); Raymond Koch and Charlotte Koch, *Educational Commune: The Story of Commonwealth College* (New York: Schocken Books, 1972), 89. "March of the Hungry Men" has recently been republished in Elizabeth Morgan, *Socialist and Labor Songs of the 1930s* (Chicago: Charles H. Kerr Publishing Company, 1997), 28.

10. See James R. Green, *Grass-Roots Socialism: Radical Movements in the Southwest, 1895–1943* (Baton Rouge: Louisiana State University Press, 1978), 360–66; Garin Burbank, *When Farmers Voted Red: The Gospel of Socialism in the Oklahoma Countryside, 1910–1924* (Westport, Conn.: Greenwood Press, 1976), 133–56; John Thompson, *Closing the Frontier: Radical Response in Oklahoma, 1889–1923* (Norman: University of Oklahoma Press, 1986), chapter 9 and passim.

11. On Thompson, with numerous references to Gordon Friesen, see Robert Polito, *Savage Art: A Biography of Jim Thompson* (New York: Alfred A. Knopf, 1995). On *Flamethrowers*, see the discussion in Teichroew, "Gordon Friesen: Writer, Radical and Ex-Mennonite," 13–16.

12. See James Gregory, *American Exodus: The Dust Bowl Migration and Okie Culture in California* (New York: Oxford University Press, 1989), 3–19; also Kenneth E. Hendrickson, ed., *Hard Times in Oklahoma: The Depression Years* (Oklahoma City: Oklahoma Historical Society, 1983).

13. Gordon Friesen, *Oklahoma Witch Hunt* (Oklahoma City: Oklahoma Committee to Defend Political Prisoners, October 1941), 23; Guy Logsdon, "Censorship in Oklahoma," *Oklahoma Librarian*, January 1969, 13–14. For a fascinating discussion of hucksters and con men of the time, see Gene Fowler and Bill Crawford, *Border Radio: Quacks, Yodelers, Pitchmen, Psychics, and Other Amazing Broadcasters of the American Airwaves* (New York: Limelight Editions, 1990).

14. Eli Jaffe, *Oklahoma Odyssey: A Memoir* (n.p., 1993): 135–36. Gordon rated a brief notice in Mary Hays Marable and Elaine Boylan, *A Handbook of Oklahoma Writers* (Norman: University of Oklahoma Press, 1939), 38 (for Bill Cunningham's write-up, see pp. 6–7).

15. Joe Klein, *Woody Guthrie: A Life* (New York: Alfred Knopf, 1980), 161–62.

16. Jaffe, *Oklahoma Odyssey*, 39–40.

17. Green, *Grass-Roots Socialism*, 423, 419–432; Lowell K. Dyson, *Red Harvest: The Communist Party and American Farmers* (Lincoln: University of Nebraska Press, 1982); chapter 8; Donald Grubbs, *Cry from the Cotton: The Southern Tenant Farmers' Union and the New Deal* (Chapel Hill: University of North Carolina Press, 1971); Robert F. Martin, *Howard Kester and the Struggle for Social Justice in the South, 1904–77* (Charlottesville: University Press of Virginia, 1991); H. L. Mitchell, *Roll the Union On: A*

Pictorial History of the Southern Tenant Farmer's Union (Chicago: Charles H. Kerr Publishing Company, 1987).

18. For the view that the Popular Front was not particularly harmonious, see Judy Kutulas, *The Long War: The Intellectual People's Front and Anti-Stalinism, 1930–1940* (Durham: Duke University Press, 1995).

19. On the VIA, see Patrick McGinnis, "'Share the Work': Ira M. Finley and the Veterans of Industry of America," in *Hard Times in Oklahoma*, ed. Hendrickson, 23–46.

20. Mary Frederickson, "A Place to Speak Our Minds," in *Working Lives: The Southern Exposure History of Labor in the South* ed. Marc Miller, (New York: Pantheon Books, 1980), 164. See also Mary Evans Frederickson, "A Place to Speak Our Minds: The Southern School for Women Workers," (Ph.D. diss., University of North Carolina, 1981).

21. For a small sampling of the recent literature, see Maurice Isserman, *Which Side Were You On?: The American Communist Party during the Second World War* (Middletown: Wesleyan University Press, 1982); Fraser M. Ottanelli, *The Communist Party of the United States: From the Depression to World War II* (New Brunswick: Rutgers University Press, 1991); Harvey Klehr, *The Heyday of American Communism: The Depression Decade* (New York: Basic Books, 1984); Harvey Klehr and John Earl Haynes, *The American Communist Movement: Storming Heaven Itself* (New York: Twayne Publishers, 1992); Michael E. Brown et al., eds., *New Studies in the Politics and Culture of U.S. Communism* (New York: Monthly Review Press, 1993); Michael Denning, *The Cultural Front: The Laboring of American Culture in the Twentieth Century* (New York: Verso, 1996).

22. Daniel Friedman, "A Brief Description of the Workers' Theatre Movement of the Thirties," in *Theatre for Working-Class Audiences in the United States, 1830–1980*, ed. Bruce A. McConachie and Daniel Friedman (Westport: Greenwood Press, 1985), 111. See also Malcolm Goldstein, *The Political Stage: American Drama and the Great Depression* (New York: Oxford University Press, 1974); Jay Williams, *Stage Left* (New York: Scribner, 1974); Eric Trumbull, "Musicals of the American Workers' Theatre Movement—1928–1941: Propaganda and Ritual in Documents of a Social Movement," (Ph.D. diss., University of Maryland, 1991); Douglas McDermott, "The Theatre Nobody Knows: Workers' Theatre in America, 1926–1942," *Theatre Survey* 1 (May 1965): 65–82.

23. Douglas McDermott, "Agitprop: Production Practice in the Workers' Theatre, 1932–1942," *Theatre Survey* 7 (November 1966): 115, 122.

24. Norris Houghton, *Advance from Broadway: 19,000 Miles of American Theatre* (New York: Harcourt, Brace & Company, 1941): 284–185.

25. Dorothy Schmidt to Sis Cunningham, June 21, 1974, Cunningham/Friesen Papers, in editor's possession.

26. Daniel Bowie, "Artist from the Dust Bowl State," *Daily Worker*, September 23, 1941, 7.

27. On the Almanacs, see Richard A. Reuss, "American Folklore and Left-Wing Politics, 1927–1957," (Ph.D. diss., Indiana University, 1971); R. Serge Denisoff, *Great Day Coming: Folk Music and the American Left* (Ur-

bana: University of Illinois Press, 1971), chapter 2; Robbie Lieberman, "*My Song Is My Weapon*": *People's Songs, American Communism, and the Politics of Culture, 1930–1950* (Urbana: University of Illinois Press, 1989), 52–60; Klein, *Woody Guthrie*, chapter 6; Doris Willens, *Lonesome Traveler: The Life of Lee Hays* (New York: Norton, 1988), chapter 6. All the Almanacs' recordings, along with a few others by Sis and elaborate notes, appear in Ronald D. Cohen and Dave Samuelson, *Songs for Political Action: Folk Music, Topical Songs and the American Left, 1926–1954*, Bear Family Records, BCD 15720, 1996.

28. Millard Lampell, "Home before Morning," unpublished manuscript in editor's possession, 214–215.

29. Gordon Friesen, "Aunt Molly Jackson," *Daily Worker*, January 10, 1942.

30. Sis Cunningham to Ronald D. Cohen, July 27, 1994, Cunningham/ Friesen Papers.

31. Klein, *Woody Guthrie*, 213.

32. Gordon Friesen, "Day Of Infamy," *Mainstream*, February 1963, 3–18; Dominic Capeci and Martha Wilkerson, *Layered Violence: The Detroit Rioters of 1943* (Jackson: University Press of Mississippi, 1991).

33. For the larger story, see in particular, Ellen Schrecker, *Many Are the Crimes: McCarthyism in America* (Boston: Little, Brown, 1998).

34. Gordon Friesen to Dick Reuss, December 10, 1965, Richard A. Reuss Papers, Indiana University Archives, Bloomington; Marty Martin, "People's Songs for Political Action," *Daily Worker*, August 2, 1946. For discussions of People's Songs and People's Artists, see Reuss, "American Folklore and Left-Wing Politics," chapters 6–7; and Lieberman, "*My Song Is My Weapon.*" For a recording of Sis doing "Parnell Thomas Blues" and much more information about these musical times, including all the Almanacs' recordings, consult Cohen and Samuelson, *Songs for Political Action*.

35. Quote from Gordon Friesen's FBI file. There is a large literature on the Red Scare; in addition to Schrecker, *Many Are the Crimes*, see Ellen Schrecker, *The Age of McCarthyism: A Brief History with Documents* (Boston: Bedford Books, 1994), which has an excellent bibliographic essay; and Richard Gid Powers, *Not without Honor: The History of American Anti-Communism* (New York: Free Press, 1995), a critique of the old Left and mushy defense of the Red Scare. See also David Caute, *The Great Fear: The Anti-Communist Purge under Truman and Eisenhower* (New York: Simon and Schuster, 1978); and Stephen J. Whitfield, *The Culture of the Cold War* (Baltimore: Johns Hopkins University Press, 1991).

36. Editorial, *Broadside*, no. 1 (1962): 1.

37. Josh Dunson, *Freedom in the Air: Song Movements of the 60's* (New York: International Publishers, 1965): 72–73.

38. Dunson, "Birth of Broadside," *Broadside*, no. 20 (1963): 8; Robert Shelton, *No Direction Home: The Life and Music of Bob Dylan* (New York: Ballantine Books, 1986): 157 and passim. See also Bob Spitz, *Dylan: A Biography* (New York: McGraw Hill, 1989); Marc Eliot, *Death of a Rebel: Staring*

Phil Ochs and a Small Circle of Friends (New York: Anchor Books, 1979); Michael Schumacher, *There But for Fortune: The Life of Phil Ochs* (New York: Hyperion, 1996).

39. Sis Cunningham [Gordon Friesen] to Richard A. Reuss, May 4, 1963, Reuss Papers. There is an extensive, enlightening Friesen-Reuss correspondence in this collection; Reuss's letters to Sis and Gordon are currently in my possession. On Broadside Records and much else, see Peter D. Goldsmith, *Making People's Music: Moe Asch and Folkways Records* (Washington: Smithsonian Institution Press, 1998), 308–310 and passim.

40. Pete Seeger, "Johnny Appleseed, Jr.," *Sing Out!* 13 (October–November 1963): 67; Seeger to Gordon Friesen, undated postcard from Japan, Cunningham/Friesen Papers.

41. "Editors' Column," *The Little Sandy Review,* no. 22: 46; Letter from Sis Cunningham, ibid., no. 25: 3–4. Gordon also described the emerging folk scene in other publications; see "Songs for Our Time," *Mainstream,* December 1962: 3–22; "Something New Has Been Added," *Sing Out!* 13 (October–November 1963): 12–23.

42. Moses Asch to *Broadside,* October 16, 1965; Gordon Friesen to Moe Asch, October 18, 1965; Moe Asch to Gordon, October 19, 1965, Smithsonian/Folkways Collection, Smithsonian Institution, Washington, D.C.

43. David A. Nobel, "A Historical Analysis of the Radical Folk Tradition as Presented in *Broadside* Magazine February, 1962–November, 1967," (graduate student paper, University of Tulsa): 35, 37. For a discussion of the radical Right's attack on folk music, see Denisoff, *Great Day Coming,* 151–163.

44. Robert Shelton, "First Edition of 'Singing Paper' Is Issued Hot Off the Guitars," *New York Times,* November 2, 1964.

45. Ralph J. Gleason to Sis Cunningham, January 23, 1965, copy in Cunningham/Friesen Papers; Ralph J. Gleason, "The Times They Are A Changin'," *Ramparts,* April 1965, 36–38, 47–48; Ralph J. Gleason, "Perspectives: 'Cover' Versions and Their Origins," *Rolling Stone,* June 7, 1973: 7.

46. Gordon Friesen to Dick Reuss, May 3, 1968; Friesen to Reuss, February 7, 1969, Reuss Papers.

47. Sis Cunningham to Pete and Toshi Seeger, December 27, 1970, carbon copy in Cunningham/Friesen Papers; Gordon Friesen and Sis Cunningham to Dick Reuss, July 27, 1971; Cunningham to Reuss, August 5, 1971, Reuss Papers.

48. Robert Shelton to Sis Cunningham and Gordon Friesen, June 16, 1970, Shelton to Friesen, June 30, 1971, Shelton to Friesen and Cunningham, August 12, 1971, in Cunningham/Friesen Papers.

49. Sis Cunningham to Wally Hille, January 22, 1971, copy in Cunningham/Friesen Papers.

50. Gordon Friesen to Irwin Silber, March 24, 1972; Sis Cunningham to Toshi Seeger, August 17, 1972, copies in Cunningham/Friesen Papers.

51. Gordon Friesen and Sis Cunningham to Pete and Toshi Seeger, "Re-

port On Status of Broadside Magazine," October 17, 1972, copy in Cunningham/Friesen Papers.

52. Gordon Friesen to Irwin Silber, June 20, 1972, Irwin Silber Papers, in possession of Silber.

53. Mark Eliot to Sis Cunningham and Gordon Friesen, March 15, 1979; copy of Sis Cunningham and Gordon Friesen to Jacques Vassal, March 18, 1979, Cunningham/Friesen Papers. See also Schumacher, *There But for Fortune*, 319–320 and passim; Jacques Vassal, *Electric Children: Roots and Branches of Modern Folkrock* (New York: Taplinger Publishing Co., 1976).

54. Jim Capaldi, "The Struggle Continues," *Folk Scene* 4 (February 1977): 22–23; Sis Cunningham to Dick Reuss, February 16, 1984, Reuss Papers. There is currently no general history of the folk revival, but when written it will have to include a lengthy account of *Broadside* and its contributions. Robert Cantwell, *When We Were Good: The Folk Revival* (Cambridge: Harvard University Press, 1996), only mentions Sis and Gordon in connection with the Almanac Singers, and has no reference to *Broadside*.

55. Gordon Friesen to Irwin Silber, June 20, 1972, Silber Papers.

56. Greg Mitchell, *Tricky Dick and the Pink Lady* (New York: Random House, 1998).

57. Sharleen Leahey, "A Life Well-Lived: Tribute to a Survivor," *Songs for Peace*, no. 15 (Fall/Winter 1997): 12. For a fascinating overview of the history of radicalism in the United States, see Paul Buhle and Edmund B. Sullivan, *Images of American Radicalism* (Hanover, Mass.: Christopher Publishing House, 1998), with a photo of Sis and the Almanacs, 287. A photo and discussion of Sis also appears in Chuck Mancuso, *Popular Music and the Underground: Foundations of Jazz, Blues, Country & Rock 1900–1950* (Dubuque: Kendall/Hunt Publishing Co., 1996), 503.

Bibliography and Discography

Books

Cunningham, Sis. *Ain't It Time We Got Mad!* New York, the author, 1962.

———. *Broadside*, vol. 1. New York: Oak Publications, 1964.

———. *Broadside*, vol. 2. New York: Oak Publications, 1968.

———. *Broadside*, vol. 3. New York: Oak Publications, 1970.

———. *Red Dust & Broadsides: A Piece of People's History in Songs, Poems & Prose.* New York, the author, 1990.

———. *Six Labor Songs.* Mena, Arkansas: Commonwealth College, n.d.

Friesen, Gordon. *Flamethrowers.* Caldwell, Idaho: Claxton Printers, 1936.

———. *Oklahoma Witch Hunt.* Oklahoma City: Oklahoma Committee to Defend Political Prisoners, 1941.

Broadside is available on microfiche through Congressional Information Service, Inc.

Recordings

Cunningham, Sis. *Red Dust & Broadsides.* n.p., n.d. Audiocassette.

———. *Sundown.* Broadside no. 9. Folkways Records FH 5319.

All of Sis's recordings with the Almanac Singers, plus a few others, can be found in *Songs for Political Action: Folkmusic, Topical Songs and the American Left, 1926–1953.* Ten compact discs and illustrated book. Bear Family Records BCD 15720.

Index

www.ingramcontent.com/pod-product-compliance
Lightning Source LLC
Chambersburg PA
CBHW071829270326
41929CB00013B/1934